Collaborative Wisdom

This book is dedicated to Iris, a quiet and practically wise leader and also Gregory and Ruairi, two of the global leaders of the future.

Collaborative Wisdom

From Pervasive Logic to Effective Operational Leadership

GREG PARK

Routledge
Taylor & Francis Group

LONDON AND NEW YORK

First published 2013 by Gower Publishing

2 Park Square, Milton Park, Abingdon, Oxfordshire OX14 4RN
52 Vanderbilt Avenue, New York, NY 10017

Routledge is an imprint of the Taylor & Francis Group, an informa business

First issued in paperback 2019

Gower Applied Business Research
Our programme provides leaders, practitioners, scholars and researchers with thought provoking, cutting edge books that combine conceptual insights, interdisciplinary rigour and practical relevance in key areas of business and management.

British Library Cataloguing in Publication Data
Park, Greg.
  Collaborative wisdom : from pervasive logic to effective
  operational leadership.
  1. Leadership. 2. Senior leadership teams. 3. Group
  decision making. 4. Executive ability. 5. Corporate
  culture. 6. Success in business.
  I. Title
  658.4'092-dc23

  ISBN 13: 978-1-4094-3460-3 (hbk)
  ISBN 13: 978-0-367-87900-6 (pbk)

Library of Congress Cataloging-in-Publication Data
Park, Greg.
  Collaborative wisdom : from pervasive logic to effective operational leadership / by Greg Park.
    p. cm.
  Includes bibliographical references and index.
  ISBN 978-1-4094-3460-3 (hardback) -- ISBN 978-1-4094-3461-0 (ebook) 1. Leadership. I. Title.
  HD57.7.P3647 2013
  658.4'092--dc23

                                                                2012025806

Contents

List of Figures

List of Tables

Acknowledgements

Many have contributed to the moulding and creation of this book but a few have been instrumental in both its inception and completion.

I would particularly like to thank Martin West, Commissioning Editor at Gower Applied Research who has exhibited an initial and ongoing personal, easygoing interest, insight and professionalism which has coaxed me ever onwards.

I would also like to acknowledge the support, advice and friendship proffered by Professors Ray Kinsella (Michael Smurfit Graduate School of Business, UCD), Philip Molyneux (Bangor Business School), Patrick Flood (Dublin City University Business School) and Dr Paddy McEvoy, recently retired Chairman of IIB Bank (now KBC Bank Ireland) during my field and desk research.

Finally, I would like to thank all those publishers and their authors, and business organisations which agreed to allow me to quote at no cost from their publications and websites. In this respect I particularly acknowledge the support of HSBC Holdings plc and its staff, who have freely given of their time in respect of lengthy interviews and provided access to valuable archival material; also The American Academy of Management, Cambridge University Press, American Psychological Association, Sloan Management Review and Procter & Gamble.

Preface

This book is written by an operational business leader for the benefit of existing and aspiring business leaders. Those who head the operational units, taking decisions and resolving operational issues on a day to day basis, rather than those who might be perceived to manage the business "dashboard", who plan and strategise. It puts forward an approach to effective operational leadership which addresses practical, pragmatic, day to day issues, written in a manner to which the reader will hopefully relate. I hope that it will both interest and inform this important audience, who comprise the group whose hands ultimately deliver on an organisation's vision, objectives and targets.

Throughout a lengthy career as technical expert, manager and operational leader I have tripped, stumbled, fumbled, perspired and adapted, with resolute determination and no small commitment to various organisations, in the absence of adequate clarity, direction and information, towards consistently achieving organisational objectives. An impatience and curiosity in respect of this suboptimal situation spurred me into resolving this situation through scholarly investigation and continuing on the job critical reflection. Through this process I found many excellent answers to questions in scholarly books and journals for which I had sought answers, which somewhat assuaged my burning curiosity. However these tended, in the vast majority of cases, to be written in a manner totally unsuited to the audience's mindset and time availability. Perhaps, most importantly, they were rarely in synch with the nature of the operational issues and therefore the nature of the process of decision-making and issue resolution with which the operational leader was faced. This tended to span a range of scholarly subject areas, all at the same time.

Whilst there will be exceptions, my experience of the reality and process of daily business communication to gain and maintain the interest and credibility of superiors to resolve business issues whilst maintaining business momentum, is as follows:

- **Discussion with superior**: answer specific question in maximum of three sentences.
- **Written communication on an issue**: maximum of 1.5 pages A4.
- **Presentation on an issue**: 20-minute presentation maximum, 10–15 minutes for clarification and discussion and then management decision.

I have found that these communication expectations apply equally as both a superior as well as communication to superiors. The requirement is therefore for clarity, brevity and provision of key information in order that an appropriate decision can be made and everyone can turn to the plethora of other pressing, urgent and important matters

As an operational leader I have therefore sought to be guided by my own experience in writing this book, particularly in respect of the nature, quantity and display of evidence required for assimilation and understanding with a view to effective decision-making and issue resolution. The structure and content of this book is therefore geared towards:

- Gaining and maintaining the interest of the practitioner.
- Briefly highlighting key perspectives and information to practitioners and thereafter allowing them to decide whether they wish to delve further into the area.

These objectives have resulted in a number of somewhat unusual features within the book:

- Perhaps of necessity this book contains significant amounts of what may be termed theory but what should be regarded by the aspiring or existing operational leader who is reading it as information for consideration. In this respect there is an emphasis less on the detail of the theory, rather on its practical and operational application, particularly in respect of developing operational leadership perspectives and priorities and the resultant impact on decision-making and issue resolution.
- A gradual move from solid theory (perhaps too quick for some, too slow for others) to insight into and examples of their practical application in the multifaceted and multitasking world of operational business leadership.
- The utilisation, as far as possible, of language more recognisable in every day usage by operational business leaders.
- The use of synopses at the beginning of book Parts, chapters and chapter sections in order to provide a brief insight for what is to follow. Readers may therefore choose to read further or skip to another section, satisfied for the moment by the information imparted by the synopsis.
- The use of boxed text to highlight key points for particular consideration.
- A preponderance of quotations, many by senior and successful business executives, to reinforce points, particularly in Parts Two and Three.
- The utilisation of operational leader quotations from interviews which I have undertaken in respect of important and pertinent issues, included under the assurance of anonymity.
- The inclusion of exercises at the end of each chapter, less as scholarly tasks, more as a means of embedding the propositions contained within the chapter into the mindset of the reader. Also providing the opportunity to spend a few minutes to consider their validity in relation to the reader's prevailing views on the perspectives, priorities, attributes and capabilities required for effective operational leadership within the organisational business context.

Whilst this book's content is founded on both field and desk research, propositions and conclusions are significantly influenced by my personal knowledge, experience, insight, intuition and judgement, developed over a period spanning four decades within the operational business context, much of it as an operational leader. In this respect I would invite readers not to take what is written as tablets of stone but rather to actively consider the content and draw their own conclusions on relevance and validity within the context of their knowledge, experience, insight, judgement and prevailing organisational environment, blending it into existing leadership principles, perspectives, priorities and practices. Hopefully there will not be substantial dissonance and the process will refine and extend your insight into the means of acting as a practically wise and effective operational leader.

I have sought to provide practical insights and examples from a number of business sectors. However, due to my particular experience and insight into operational leadership perspectives and practices within the financial services sector, readers may perhaps tire of frequent reference to examples within this sector. If so, I apologise; but trust that readers will nevertheless gain significantly from such insights and general applicability across business sectors and leadership contexts.

Finally, it is important to stress that this is a book whose contents should be absorbed rather than learnt. It is aimed towards changing mindsets and perspectives, to some small or great degree; to enhance practical, operational decision-making and issue resolution, rather than passing tests or examinations. It is therefore not a textbook in the accepted interpretation of that term. Whilst there will be useful and interesting facts and information which you might wish to remember and utilise at some stage, in projects, examinations, reports, presentations, this is not the primary purpose of this book.

May I end this Preface by wishing you well as operational leaders and hope that it provides not only an insight but an edge at the beginning of your business career. Whilst operational leadership will always be like pushing a boulder up a steep hill, perhaps you will now be able to see beyond the boulder, gain enhanced traction and energise others to provide support and encouragement along the way to the top.

Reviews for
Collaborative Wisdom

Greg Park's book Collaborative Wisdom: From Pervasive Logic to Effective Operational Leadership *engagingly connects the world of the practitioner to relevant scholarly concepts in this welcome practical contribution to effective operational leadership. Moreover, it is particularly timely within the context of today's increasing questioning of prevailing leadership values, principles, and practices. It does so by clearly illustrating how "best in class" organisational performance can be consistent with universal values and communal principles, through the application of practical and collaborative wisdom. I warmly recommend this thought-provoking, sometimes contentious, and always insightful book which replaces the prevailing emphasis on "smart" thinking with an emphasis upon the "wise" in the process of the operational leadership decision-making process.*

Patrick C McEvoy, Former Chairman, K and H Bank, Hungary and former Chief Executive and Chairman, IIB Bank plc, Ireland

Dr Greg Park has produced a highly readable and useful account of what ethical collaborative wisdom is and its importance to strategic leadership of the modern enterprise. In doing so, he provides many deep insights into leadership and management based upon research and over thirty years of international business experience. I expect his advocacy of soft hearted, hard headed pragmatism will resonate with managers, post experience business students and leaders alike. I very much enjoyed this book.

Professor Patrick C. Flood, Dublin City University Business School, Ireland

Introduction

What's this Book About?

The title of this book aptly describes the focus and balance of its contents. Whilst there is much emphasis throughout the text on the leadership of people, the key point to initially acknowledge and understand is rather the logic, dare I say the wisdom, which draws us to this conclusion. In essence, it is practically wise, pragmatic, hard-headed operational business leadership to take a people and organisational community focus. This book is however not about a people perspective, which is merely the result or by-product rather than the purpose of the book. Its primary objective concerns the development of a leadership cognitive mental process which ensures the effective application of those principles, priorities, perspectives and practices of the practically wise leader within the operational business context.

In essence this book reflects, translates and tangibilises the principles and process of practical and collaborative wisdom into the perspectives, priorities and practices, the attributes and capabilities of effective operational leadership. It thereby explains and illustrates the dominant logic which pervades those business organisations which consistently achieve operational effectiveness and optimal performance over decades, indeed beyond; for these are the central and ultimate priorities and responsibilities of the operational leader.

But Wisdom is Only for Sages and Philosophers

In today's lexicon the term wisdom is rarely if ever linked to the terms business and/or leadership. It is rather referred to only in the same breath as the philosophers who cast their shadow before the advent of global religions, such as Plato and Aristotle. However, as we will see, wisdom lives, albeit cloaked in different terminology and perhaps only applied by leadership cadres in a very few business organisations. There is a justification to reintroduce wisdom in the form of its practical and collaborative components, as an operational leadership aid, acting as an anchor and compass in order to furnish leaders with clear principles and perspectives by which they might consistently take decisions and resolve issues. Practical and collaborative wisdom is essentially comprised of specific fundamental values, principles and cognitive mental processes.

Practical and collaborative wisdom is relevant, indeed critical in the realisation of effective operational leadership. The objective of this book is therefore to explain and illustrate this relevance and the considerations, components, implications and obstacles to the effective implementation of practical and collaborative wisdom. Utilising a process of interpretation and translation from what might initially appear abstract and obscure theories and concepts, we gradually move to the development of a framework of practical, pragmatic, hard-headed but soft-hearted leadership perspectives, priorities and practices, attributes and capabilities, which will consistently achieve optimal operational effectiveness and long-term organisational performance.

How Does Wisdom Deliver on the Shop Floor?

This book addresses a mental process by which a defined framework of values, principles, perspectives and priorities, leadership attributes and capabilities are applied to consistently deliver practically "wise" decisions, practices and actions, within the day to day, operational business context. The result is a focused, energised cohesive, dedicated and inculcated leadership cadre, workforce and stakeholder community, consistently delivering optimal productivity, operational effectiveness and long-term organisational performance, as committed members and advocates of the organisation. Regrettably, the path to such organisational nirvana is not clear, smooth, straight or indeed short. However, this book describes and details the path and the milestones along the way which must be passed in a manner which the operational leader will comprehend, relate to and acknowledge as practical and realistic in achieving the above desirable objectives.

In its simplest terms this book is about the process of developing amongst the leadership cadre of an organisation a particular type of practical wisdom which is driven by a constant mental state of collaboration. Its overall primary objective is to make a contribution to changing the logic, the perspectives and priorities of business management scholars, also aspiring and practicing leaders. My desire is that readers consider and absorb the themes and logic rather than remember the detail contained within this book. There is an understanding, although perhaps not a widespread acknowledgement that the fundamental logic, the principles, perspectives and priorities by which business has been driven, particularly but not limited to the Anglo-American economies, in the latter half of the twentieth century and into the twenty-first century, has been aberrant and are increasingly redundant. This has resulted in all too evident negative repercussions for economic and social stability, the final outcome of which will not become clear for decades yet. It is therefore important that aspiring and junior business leaders are no longer imbued with these aberrant perspectives and priorities which will become hard coded into new generations of leaders, with the resultant impact on operational decision-making and issue resolution. It is proposed that only through the development and consistent application of the principles and process of practical and collaborative wisdom by the operational leadership cadre of an organisation will it be possible for an organisation to survive and achieve consistent optimal performance over the long term.

Will it Take Away the Pain and Confusion?

The key point to appreciate is that operational leadership is not only highly complex but also confusing and often psychologically painful. The application of practical and collaborative wisdom seeks to diminish the complexity, confusion, pain and anguish of operational leadership. It does not offer a recipe, rather an anchor and a compass for effective operational leadership. It offers a foundation of values, principles, perspectives and priorities and a guide on how to develop the appropriate attributes and capabilities of effective leadership in order to take decisions and resolve issues with clarity and purpose towards operational effectiveness and organisational performance over the long term.

This book is about practical, pragmatic effective, operational leadership and all that is required to achieve that end. It is about the development of simplicity, clarity of thought and purpose in the face of constant operational chaos and confusion. Leading within an organisation is very much like leading in a war – very few spontaneously or voluntarily discuss the process and decisions made amongst themselves, much less to those who do not have experience of it in practice. This is due to the often adverse effects which pragmatic, practical, operational decision making has on individuals and groups, many with whom you have developed close bonds of friendship, camaraderie and dependency, through working closely to resolve serious issues and not a few crises in the past.

The reality of the application of practical wisdom is that operational decisions are in practice at variance with any set of values and principles you or anyone might espouse and apply, causing pain and hurt to many for the espoused benefit of the organisational community or key stakeholder groups (e.g. the laying off of 6,000 for the survival of the organisation or to make it more attractive for acquisition suitors, impacting on a total of perhaps 25,000 individuals). The application of a framework of values, principles, perspectives and priorities provide a compass and framework which facilitates and against which you take practical, pragmatic, contextually-based decisions. Where you cannot be said to have taken decisions which support these principles you at least understand and appreciate that you have not and the reasons why. It is about seeking to consistently apply a framework of principles, perspectives and priorities in which you believe, to a constantly changing leadership context; getting ever closer, but never attaining this goal, which is ultimately unattainable. It is perhaps about what I pointed out to a retired criminal trial judge during a function in Colorado. Practically wise operational leadership is having a foundation of values and principles and believing in them, yet not applying them, but knowing that you have not and being able to justify it in this particular case, because this was their optimal practical interpretation and application, in this particular case. At the same time the practically wise operational leader remains committed to constantly trying to take decisions on the basis of this anchor and foundation of values, principles and perspectives. This approach is far superior in achieving operational effectiveness and optimal performance than taking decisions in the absence of a compass and anchor of principles and priorities, merely applying those which seem appropriate and convenient at the time. The problem with this latter decision-making option is that individual issues, resolved on an ad hoc basis, are linked in the minds of stakeholders and, in the absence of the consistent application of principles, perspectives and priorities, result in a diminution in credibility of, commitment and allegiance to and energy expended on behalf of such leaders.

Why Should I Believe It?

The evidence and conclusions contained within this book are based upon research and evidence from established and published scholars and my own scholarly investigations. Equally, if not more importantly, they are based upon the views and experiences of senior executive practitioners who have critically reflected upon their substantial experiences leading complex, often multinational organisations. They also reflect my own career experiences working within a range of functions and leadership roles within a number of national, international and global banking organisations. It is therefore considered that by a process of triangulation of these views and results we are able to gain an insight into the value of the application of the attributes of practical and collaborative wisdom in the effective operational leadership of the business organisation.

Increasingly I take the view that leaders and managers across any organisation recognise the key issues and know how to address them, in other words they know the key questions to address optimal performance and they know the answers. They know how to and have the tools available to cut costs, increase productivity, enhance performance, motivate staff, maintain the confidence of stakeholders, etc. They just can't do it in practice. They, as individuals or as groups within the organisation cannot effectively implement recognised solutions. This is due to the absence of a development process which fosters the perspectives, attributes and capabilities amongst the leadership cadre which provide insight and judgement towards a state of practical and collaborative wisdom. It is fair to say that the vast majority of organisations fail to optimise performance over the long term, indeed many merely stumble from one crisis to another, prey to market and economic cycles for their success or eventual demise, in the absence of the embedded leadership principles, perspectives, attributes and capabilities provided by practical and collaborative wisdom, to control their destiny. The majority of organisations rely more on application, determination and perspiration on the part of their management and staff to achieve annual and longer term objectives than the consistent and effective application of a framework of principles, perspectives, priorities and objectives which address key organisational issues in a structured and methodical manner. Many might indeed prefer a state of disorganised and confused myopia, since it provides wiggle room to explain suboptimal results and performance. To bring this point home, how many of those reading this Introduction could state the principles, perspectives and priorities upon which decisions are made and issues resolved in an organisation with which they are familiar?

Some readers will deny that this is the case. Some will already see me as a heretic by making such a statement publicly and be fearful of what is to come in the rest of this book. Others, hopefully the majority, will agree, but may respond that this is the reality, reflecting, in practice, the pragmatic management of organisations, encapsulating the real challenge of operational leadership. This comprises of a continuing process of compromise and "satisficing" with regard to effective organisational leadership and performance, whilst simultaneously maintaining the confidence and satisfying the expectations of key stakeholder groups. To this group I say that whilst operational leadership will always be like pushing a boulder up a mountain I propose a leadership perspective and management process which ensures maximum clarity, cohesion, energy, traction and progress for each unit of effort and a means of scaling higher peaks than one previously thought possible.

OK, Let's Plug and Play

For good or for ill this perspective and process will not be successfully achieved through sending staff on training courses or including on the syllabus of any MBA. Rather than being something which can be added, like a piece of software, it is fundamental to the principles, perspectives, priorities and operational practices of organisational leadership, coded into the hardware of the organisation's dominant logic and most importantly in the mindset of the operational leadership cadre. This is achieved through clear definition, reinforcement, continuous and appropriate experience gathering, constant example and reward. This book will be discussing a process of inculcation, in its most positive interpretation, rather than in its mindless "Borg-like" interpretation. This will be undertaken in order to embed key principles, perspectives and priorities in not only the leaders of today and tomorrow, but all employees within the organisation. It is a process of positive inculcation which has stood as the foundation stone of the optimal performance of a small number of organisations globally for a sustained period, spanning many decades, in a few cases over a century.

Start Young and Optimise Your Contribution

As a new entrant to banking in the 1970s I didn't have a clue. At 21, after learning at college about the principles of monetary economics I entered banking and found myself opening deposit accounts, taking money over the counter, checking bills of exchange to finance foreign trade, buying and selling shares, printing chequebooks, managing a branch back office, managing a branch office and analysing corporate defaults. I was confused. In addition to instructions on how to excel in my day to day technical duties I also sought and expected guidance on those principles, perspectives and priorities which guided the leadership of the organisation and upon which I should base my approach to issues arising and decision making throughout my career. In my case this confusion probably lasted some 8–10 years, maybe longer if I were to be honest. I consoled myself with the thought that someone higher up the organisational food chain has this all worked out and they would enlighten me when they considered it necessary in order to enhance my performance and contribution.

Whilst I would like to think that I was unique in being a little slow on the uptake regarding the direction which was available and the communication of key principles, perspectives and priorities, my experience leads me to the conclusion that I am pretty typical of the new entrant in most organisations, with the resultant impact on individual contribution to the organisation over the first 5–10 years. There is a common perception that furnished with the basic ingredients of reasonable intelligence and analytical ability the priority for new entrants is to learn the technical side of any role and the rest will follow. Such matters as interpersonal skills, decision making, insight, judgement, direction, motivation, drive, determination and loyalty, are all the perceived intangibles of success. In my case, the lack of a vision, direction, a compass or anchor left me dissatisfied and dispirited and my productivity and dedication pretty much hit rock bottom. Admittedly this was over 30 years ago. Regrettably, having eventually found my feet and attained senior leadership roles I find that at the operational level the change has not been dramatic in clearly communicating the key values and principles which new entrants should use to provide clarity of purpose and direction to enhance their contribution beyond short-term technical requirements and proficiency. The focus of operational, day to day leadership continues to be focused on achieving output targets and objectives through the development and management of technical expertise and capability. In the twenty-first century this is a perspective which results in mediocre operational practices, productivity and long-term performance. The implications of the contents of this book are therefore a radical realignment in the perspectives, priorities, capabilities and role of operational management as, day to day, they take decisions and direct resources, particularly human, towards optimising organisational performance.

One of the key objectives of this book is therefore to support new entrants to business organisations, to ensure that they make a contribution to the output and management of the organisation from the word go. This is achieved by providing clarity on those principles, perspectives and priorities which must direct decision making, and the attributes and capabilities which they must develop in themselves and others in order to become wise and effective leaders; also to support potential leaders at all stages of their career to ensure that they are making the optimal contribution to the organisational vision from the outset. That they are part of a holistic organisational community, rather than an isolated, minor cog of a giant machine which has some purpose and objective, which is only known by and the responsibility of someone somewhere who is all knowing and omnipotent.

But Someone Else Looks After All This Stuff

Many readers might by now be saying that this book is about "nice to have", aspirational, "pie in the sky", hard to achieve, almost philosophical issues, for consideration by business scholars and media commentators, rather than operational organisational leaders who could work 24 hours a day, effectively firefighting and still have a full in-tray in the morning dealing with today's budgetary, planning, personnel, IT, finance, customer service, sales, risk, compliance, interpersonal, political, or any one of an array of other urgent and pressing issues. As I have said previously, many experienced leaders within an organisation know both the key questions and the answers; the problem is that the majority of leaders within the organisation can only manage within the environment in which they find themselves, this is the reality. Each organisation has developed a dominant logic of principles, perspectives, priorities and practices that have become accepted, embedded, often sacrosanct, only to be reappraised by senior executive leaders and board members in times of organisational crisis or in an evolutionary manner over an extended period. There is much evidence to suggest that behind the prevailing economic crisis lies a more critical and chronic leadership crisis spanning business sectors based upon a primary focus on short-term gain for key stakeholder groups (predominantly senior executives and institutional shareholders and bondholders) and technical expertise.

It is important to acknowledge and understand that the constant reference to operational leadership principles, perspectives, priorities, attributes and capabilities is not directed to others, it is directed to you, the reader, the operational leaders of today and tomorrow. I leave others better qualified to ruminate and expound at length on the reasons for the prevailing economic and social collapse. However, this economic and financial crisis is in many respects fortuitous, if it manages to realign these prevailing aberrant leadership priorities to which we have already alluded. In such a situation senior executive leaders have a responsibility to their stakeholders to reconsider the organisation's dominant logic in respect of key leadership principles, perspectives and priorities. Divisional and departmental operational leaders also have an opportunity and more importantly, a responsibility, to participate in this fluid environment, where boards and executive committee members are under pressure to be seen to be taking a broader stakeholder and longer-term perspective which is fundamental to the objectives of this book. Ultimately you will be in the driving seat, operationally responsible for implementing changes to perspectives, priorities and practices on a day to day basis throughout the organisation.

OK, What Do I Have to Do?

It is within this context that I make, what might seem to many, to be a radical statement. In order to optimise organisational performance the primary role, central area of focus, the priority requirement of any operational leader, no matter your role and level of responsibility is to lead people effectively. However, unlike other areas of expertise operational people management is less about principles, standards and practices, and more about perspectives, attitudes, characteristics, attributes and capabilities. This is not a revolutionary idea, many scholars have pronounced on this over the last decades. This is not about tea and sympathy. This is hard-headed, pragmatic, realistic organisational management as a means of achieving operational efficiency and optimal organisational performance. It is about a realisation that no matter how well you "manage" your products, your distribution channels, your IT systems, your treasury management, cost/income ratio, ultimately an organisation's long-term success will be based upon clarity and unity of purpose, loyalty, motivation, cohesion, energy and a communal atmosphere, particularly within the leadership cadre but also within the broad employee and stakeholder base. At the operational leadership level, the significance and implications of this statement have rarely in my experience been recognised in an operational sense to date. The content of this book illustrates how only through the application of the principles and cognitive mental process of practical and collaborative wisdom can this perspective consistently result in operational effectiveness and optimal long-term performance.

What does this mean in terms of operational practice? It means that when leaders come into the office each morning they must recognise that they should view the resolution of prevalent operational issues critical to the performance of the organisation primarily through the lens of the proactive management of people, as the central focus, at front of mind. The problem with this statement is that in practice people management continues not to be recognised as a fundamental and dominant leadership requirement and expert proficiency for optimal operational effectiveness, long-term organisational performance and elevation to increasingly responsible positions of authority within the organisation. It is not lauded in the same terms as proficiency, an expertise in, for example, marketing, finance, IT and R&D. Alternatively there may be a realisation that expert leadership is far more complex than any of these areas of functional expertise and cannot be taught but rather merely prompted, realised and absorbed over time as a result of critical reasoning. What makes it even more complex is that the effective leadership of people requires the inclusion of appropriate values and principles within the dominant logic and their effective communication and consistent reinforcement. The absence of an appropriate dominant logic and/or its ineffective communication and reinforcement leads to isolated islands of effective people leadership throughout the organisation, resulting in suboptimal operational effectiveness. It is the contention of this book that organisations which make the effort to communicate a dominant logic based upon values and principles which foster effective people leadership to new entrants, whilst proactively developing people leadership attributes and capabilities will quickly reap tangible rewards in productivity as a result of enhanced clarity of direction and purpose, energy, excitement, commitment and dynamism.

In practice it means that at the operational people interface leaders need to define and consistently apply a psychological covenant which satisfies the requirements and expectations of employees and that this covenant is reinforced within the operational management context on a day to day basis. It requires a refocus of how operational issues are viewed and resolved. In practical terms the priority of operational leaders is to build trust, cohesion, motivation, enthusiasm, and then sales and profits will be achieved. If you are launching a new product or service the priority is not to make sure that the IT, procedures, sales scripts, terms and conditions are in place. Rather, it is to ensure that the disparate groups of individuals involved in the launch are instinctively working positively together as a single community with clarity of purpose and energy, that it is intrinsically satisfying their individual aspirations and expectations. In this respect, in the text, we go on to question whether Alexander was indeed Great, why Magellan exhibited the attributes and capabilities of practical and collaborative wisdom, why the Hittites are but a semicolon in global history and how Procter & Gamble have developed global leadership capabilities which have resulted in optimal long-term performance.

Where are the Leaders in the Organisation?

How many leaders within the organisation (when I talk of leaders I refer to anyone within the organisation who is responsible for directing the energies and time of one or more other persons) can honestly say that they are people managers, with specific people management focus and capabilities, as opposed to managing tasks or technical functions which require the utilisation of human resources to attain targets and objectives?

The development and nurturing of such a dedicated focus and capability is ultimately less the responsibility of operational management and more that of the dominant coalition, the executive management, who tend to look more at the "numbers" and look at and run the organisation in a functional and technical rather than holistic and organic manner. I am increasingly bemused to find that the higher that one looks within an organisation's leadership hierarchy the less one sees individuals with capabilities in and a focus on people management. Rather, the focus, as I have already stated, is on the numbers, sales, revenue, profit, cost and income, capital ratios, on technical, tangible issues, such as statutory requirements, IT development, compliance, operational risk and property.

Many readers may consider that this is entirely appropriate, that at the end of the day the role of executive management is to monitor the numbers "dashboard" and deal with urgent/important "macro" issues. People management is, after all, operational. If, as I suggest, long-term optimal performance and organisational survival is dependent upon effective people management then senior management are, in fact, not in control of the organisation's engine, gears and steering; they are in the majority of cases merely holding the map and watching the speedometer.

I am minded in respect of the primacy of people leadership by Tarantino (1998) who concluded that if an organisation succeeds in efficiently and effectively satisfying the requirements and expectations of its key stakeholder groups, internal and external, then concomitant profits will accrue. The focus of executive leadership time, energy and attention should therefore be focused upon ensuring that all the factors are in place to ensure stakeholder cohesion, loyalty, motivation and advocacy rather than a focus on managing the organisational numbers and technical table stakes of organisational management; in essence, a primary focus on creating and managing an environment to encourage and foster organisational leadership. The role of the operational leadership cadre is to proactively manage these factors to achieve operational effectiveness and optimal performance. This requires a preponderance of "engineers" rather than "mechanics" in positions of operational leadership, a point which we will expand upon within the text. Practical wisdom informs the operational leader that this is primarily achieved through a focus on people.

These are controversial statements and of course in organisational leadership there are no absolutes. Of course executive committee members as individuals and as a group, perhaps subconsciously, at the back of their mind, understand the importance of and consider the "soft" issues of employee motivation, cohesion, dedication and loyalty and shareholder confidence. Yet too often there is a tendency to manage at "front of mind", the easier to grasp and control tangible issues which always seem to be pressing for resolution. This priority leaves the more complex people issues, in which experience and insight is limited, to be resolved later, when it is perceived to have become critical to organisational survival and long-term performance.

It's Tough, But It Works

Such a realignment in leadership focus to what might be termed soft-hearted, hard-headed perspectives requires a paradigm shift in the culture of operational management. Such a paradigm shift battles against a generation of leaders who presently populate middle and senior positions, and have been inculcated in a predominantly technical, functional and profit management perspective and priority. Even if they considered that there was some validity in the people management perspective and priority to drive profit optimisation, they might still resist implementation because it required such a radical change in mindset across the leadership cadre within the organisation that for many it is a mountain peak too difficult to scale. This book proposes and illustrates the application of the principles, perspectives, process, attributes and capabilities of practical and collaborative wisdom, thereby facilitating the required realignment to consistently achieve operational effectiveness and optimal organisational performance over the long term.

However, what of those few organisations which have, over decades already scaled this peak and embedded principles, perspectives, priorities and key practices of practical and collaborative wisdom in relation to optimising long-term performance, based upon an operational leadership focus on and capabilities in people management? This book will illustrate how a number of these organisations have developed, nurtured and maintained this dynamic capability and, equally importantly, how the leadership cadres within these organisations who acknowledge its value in enhancing long-term performance, can replicate such capabilities over generations of leadership coalitions. We therefore begin this book by describing and illustrating the fundamental values, principles and process, the building blocks, upon which a robust organisation is founded in order to resist adversity and take advantage of opportunities over the longer term. This is the existence within the organisational dominant coalition and its operational leadership cadre of wisdom, more particularly, practical and collaborative wisdom.

1 *Who Needs Wisdom?*

The purpose of Part One is to gain a broad understanding of the meaning and dynamics of wisdom and insights into its potential relevance, operational and practical contribution to effective operational leadership. Having achieved this objective, the remainder of the book will be dedicated to translating the principles, perspectives, priorities and processes upon which wisdom is founded into practical, pragmatic and operational leadership characteristics, attributes and capabilities. By this means the leadership cadre is able to effectively nurture, develop and reinforce the application of practical and collaborative wisdom within the operational business context in support of the attainment of the long-term organisational vision, objectives and optimal performance.

1 *Wisdom and Leadership*

This first chapter sets the scene for a detailed discussion of the merits, perspectives, processes and attributes of a leadership mindset founded on practical and collaborative wisdom. In this respect it briefly portrays the organisational context within which operational leadership is presently expected to perform, predominantly one of chaos, crisis, myopia and a focus on technical rather than leadership excellence. The result is, in most, although not all cases, an ineffective operational context and suboptimal organisational performance, based primarily upon pragmatism and perspiration. Given this prevailing context we consider the critical importance of initiating the process of inculcation even before the aspiring leader begins their career. In this respect we address the contribution which business schools make to this suboptimal scenario and what is required in order that their contribution is enhanced at this critical stage in the development of the leadership mindset.

The Leadership of Chaos and Pragmatism

The majority of experienced organisational leaders know both the key questions to ask and the answers to achieve operational effectiveness and performance. It is, however, the individual and also the organisational mindset which stunts the ability to implement and deliver. In the absence of the appropriate perspectives, attributes and capabilities of wisdom, which act as a foundation stone, an anchor, a compass for effective decision making, we find that we are faced with shallow leadership logic, perspectives and practices, largely based upon a reliance on pragmatism, perspiration and chaos management, resulting in suboptimal organisational performance over the long term.

Increasingly, based upon my experience as a business executive, I take the view that the majority of leaders of business organisational units (be it a section, department, division or the whole organisation), with perhaps 15–20 years of experience clocked up in their career, pretty much recognise the key issues which affect their unit's performance and know how to address them. In other words they know the key questions in order to address optimal performance and they know the answers. They know how to cut costs, increase productivity, enhance performance, motivate staff, maintain the confidence of stakeholders, etc. The problem is that despite their significant intelligence, experience, insight and judgement the majority just can't translate their knowledge into practice. They, as individuals or as groups within the organisation, cannot effectively implement recognised solutions.

It is fair to say that the vast majority of organisations fail to optimise performance over the long term, indeed many stumble from one crisis to another, largely prey to and dependent upon market and economic cycles for their success or eventual demise. In reality, the majority of organisations rely more on application, determination, instinct and particularly perspiration on the part of their operational management cadre and staff to achieve annual and longer term objectives. This, rather than the effective and structured application of a plan, based upon consistently applied principles, perspectives and priorities which address key organisational issues in an insightful, purposeful and methodical manner. Some readers will deny that this is the case and contend that plans are executed with clarity and precision, but are frequently blown off course by external, unanticipated events. Others will align themselves with a "managing in chaos" perspective, focusing on the important, almost heroic, leadership attributes of experience, insight, judgement, adaptability, flexibility, pragmatism and particularly persuasive skills to create order, direction and consistent achievement from chaos. From the perspective of organisational leaders there is some advantage in creating the impression that leadership has a mystical ingredient, difficult to grasp, elusive and transitory, and that those individuals or organisations which consistently perform are verging on the supernatural, which mere mortals cannot comprehend, much less replicate.

I must admit to being a bit of a chaos management adherent and having a great respect for practitioners who do not overly think consciously much about or discuss management and leadership. They just do it (in the majority of cases much better than they can explain it), year in year out on the basis of experience, insight, instinct, intuition and hard graft. Their operational role, indeed responsibility is to realise a strategic plan, most often based on flawed information and organisational insight, unrealistic aspirations, ego and best intentions. This in an organisation with an unclear vision, limited resources and focus, flawed internal communication, limited leadership vision and capabilities and diverse personal and group priorities and loyalties. This is the reality of the chaotic, suboptimal environment in which the majority of leaders find themselves and where the new entrant is dropped, either directly from school or increasingly as a business graduate, expected to find his/her way and make their mark as experts and leaders ASAP. This is to be achieved, in the majority of cases, presumably on the basis of osmosis, rather than on the basis of example or structured development and training.

On reflection, I believe that the various theories revolving around managing in chaos, such as Tom Peters (1988), have much to commend them and strangely add clarity to and aptly describe the holistic reality of organisational management as it is experienced by operational leaders today. It should also be commended for explaining in a clear and realistic manner the process and practices of leadership, in a form and terminology which is recognised, acknowledged and most of all understood by practicing managers. However, in practice, such theories, although portraying the reality of organisational management at the dawn of the twenty-first century do not provide guidance on how to achieve optimal effectiveness and performance. They are somewhat like providing a length of rope for someone who stumbles into one deep hole after another, very useful but of no value in avoiding the holes.

Regrettably much of what is written within the area of organisational management is of even less value to the organisational leader. It is largely aspirational, barely understandable or recognisable to the practicing leader and of minimal practical value to the practice of management because it fails to reflect the complex, dynamic realities of operational organisational management. Many, I would suggest the vast majority, of leadership "practitioners" would contend that scholarly research and texts tend to reflect the priority of rigour rather than practical relevance, failing to add value to effective leadership. In this respect I am reminded of a quote by Stewart:

> *Oh sure, there are a few points of insight, and one or two stories about hero-CEOs that can hook you like bad popcorn. But the rest is just inane (Stewart, 2006, p. 82).*

Operational leaders consider that on the basis of the evidence with which they are provided by scholars, clarity and direction are desirable yet unachievable and the most successful leader is the pragmatist who takes decisions, resolves issues as they arise, fixing and repairing and shall we say, adapting, the principles, perspectives, priorities and practices of the organisation on the hoof, on the basis of experience, intuition, practical insight and judgement. This is a sad and calamitous perspective for both the scholar and practitioner, since it is much akin to repairing a desktop computer with a hammer and monkey wrench, totally outdated and inappropriate tools for the purpose, when appropriate tools are available, if only they were acknowledged as capable of resolving practical, operational leadership issues. My practitioner/scholar experience has convinced me that the embryonic solution to many fundamental and intractable leadership issues are contained within the results and conclusions of scholarly research. Yet the complexity, dynamism, most importantly the urgency of organisational management dictates that organisational leaders do not have the time, patience or the mindset to delve into scholarly literature to seek out any practical solutions. Indeed, in the majority of cases the objective of such documents is not the resolution of operational management issues and the terminology and train of thought is not in congruence with the mindset of the practicing organisational leader.

"Chaos" and "pragmatism" are words which reflect the mindset, perspectives and terminology of practicing managers and leaders at all levels of management and across the majority of functional divisions. Other similar terms might be tasks, projects, targets, revenue, profits, costs, sales, products, distribution. I have no major issue with these words; they are all appropriate within the operational context. However, they encourage what I would term "shallow", second division, rather than "wise" thinking, which inevitably lead to suboptimal performance over the long term.

A major objective of this book is to change the mindset and perspective of the practicing and aspiring organisational leader, by putting forward ideas which, whilst initially appearing to be outside their normal frame of reference, will resonate with them. Ideas which will be acknowledged as potentially valid will be more easily understood and regarded as implementable. Remoulding the mindset of the aspiring and practicing operational leader to a situation where leadership is less about constantly breaking, managing and controlling a bucking bronco in the Wild West and more about optimising the performance of a Lipizzaner horse at the Spanish Riding School in Vienna. Both practitioners and scholars, in seeking to build an effective management framework of concepts, perspectives, priorities and practices have managed to develop its bricks, doors, windows, etc. However, the foundation stones of effective leadership logic, which links, coordinates and makes operational and practical sense of these component parts has so far eluded them or been lost in a form of myopia which will be briefly addressed at a later stage.

This book acknowledges, recognises and proposes practical "wisdom", its attributes and capabilities to be these missing foundation stones. What we shall term practical wisdom precludes the onset and continuance of chaos management. Instead it provides a compass, an anchor, clarity of direction and purpose, principles, perspectives and priorities, to consistently aid optimal operational decision making in the operational leadership process. Collaborative wisdom lies at the centre of practical wisdom, as a means of consistently energising stakeholders and thereby optimising operational productivity and organisational performance.

I have for many years struggled in my leadership perspectives with the term "pragmatic". I have used it myself frequently in the past as a primary defence against the perspectives of those whom I considered to be proposing impractical and unrealistic solutions for "real" operational issues and situations. It was a matter of the real and practical versus the application of some theoretical solution. Yet, in reality whipping out the "practical" or "pragmatic" card is limp and lazy leadership thinking. I have a good friend who has attained the very highest positions in banking organisations and is respected as highly principled within the sector. I am not suggesting that these attributes are mutually exclusive, yet his view is that in business, in order to practice effective leadership, you have to "manage" your principles in a pragmatic manner in order to consistently attain an optimal and "pragmatic" solution to operational issues. In principle I do not object to this perspective. However, this perspective often appears to be inadequate as a means of decision making where it results in aberrant outcomes in the eyes of the fair minded. As an example, I am sure that those who advocated apartheid in South Africa, the Holocaust in Europe, ethnic cleansing in the former Yugoslavia and in Rwanda, dropping atomic bombs on Japan, invading Iraq, considered this pragmatic within the context of their situation. I am sure that if you could speak to Hitler, Stalin, Idi Amin, Saddam Hussein, Mao Tse Tung, Harry Truman or George Bush (Senior and Junior) they would say that they took pragmatic decisions within the context of the prevailing socio-economic and political priorities, and each would have their own followers and adherents, dependent upon their dominant logic, principles, perspectives and priorities.

As we will show in Part Three, business leadership has strong parallels with building and maintaining other communities, including countries and empires. The fundamental issues and principle involved in effective leadership in business are very similar, if not identical, to those involved in decision making during the above much commented upon and analysed episodes in recent history. In this respect it is important from the perspective of understanding and appreciation of the content of this book that readers view it from an holistic and universal perspective rather than related to the business leadership silo. To create a separate body of thought and theory for business leadership is a false and unnecessary complexity which is counterproductive in the understanding and implementation of effective leadership principles and practices. This is particularly the case for those at the initial stages in their leadership careers, looking for foundation stones and a compass by which to base their core principles, perspectives and priorities which will direct operational decision making. Whilst there may (or may not) be differences in the leadership of different societal sectors, an understanding of the fundamental and critical aspects of effective operational leadership within the business context is primarily founded on universal principles and practices rather than a focus and emphasis on detailed differences.

In the same manner that some or indeed many might, rightly or wrongly question the dominant logic, the principles, perspectives and priorities, the decisions of the above mentioned political figures, so we have recently begun to question the dominant logic, principles, perspectives and priorities of business leaders who have effectively destroyed the credibility and continuing pre-eminence of the Anglo-American economic model and the dominance of the Western financial services sector. In this respect we must look beneath the headlines, sound bites and media analysis attending the rapid collapse of so many financial institutions who had been dominant players in their national and global markets (see Table 1.1). We must rather assess whether there were fundamental flaws in the dominant logic (i.e. values, principles, perspectives, priorities and core practices) of large parts of the industry, which in turn influenced, indeed dictated the perspectives and priorities of individual leaders and dominant coalitions within these organisations in respect of their approaches to operational decision-making and issue resolution.

It is not the purpose of this book in any way to rake over the coals of the calamity which has befallen the Western economy and society during the first decade of the twenty-first century. I leave this to the analysts and commentators who consider themselves gifted with an insight gained through practical inexperience of the realities of operational leadership within the sector. It is, however, reasonable to propose that the fundamental causes of this crisis are ultimately the application of the wrong leadership principles, perspectives and priorities, which we will term dominant logic, rather than the "symptoms" (e.g. greed, corruption, cronyism, incompetence, short-termism, lack of capital reserves, liquidity and weak regulation), upon which commentators have tended to focus. A continuing focus on proposed remedies for such symptoms fails to address the continuing application of a dominant logic comprising of aberrant principles, perspectives and priorities of not only senior leaders within business, but also within the broader society. These were ultimately reflected in the multitude of individual, often unconnected decisions, practices and actions of operational leadership on a day to day basis, culminating in a calamitous economic and social train crash within large sectors of the developed economies. In seeking to describe the prevalent societal and business mindset which was a prelude to the economic and financial crisis of the first decade of the twenty-first century one is reminded of the oft quoted statement from "Barbarians at the Gate", differentiating between the previous market pre-eminence of the long-term "investor" and their recent usurpation by the short-term "trader" perspective and priority of individual and institutional shareholders.

Table 1.1   Armageddon for the Financial Services Sector

Wall Street	City of London and Western Europe
• Lehman Bothers	• Royal Bank of Scotland (RBS)
• Morgan Stanley	• Halifax Bank of Scotland (HBOS)
• Bear Stearns	• Northern Rock
• Wachovia	• Fortis
• Washington Mutual	• Anglo Irish Bank
• CitiGroup	• Depfa
• AIG	• Hypo

He shredded traditions, jettisoned divisions, and roiled management. He was one of a whole breed of noncompany men who came to maturity in the 1970s and 1980s; a deal driven, yield driven nomadic lot. They said their mission was to serve company investors, not company tradition. They also tended to handsomely serve themselves (Burrough and Helyar, 1990, p. 28).

So, in effect the term "pragmatic" leadership is an excuse for a mediocre, narrow and superficial leadership perspective. More importantly, a cloak which covers a framework of assumed and embedded principles, perspectives and priorities which it is preferred are not exposed to daylight. Interestingly, there were a number of banks which, in contrast to those contained in Table 1.1, whilst not entirely innocent of the symptoms and stumbling amid the market aftershocks, were able not only to survive but, some would argue, take advantage of the crisis to promote their long-term business visions. This group might arguably include such banking organisations as HSBC Holdings plc, Barclays plc, Santander Group, JP Morgan, perhaps Goldman Sachs & Co. This book will seek to show that the embedded principles, perspectives, priorities and practices which direct operational leadership decision making within such organisations are founded upon "wise" principles and cognitive processes which ensure consistently effective and optimal-issue resolution throughout the various stages of the business cycle. This is not to say that these organisations or members of its dominant coalition do not occasionally drift to the "dark side". However, as we will later discuss, the foundation of values, principles, perspectives and priorities is embedded to act as a compass to bring them back on course (although as we will also discuss later, perhaps not always).

Nurturing the Attributes and Capabilities of Wisdom – The Role of Business Schools

Business schools have both a responsibility and opportunity to prepare their students to become wise leaders. This will be achieved by developing academic policies, course programmes and teaching capabilities which support aspiring leaders in the development of a mindset and wise decision-making process which supports the resolution of complex, contextually driven operational issues, rather than the more limited objective of the furnishing of explicit knowledge to create technically competent managers.

Prior to immersing ourselves in the principles, perspectives, processes, attributes and capabilities of practically wise leadership it is necessary to briefly address the important role of those institutions which have a critical role to play in the initial development of an appropriate leadership mindset at the beginning of what is a lengthy inculcation process. Given the increasing number of aspiring and practicing business leaders who are attending undergraduate and postgraduate business and management programmes, it is important to emphasise at this early stage in the book that the role and involvement of academic institutions, in preparing their students for a career of wise leadership, could be, but is not, critical. Academic leaders, teachers and research scholars are therefore included as key readership groups with regard to a consequential review of business school vision, policy and course programmes, and a concomitant impact on teaching staff, business insight, experience and capabilities.

Business colleges and schools have a critical role, responsibility and opportunity to nurture the appropriate mindset, perspectives and priorities in tomorrow's organisational leaders. James C. Worthy in 1955 considered that business schools had poorly equipped graduates for business. The reasons arguably persist today; an undue amount of specialisation and an undue emphasis on creating "technicians" competent in specific areas of management (e.g. finance treasury, marketing, HR). This has resulted in a good supply of narrow, technical "management" experts, well versed in the table stakes of managing an organisation, but not of individuals who have the necessary insights into organisational leadership from an holistic and "people" leadership perspective and within a broader socio-economic context. Business schools must focus on inculcating their students with the principles and practices of operational leadership which are clearly seen to be relevant and applicable in day to day decision-making and issue resolution.

Worthy explained the basis for the prevailing emphasis by the fact that the teaching resources available made it very difficult to teach anything more relevant to effective organisational leadership than the technical. Also that this was what business organisations demanded, on the basis of their own perspectives that the key to organisational performance in the era of mass production lay in technical expertise. He argued that business schools essentially "grew" the management capabilities required by the dominant coalitions' leaders in organisations and industrial sectors (a bit like beef for supermarkets) and failed to show the kind of intellectual leadership and moral courage required to make wise curriculum choices in the interests of the wider society. Bennis (1999) argues that organisational leaders do not lack technical expertise and skills, nor do they lack experience or an ability to understand concepts. Rather they lack the "softer" skills, characteristics, judgement and people management skills of the effective leader.

Many would argue that such characteristics, capabilities, insight, judgement, cannot be taught, but rather is "hard won from engagement with life" (McAdams, 2005) and I would not argue with this point. However, in ostensibly addressing key points in nurturing effective organisational leadership within business schools it is appropriate to emphasise that what is being taught is in the majority of cases merely the technical table stakes and is of marginal value in developing effective leadership skills, preparing them for "management" rather than "leadership" roles (the critical differences which will subsequently be described). Therefore, aspiring leaders must expend substantial time and effort over their careers to develop these foundational perspectives, priorities and soft skills if are they are eventually to develop into effective leaders, when this might have been "kick started" at a much earlier stage in their career development.

Colleges and particularly business schools have a critical role to play in the development of practical wisdom amongst existing and aspiring leaders. There must be a recognition and understanding amongst both scholars and students alike that the accumulation of explicit knowledge, which you get out of books, is not the ultimate achievement or end product in readying students for a career in business. Rather it is to provide "scaffolding" (Sternberg, 2001), learning structures and experiences which will allow individuals to utilise the explicit knowledge to take practically wise decisions in specific practical business situations. The ultimate test of the value of any business management programme or book/article is whether it substantively supports the operational leadership decision-making and issue resolution process. If the answer is no, but it adds to the body of technical expertise and/or business knowledge, this is fine.

However, it must be recognised as of lesser significance and priority in the enhancement of operational effectiveness and organisational performance.

This is a perspective which is likely to lack universal support and result in much consternation amongst groups within both scholarly and business organisations. Yet few would argue that technical expertise is rarely in short supply in organisations. Nor is there a shortage of written business knowledge. What is lacking is leadership perspectives, skills, attributes and capabilities, to apply knowledge in a contextually focused manner in order to optimise organisational performance. In this respect what is proposed is to take business education to another level, beyond a primary focus on technical excellence. Case studies which presently tend to be utilised to reinforce, for example, theories of marketing, organisational behaviour, HR management, financial, risk or supply chain management might be reconfigured and focused to "kick start" a mindset to support the operational leadership decision-making and issue resolution process.

Academic institutions can and should play a critical role in the development of practical wisdom, through the dynamic process of not only transmitting valuable knowledge, but taking a further step in converting facts and information into tacit knowledge of how to act and take optimal decisions within the operational leadership, rather than management context. Rather than providing insight to appropriate business and management knowledge and how these have been applied in case studies, the primary objective should be to dynamically provide clear insight with respect to why, when, where, how and to whom this knowledge should be applied. In this way academic institutions provide organisations not only with potential technical experts but individuals who are nascent leaders, with a mindset which will provide effective general management and support optimal performance.

This will require not only a change in perspectives and priorities in respect of the objectives of educating business students by both academic institutions and business organisations but a concomitant change in teaching staff experience and capabilities, from the technical to the holistic and organisational. The implications for business school policy and leadership are equally substantial, requiring a holistic, daring, dynamic and innovative approach in order to move away from a mass production approach to education to a more R&D approach, embedding broad leadership principles and logic rather than technical expertise. Fundamentally this requires teaching staff to have significant business management experience and insight; otherwise their capabilities are limited to the transmission of technical knowledge. It also requires a focus on research which is primarily focused on and directed towards enhancing and supporting operational leadership capability, rather than adding to the sum of knowledge. This is an approach already increasingly applied by those few business schools which are globally recognised and respected for nurturing and developing individuals who have a mindset to take practically "wise" approaches to leadership issues. These institutions, rather than waiting for business to redefine their requirements, are proactively recognising their role as providers of nascent business leaders who have the required technical expertise, rather than merely technically expert managers, thereby redefining and helping to re-configure the leadership capabilities required of the business organisation in the twenty-first century.

2 *Understanding Practical Wisdom*

What Happened to the Phronimos?

Over time, the attributes of the leader who exhibited the principles, perspectives and capabilities of wisdom, from being venerated, have become devalued and largely ignored, in favour of the dominance of scientific, rational, utilitarian and impersonal perspectives and priorities. The consequence has been diminishing cohesion, loyalty, dedication and performance, increasingly resulting in suboptimal performance, organisational collapse, social and economic crisis.

As stated in Chapter 1, in order to understand and gain insight into the attributes and process of wise operational business leadership one has first to stand outside the silo of business management knowledge and view it from an holistic and universal perspective. The concept of wisdom has been venerated since classical Greek times, but also in Chinese and Islamic texts, recognised as encapsulating the peak of human knowledge and excellence. All texts identify the critical attributes of practical wisdom to include such "soft" characteristics as humility, persuasiveness, sincerity, dignity, honesty. They also include such intangibles as intuition and imagination as capabilities enhancing wise decision making. Aristotle, in his *The Nicomachean Ethics* (1998) distinguishes between:

- *Sophia* which involves the contemplation of universal truths.
- *Episteme*, a more scientific, rationalist approach to knowledge; and, more relevant to our deliberations.
- *Phronesis*, which relates to sound judgement and wisdom when deciding on actions to resolve practical operational, day to day issues. Phronesis requires consideration of all aspects of knowledge, experience, insight and intuition, taking into consideration both rational and emotional considerations in coming to any single decision.

The individual who had phronesis was termed the Phronimos, the individual who could be trusted to come up with the optimal practical solution in the interests of the "polis" or community, at that time in history, usually in relation to the areas of politics or war.

We can easily relate this description of the Phronimos to some of the much lauded business leaders of the twentieth century and indeed those whom from our personal experience we recognise as excellent leaders of people, organisations and communities. However, from a position of prominence and veneration wisdom has continued to be respected as a desirable attribute or characteristic, although more from a philosophical, abstract perspective, rather than as a pre-eminent attribute, capability and fundamental requirement for optimally resolving practical, operational issues. This development has now progressed to such an extent that wisdom as an attribute or characteristic is no longer considered relevant and the terminology used to discuss wisdom is considered inappropriate for discussion and to the development of concepts in relation to effective leadership and organisational management (Case and Gosling, 2007).

The reasons for this fall from pre-eminence could be the subject of a separate chapter, if not a book, and involve many converging strands of the dynamic route by which society's balance of perspectives and priorities, particularly in the Anglo-American culture(s), has developed, in particular over the last millennium. Such strands include the spread of the global religions, which sought to portray wisdom as steeped in archaic metaphysics and therefore a corrupting influence. Latterly, developments in science, economics, philosophy, administration and industrialisation, with their focus on the rational, tangible and utilitarian have sidelined an attribute which, whilst prizing rational intelligence also put great store by the intangible, on universal values, on imagination, intuition and emotion, to arrive at optimal decisions in the interests of the "polis". Rooney and McKenna succinctly describe the waves of rational, utilitarian, scientific and disciplined thought which swept issues of morality, humanity and practical wisdom aside as priorities for consideration, increasingly redundant concepts in the process of socio-economic evolution,

> From the Enlightenment came "value free" empirical science; from Protestantism came social utilitarianism; from the secular liberalism of JS Mill and Adam Smith came an incipient economic rationalism and a view of humans as homo economicus; from mercantilism came the need for increasingly complex government and business administration; from the Industrial Revolution came the normalisation of disciplined regularity and order in the production process (Rooney and McKenna, 2007, pp. 118–119).

During the 1920s onwards we have experienced the onset of highly structured, scientific management approaches and models based upon structures, strategies, processes, procedures and programmes supported by an emphasis on technical expertise as the means to maximise productivity and organisational performance. This development is not to be decried as an irrational response to what was a phenomenal increase in organisational scale and management complexity. However, when rational, value-free utilitarianism replaces the "balanced" hard-headed yet soft-hearted, practical wisdom approach, based as it is on resolving practical issues on the basis of universally acknowledged values, utilising accumulated knowledge, experience, judgement, and intuition in a balanced and sensitive manner, in the interests of all stakeholders, the result is likely to be a diminution in cohesion, loyalty and motivation.

As a result, today, actions and practices are therefore now frequently perceived of as impersonal and degrading to the self-respect and self-esteem of the individual and the pre-eminence of the broader community. This has arguably resulted in lacklustre and suboptimal performance and ultimately, where this perspective has become a dominant feature of policy and practice, a collapse at the organisational level and economic crisis, leading to social fragmentation at the macro level. Whilst there is no doubt that the technical innovations of the twentieth and twenty-first centuries have substantially increased the potential and capability for enhanced performance wellbeing, the response in respect of the selection and application of relevant principles, perspectives and priorities which have developed within the organisational dominant logic have arguably resulted in a suboptimal realisation of such potential over the long term.

The application of "phronesis" or practical wisdom and the creation of a cadre of leaders which correspond to the profile of the Phronimos make it possible to rebalance the leadership logic. The potential also exists to have a dramatic and positive impact on the quality of leadership and the cohesion of the community, whether it is the organisation or society, with a concomitant impact upon productivity and performance within the organisation and community (whose interests and performance are intertwined). Whilst this book is most certainly not a philosophical treatise it is necessary to recognise and take stock of the relevance and validity of key, "universal" principles, perspectives and priorities which underpin, act as an anchor and determine decision making within all sectors of society, thereby creating clarity, confidence and cohesion throughout the organisation. In this respect it is appropriate that we clearly understand both the relevance and fundamental components of wisdom and more specifically practical and collaborative wisdom. Building on this knowledge we can then look in greater detail at how it can be translated into, impacts upon and can be utilised within the operational leadership practice.

Wisdom Through Adversity

The attributes and capabilities of wisdom are developed largely as a result of experiencing life's severe adverse and traumatic episodes. Such experiences result in one taking a critically reflective, calm, yet empathetic perspective, considering any issue from a holistic rather than specific perspective, allowing one to apply these attributes within a multiplicity of contexts.

When one implicitly considers wisdom and wise individuals one develops an impression of a self-assured, confident, content and satisfied individual with an experience of and understanding of the vagaries of life. Someone who is able to recover from, and rationalise and transcend personal crisis and tragedy, where others are permanently scarred, if not psychologically incapacitated. Perhaps due to the above impressions such individuals are considered capable of dealing effectively with any crisis that they encounter or in which they are asked to become involved, be it personal or occupational/professional. Ardelt (2005) proposes that the ability to cope with such situations is not only a mark of the wise individual but a route by which one attains a state of wisdom. Without wishing to denigrate the problems, stresses and hardships of senior executives within their organisational roles, it is unlikely that they attain a state of wisdom on the basis of "crises" which they have experienced in business. It is more likely that they are able to take wise decisions within the organisational context on the basis of situations in their "private" lives which have taken them to the brink of their ability to cope with life, such as death, oppression, extreme poverty, guilt, absolute failure or uncontrollable fear within other contexts, which they have survived and had the strength to reflect upon in a critical manner.

However, given the centrality of their profession and career within their lives it is likely that in many instances these personal traumatic episodes may occur or be experienced during the carrying out of their leadership role, impacting the generation of wisdom on the part of the participants and also their close relatives and colleagues. In respect of those institutions within which I have been employed I am aware of traumatic incidents experienced by individuals or their close colleagues which are likely to have generated intense periods of critical reflection. These include assassination in Ireland, execution in Singapore, being shot by terrorists in Argentina, bombed by terrorists in Turkey, self and/or family members kidnapped in Mexico and Ireland, long-term hospitalisation as a result of rioting staff in the Philippines, 9/11 survival and imprisonment for apostasy in Saudi Arabia. These individuals and others have thereby likely developed experience, knowledge and insight, creating a cognitive and motivational problem-solving capability for critical reflection of a higher order than others to resolve crises within the business context. This may well be why some individuals who have managed to extract themselves from disadvantaged environments go on to be successful in business and life in general.

Ardelt provides a penetrating insight into the mindset and perspectives of those perceived from her research into this issue to be relatively high wisdom respondents.

PERSONAL TRAITS OF WISDOM AS A RESULT OF CRITICAL REFLECTION

- Such individuals exhibited a positive, optimistic perspective and did not consider that they had encountered many, if indeed any recent unpleasant occurrences.
- Where a crisis had occurred they would not take it personally but rather objectively and view it from a psychological distance, taking a calm, reflective approach, confident that the application of their experience and knowledge would result in an optimal solution.
- Such crises were rather regarded as a puzzle or challenge to be resolved, rather than a personal attack or injury.
- Where a tangible loss had occurred the perspective was to take a holistic approach, placing the loss within the wider life context, moving on and continuing to apply time proven values and principles in order to optimise the overall benefit of key stakeholders, even though some individuals might suffer or be disadvantaged.
- These individuals never considered that they had lost control and were mere pawns, but considered that their actions and perspectives could always make a difference and that they were active participants in and contributors to the outcome.

Source: adapted from Ardelt (2005).

Whilst there is a body of thought which indicates that it is not possible to be "wise" in response to all issues and contexts (Ardelt, 2004a), we propose at this juncture in the development of our propositions a holistic rather than sectoral perspective to the capabilities of "wise" individuals. The attributes of practical wisdom, essentially a balance of intelligence, knowledge, experience, insight, empathy and judgement, with an ability to be both reflective and affective, are those characteristics required of individuals who effectively lead any unit of a community or society towards optimal performance over the long term. If you can imagine the attributes of great leaders of countries, cultures or empires which have survived over an extended period throughout history, these are the attributes required to lead an organisation effectively, because a business organisation is merely a microcosm of society. Naturally, if you are leading within a pharmaceutical company it does require specific expert technical knowledge and insight rather than if you were leading within a bank or mining company. However, the characteristics of wisdom which drive effective leadership are to all intents and purposes identical. The wise individual is potentially an effective leader and individual within all groups of which he is a member (e.g. business organisation, family, political party, sports club) because the traits, attributes, capabilities, perspectives and mental processes of practical wisdom are universal, no matter the context. Regrettably many business leaders who are lauded by commentators and analysts due to short-term successes do not fulfil this criterion. They lack the attributes comprising practical wisdom to achieve holistic "success", making suboptimal assessments and decisions on individual issues and occasions where effective leadership is required, with the resultant impact on long-term optimal performance and survival of the organisation.

Wisdom in the Modern Business Organisation

Wisdom must become established as the fundamental cornerstone of effective organisational leadership. The application of the perspective, attributes and capabilities of wisdom will enable leaders within the business organisation to achieve economic objectives whilst simultaneously optimally satisfying the requirements and expectations of all key stakeholder groups within the "community", without the requirement to resort to unethical practices.

HARD CODING PRACTICAL WISDOM

Rather than being something which can be added, like a piece of software, wisdom is fundamental to the principles, perspectives, priorities and operational practices of organisational leadership, coded into the hardware of the organisation's and individual's dominant logic. It looks beyond the operational perspectives, priorities and practices which are most apparent to the casual viewer and analyst, to those fundamental values, principles and logic deeply embedded within and which subconsciously, perhaps unknowingly by the dominant coalition, drive an organisation's decision making. This book will be discussing a process of inculcation, in its most positive interpretation, rather in its mindless "Borg-like" interpretation, in order to embed key principles, perspectives and priorities in not only the leaders of today and tomorrow, but all employees within the organisation. It is a process of positive inculcation which has stood as the foundation stone of the optimal performance of a small number of business organisations for a sustained period (to which we will refer subsequently in the text), spanning many decades, in a few cases over a century.

This book sets out to provide clarity and simplicity vis-à-vis a route map which existing and aspiring operational leaders can easily understand, follow and implement. The milestones are universally applicable but, very much in line with the "pragmatic" approach require to be read contextually and "practically". This does not mean that where they are seemingly difficult to apply then they are impractical to apply. Merely that the organisation's leadership has deviated from the optimal operational priorities and practices consistent with a dominant logic which reflects the principles, perspectives, attributes and capabilities of practical wisdom.

CONTRADICTORY LEADERSHIP IMPERATIVES

Leaders in organisations of the twenty-first century, in the eyes of many, are facing contradictory performance imperatives (Margolis and Walsh, 2003). On the one hand, they are expected by their superiors to manage business performance imperatives. On the other, they are compelled by the mission statements and pronouncements of the corporation and increasing legislation to deal with and deliver on complex social and macro ethical dilemmas (Dawes, 1980) during the decision-making process of day to day operational management. Whilst some operational leaders do have the personal attributes, capabilities and experience, and are also working within an appropriate organisational dominant logic, others have neither the personal capabilities nor operate within an appropriate organisational set of dominant principles and priorities to balance and achieve what are perceived to be contradictory, indeed often conflicting imperatives. This conflict and absence of appropriate leadership perspectives and capabilities often leads to unethical and frequently illegal decision-making behaviour when considering and seeking to satisfy the requirements and expectations of key stakeholder groups.

In the short term such behaviour leads amongst the stakeholder community to confusion, diminishing loyalty to the organisation and its management, a fracture in optimal cooperation, coordination, motivation and suboptimal productivity. Ultimately this leads to open conflict between stakeholder groups, intransigence, a lack of cohesion and the voluntary or involuntary exit of stakeholder members, leading to the destruction of the organisation in the form of collapse, merger or acquisition. Thus, the current state of organisational logic and practice calls on leaders to optimise economic value creation whilst simultaneously considering how to organise and lead ethically (Kupers, 2007). The proposals contained within this book ensure that through the consistent application of practical and collaborative wisdom the primary objectives of the organisation in respect of optimal operational effectiveness and performance and the satisfaction of both the tangible and intangible requirements and expectations of the stakeholder community and society at large are both compatible and achievable.

This seems like a panacea and certainly will not be achieved within many organisations without a substantial reorientation in principles, perspectives and priorities on the part of the dominant players and peer group leaders, be they senior executives and/or non-executive directors. However, in the absence of the components of practical and collaborative wisdom organisations will be unable to consistently apply the appropriate principles and values which ensure the ongoing trust, dedication and cohesion of all stakeholder groups, thereby failing to ensure survival and optimal performance over the long term. It is important to stress at this juncture that in contrast to what impressions one might have gained from operational experience, peer group leader example, or other influences to date in one's career, these components of practical and collaborative wisdom are the practical, pragmatic, hard-headed, though "soft-hearted" realities, requirements and priorities for effective operational leadership, if indeed the primary objectives are organisational survival and optimal long-term performance of the organisation (this is however an assumption perhaps no longer to be taken for granted). The proactive leadership of people, of stakeholders, must hold centre stage in the mindset and issue resolution process of the operational leader in order to ensure optimal effectiveness and performance over the long term. In practice, this requires in many cases a radical realignment in perceived priorities to optimally achieve organisational targets and objectives.

WISDOM – A CORNERSTONE OF LEADERSHIP

At the core of the proposals within this book are two key terms "practical" and "collaborative". The terms practical and collaborative applied on their own are well understood and indeed utilised by the majority of leadership practitioners. In the four decades that I have operated within business I do not recall ever using the word "wisdom" in conversation, or indeed thinking of the word "wisdom" to consider or explain the solution to an operational or strategic management issue. In all honesty, and regrettably, I would be hard pressed to think of a truly "wise" person that I have met within the business context.

However, as I have travelled on my journey of desk and empirical research to ascertain the core component(s) of effective organisational leadership, beyond strategy, core competence, culture, dominant logic, values, and many other terms I have arrived at the term "wisdom" as the attribute which ultimately determines whether an organisation is most likely to be effectively led and will ultimately survive and prosper over the long term. This is somewhat unfortunate, since the term "wisdom" carries much baggage and conjures up the image of a man, sage-like, with a long white beard, somewhat dishevelled. It nostalgically brings to mind Aristotle, Socrates, the Stoics and the philosophy of classical times, propounding on interesting yet patently not very relevant or practical issues within the context of today's operational business priorities. The concept of wisdom therefore hardly appears appropriate to be considered as fundamental or essential to the leadership of a dynamic, complex business context.

However, it is the contention of this book that practical and collaborative wisdom be established as the fundamental cornerstone of effective organisational leadership. On this basis considerable time, focus and resources should be expended to create an environment for the development of practical and collaborative wisdom within the organisation, particularly amongst its leadership cadre. This initially comprises of the recruitment of appropriate individuals and thereafter the active and structured development of the appropriate framework of experience, insight, principles, perspectives and priorities to generate an organisational logic and mindset consistent with the application of practical and collaborative wisdom. The primary focus of this book will therefore be to gain a clear operational understanding of what the wisdom attribute or capability comprises and describe the key steps in its nurturing, development, management and operational day to day application within the business organisation.

Wisdom: A Balance of Attributes and Capabilities

Wise individuals balance the rational with the intuitive and empathetic, applying universal values for the overall benefit of the wider community. Wisdom develops best in leaders within environments where they must optimise performance through the continuous resolution of adverse life experiences amongst a multiplicity of individuals. However, the objectives and priorities of many organisations are such as to ensure that their dominant leadership coalitions are populated by the savant and/or the ignoramus rather than the sage.

If there is a word which might appropriately describe the attribute or capability of wisdom it is balance; a balance of intelligence, insight, experience and perspective, a balance which few possess and only a few accurately recognise in others. Sternberg undertook a series of studies to distinguish and differentiate between the conceptions which people had of intelligence in comparison with wisdom. These are shown in Table 2.1. Overall, the difference appears to be a more balanced, dynamic, vibrant and "deeper" thought process in favour of the wisdom attribute.

Table 2.1   Implicit Theories of Wisdom and Intelligence

Intelligence	Wisdom
• Practical problem-solving ability	• Reasoning ability
• Verbal ability	• Clarity of vision
• Intellectual balance and integration	• Learning from ideas and environment
• Goal orientation and attainment	• Judgement
• Contextual intelligence	• Prompt and efficient use of information
• Fluid thought	• Keen discernment and foresight

Source: adapted from Sternberg 1985, 1990.

Sternberg (2005) further considers that wisdom is a critical component of effective leadership, which he considers occurs primarily as a result of those attributes contained within the boxed text below.

KEY COMPONENTS IN THE APPLICATION OF WISDOM FOR EFFECTIVE LEADERSHIP

- A creative ability to generate ideas.
- The analytical intelligence to evaluate the quality of those ideas.
- The intelligence to effectively implement the most appropriate ideas.
- The ability to persuade others of the value and viability of the selected ideas, enough to facilitate their implementation.
- The wisdom to ensure that implementation of the selected decisions ultimately optimises the benefit to all stakeholders.

Source: adapted from Sternberg (2005).

Perhaps the most salient leadership attribute is the final one, which focuses primarily on attitude and perspective, rather than skills and competencies. This attribute focuses upon how one thinks, one's perspectives and priorities, rather than one's technical expertise in completing the tasks and functions of leadership. In this respect a key attribute of wisdom is the focus on the optimal benefit for the community of stakeholders, rather than the attributes of intelligence, which can be applied for the benefit of individual or limited stakeholder groups. By implication, an organisational leader who applies principles, perspectives and priorities to individual operational issues which are not ultimately in the interests of the "common good" of the community of stakeholders is not wise. Ultimately such decisions are likely to be detrimental to the community (i.e. organisation and society as a whole) and also adversely affect upon those stakeholders who had been preferred.

Wisdom requires the balancing of personal interests, the interests of others and the environment and context which support pertinent stakeholder groups, to reach a decision which creates the optimal overall benefit, rather than the maximum benefit for self and/ or limited stakeholder groups. This is achieved by consistently applying a set of universal values which are understood, respected and acknowledged within all communities as the basis upon which all communities fundamentally operate (Schwartz, 1992; Schwartz and Bardi, 2001), rather than those peculiar to an individual, a particular group, culture or society. This is a somewhat controversial statement, to which we will return at a later juncture in order to provide robust empirical evidence, but for the moment we might accept it to facilitate the development of the overall proposition.

In order to gain an initial understanding of the attributes of practical wisdom, we can distil pertinent research on the subject of wisdom to date and propose that it comprises of a number of fundamental components contained within the boxed text below.

THE ATTRIBUTES OF PRACTICAL WISDOM

- The rational: based upon justified reason and empirical evidence.
- The intangible: takes into account intuition, emotion, empathy, imagination and other similar aspects of human experience.
- Core principles: an understanding of universally applicable values, principles, perspectives and priorities.
- Practical application: ability to utilise this understanding in an analytical manner and apply sound judgement, intuition and insight in order to resolve individual, practical, context driven issues in an optimal manner.
- The interests of the polis: this, in the interests of the broader community, rather than merely individual or narrow stakeholder interests.

Sources: adapted from Baltes and Kunzmann, 2004; Baltes and Staudinger, 2000; Kupers, 2007; McAdams, 2005; Rooney and McKenna, 2007; Sternberg, 2001.

Within this context the attributes, process and practice of wisdom are not abstract, theoretical and only involved with principles and philosophy. It is rather critical in the optimal resolution of practical, operational, day to day issues and effective leadership decision making. What we shall term practical wisdom is the key skill and capability, possessed by very few individuals, of effectively utilising the intelligence, knowledge, experience and insight, also possessed by many others, but who lack the appropriate perspectives, attributes and capabilities, within the practical context, to optimal effect. Practical wisdom has been described as,

An ability to conduct oneself prudently and well and to judge correctly and soundly by applying reason to putative fact, tempered by intuition and insight. Wisdom must be infused by ethical judgment and is directed to soundly based practical outcomes (Rooney and McKenna, 2005, p. 308).

Practical wisdom may therefore be considered to be the ultimate state for decision-making and issue resolution, transcending those who are endowed with all or a combination of:

- Intelligence
- Knowledge
- Experience
- Insight
- Sound judgement.

The unwise are therefore so for one or a number of reasons:

THE ATTRIBUTES AND CHARACTERISTICS OF THE "UNWISE"

- They apply inappropriate values and principles as the basis of their decision making.
- They lack the ability and/or personal characteristics to combine experience, insight, judgement judgment and knowledge to apply appropriate values and principles to specific practical contexts.
- They have a purely rational, scientific and technical approach to issue resolution, failing to recognise the value of intuition, empathy and emotion in what are ultimately people-related and oriented solutions.
- They have a narrow view of the stakeholders to be considered when considering issues for resolution in order to have arrived at the most appropriate optimal contextual solution.

Practical wisdom is in many respects the overarching attribute or capability in an individual or group of individuals, without which other attributes or capabilities cannot ensure that optimal decisions and actions are taken within a specific operational context. Baltes and Staudinger (2000) consider that wisdom constitutes an exceptional level of human functioning, which requires the balanced and coordinated utilisation of intellect, experience, insight and empathetic aspects of the individual's mental functioning. This with a view to the benefit of self and a broad range of significant others. It is a critical attribute of those who lack wisdom that they fail to acknowledge, take into account, comprehend and/or care about the broad impact of decisions on the wider community. Equally, such individuals fail to comprehend and/or appreciate the potential negative response of stakeholders adversely affected by the results of such decisions who recognise that they have been taken for the benefit of specific individuals and a narrow range of stakeholders.

Rooney and McKenna (2005) aptly describe such individuals as either:

- **The Savant**, who takes a straight line approach, applying general rules to specific contexts; or
- **The Ignoramus**, who knows how to personally succeed, but ultimately fails in the most important matters due to an absence of humane reflexive wisdom.

In contrast, wisdom is a problem-solving and decision-making technique and expert system of a higher order which translates human capability towards optimal human development, growth and performance.

The possession of practical wisdom not only indicates a knowledge of what is the most appropriate decision and action, it also requires the will, the courage (the word courage comes from the Latin "cor", which means heart) and skill to effect what may be an onerous or controversial decision, which has significant negative repercussions for some stakeholders, including, in some circumstances, the decision maker and close confidantes. Practical wisdom importantly allows the individual or group to decide which universal value or principle is most relevant within a specific practical context. In this respect the example is offered by Schwartz and Sharpe (2006) of how one might respond to a request to comment on a friend's outfit for an important occasion; should one be kind, supportive, compassionate or courageous and honest? So it is also in acts of business leadership, with, for example, a plant closure, staff appraisal and discipline, downsizing, redundancy, bonus payments or increment distribution. In essence, practical wisdom is a capability to engage insight, experience and judgement within the context of incomplete information and significant levels of ambiguity and uncertainty, by which individual decisions and actions are undertaken to consistently benefit the relevant "community", rather than specific individuals or stakeholder groups. An individual with practical wisdom is a "fine tuner", capable of judging between two apparently appropriate options to resolve a specific practical issue in order to decide on the optimal solution. Similarly, listen to two persons, both with apparently viable solutions and decide which is the most reliable (Hursthouse, 2006) and therefore to reach the optimal solution to resolve a particular issue.

The application of practical wisdom in leadership is a super ordinate attribute or capability, beyond the technical skills, techniques and practices consistently applied to manage effectively on a day to day basis. Ultimately the leadership mindset of an organisation or a unit thereof should not be primarily concerned with or merely focus upon the technically excellent in respect of, for example, accounts, programmes, procedures, processes, structures, specifications, policy, functional specialisms, instrumentality or scientific logic. These are useful, indeed necessary aids or tools in implementing the technical table stakes of operating an organisation, but are ultimately distractions and have no significant relationship with the process of effective operational leadership. Hofstede (1999) would contend that management only occurs when one is dealing with the coordination of people, rather than accounts, criteria, policy, processes, procedures or specifications. Those whose time and efforts are primarily focused on the latter issues are technicians rather than leaders, no matter their formal title. As we have already noted, wisdom-related performance is significantly correlated with life and personal experiences and a primary career focus on the intricacies of the expert technical provision of finance, treasury, IT, risk, compliance, or other such technical function, is most unlikely to support the development of significant levels of practical wisdom. Fundamentally, effective leadership and ultimately optimal organisational performance is predicated upon a people, personal and interpersonal perspective and priority, where judgement, balance, proportion, feeling, emotion are the most appropriate and important personal characteristics (Case and Gosling 2007).

The above statement may be regarded by many managing "technical" functions as both offensive and more importantly inaccurate and a generalisation in many instances, since their personal experiences outside of work may well enhance their insight into "soft" attributes such as balance, proportion, empathy and appropriateness, compared with following rules, procedures and processes. However, practical wisdom requires not only the appropriate experience and insight but also a realisation of its importance and relevance for the practice of effective operational leadership. By this I mean that there are many who experience yet appear to compartmentalise their personal crises and traumas (for many justifiable reasons) and do not thereby leverage these experiences to enhance leadership capabilities.

Whilst the statement may be considered contentious, perhaps requiring further elaboration and refinement, it is nevertheless important to raise the issue. If senior leadership positions are indeed in many cases populated by technical experts, rather than those with technical competence but a primary focus upon and capability in people management, then it is most unlikely that organisations are directed by those with practical wisdom, with the resultant implications for effective operational leadership and optimal performance. Baltes and Staudinger (2000); Staudinger and colleagues (1998) intimate that it is those occupations or professions which frequently come into contact and deal with the crises and trauma of human experience (e.g. clinical psychologists, judges, social workers, HR managers) where the attributes of wisdom are most likely to develop. This might suggest that functions within a business organisation where individuals are exposed to a wide variety of personal experiences, issues and deep interaction, where the effective resolution of troubling personal issues is important to optimise performance are likely to contain individuals with the perspectives, priorities, attributes and capabilities of practical wisdom. Functions such as sales, distribution, production, HR, customer service, rather than finance, IT, treasury, risk, legal, corporate finance, where optimal performance is considered more dependent upon technical expertise and from where a great many members of the dominant coalitions and executive committees of organisations tend to emanate. Naturally, there will be individuals from these technical functions whose life experiences have generated the required attributes and capabilities of wisdom. However, if members of dominant coalitions are appointed primarily on the basis of their technical expertise and its perceived impact on short-term performance, then this ensures that the top echelons of organisations are unlikely to be populated by the practically wise.

The Development of Wise Leadership within the Organisation

Senior executives have the ability to dramatically enhance the attributes and capabilities of wisdom amongst the leadership cadre and indeed the overall repository of wisdom held within the organisation, this in order to focus on key priorities and practices which will optimise performance. It is important that "sages" do not merely populate the top leadership positions, or that they are restricted in their ability to optimise performance by conscious and active obstruction by the dominant coalition.

CHARACTERISTICS OF INDIVIDUAL WISDOM

So, assuming that you are now convinced that wisdom is an important attribute in the effective business leader, how does one develop the appropriate attributes? As we have already discovered, research has concluded that some of the most effective business leaders are likely to have experienced a series of personal crises or a single tragedy, for example, the death of a parent or significant other in their early life. Ardelt (2004b) contends that one or a number of crises have the ability to force one to take stock, reflect, self-examine and become aware of the realities and priorities of life, to increasingly recognise appropriate personal characteristics and modes of relationships towards other individuals with whom one comes into contact. Over one's life such crises and other major events inevitably occur which cause one to consciously or subconsciously reflect on these universal realities and priorities, leading to a lesser inner directed, self-centred, egocentric perspective and a more "joined up", holistic, both reflective and affective, approach to others and the world around you. Given that leadership is primarily concerned with people management, rather than technical table stakes issues, such experience and insight allows the practically wise to empathically understand the issues on which others seek assistance, require direction, reassurance and motivation, whilst providing a rounded, holistic perspective and optimal solution for all concerned.

Baltes and Kunzmann (2004); Baltes and Staudinger (2000) undertook research to determine those factors which determine the extent of individual wisdom, which they define as "expert knowledge and judgement in the fundamental pragmatics (and conduct) of life". In this respect they have identified three sets of key factors.

DRIVERS IN THE DEVELOPMENT OF INDIVIDUAL WISDOM

- "Facilitative" or contextual factors as the historical context within which you live, for example, your age, your education, parental profile, the work or professional context and the provision and nature of mentorship.
- Personal characteristics, such as the manner by which the individual acquires and processes information, awareness, judgement, creativity, openness to new experiences and strength of ego.
- Factors involved in gaining life expertise, including the extent and nature of guidance and mentoring provided in dealing with life's problems and motivational disposition, including a desire to strive for excellence.

Whilst therefore there are some factors which are fixed, there are a large number which the individual or other interested parties can influence and refine. As far as effective business leadership is concerned business schools, organisational mentors and training programmes could follow the example of research by Staudinger and Baltes (1996) to introduce short-term interventions, by introducing participants to prevailing life problems (e.g. teenage pregnancy and marriage, euthanasia, unequal wealth distribution, political corruption) and getting them to discuss with peers and reflect on the nature and outcome of such conversations as a contribution to the development of wise attributes. This equates in some respects to the personal crises discussed above. Reflection on such serious issues requires the ability and willingness to look at issues from different perspectives and an absence of subjectivity, this through the application of all of one's intelligence, knowledge, experience, affective and empathetic attributes to reach an optimal, "practically wise" solution. Understanding the dynamics of such a process is important to comprehend the value of practical wisdom in effective leadership of a business organisation. Baltes and Staudinger developed a model of wisdom-related criteria which they used to assess the profile of wise individuals. This provides a clear profile of the reflective process, which has been adapted in Table 2.2.

Table 2.2 Wisdom-Related Criteria for Effective Issue Resolution

Criterion	Examples
Factual knowledge	Collection of facts on who, when, where, why, how
	Consideration of different situations and options in respect of specific issue
Procedural knowledge	Strategies for information search, decision making and advice giving
	Monitoring and response to emotional responses
	Cost-benefit analysis of alternative scenarios
	Analysis of optional means to achieve defined ends
Lifespan contextualism	Cultural norms and ongoing changes vis-à-vis adolescence
	Impact on future life stages and personal ambitions
Relativism	Personal and changing societal values
	Religious principles and perspectives
	Role of participant within life of subject
	Subject circumstances and justification
	Family context
Uncertainty	Acknowledge no ideal solution
	Unpredictable future
	Incomplete information

Source: adapted from Baltes and Staudinger (1993).

Whilst one might perhaps wish to change or refine the criteria to one extent or another, they do provide a clear and sound foundation by which to not only assess wisdom in individuals but also to develop the capabilities and perspectives of practical wisdom within the leadership cadre of the organisation. The Baltes and Staudinger criteria, tangibilise and operationalise wisdom into something which can be worked on, managed and nurtured in a practical manner.

WISDOM VERSUS CODES OF ETHICS

In long-term successful business organisations there is a recognition by the dominant coalition of executives, who set and manage its embedded logic, that a fundamental requirement for the achievement of the organisation's long-term vision is the creation of an organisational environment and culture which fosters the capability of its existing and aspiring leaders to develop and foster the consistent, logical development and application of practical wisdom. This book takes a step by step approach in detailing how this might be and indeed has been achieved by a number of prominent business organisations. It contrasts the principles, perspectives, priorities of the dominant coalitions of many organisations with those which should prevail on the basis of the application of the perspectives, components and processes of practical wisdom.

Much of what has been written on the steps taken to resolve the recent financial and economic crises in the USA, UK, Western Europe and other countries referred to the requirement for the development and stringent application of codes of conduct or ethics. Yet this exhibits a shallow and peripheral understanding of the fundamental issue which has created this cancer. I have myself been roped in to review the code of practice of a number of institutions. However, I have responded that such a process will do little to resolve the long-term malaise, merely acting to paper over the cracks and creating an ability to quickly and confidently produce a cogent and comprehensive document from the bottom drawer when regulators come calling. I have been equally surprised to find in the Situations Vacant sections of newspapers and dedicated websites a growing demand for risk specialists in financial institutions, when patently the problem was not the number of risk managers, not the risk policies and parameters themselves. Rather it was and remains the absence of an understanding and the consistent practical application of appropriate underlying values, principles, perspectives and priorities embedded within the dominant logic of the organisation, based upon the fundamental components of practical wisdom, as described in the previous chapter sections. The recruitment of more risk managers is a management solution to a leadership issue and will ultimately be more costly and less effective than the embedding of the components of practical and collaborative wisdom.

A code of ethics is a wooden, inflexible, narrow, inanimate substitute in the absence of practical wisdom. The application of practical wisdom ensures that in each instance and case an appropriate decision is taken in the optimal interests of the relevant community, based upon "wise" values, principles, perspectives and priorities. Unless a principle, perspective or priority is embedded in the fundamental logic of an individual or group of individuals, which make a community or organisation, then it will not be applied consistently or with understanding and purpose, with commitment and conviction. Moreover, the complexity of society and the twenty-first century business organisation defies the application of a set of "ethical" priorities and perspectives which are inflexible and based upon either right and wrong, making them idealistic rather than realistic, pragmatic and practical (Nyberg, 2008). Equally important, if such ethical codes are not understood, acknowledged and clearly communicated as anchored to widely accepted values and principles then they will not be intuitively recognised and applied when relevant situations and issues arise on a day to day basis. There was no shortage of ethical codes in Enron, WorldCom and many of the banks which recently collapsed, partially or wholly, due to unethical practices and/or a convenient interpretation of regulations by corporations and regulators and in a few cases outright corruption, greed and cronyism. The application of practical wisdom would undoubtedly have avoided this and indeed many other prior and recurrent financial crises over preceding decades and centuries.

THE NURTURING AND MANAGEMENT OF WISDOM

A key attribute of the "wise" executive team within an organisation is to set an example vis-à-vis the perspectives and priorities by which they as leaders are seen to take decisions. Equally, it is to acknowledge the importance of generating an ever-increasing mass of wisdom within the organisation. This is achieved by recognising that wisdom requires and reflects the integration and balancing of several aspects of the functioning of the individual (Baltes and Staudinger, 2000). Perhaps more importantly to recognise that the organisation has the opportunity and ability to dynamically manage the development of the body of wisdom within the organisation, through its staff selection and development policies. Baltes and Staudinger identified four "correlates" which impacted on wisdom-related performance in adults, allocating a percentage impact for each.

FOUR CORRELATES WHICH INFLUENCE WISDOM-RELATED PERFORMANCE

Age and life experience: somewhat surprisingly (and disappointingly for many) there was no direct correlation between age and wisdom-related performance. Rather, age was important due to the opportunity to generate general life experience and gather specific professional experience. Naturally there will be many individuals over their lives who, due to their perspective, limited opportunities and other factors, will generate low to moderate experience in one or both correlates. As already alluded to Baltes and Staudinger proposed that some professions and other groups (e.g. clinical psychologists, HR professionals, family and tribal leaders) may have a higher propensity to generate enhanced levels of wisdom due to their personal involvement with and experience in seeking to resolve the serious issues related to a broad swath of individuals. This thereby allows them the opportunity to enhance their life experience, insight and judgement at an earlier age than other groups, so it will be for other groups and individuals.

The key point in respect of life and professional experience for organisational leadership is the ability to nurture, develop and manage its continuing generation, particularly amongst its constantly developing leadership cadre. A number of successful organisations, which we will discuss in greater depth at a later stage, closely manage the generation of life experience and insight by regularly exposing their leadership cadre to different life and professional experiences. This is engineered in order that they are compelled to encounter new issues, both from a professional but also broader life context. This is undertaken in order to enhance their capability to respond with insight and judgement and not be phased by any new eventuality perceived to be outside the framework of their experience, knowledge and reference to date.

One successful organisation has for over a century had a policy of moving their top 400–500 leaders to new and increasingly challenging roles, usually in new countries, every 3 years. The accumulation of new experiences over a career spanning 35–40 years must inevitably enhance the opportunity and also the capability of the individual (indeed, the organisation) to take decisions with enhanced insight and sound judgement within a broader range of practical business situations, to the ultimate benefit of long-term performance. Baltes and Staudinger's research at the Max Planck Institute in Berlin indicated that the life experience correlate scored at 26 per cent in respect of wisdom-related performance.

Personality traits: the research gave examples of personality traits such as an openness to experience, a desire for personal growth, but one might also include self-importance, individualism or a collegiate approach to tasks. Once more these traits are malleable to the benefit of the organisation on the basis of example by and exposure to respected peers and superiors. Also the recognition during the recruitment and selection process for leadership positions of those personality traits required in order to achieve personal objectives within a preferred business and social environment. Personality traits scored 21 per cent in respect of wisdom-related performance.

Intelligence and the personality-intelligence interface: these two comprise 50 per cent of the impact on wisdom-related performance and include such attributes as creativity, cognitive style and social intelligence, attributes which may prove difficult for an organisation to significantly modify. However, if the organisation recognises those attributes contained within these correlates which enhance wisdom-related performance then these should be sought out as priority characteristics during the recruitment process and subsequent selection processes for appointment to leadership positions.

Source: adapted from Baltes and Staudinger (2000).

The key point for consideration on the basis of these findings is that if wisdom is the key determinant in the long-term effective management and optimal performance of an organisation, then senior executives who determine the dominant logic, key principles and priorities of the organisation, have the ability to develop and manage the mass of wisdom contained within the organisation and an ability to enhance it substantially, over time. A key issue, however, is that an organisation with sages only at the top is just as likely to fail as one with none at the top. There is a requirement that wisdom capabilities pervade the organisation beyond the top echelons of leadership, since some decisions may appear perverse to individuals who do not recognise the implications of the decision-making principles, perspectives and process of practical wisdom.

If, for instance, in order for an organisation to survive it is considered necessary to close a division, major production centre and/or distribution network, based strictly upon the perspectives and decision-making processes of practical wisdom, this may result in obstruction, demotivation and suboptimal performance amongst the remaining staff. If however, efforts have been made to inculcate the leadership cadre at all levels of the organisation, in the logic of practical wisdom and its cognitive mental processing, then there will be a more uniform acknowledgement, understanding, consideration and application of the principles, perspectives and priorities in such difficult circumstances and a more uniform message communication cascade. This will thereby minimise demotivation, disharmony and potential obstruction and conflict by those who are not yet in a position to possess the attributes of practical wisdom, on the basis of experience, insight and/or training and development.

Equally important for both the organisation and the individual is the frequent scenario where "wise" individuals populate the organisation in positions below the dominant coalition of senior executives. If we accept that those who take decisions based on the key criteria detailed in previous chapter sections are most likely to optimise long-term performance, how are they able to do so where the predominant organisational logic in the form of core principles, perspectives, priorities, translated into practices, are contrary to the principles and processes of practical and collaborative wisdom and thereby suboptimal and permeate all functions, which are increasingly inter-related and inter-dependent? Such individuals may be located within any function of the organisation, since it is based upon life rather than occupational or professional experience. In such a scenario these "wise" individuals have the option:

- To try to apply their wisdom to achieve optimal solutions for the organisation on the basis of their area of responsibility and authority, where this does not blatantly clash with the dominant logic of the organisation.
- Seek to "convert" other functions over time.
- Seek to "convert" the dominant coalition over time.

Alternatively, where the values, principles, perspectives and priorities of the organisation and "wise" individual are inconsistent, the result is disillusionment and a likely voluntary or invited early exit. Even if such individuals remain within the organisation, they will likely find themselves able to make only a suboptimal contribution to organisational performance due to a dissonance with the dominant logic. They are therefore likely to find progress to roles where they can maximise the contribution of their wisdom blocked, this through an impression that their perspectives and priorities are misaligned with those of the dominant coalition, even though their technical expertise may ensure continuing employment over the long term. Such a situation is suboptimal for the individual, the organisation as an entity and the broader range of stakeholders, who look to the performance of the organisation to satisfy their individual requirements and long-term expectations.

Collaborative Wisdom and the Collective Vision

Rather than develop the wisdom of individuals the objective should be to create and enhance an organisational repository of wisdom and a collective vision which enhances stakeholder cohesion, dedication, confidence and motivation, leading to optimal long-term performance. Profit, rather than being fundamental to this vision is merely a by-product. A critical attribute of practical wisdom is the ability to appropriately communicate the collective vision.

Given the size and complexity of many organisations, it would be impossible for any wise individual to have the time and energy to take all the individual leadership decisions which are required to resolve the plethora of leadership issues which must be resolved across the organisation on an ongoing basis. Furthermore, it is increasingly understood and accepted that no individual has the knowledge, experience and technical expertise to take the wise, optimal decisions across all aspects of the practical and operational leadership of the organisation. A number of theories have therefore recently been developed (collective mind, collaborative memory, mutual knowledge) which encapsulate the concept that the capability of an organisation to optimise performance is dependent upon the repository of leadership knowledge and wisdom being held by a collective of leaders. These individuals collaborate to exchange views and take decisions in a collaborative manner in order to optimise the benefits to the organisation of available leadership knowledge and reflective capabilities.

Staudinger and Baltes (1996) stress the need to extend scholarly development in this area beyond the single individual and that the ability to take wise decisions is fundamentally tied to a collective and collaborative rather than individual repository of knowledge. This is the case not only to gain a better understanding of the repository of knowledge and wisdom, but also to better understand how wisdom is generated, primarily by interactions between individuals who have critically reflected on an issue, utilising their collective knowledge, experience and insight. Their research indicated that an interactive approach to issue resolution significantly increased wisdom-related performance.

In many respects this interaction and exchange may be real or internalised as a result of previous conversations and mentorship, such that an individual might consider an issue and reflect on how a wise peer, superior or mentor might have responded, as if they were present. Later in this book we will go on to give examples of how, having created an environment to nurture and develop practical wisdom within the leadership cadre, a collegiate management approach is applied to leverage the pool of wisdom in a collaborative manner, this in order to facilitate consistently effective organisational management and optimise performance over the long term.

The point that I would like to make at this early stage in the book is that what is being proposed in this text is not scholarly aspirations which, when it meets the complex practice of operational organisational leadership is quickly considered by those who seek its implementation as simplistic, naive, impractical and unrealistic. In order to achieve significant operational impact the practical and collaborative proposition requires a determined and resolute effort to question the logic of those principles, perspectives, priorities and practices which have become deeply embedded in the management and leadership psyche and mindset. Such an approach is required in order to initiate what might be considered a radical realignment in organisational dominant logic. Fundamental to the application of practical and collaborative wisdom and optimal performance in long-term, successful business organisations is a common, collective and collegiate mindset, not just within the dominant coalition of the executive team, but within all staff. Also fundamental to a successful leadership approach based on practical and collaborative wisdom is a common vision, which is understood and accepted by all staff because it is consistent with their individual life objectives. The implications of these two latter sentences for the practice of operational leadership cannot be underestimated and will be referred to throughout the remainder of the text.

As I indicated at the beginning of this book, experienced leaders fundamentally know, consciously or subconsciously, what is required to lead effectively, what the questions to ask are and what are the answers. However, consistent application is complex, resource and energy hungry, and requires an appropriate value-based foundation and the corresponding leadership perspectives, attributes and capabilities. Certainly you require as table stakes a good product or service to offer, a cost-efficient operation, appropriate technical experts, but most of all you require a leadership which nurtures, develops and manages on an ongoing basis a common vision and purpose in order that everyone understands their role in the achievement of a common purpose.

I acknowledge that it is much simpler to envisage and manage a tangible vision of increasing net revenue by 12% every year for the next 3 years than the more intangible ones which we will discuss in later chapters, which reinforce a loyalty, dedication, motivation and advocacy amongst key stakeholder groups, which increases productivity without a concomitant increase in cost. Practical wisdom dictates decisions which optimise the benefit for the community of stakeholders. As Nonaka and Toyama (2007) contend, this is not the same as the profit maximisation priority of neoclassical economics, which continues to be the foundation of so many organisations and industries throughout the developed, particularly Western economies.

On the basis of both my practitioner experience and scholarly research, if you ask members of dominant coalitions within consistently successful organisations to comment on the organisation's vision they will talk about becoming global players, becoming the number one in the industry and/or specific markets or successfully moving into a new market sector(s). They may also talk about consistent growth in revenues of x% or a shareholder return of y%. However, once they have become relaxed and comfortable in your company and you have gained their confidence, when you ask them how this will ultimately be achieved, their response is that you must consistently satisfy the tangible and intangible requirements and expectations of all major stakeholder groups, because this is how you retain the confidence, loyalty, dedication and advocacy of all stakeholders. By this means optimal cohesion, teamwork, allegiance, energy and ultimately productivity is achieved.

However, crucially, I have found that this perspective is pretty much a secret, hidden and embedded in the psyche or logic of these senior executives and directors. It is as if it is a fundamental building block which is no longer discussed because it is acknowledged and understood, embedded deep in the psyche and mindset of the dominant coalition, deeply embedded in the dominant logic of the organisation, passed down from generation to generation of its executive leadership. This process of inculcation to ensure the ongoing application of the principles and process of practical and collaborative wisdom is a subject to which we will return in greater depth. This leadership mindset is best summarised by Tarantino (1998) when he contends,

> *Profit is not the legitimate purpose of business. Its purpose is to provide a service needed by society. If this is done efficiently, companies will be profitable (Tarantino, 1998, p. 560).*

Whether this is in practice a means to a more tangible end for the organisation, or is a fundamental end in itself, as the key perspective comprising and directing the application of practical wisdom, is perhaps incidental. In either respect the common good, through a common vision and collaborative leadership does constitute a driving force of effective, practical and context-driven organisational leadership.

Interestingly, it is a reflection of the prevalent mindset, embedded perspectives and priorities within both the scholarly business community and the practitioner business community that on the two previous occasions when I cited the above quote there was a response that such a statement was unrealistic and "naive". This may be a response based upon both emotion and fear; that principles, perspectives, priorities and practices which have guided the decisions and actions of individuals and organisations over a sustained period are in practice synonymous with the emperor's new clothes, found to be lacking in substance and validity.

However, Tarantino does have credible advocates for his apparently heretical views amongst indisputably successful business leaders. Whilst we will explore in greater detail the principles, perspectives and priorities of senior executives of HSBC Holdings plc later in this book it is pertinent to quote from a speech by Stephen Green, until 2010 Executive Chairman of this global organisation and prior to that its Group Chief Executive,

> Some still think that the concept of corporate social responsibility is somehow incompatible with shareholder value maximisation, or fear it can be an excuse for poor competitive positioning, operational inefficiency and low returns to investors ... Sustained shareholder value creation is absolutely critical to any discussion of wider responsibilities in business. And yet it should not be – as has been the case – the over-arching objective of management in business. It should rather, be the hallmark of business well done (Green, 2009, p. 3).

In a similar manner to the extinction of the attributes of wisdom as a prerequisite in the wise business leader over the last century, so we have seen a perspective of the organisation as part of and a contributor to the overall growth and well-being of the broader society of stakeholders replaced by a narrower, financial, key stakeholder approach, which has become the normal, logical, rational, "pragmatic" perspective and priority. In a 2010 speech Green does address this change, citing as an example the openly holistic, communal objectives of a global chemicals company in the mid-1980s contained in its mission statement, which declared its goal,

> to be the world's leading chemical company serving customers internationally through the innovative and responsible application of chemistry and related science. Through achievement of our aim, we will enhance the wealth and wellbeing of our shareholders, our employees, our customers and the communities in which we serve and where we operate.

In the 1990s the mission statement of the same company described its sole objective as,

> to maximise value for our shareholders by focusing on businesses where we have market leadership, a technological edge and a world competitive cost base (Green, 2010, p. 1).

It is a mark of the effective inculcation by business organisations and business schools which has taken place over the last 30 years that many, perhaps the great majority of readers will regard the latter quotation as fundamentally logical and rational, based upon the realities of the business environment of the latter stages of the twentieth and the first decades of the twenty-first century. Similarly, they might find the former quote as aspirational, unrealistic, impractical and soft headed, dare I say naive. In fact, the former quote reflects a wise approach to leadership which results in optimal performance over the long term, better avoiding the economic and social trauma of recent years, which was arguably created by the mindset underpinning the latter quote.

Wise organisational leaders understand that revenue, income, profit, cost are tangible, numerate verbal representations which describe the performance of the organisation for short-term stakeholders and those imbued with the short-term profit perspective and priority. However Nonaka and Toyama (2007) contend that profit is a by-product of applying practical wisdom consistently towards the fundamental organisational or "community" and individual priority of self-realisation. I acknowledge that given the prevalent and embedded framework of societal perspectives and priorities, if you as a leader had to decide whether to explain the objectives of the organisation in terms of:

- Market share, net revenue, capital growth, shareholder value; or
- The development of a process of "distributed phronesis" throughout the organisation as a means of creating common knowledge and purpose and ultimately organisational and self-realisation, which will also, as a by-product, result in optimal organisational performance.

I suspect career opportunities would be curtailed if one chose the latter approach.

However, this is why we have the "practical" in practical wisdom. Whilst leading based upon the application of universal values for the ultimate benefit of the broad community of stakeholders, you apply your personal experience, knowledge, insight, reflective and affective capabilities to communicate different messages to diverse audiences in order to nurture, develop and manage a common vision, a common mind, knowledge and memory to engender a common and uniform purpose towards self and organisational realisation. In subsequent chapters we will exhibit how this insight and judgement is broken down into key leadership practices in order to create a collaborative wisdom throughout the organisation, which results in what may be termed an inculcated leadership cadre, fostering collegiate management.

PRACTICAL AND COLLABORATIVE WISDOM: A SYNOPSIS AND TRIGGER MEMORY MECHANISM

In this and the previous chapter we have introduced much new theory and sought to reinvigorate a concept better recognised as part of classical philosophy into one which is acknowledged as relevant, indeed critical to the effective operational leadership process and the long-term performance of the twenty-first century business organisation. As a practitioner I recognise that less is more in seeking to ensure that new ideas and propositions are combined with prevailing perspectives and practices within the operational business environment. Before we move on to the means and manner by which the concept of practical and collaborative wisdom is applied within the operational business leadership context, I have encompassed what I consider are the key points of this and the preceding chapter into Figure 2.1. This will act as both a useful memory trigger and bridge into the content of subsequent sections of the book.

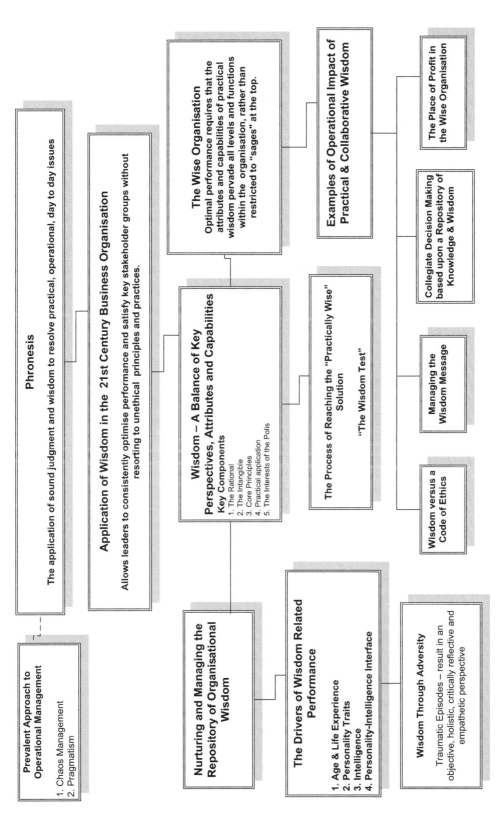

Figure 2.1   Practical and Collaborative Wisdom – A Route Map to Optimal Organisational Leadership

Exercises

1. Select an individual whom you consider to be wise from any walk of life (from personal experience or knowledge). Detail what are the characteristics or individual attributes which you consider justify such a description.
2. Imagine that you have been asked to advise a family friend who has a terminal condition and has decided to make arrangements for assisted suicide. Working with two of your peers, describe the criteria which you consider relevant in advising on this personal issue and the logic of argument that you would present. Once completed, consider how an individual with practical wisdom might respond to the family friend.
3. Consider how a programme might be developed within a college or business school to engender attributes and capabilities of practical wisdom in aspiring business leaders.
4. Describe what six practical initiatives you would undertake to embed a leadership perspective based upon the attributes and capabilities of practical wisdom in a business organisation, club or other group of which you have personal knowledge and experience.

2 *Wisdom and Leadership Practice*

In order to achieve optimal organisational performance it is necessary that the leadership of people is regarded as a profession, an attribute and capability of primary importance in the attainment of operational effectiveness and optimal organisational performance. Effective leaders are required to exhibit excellence in both their selected technical specialism but, more importantly, in people leadership.

To be optimally effective the practical application of the perspectives, attributes and capabilities of practical and collaborative wisdom must be exhibited, encouraged and supported by the dominant coalition within the organisation. In the absence of such open support individuals applying these attributes will become isolated and frustrated, leading to conflict, ineffectual organisational leadership and suboptimal organisational performance.

In Part One we described the attributes and capabilities of wisdom, this in order to justify its inclusion as the foundation of effective "practical" leadership. Of necessity, the content bordered on the philosophical, conceptual and theoretical. This is of little practical value to the practitioner, who rarely has the time to consider additional input, unless it is patently, directly relevant and assists in the resolution of an urgent and/or important operational issue which lies waiting for attention on his/her desk. In Part Two we turn to clearly show how the perspectives, priorities, attributes and capabilities of the "wise" dominant coalition or "wise" individual have direct practical relevance to the day to day practice of effective operational leadership within the business organisation.

Fundamental to the successful application of the content of Part Two is the requirement that the leader does not necessarily think outside of the leadership box, but rather has a clear understanding of the nature of the box within which he is operating in the quest for optimal decision-making and issue resolution. In order to ensure optimal effectiveness and long-term organisational performance it is critical to be aware of and clear on the operational decision-making environment, the priorities, the perspectives, attributes and capabilities of wise operational leadership. Practical wisdom provides clarity and consistency in decision making. It does so through clearly defining those groups which should benefit and the values and principles upon which decisions should be based. Further, it defines the cognitive process by which the leader utilises his/her knowledge, experience, intuition and insight to reach the optimal solution in respect of context-based issues.

The operational reality is that the majority of leaders take decisions in a myopic and chaotic state of mind:

- Over reliant on inexpert intuition in key areas to which we will refer later.
- Unsure of the values and principles to be applied.

- Who are the primary beneficiary stakeholder groups of any decision.
- The key issues for consideration in the decision-making process.

The result is that leadership mindsets are at the mercy of those who prefer to maintain this myopia and ambivalence concerning core values, principles to be applied and primary stakeholder groups for whose benefit the resources of the organisation are dedicated.

In order to be effective leadership must be regarded as a defined body of expertise and as a dedicated profession, rather than as an individual talent. The professional (people) leader needs to have an embedded and comprehensive grasp of the fundamental principles, perspectives and priorities of that profession, as in any other body of expertise. A scientist, engineer, accountant builds his rational analysis and bases his decisions on proven foundational concepts and principles. Given the importance of effective people leadership for the achievement of organisational objectives and the satisfaction of individual requirements and expectations, leadership must be built upon the consistent application of principles which are more than the sum of an individual's experience, instinct and intuition, important as these are for providing operational and practical flexibility and relevance. However, much more important than understanding the principles and priorities is that you are proactively thinking about leadership in relation to contextual, operational issues, rather than merely achieving technical competence. The defined profession and context-based practice of people leadership should stand four square and central in the assessment and analysis of the majority of operational decisions and actions taken as an operational leader within the organisation.

Effective leaders are required to be professionals in at least two areas, their technical specialism and more importantly in their (people) leadership capabilities. (People) leadership is the primary role, priority and active, rather than secondary and passive in the management of any function, be it you and an assistant, a department, division, a national multinational or global business organisation. This realisation makes such roles much more complex than merely the requirement to apply one's technical skills and do one's best as a leader, because effective leadership, which, as we will discuss later in greater depth, revolves around the direction, motivation and energising of individuals, is generally presently perceived as of secondary importance, as a bonus in the attainment of organisational objectives and targets. Management practitioners might protest that people leadership capabilities are considered and assessed in the appraisal process under such titles as "interpersonal skills". However, apart from the continuing debate on the link between appraisal, focused development and promotion, I have yet to see evidence of promotion to senior executive roles based to any significant extent on people management skills, particularly to Executive Committee roles. To run a function effectively you have to excel as a technician but also as a leader of people, this in order to optimise the productivity of your people resource. Given the proposed importance of the leadership of people for achieving optimal performance this is achieved primarily by gaining and maintaining the credibility, trust, confidence and allegiance of key stakeholder groups. At a minimum, this is not only amongst your superiors, but equally, if not more so, amongst your peers and subordinates. Dependent upon role, those stakeholders of which you must be consciously aware during the process of operational leadership, in order to ultimately make wise decisions in respect of issue resolution, might also include the broader spectrum of stakeholders, which often also includes customers, suppliers, statutory bodies and shareholders.

Part Two proposes a solid foundation of operational leadership perspectives, priorities and practices, which act as a logical and consistent base for operational decision making on a daily basis. These people leadership attributes have become embedded in the psyche and dominant logic of the leadership cadre of the few long-term successful organisations, a number of which we will describe in greater detail throughout the book. We will clearly see the translation of characteristics of wisdom contained within Part One into the leadership principles, perspectives and priorities of successful organisations. These perspectives and priorities are not necessarily revolutionary and/or novel, since many practitioners and leaders recognise the value of their own volition, sometime in mid to late career. Regrettably, this is often when they have lost the energy, motivation, willpower and powers of adaptability to apply them.

Whilst this book advocates that aspiring and individual leaders apply the characteristics of practical and collaborative wisdom within their own areas of responsibility it is more important for optimal performance that dominant coalitions within organisations create an environment conducive to the principles and attributes of practical wisdom. In the absence of an organisational culture based upon the principles and priorities of practical and collaborative wisdom, exhibited, actively encouraged and supported by the dominant coalition, individual wise leaders throughout the organisation will quickly become isolated and frustrated. This will lead to fractured, dysfunctional organisational management, open conflict and suboptimal organisational performance. Long-term successful organisations take steps to embed this logic, these perspectives and priorities in aspiring leaders at the beginning of their careers, this in order to create a leadership consensus based upon "wise" leadership principles, perspectives and priorities . The purpose of this book is therefore, in the same way, to provide its readers with a head start to effective leadership, by providing them with the opportunity to consider the priorities of the effective leader at an early stage in their career development. To develop leadership logic, insight and reach a state of practical and collaborative wisdom in order to optimise their career potential whilst optimising their contribution to organisational performance. Once convinced and inculcated with the logic and capability of the wise leader they must decide for themselves if they are both willing and able to apply them in their present organisational environment.

In order to initiate this significant change in mindset I have decided to introduce at this early stage two figures which encapsulate the key principles, perspectives, priorities and practices of effective leadership. These take us from:

Step One: the attributes of practical wisdom, which we addressed in Part One to

Step Two: the clarification of operational leadership principles and priorities;

resulting in:

Step Three: those individual leadership characteristics, perspectives, attributes and capabilities which result in optimal performance.

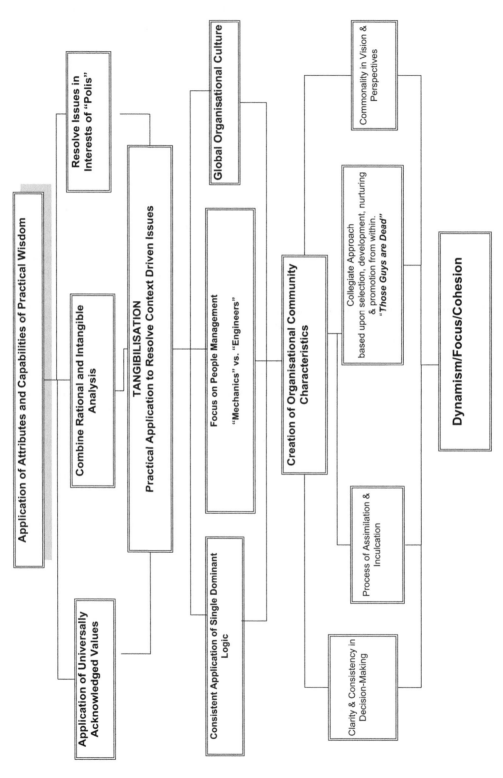

Figure P2.1 The Foundations of Optimal Long-Term Performance

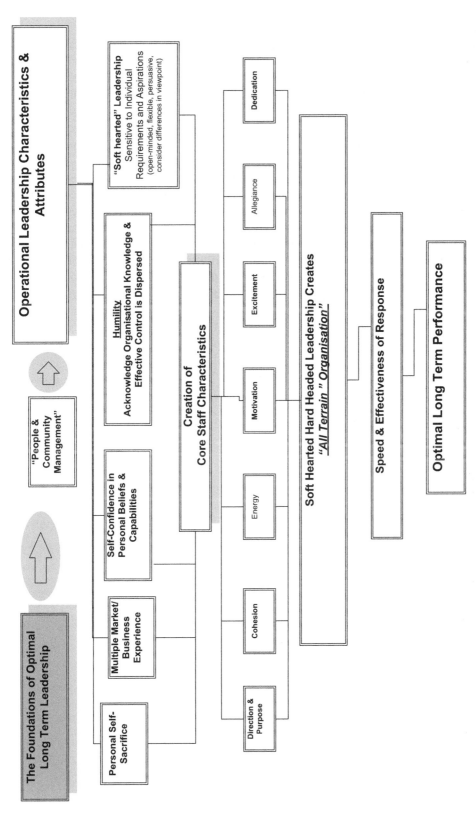

Figure P2.2 The Application of "Universal" Management Perspectives and Practices

At this stage I would ask the reader to peruse the figures to gain a broad appreciation of the proposed process. Thereafter to periodically return to these figures in order to gradually visualise how each proposition coalesces into an effective, dynamic, practically wise, operational leadership mindset and cognitive process, which achieves operational effectiveness and directs the organisation towards optimal long-term organisational performance. As we describe the key attributes and capabilities of effective leadership in the following chapter we will gradually recognise, acknowledge and understand a correlation between these and those which we have described as fundamental to the practical application of practical and collaborative wisdom.

It is important to emphasise before we delve into the detail contained within the following chapters that this book is proposing that leaders take a "wise" approach to leading at the operational level within the organisation. Such an approach does not exclude consideration of technical expertise as a significant contributor to optimal long-term performance. However, it displaces technical expertise from centre stage, as the primary attribute for consideration in the credentials, attributes and capabilities of individuals considered for appointment to the leadership cadre of organisations. It proposes that leaders must gain and exhibit specific, dedicated operational expertise in the leadership of people. Also that the effective practical application of such expertise be acknowledged and understood by the dominant coalition to be the primary and central attribute and capability in the effective leadership and optimal performance of the organisation.

3 *Operational Leadership: The Development of Credibility and Trust*

The dominant theme of this book is that the primary and central focus of the practically wise leader is the effective direction and motivation of people, rather than the technical component of their respective roles. If wise, effective leadership is indeed concerned with the development and maintenance of the "polis", then the focus of the leader's thoughts and actions must revolve around the principles, perspectives, priorities and practices which are most likely to create cohesion, dedication, teamwork and allegience amongst the community of stakeholders. This is achieved by generating optimal credibility and trust. This chapter therefore sets out the fundamental perspectives and priorities of the practically wise leader in order to generate optimal credibility and trust.

Leadership in a "Global" Cultural Context

Successful global organisations have developed a dominant logic of leadership values and principles which they consistently apply, no matter the organisational or market context. "Sympathetic" adaptation to the local business context occurs at the level of local practices, as long as they do not significantly impact on the application of the dominant logic. It is important that practitioners recognise how the consistent application of such values and principles both simplifies and enhances operational decision making.

A significant test of the effectiveness of an individual's embedded leadership attributes and capabilities, or indeed an organisation's embedded leadership principles, perspectives and priorities is the ability to transfer them across "cultures". In a successful leader's career he/she will be tested by leading in one or a number of different cultural contexts:

- Different departments and divisions of the same organisation where different professional cultures are predominant.
- Different organisations, with their individual cultures.
- Different industrial sectors, with their specific cultural perspectives and priorities.
- Leading within organisations in dramatically different social cultures.
- An amalgam of two or more of the above at the same time.

A veritable industry of scholars, authors and consultants has developed over the last 2 or 3 decades around the need to and extent to which cross-cultural adaptability is required in leadership principles, perspectives, priorities and practices in respect of organisational cultures. This is particularly relevant with regard to merger and acquisition, predominantly in the field of multinational expansion across societal cultures, this is due to the perceived differences in societal perspectives and priorities. Readers are directed to such prominent authors in this field as Cartwright and Cooper (1993); Hofstede (1997); Lubatkin, Calori, Very and Veiga (1998); Trompenaars and Hampden-Turner (2003) if they wish to look into this issue in greater detail.

Whilst the jury is still out, there appears to be a growing consensus that if any adaptability is required it is at what might be termed "downstream" operational units, within each organisation, in what might be termed practices, rather than any significant changes in embedded organisational principles, perspectives and priorities. This is confirmed by my own research amongst senior executives and executive board members of global banks. These highly experienced practitioners looked quizzically when I asked them to comment on the extent to which they adapted core organisational principles, perspectives, priorities and practices in order to gain acceptance, loyalty and credibility amongst the management cadre of an acquired organisation, particularly as a means of optimising the performance of that unit. The view was that successful organisations have developed a dominant logic of principles, perspectives and priorities which have been tried over time in the crucible of business. The secret of long-term global success is to continue to consistently apply this dominant logic, but in a manner which is sympathetic to context, this is in order to leverage local management expertise, knowledge and insight and thereby optimise performance of both the local business unit and group operation,

> *HSBC is like Sony or any other international brand, it applies universal business values and practices but adapts to local operational context. Each local organisation is now part of a global business network and plan. Many decisions of an operational and strategic nature at local level will be affected by universal global plans, particularly in the areas of cost efficiency, systems, sales management and delivery to which local business must comply, unless there are good reasons to do otherwise (Interviewee D).*

The principles and perspectives which constitute this dominant logic will change in an evolutionery manner over time in the face of new challenges. However, it would be counterproductive in overall group coordination to apply different principles, perspectives and priorities in different business units, with the resultant adverse impact on operational efficiency and effectiveness, optimal performance and long-term survival. The implications of this approach are that as long as you and your organisation's decisions are based upon a dominant logic of appropriate principles, perspectives and priorities, founded upon the dynamic application of the process of practical and collaborative wisdom (which we will clarify and elucidate upon throughout the rest of the book), you should approach leadership in Beijing, Riyadh, Mumbai or Ulan Bator as you would in London, New York, Copenhagen and Rio. This is admittedly easier said than done. However, it is at the intersection of the organisation's dominant logic and the requirements of the local business context where the attributes and capabilities of the practically wise leader are both most evident and critical. It is the mismanagement (or in this case mis-leadership) of this intersection which lies at the core of the outright failure or suboptimal performance of operational leaders and, at the organisational level, many mergers and acquisitions, rather than the often cited inability to achieve anticipated economies or enhance market share.

As an introduction to this mindset, good examples of such embedded principles and priorities were elicited from the interview of a senior executive of HSBC Holdings plc. These clearly profile the values which are applied globally, no matter the cultural context and clearly direct leadership perspective and decison making in key areas, no matter the organisational context.

KEY BUSINESS VALUES: HSBC HOLDINGS PLC (EXAMPLES)

- Highest personal standards of integrity at all levels
- Commitment to truth and fair dealing
- Openly esteemed commitment to quality and competence
- Minimum of bureaucracy
- Fast decisions and implementation
- Putting team's interests ahead of individuals
- Appropriate delegation of authority with accountability
- Fair and objective employer
- Diversity underpinned by a meritocratic approach to recruitment, promotion and selection

Source: provided by Interviewee (A) from HSBC Group Standards Manual.

Practitioners may initially consider that these values are both aspirational and top line to be of any practical operational value. However, we must recognise, acknowledge and understand that these values are to be consistently and consciously applied within the context of managing the direction, motivation and behaviour of people within the operational, day to day context of decision-making and issue resolution by the functional leader, be it a unit of two or a division of thousands. Once acknowledged, understood, accepted and embedded in the individual leadership cognitive mental process, these will act as an anchor or foundation for effectively taking a view on and assessing individual operational leadership issues, situations and decision making. We can then see their operational value, acting as they do as both anchor and compass, clarifying priority issues and considerations in the decision-making process, on a day to day basis. Their true value is exposed once they are inculcated in the psyche of the individual leader or leadership cadre, thereby facilitating a spontaneous, intuitive response. This is an important issue in the development of a framework of effective and consistent leadership, founded upon practical and collaborative wisdom. It is perhaps therefore appropriate at this juncture for readers to pause for a couple of minutes to consider how the consistent application of these values would apply in an operational issue in which you are presently involved or with which you are conversant, in order to fully recognise the impact on the process of decision-making, issue resolution and unit productivity and performance.

Another long-term successful business organisation which has historically been seen to consistently apply a universal set of business principles, with an emphasis on active, front of mind, people leadership, no matter the banking sector or geographic location, is Goldman Sachs & Co. Whilst some might argue from recent revelations that this organisation has failed to live up to some of the principles stated in the boxed text:

Goldman Sachs – "Our Business Principles below (note: I have highlighted those points which I believe are most pertinent) there is little doubt that these principles have acted as both the anchor and compass of leadership decision making for over a century, bringing clarity to the priorities and standards by which all employees were directed to carry out their duties. Whilst each principle has a strong resonance, given the prevailing struggle of Goldman Sachs & Co to regain its long held reputation for professionalism and principled banking practices, perhaps the first principle is most resonant, particularly when we see its impact on what had previously been stellar performance. Goldman Sachs & Co may be an example of an organisation which had achieved consistent success over a sustained period based upon the application of the principles and cognitive mental process of practical and collaborative wisdom changing fundamental values and principles, this is in response to a paradigm shift in market and business context in order to leverage new opportunities. Such a change in context, in the absence of the appropriate expert intuition and insight (to which we will refer in some depth at a later stage) leads to decisions and the resolutions of operational issues inconsistent with the cognitive mental processes of practical and collaborative wisdom. In the case of Goldman Sachs & Co there is increasing agreement that the changed financial market context finally encouraged the leadership cadre to convert from a partnership to public company, radically recalibrating key principles, perspectives and priorities. A similar case in point is illustrated by Barbara Ley Toffler in her book (2003) recounting the change in cultural perspectives and the resultant collapse and demise of Arthur Andersen. However, for the present let us look benignly on the dominant logic of the Goldman Sachs leadership cadre and focus upon their cited "Business Principles".

GOLDMAN SACHS – "OUR BUSINESS PRINCIPLES"

1. **Our assets are people**, capital, and **reputation**. If any of these are ever lost, the last is the most difficult to regain
2. **We make an unusual effort to identify and recruit the very best person for every job. Although our activities are measured in billions of dollars, we select our people one by one.** In a service business, we know that **without the best people, we cannot be the best firm**.
3. We offer our people the opportunity to move ahead more rapidly than is possible at most other places. We have yet to find the limits to the responsibility that our best people are able to assume. **Advancement depends solely on ability, performance, and contribution to the firm's success, without regard to race, colour, age, creed, sex or national origin.**
4. **We stress teamwork in everything we do.** While individual creativity is always encouraged, we have found that team effort often produces the best results. We have no room for those who put their personal interests ahead of the interests of the firm and its clients.
5. The **dedication of our people to the firm and the intense effort they give their jobs are greater than one finds in most other organisations. We think that this is an important part of our success.**
6. Our profits are a key to our success. They replenish our capital and attract and keep our best people. **It is our practice to share our profits generously with all who helped create them. Profitability is crucial to our future**.

7. We **consider our size an asset that we try hard to preserve**. We want to be big enough to undertake the largest project that any of our clients could contemplate, **yet small enough to maintain the loyalty, the intimacy, and the esprit de corps that we all treasure and that contributes greatly to our success**.
8. We regularly receive confidential information as part of our normal client relationships. **To breach a confidence or to use confidential information improperly would be unthinkable**.
9. **Integrity and honesty are at the heart of our business**. We expect our people **to maintain high ethical standards in everything they do, both in their work for the firm and in their personal lives**.

Source: adapted from Goldman Sachs website (Who We Are – Goldman Sachs Business Principles).

The objective of this section, at the beginning of this chapter, is to emphasise that there are leadership principles, perspectives and characteristics which have universal application, no matter the context. Effective leadership requires practical wisdom to apply an organisational dominant logic in a sympathetic manner, dependent upon context, in order to achieve optimal performance. Due to the fact that effective leadership revolves around people management the predominant objective of the leader is to develop, maintain and proactively manage the levels of credibility and trust which they are able to generate amongst key individuals and stakeholder groups. The ability to understand and apply the key principles of an organisation's dominant logic within a specific context, in order to generate credibility and trust, requires the application of the principles, perspectives, priorities and individual attributes and capabilities of practical wisdom.

A natural output of a universally applied and effectively communicated dominant logic of organisational values, principles and priorities is a framework of universally applied, operational leadership attributes and capabilities by individual leaders. Figure 3.1 represents and encompasses those fundamental components of effective operational leadership which are required in an individual in order to create and manage the requisite levels of credibility and trust which optimise motivation and productivity on a day to day basis.

The key questions in this book are,

How important is practical and collaborative wisdom in the effective leadership of the organisation?

and

How does one develop in the individual and in the organisation as a community the attributes and capabilities of practical and collaborative wisdom?

Therefore, as scholars of business management, aspiring and practicing leaders, perusing the required attributes, capabilities, perspectives and priorities of the effective leader, contained within Figure 3.1, our ongoing question must be, *"How do we develop such traits in ourselves and others?"* More importantly how does the organisation successfully and

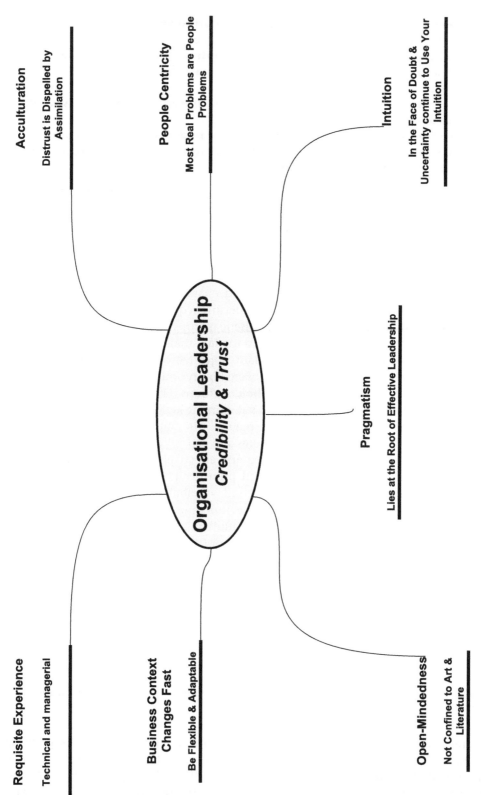

Figure 3.1 Organisational Leadership – The Creation of Credibility and Trust

consistently inculcate its leadership cadre with such traits? Whilst we will specifically address this issue later in the book it is desirable that this is an ongoing question in the mind of the reader, to aid the development of new perspectives and insights.

The following chapter sections discuss in greater detail these perspectives and the attributes of the effective operational leader.

Requisite Experience

In order to be a credible and effective leader within an organisation it is not enough to exhibit a broad understanding and insight of the market context, technical experience and an ability to manage. Such attributes and capabilities produce "mechanics" whose perspectives and priorities cannot ensure the survival and optimal performance of the organisation. Organisations are required to be led by "engineers".

As already mentioned in Chapter 2 the effective leader has to be an experienced professional and exhibit expertise as both a technician and as a leader of individuals. In order to appear credible and evoke widespread respect and trust a prerequisite is that you, as a people leader:

- **Exhibit a broad understanding, knowledge and insight in respect of the dynamics and current key issues and priorities of the industry**, its market and competitive environment (e.g. pharmaceuticals, banking, telecommunications, retailing).
- **Exhibit an in-depth insight in at least one key area of functional expertise** which is considered fundamental and intrinsic to the optimal performance of the organisation, (e.g. in banking – finance, corporate banking, treasury and wholesale banking, risk, marketing, sales, IT, HR). However, you are likely to be required to become a perceived technical expert in more than one of these functions in order to gain organisation wide credibility in preparation for appointment to a senior executive position.
- **Exhibit an ability to "manage"**, an ability to use the expert and professional knowledge encapsulated in both of the above areas for the benefit of the organisation towards achieving predetermined organisational goals within the operational context. An inability to perform in this arena generally precludes an individual from taking a leadership position, limiting that person to a role based purely on technical expertise (such roles exist in such funtions as IT, finance, treasury, R&D, HR, compliance, risk management). This attribute is essentially an ability to utilise resources, capabilities available within the organisation and established tools and frameworks of operational management to achieve individual targets and objectives set by the organisation. This is achieved through, for example, an ability to be technically proficient in managing one on one meetings, larger meetings, project management, written documentation such as plans, strategies, memoranda. It is an ability to direct individuals in order that tangible progress is consistently achieved. Progress, in this respect, is achieved primarily on the basis that individuals accept that you are following agreed processes and procedures and interpreting information and data in a

logical manner, rather than on the basis of an ability to lead, direct and persuade effectively.

- **Exhibit an ability to "lead"**. Effective leaders are those who combine:
  - Industry insight;
  - Technical expertise;
  - An ability to manage;
  - With expert people management through the satisfaction of the requirements and expectations of a broad spectrum of stakeholders;
  - A holistic perspective of how every unit of the organisation must be coordinated to optimise performance for all key stakeholders who impact on or are impacted by the organisation.

All require the perspectives, attributes, capabilities and cognitive processes of practical and collaborative wisdom in order to achieve operational effectiveness and optimal long-term performance.

In this respect it is important to distinguish the implications for the organisation between the mindsets, perspectives and priorities of:

- Effective technical managers, who exhibit an ability to "manage" as described above, whom I term "mechanics". These individuals exhibit an ability to manage individual technical tasks effectively. Their primary focus is technical excellence.
- Effective leaders, whom I term "engineers", who exhibit an ability to lead as described above, able to take an organisation wide perspective.

A pencil picture profile of the perspectives and priorities of these two groups is displayed in Table 3.1.

Table 3.1 Mechanics versus Engineers – Perspectives and Priorities

Mechanics	Engineers
• Piecemeal and limited understanding of the dynamics of the organisation	• Holistic understanding of logic and dynamics of the organisation and its position/role within wider societal/economic context
• In the absence of a holistic perspective primary motivations are technical excellence, making a living and maximising remuneration	• Due to broader perspective they view their role more as a vocation than a job. More likely to sacrifice self and dependents best interests for the broader good
• Perceives primary role and responsibility as keeping their unit within the organisation efficiently performing through an ongoing process of "replace" and "repair"	• See their role as optimising long-term performance rather than maximising short-term profit to impact positively on personal remuneration
	• Perceives their responsibility as building and improving the organisation over the long term through continuous adaptation and innovation

I do not wish to appear to be "knocking" mechanics, who are crucial in managing the "table stakes" requirements for the effective management of the organisation. Table stakes are the individual and organisational knowledge, expertise and capabilities which are required to create and maintain the fabric and ongoing operation of the organisation (e.g. finance, treasury, risk, compliance, marketing, IT, HR, legal, R&D). However, we need to be quite clear that it is not these areas of knowledge, expertise and capability which generate optimal productivity and performance. This is down to a more intangible, elusive capability, frequently in scarce supply within organisations; the ability to lead, direct, motivate and energise people effectively.

Everyone, including myself, is likely to go through the mechanic stage of focusing on a narrow field of expertise in order to attain technical excellence and thereby gain initial, individual credibility. At some stage, however, those individuals who have developed the appropriate leadership perspectives and attributes move beyond this stage to a more holistic mindset, creating a broader "community" emphasis. This provides a means of optimising individual aspirations, but through the satisfaction of the requirements and expectations of all stakeholder groups within the organisational community, rather than in a self and narrow significant others perspective.

I make these somewhat controversial and perhaps inflammatory comments on the basis of my operational experience, insight and reflections, during a career spanning four decades, rather than on the basis of empirical research. We will note later in this chapter the predominant utilisation by practitioners of expert intuition, rather than solely hard facts and evidence to draw conclusions, taking decisions and resolving issues with the required speed in order to maintain the expected or required business progress. As we noted in Part One of this book, the inclusion of the Intangible, in the form of emotions, insight, intuition, is a critical aspect in the application of practical wisdom.

Perhaps I am unlucky, but during my career I have rarely identified more than one leader on the basis of this profile in any organisation within which I have been employed, and, more ominously, rarely holding one of the senior executive positions. Senior executive positions tended, in my experience, in the main, to be taken by expert technicians and "mechanics". Capable in fields of knowledge more attuned to the dominant priority of individual and institutional shareholders for "trading" for short-term gain rather than "investing" for the long term. Able to manage effectively, but lacking the appropriate personal principles, perspectives and priorities, attributes and capabilities to lead effectively.

This point is not based upon any social, political or philosophical standpoint. Rather it is made from the pragmatic, hard-headed standpoint that this "trader" perspective, priority and profile of individual characteristics, attributes and capabilities will not result in operational effectiveness and therefore optimal long-term organisational performance. Whilst the process of managing an organisation is much simpler to understand and undertake when it is judged based upon technical experience, short-term objectives and the satisfaction of a limited group of stakeholders, optimal performance is based upon a holistic, long-term perspective, based upon the application of the principles, perspectives and cognitive processes of practical and collaborative wisdom. The logic of practical and collaborative wisdom dictates a direct link between effective people leadership, effective operational leadership and optimal organisational performance.

During my career in the Arabian Gulf the demand for expatriate executives was primarily related to a requirement for technicians and "mechanics". However, given the dynamic and changing nature of the industries, economies and society within the Gulf, they particularly appreciated those expatriates who exhibited "engineer" characteristics, particularly those taking a holistic perspective of their role and organisation within the broader economic and social context of the region. The atttributes and capabilities of effective people leadership were particularly prized by a complex stakeholder community and resulted in tangible enhancements in motivation, energy and advocacy.

Open-Minded and Pragmatic Leadership

In order to be credible as a leader, evoke trust and engender allegience, dedication and motivation, it is necessary to be a "quiet leader". Whilst confident of their developed schema of perspectives, based on their experience, knowledege and insight, they must acknowledge that such schema are unique and contextually based rather than universally applicable. In order to reach optimal solutions they must therefore take the views of credible and respected others, listen enthusiastically, be inclusive, thoughtful, patient, focusing on persuasion rather than direction. Such a disposition is achieved through experience of resolving issues within a wide variety of different management and leadership contexts, this in order to become an "all-terrain" leader.

It is a mark of a good leader that they have a confidence in their roots, their culture, their intellect, knowledge, instinct, intuition and analytical powers, this in order to be convincing and decisive. Throw in technical proficiency, a healthy dash of drive and motivation, self-importance and political savvy and you have a pretty accurate pencil profile of your average member of an Executive Committee. The possession of these perspectives and attributes is a substantial individual achievement and the mark of an individual of considerable talent and capability. However, the effective leader, who has the attributes and capabilities of practical and collaborative wisdom, exhibits additional key traits, perspectives, attributes and capabilities in order to consistently take optimal decisions in the resolution of context specific issues and achieve optimal performance. Whilst they are confident and assertive, they are also thoughtful, adaptable, patient, sympathetic, persuasive and inclusive. They are highly pragmatic, recognising the limitations of their knowledge and insight; also the limitations prescribed by the wider environment. This is dictated by the requirement to utilise all available resources, tangible and intangible, to optimise performance. Sustained success requires an open-minded, reflective, sensitive, nimbleness of management perspective, which is ready to adapt, accept change and operationalise its implications in order to optimise the advantages and minimise the downside. The predominant result is trust, respect and acceptance amongst involved and affected stakeholder groups, even if ultimately the decision may be contrary to an individual's views and personal recommendations.

Badarocco (2002) has coined the term "Quiet Leadership" to describe this operational management perspective, which emphasises the achievement of optimal performance through a primary focus on people dynamics and the possession of people leadership perspectives, attributes and capabilities. Quiet leaders are not individuals who are distant, superior and omnipotent, communicating through brief, often curt communications, by remote channels, such as telephone and email. Quiet leaders understand and practice positive psychology as a primary and central means of attaining operational effectiveness.

In this respect Badarocco contends that their leadership approach focuses upon the following attributes, perspectives and practices,

---

ATTRIBUTES OF THE "QUIET LEADER"

- They are confident, thoughtful, assertive, adaptable and persuasive.
- They are flexible, highly pragmatic, often opportunistic.
- They focus on what is reasonably attainable rather than what is ideal. Quiet leaders accept the limits to their knowledge and understanding; they therefore recognise the benefits of listening, judging, a teamwork and collegiate approach.
- They make sure that their motives are strong enough to carry them through difficulties.
- They nudge, test and escalate gradually.
- They find ways, when considered absolutely necessary, to bend the rules.
- They view compromise as a high form of leadership and creativity.

Banutu-Gomez (2002) and Miroshnik (2002) have added the following attributes:

- Recognising differences of viewpoint but not judging.
- To listen and consider context specific alternatives.
- To adapt practices and processes to local context requirements.

Effective management in the complex global business environment of the twenty-first century requires an individual who is confident of his/her own embedded logic, based on his/her own experiences, knowledge, insight and "home" communal values and context, whilst also accepting that they are unique and contextual, rather than universal in their practical applications. To attain such a perspective requires an open mind, willing to listen to alternative views and compromise on the basis of circumstance and context. Such characteristics can only effectively be developed as a result of experience, of managing, leading, taking responsibility for decision-making and issue resolution in a variety of business contexts. Leadership in the new global business context requires the creation of a "mental map", which allows executives to anticipate and quickly respond to developments across an ever wider and deeper spectrum of business contexts. Global leaders are "all-terrain vehicles", possessing the mental "technology" and capabilities to adapt to any business and organisational context, without jeopardising the dominant logic of the organisation which has consistently ensured its survival and long-term performance,

> Global leaders have exceptionally open minds, respect how things are different and can imagine why these things are different. Global leaders are incisive as well as generous and patient ... They have an understanding of their own roots, are sensitive and adaptable to global issues/cultures and are adaptable to new things" (Stanek, 2000, p. 232).

In many respects the leadership perspectives and priories embodied in "quiet leadership" are reflected in the views of Henry M. "Hank" Paulson, until January 2009 United States

Secretary of the Treasury, but prior to that Chief Executive of Goldman Sachs & Co. When reflecting on the attributes of successful leaders, he says,

> *The things that make a good leader are being open-minded, having a willingness to really ask for and accept advice, showing a sense of humility ... and his ability to evaluate people and match them with the responsibilities best suited to their development. Business failures are always linked to people failures ... Often I'll say to them ... and they always appreciate the candor ... I'm not sure you're in the right job for you. Let's repot you and see how you do (Ellis, 2008, p. 648).*

The key points within this quote are a pragmatic willingness to ask and listen, an interest in proactively placing talent and to try out people who are considered to have the required management and/or leadership talent in alternative positions, in order to enhance and leverage their talents. Rather than taking a short-term "human resource" perspective of their potential and ability to contribute to organisational performance on the basis of their existing role. These are all perspectives geared to the long-term benefit of the organisation, all key stakeholder groups and the achievement of individual aspirations, including those of self-esteem and self-respect. Most importantly, this quote reflects an acceptance of the importance of the individual in the optimal performance of the organisation and by implication the criticality of excellence in people leadership in its achievement. An acknowledgement that ultimately business failure emanates from an inability to focus upon and actively manage the people resource, rather than a focus on managing capital, products and other inanimate resources, structures and processes.

In all honesty, the management of the "table stakes" technical issues to which we have already referred is onerous, increasingly complicated, time-consuming and fraught with danger to an individual's long-term career. Yet effective leaders, who are specifically responsible for or directing such functions, have an ability to accommodate and priortise such technical proficiency requirements in a holistic manner, whilst recognising the centrality of people leadership in the resolution of critical operational business issues and ultimately the survival and optimal performance of the organisation. Aspiring leaders are advised to take this on board at the earliest opportunity in order that it is in place to direct their perspectives and priorities in the face of the day to day clamour, demands for speedy, intuitive responses, strident alternative views of those in whom the principles and process, attributes and capabilities of the practically wise are not in evidence.

Wise Decisions Require Light and Fast Feet

Effective leaders acknowledge and understand that control of one's environment and key resources, particularly human, is illusory, tenuous and transient. It is bestowed rather than claimed. Successful leadership is a light touch, deft, almost imperceptible, focusing upon the achievable rather than the ideal, based upon a pragmatic evaluation of one's ability to effect change. It is about taking responsibility for decisions whilst encouraging collegiate decision making to engender a common vision and optimise team cohesion.

The role of the individual leader or dominant leadership coalition would be relatively simple if it were merely to apply a business vision, utilising an agreed dominant logic, through the application of a standard set of priorities, procedures, processes and practices. Indeed many leaders wish and continue to manage their functions as if it were so. The two primary factors which dictate a more dynamic, subtle, flexible and adaptable approach are:

- Predicting and responding to the behaviour of individuals and stakeholder groups.
- The realisation that ultimately the business, being an intrinsic part, is hostage to rapid and unpredictable changes in the broader social, economic and business context.

The truly effective leader is often discovered, if not necessarily acknowledged, during a period of a radical downturn in market demand, usually without a concomitant decrease in organisational targets and objectives. During such periods he/she is able to enhance teamwork, cohesion and motivation in order to enhance productivity, often with diminishing resources. It is therefore an ability to effectively manage the behaviour of others, through a balanced, flexible and adaptable response to context, utilising an analytical yet affective cognitive mindset as detailed in Chapter 2. This, rather than efficiently managing costs, introducing new products, sales strategies and downsizing plans, is ultimately the critical mark of practical and collaborative wisdom and effective organisational leadership. During such periods of crisis the practically wise and effective leader retains credibility, trust and confidence, thereby maintaining the cohesion, allegience and dedication of key stakeholder groups which is so important for long-term optimal productivity.

Business organisations in the twenty-first century are highly complex, where leadership control is, in practice, both tenuous and illusory, requiring a light, deft, almost impercerptible touch. The attributes of practical wisdom as described in Chapter 2 are therefore critical in the effective management and survival of the organisation throughout the business cycle. As an example of such deft leadership Geringer and Herbert (1989) conclude that effective leaders within the multinational context recognise and emphasise their remit as one of directing selective change and, more importantly, selective control over functions and business issues which are considered critical and over which effective control is considered feasible in practice. Other functions and business issues will be managed effectively to optimise performance through their control by "local" leadership, who are able to leverage local tacit knowledge and insight. In the most successful business organisations leadership dynamics are not a black and white issue. It is rather a melding of control mechanisms, a consensus on the most appropriate balance of control for the effective management of the individual business unit and the overall group entity. In this respect, for example, control of and responsibility for various aspects of R&D , marketing, finance, risk, HR, customer service and sales may lie with either group or local management. In practice, whilst group management may define standards to be consistently applied, operational implementation and control of those functions (e.g. HR, marketing, sales, distribution, customer service), which have a significant impact on large numbers of people (i.e. staff, customers and stakeholders), will be left in the hands of local leadership who have the knowledge and insight to be fleet of foot and mind to adapt to frequently, often constantly, changing behaviour and responses.

In this respect effective leaders take pragmatic views on control mechanisms, decisions and issue resolution on the basis of what is practically achievable, rather than the ideal. They recognise the significant negative impact on productivity and organisational performance, in terms of such intangibles as motivation, cohesion and allegience, of seeking to achieve what might appear on the surface or from afar as the ideal. This open-minded, flexible perspective is particularly valuable within the global leadership context, where the individual is dealing with situations and perspectives which are different from the "home" context, perspectives and priorities, corresponding to the cognitive mental process which was illustrated in Chapter 2. As leaders they must recognise that they are not there as missionaries to change embedded, beliefs, but rather to lead successfully within a given social, economic and business environment. Stanek (2000) concludes that global leaders are sensitive and adaptable to local cultural contexts, acknowledging and accepting such differences as some of the key variables for consideration in the optimal resolution of individual issues.

In order to tangibilise and bring into relief the operational implications for the business leader faced with the requirement to optimise performance, whilst accomodating and adapting to local "differences" in an open-minded and pragmatic manner, this in order to optimise energy, cohesion, allegience, dedication and motivation, the boxed text below provides examples of some of the people management realities faced by the expatriate leader in the Arabian Gulf.

PEOPLE MANAGEMENT – ARABIAN GULF CONTEXT

- Multicultural management: managing nationalities within a single organisation might include – local nationals, Indians, Pakistanis, Lebanese, Jordanian, Palestinian, Syrian, Iraqi, Egyptian, Sudanese, Somali, British, South African, American, Chinese – potentially resulting in antipathy on the part of individuals related to cultural conflicts and superiority/inferiority perspectives.
- Cultural emphasis on wider and extended family responsibilities rather than work priorities leading in some states to significant impact on daily hours worked and work task focus.
- Some male employees having more than one wife, creating potential disharmony and conflict within the work context (how would you respond if a manager wished to take one of his female staff as his second or third wife?) – impact on morale and cohesion.
- Male employees in some states generally lackadaisical and disinterested, taking on roles primarily for social status, with employment income bolstered by significant additional income from state, family income and second job, usually small business in trading or property development – management of productivity/output.
- Segregation of genders (separate office/working space, separate lifts, separate entrances) – impact on daily work coordination and teamwork.
- Termination of employment for expatriates due to conviction on charges of apostasy or other criteria not recognised as appropriate or justified on the basis of "home" embedded values and experience to date.
- 1–3 month notice of termination of employment also resulting in withdrawal of residency permit, with knock on impact for working wife and schooling of children.
- High turnover due to demand for talented nationals, experienced expatriate technicians – impact on salaries and team building.
- Recruitment and promotion on the basis of family or tribal affiliations – impact on staff morale, particularly in respect of experienced and talented.

It is the role of the effective leader to optimise performance by effectively managing within the context of the opportunities and limitations of such differences in the local environment, mindful at all times of the stringent requirement to consistently operate within the context of the embedded dominant business logic. This is a task which requires all of the leadership perspectives, attributes and capabilities of practical and collaborative wisdom, particularly the ability to consider, analyse and process information in a practically wise manner, as described in Chapter 2. This is required in order to maintain confidence, respect and allegience, whilst appearing to satisfy the requirements and expectations of the plethora of stakeholders. It is at this intersection of often apparently conflicting imperatives and priorities that defective leadership and organisational failure often becomes evident, as suboptimal values, principles and perspectives are applied. This leads to an often silent, difficult to discern disintegration of stakeholder confidence and allegience in organisational leadership, their vision, objectives, priorities and capabilities. In practice, these intersections occur on a daily basis and leadership responses to individual issue resolution in respect of the changing business context are subconscious and intuitive, based upon the embedded values and principles of the individual leader and the prevailing organisational dominant logic.

My own experience of working in the Arabian Gulf is that one can quickly adapt, within the business environment at least, to even radical differences in cultural perspectives. As long as one is open-minded in practice, rather than merely saying one is but not taking decisions with a truly open mind. Listening, considering and as a result changing perspectives, priorities and resolving issues, implementing solutions in a manner different to what one might initially have considered optimal. When one is able to distinguish and differentiate between one's leadership role, private perspectives and priorities and the extent of one's ability to generate change, only then can you take a pragmatic and realistic approach to context and issue resolution, within the framework of an overarching dominant logic.

To be an "engineer" leader within such a multicultural context it is necessary to take a step further. This requires a truly holistic and open-minded perspective, to realistically, rather than stereotypically, compare "home" and "host" contexts, in order to practically evaluate issues for optimal resolution. As an example, whilst there may be some merit in a view of inequality of genders within some Middle East states there are an in fact an increasing number of senior executives and chief executives in the Gulf who are females and, as in the West, females "quietly" hold positions of substantial economic, social and political power. Increasingly, economic imperatives and pragmatism do and will increasingly dictate that the talents and particularly the energy and motivation of a highly educated female population are exploited, to enhance and sustain economic growth in the Arabian Gulf, just as it did in the USA and Europe in the early twentieth century. It should be recalled that it is less than a century since many Western governments gave women the vote and many western states continue to struggle with female representation on boards. Similarly, affiliations or connections with schools, colleges, institutes, clubs or similar bodies continue (albeit increasingly "under the counter") to often be the route to selection and promotion, from interns up to chairmen of boards of corporations across the globe, including within Europe and USA. This reality places the alleged endemic nepotism and tribal influence in respect of appointments into broader context. The practically wise leader appreciates the requirement to go outside the normal boundaries of what are termed by the majority as open-mindedness and pragmatism to find clarity in such complex and controversial issues when seeking optimal practical perspectives and solutions to context-driven issues. When we speak of global leadership it is important to recognise that we refer to a holistic, cognitive mental process reflecting practical wisdom, rather than merely differing management approaches as a result of differences in the scope of responsibility and/or global context. This is an issue to which we will subsequently return.

Effective leaders recognise that they cannot hope to have all of the technical and contextual knowledge required to take optimal decisions in all circumstances. They therefore take into account those around them who are generally recognised to have valuable information and perspectives. They acknowledge the value of recognising and respecting differences of viewpoint without judging (Banutu-Gomez, 2002), assessing the information and perspectives of individuals within the context of the issue to be resolved, rather than any personal motivations or relationships. Many of the most successful organisations therefore operate a formal or informal collegiate, rather than individual management perspective. Decisions of fundamental importance to the organisation are not taken on the basis of hierachical authority, perceived technical expertise and/or responsibility in the area, but rather on a consensual basis. This is due to the fact that there is a recognition by all members of the dominant coalition of the logic that the optimal decision should be taken or solution reached on the basis of collective knowledge, experience, insight, judgement and ultimately the sum total of their wisdom.

This approach is facilitated by an acknowledgement by all members of a common organisational vision, ensuring consistency and continuity in decision making. Such a decision-making foundation is achieved in successful organisations through proactive inculcation and years of supporting and relying on each other to resolve critical situations, which we will discuss in greater detail at a later juncture. This process is encapsulated in a quote by Sir John Bond, formerly Executive Chairman of HSBC Holdings plc in a retirement interview with Lucy Kellaway of the *Financial Times*,

> *The top 50 people in HSBC have been here 1,000 years. We know each other extraordinarily well, which is what makes teamwork possible (Kellaway, 2006, p. 10).*

This consensual approach in no way affects the formal and functional responsibilities and authority of individual executives and in the unlikely, rare and unfortunate event of continuing disagreement, the CEO retains the right of ultimate decision. The important point to consider is that this open-minded and collegiate approach is not founded on the "hard", formal, structured and hierarchical. It is rather based upon "soft" attributes which define the people and interpersonal dynamic, dominated by a consideration and balancing of diverse perspectives and attitudes, of respect and trust, created through mutual support in critical times, all of this as a means of consistently reaching optimal solutions. It would be very difficult to discern from the outside the difference between:

- The CEO who institutes regular discussions amongst his executive team and others within the leadership cadre, to appear to listen to views and consult on important organisational issues, but who makes decisions based solely upon his own views, perspectives and priorities or those of a favoured clique.

- The CEO who institutes regular discussions amongst his executive team and others within the leadership cadre and takes them into account in the decision-making process.

However, internally, there is a tangible recognition of inclusiveness and collegiate decision-making, resulting in enhanced self-esteem, dignity, self-respect and pride, which, in turn results in optimal cohesion, loyalty, motivation, a sense of a common vision and clear, uniform direction, ultimately leading to optimal performance.

The following case provides a clear example of a leadership ability to balance, to evaluate a multiplicity of often competing priorities through applying the principles and perspectives of practical and collaborative wisdom. This is achieved by the consistent and embedded organisational attributes and capabilities of leadership adaptability and flexibility, thereby ensuring long-term survival and growth over the long term. The subject organisation has become a global banking force on the basis of achieving widespread confidence, credibility and trust amongst all stakeholder groups, from employees to national governments and statutory authorities over a period of 150 years (with periodic exceptions, as in 2012 in respect of USA financial regulators). This has been attained through the development of both technical banking expertise but also an ability to look at situations from a holistic perspective and be seen to be both willing and capable of taking wise decisions in a practical, pragmatic context-driven manner, in the interests of all key stakeholder groups, no matter the circumstances and context.

SURVIVAL AND GLOBAL EXPANSION THROUGH EMBEDDED ADAPTABILITY

The century and a half history of HSBC Holdings plc is dotted with operational examples of an ability to adapt business focus and policy, ensuring its continuing survival and creating opportunity out of market calamity. HSBC (formerly Hongkong and Shanghai Banking Corporation) was established in Hong Kong and China in 1865, an environment subject to regular climatic, economic and political crises, resulting in civil war, epidemics, administrative and infrastructural collapse. This created severe business dislocation, resulting in the downfall and bankruptcy of the vast majority of banks in the region during the late nineteenth and early decades of the twentieth century. After the Second World War. HSBC was excluded from its primary market in China due to a policy of nationalisation. Also from Persia in the early 1950s, where it had opened in 1889, becoming the state bank (Imperial Bank of Persia), issuing banknotes. Realising the value of maintaining a presence in the oil states it pioneered banking in the Arabian Gulf states in the 1940s and developed a multiregional business perspective.

HSBC's head office has been located in London since 1993 and is now widely recognised as a universal bank, offering services across all banking sectors, with global reach spanning every continent and subcontinent. However, prior to 1959 HSBC was a bank with a regional focus in the Middle/Far East and Asian Pacific, with agencies and representative offices in key global trading locations to support its international trade finance activities, which had been at the core of its business focus and expertise until the 1970s. As Lord Sandberg, Chairman and Chief Executive of the HSBC Group stated,

The most obvious development is that we are enlarging the Group from being a major regional bank with international connections. This is not a process which will happen overnight. We still remain fundamentally a major regional bank with particular strengths in Asia and the Middle East rather than a truly international bank such as Barclays International and Citibank (Sandberg, 1978, p .8).

The significance of such adaptability, flexibility and improvisation lies not in the strategy, since international/global expansion is not not a unique strategy but rather in its consistency and success. Over the intervening years HSBC, unlike others, has expanded and expanded, without the crisis, retrenchment and in some cases collapse experienced by many other institutions. It has expanded to create major network banking presences in such areas as France, Brazil, Argentina, Turkey, Canada, USA, UK, Malaysia, Mexico and Australia plus private banking operations in Switzerland, Germany and New York.

The ability to survive by changing policy on the basis of market challenges and opportunities is due to that attribute in the organisation's dominant logic which allows it to anticipate and adapt, implementing new business strategy and to move forward intuitively, as if such market situations were part of the day to day realities of organisational management for which leaders must be prepared.

The need and ability to be light of foot is evidenced by the fact that during the period of HSBC's major expansion, a period of the last 30 years, except for one bank (Barclays plc), we have witnessed the demise, acquisition or part nationalisation of all of the major banks in the UK, many also established in the nineteenth century, and many of which dwarfed HSBC only 20 years ago (e.g. Midland Bank, National Westminster Bank, Bank of Scotland, Royal Bank of Scotland, Halifax, Abbey National, Bradford & Bingley and Lloyds Bank). This is therefore not an attribute and capability which should be taken for granted and is something which organisations require to prioritise at the very highest levels. As Sir John Bond has recently said in an interview,

You're looking at a firm believer that every company should have a board member who is responsible for "corporate insecurity"… that is his job: to remind people that a quarter of the FTSE 100 from 20 years ago have gone, and that if the 141 year old bank does not keep changing it could face the same fate (Kellaway, 2006, p. 10).

A proven ability to adapt to, indeed benefit from, a changing market context evokes confidence in the ability of organisational leaders to satisfy stakeholder requirements and expectations. This allows leaders to implement policy over the long term without unnecessary and unwelcome intervention. It can also potentially have a dramatic impact on the share price and the cost of finance as stakeholders maintain their trust during crises caused by market developments or indeed errors of judgement on the part of the dominant coalition.

Source: adapted from Park (2006).

However, the ability to anticipate and adapt has two practical components; the ability to take appropriate action, such as global expansion through acquisition and, more importantly, to successfully deliver the benefits of such a policy over the long term. As we will see throughout the rest of this book, consistent, long-term success in this respect requires a dominant logic based primarily upon the management of people, rather than a dominance of management by the numbers, supported by technical and procedural expertise.

Practical Wisdom: The Logic of People Centricity

Organisational crisis and collapse occurs when the people and communal components of leadership become incidental rather than central to its guiding principles and priorities. In the twenty-first century optimal performance relies upon a pragmatic, "feminine" approach to leadership, a focus on nurturing and enhancing intellectual capital and tacit knowledge rather than a hard "masculine" approach based on firm direction, obedience, structure and procedure. This is the primary responsibility of each individual leader, from an individual with an assistant, a departmental or divisional head, to the chief executive. Success is achieved in this regard through an acknowledgement that people issues are central to the optimal resolution of day to day operational issues, rather than the more tangible technical component. People centricity is the twenty-first century interpretation and application of the values, principles and cognitive mental process which underpin practical and collaborative wisdom.

The management of the *"global"* organisation is increasingly complex. It is therefore doubly important that the foundation stones are clearly acknowledged, understood, defined and effectively communicated, in the form of key management principles, perspectives and priorities, consistently reinforced by consistent operational practice. In many financial services organisations it appears that shareholder value, ROE, ROA, cost/income ratio, capital adequacy, Basle II/III requirements and the like constitute the central focus and the guiding priorities by which they are managed, rather than merely a number of the dashboard indicators of prevailing organisational performance. Such executive leadership priorities and emphasis are indicative of a superficial, short-term, *"trader"* perspective, which is likely to lie at the root of the present financial and economic crisis.

The problem arises when the "mechanics", who are accomplished at managing the technical *"table stakes"* and tend to interpret these dashboard indicators as marks of absolute organisational management success, are selected as organisational leaders, having delivered to the "primary" stakeholder groups (e.g. senior executives, board members and institutional shareholders) what is effectively short-term value enhancement. This in preference to "engineers", who, as we have already mentioned, have a holistic understanding of the organisation, who seek to optimise rather than maximise performance over the long term, through an ongoing build and improve approach, for the benefit of the broad community of organisational stakeholders. This issue is fundamental to the central theme of this book. The application of the principles and attributes of practical and collaborative wisdom is inconsistent with the prevailing dominant logic of the majority of business organisations, where there is a limited long-term perspective and emphasis amongst the leadership cadre. Rather there is a vision which is to be achieved through a series of short-term profit generation strategies which benefit primary but transient stakeholders which, at the macro level, is likely to reflect the prevalent ideologies of peer group leaders within society. Long-term successful organisations take a long-term "marathon" rather than sprint perspective vis-à-vis performance and profits. It is for this reason that they recognise the benefit of investing in people and acknowledge the centrality of people leadership within their dominant logic.

The "mechanic" approach fails to appreciate that the fundamental role of operational management is not to optimise profit. It is to manage a group of people who have come together for a common purpose. To make such a statement, even after much widespread reflection on the drivers of the prevailing financial crisis, doubtless meets with much disbelief and incredulity, if not horror and fear, amongst a multitude of senior executive practitioners, not to mention a few consultants and scholars. This is due to the fact that for many it undermines the fundamental principles, perspectives and priorities in which they have been inculcated and which they have applied throughout their careers as organisational leaders. However, as Sir John Bond states,

> A company is an abstract concept, the product of a lawyer's mind. Human beings are what bring a company to life and shape its destiny (Sir Bond, 2001, p. 1).

The art of the effective business leader lies not in making a profit per se, but rather in recognition that if they produce:

- A "product" attractive to the market;
- Material and psychological remuneration "packages" attractive to staff and other stakeholder groups;
- Whilst satisfying the "legitimacy imperatives" required by the local and increasingly global society.

only then will an optimal long-term profit stream occur. Long-term success is possible only when the leadership philosophy by which an organisation is led acknowledges these tenets in both policy and practice, through recognition of the organisation as *a part of* rather than *apart from* the overall socio-economic community. On the basis of the nature of much of the embedded theory, thought, assumptions and practice of business management over the last 20 to 30 years such a statement is likely to generate considerable dissonance if not incredulity, trepidation and resistance amongst practitioners. Yet it is apparent to all organisational leaders, if perhaps not universally accepted, that a fundamental realignment in values, principles, perspectives and priorities is required if business organisations are to survive and perform optimally in the twenty-first century knowledge-based environment.

The focus upon speed of market response to survive and prosper in the twenty-first century dictates a focus on people management, this in order to develop, retain and enhance intellectual capital and tacit knowledge; to be in a position to respond to the rapidly changing business environment. Such a conclusion is the inevitable result of critical reflection, based upon the selection of key principles, perspectives and priorities, issues and information in a cognitive mental process to which we have referred when describing practical wisdom in Chapter 2.

Therefore, rather than strategy, structure/hierarchy and process, which looks to obedience and subservience, practical, pragmatic, business-focused operational leaders must now rely on the intelligence, drive, determination, loyalty and energy of individuals as the primary means of sustained organisational success. Effective implementation of such an approach does not require leaders who are distant, superior and omnipotent, directing by email from some remote, location on the 40th floor. Rather, every manager must be able to engender trust, energy, dedication, through practicing the universally accepted values in resolving day to day issues. How many leaders can honestly say that:

- This is their primary leadership priority and focus as the means of achieving operational effectiveness and optimal performance.
- They possess the required people leadership perspectives, attributes, skills and capabilities.

These perspectives and conclusions are gaining increasing traction and advocacy amongst operational leaders. This book proposes how these perspectives and priorities might effectively be embedded within the leadership cadre of the organisation, through the development and application of practical and collaborative wisdom. This leadership approach is not woolly. It is feminine but does not threaten any desired image of leaders as dynamic, hard– nosed individuals. It is rather wise, smart, realistic, practical, pragmatic, soft-hearted (but not soft-headed) and contextually relevant.

The key requirements for sustained success over the long term are primarily "soft", qualitative, people-focused attributes; this in a market where everyone has ready access to the information, technical, quantitative, structural and procedural management tools to aid performance. If people are the key to optimal performance then leaders must develop attributes and capabilities to engender trust, dedication and allegiance,

Leadership is a combination of personal behaviours which focus on the soft stuff which enables the leader to gain the allegiance and dedication of others. Leaders demonstrate integrity, generate trust and communicate vision and values. By this means they create energy and motivation (Bennis and O'Toole, 2000, p. 172).

People centricity is an issue which has already been discussed and will continue to arise throughout the text as a central theme and an output of practical and collaborative wisdom. Given the importance for the organisation of effective people management it is critical that it is managed proactively, centre stage, at both the strategic and operational levels, rather than an assumption that it occurs by some form of osmotic effect, quietly and automatically in the background.

Alternatively, the view may prevail that whilst this is indeed an important issue for effective leadership of the organisation, it is rather the primary responsibility of someone else, somewhere else in the organisation, probably HR, whilst managers and senior executives are concentrating upon their "technical" responsibilities (e.g. marketing, compliance, IT, risk, finance).Whilst some technical experts might be loathe to openly admit it, many are increasingly likely to accept that people are the most difficult yet the most critical "resources" to manage effectively. Senior executives and managers prefer to place the tangible and the technical at the centre of organisational objectives and targets (e.g. revenue, turnover, sales, costs/income, assets, products/systems launched) because they do not wish to ultimately be assessed on their people management ability. This is disastrous for the performance and ultimate survival of the organisation, which is ultimately,

> *a human endeavour ... the corporate branch of society (Sir Bond, 2000a, p. 1).*

dependent not on prevailing sales and profits but rather on the cohesion, motivation, dedication and energy of people and for this reason are critical in the development of credibility ad trust. The indicators of success in this critical area are however more difficult, yet not impossible, to recognise, measure and certainly highly complicated to manage. There has been an increasing trend in the measurement of employee satisfaction, allegience, dedication and motivation amongst some organisations. However, unless there is a centric focus and substantial competency in people management throughout the organisation many of those businesses which we recognise and laud as highly successful, whose senior executives we claim to be inspired leaders, are merely shooting stars.

Despite the fact that someone may be titled or described as a manager of a unit, if they perceive that the direction, motivation and energising of individuals is a minor component in their role and this is translated in the manner of decision-making and issue resolution, then they are not managers, but rather technicians. This point is succinctly stated by Geert Hofstede when he says,

> *I prefer the general definition of "getting things done through other people", or, more specifically, "coordinating the efforts of other people towards common goals" ... Jobs in which no other people are involved are technical, not management ... because management is always about people, its essence is dealing with human nature (Hofstede, 1999, p. 34).*

This is a somewhat controversial viewpoint, due to issues of status and egoism and the counterpoint that no matter if you are an accountant or IT expert the attainment of organisational objectives requires significant to substantial people interface and direction. My response would be that if this is the case then a focus on developing expert people leadership skills and capabilities are equally if not more central to the effective execution of that role. Regrettably, in the majority of organisations, the emphasis continues to remain on the development of technical skills, with a subsidiary effort at nurturing the perspectives, attributes and capabilities which are a prerequisite for effective people leadership. It is undoubtedly true that people management is learned rather than taught, largely through a process of experience and reflection of what is the best way to enhance performance. However, it is important that its centrality is reflected in the key leadership principles, perspectives and priorities which must be inculcated in aspiring leaders at the early stages of their careers and in the embedded organisational logic which directs decision-making and issue resolution. Any acknowledgement and recognition of an individual as an effective manager/leader must therefore be based upon an expertise in a technical area, but also the possession and the consistent application of the attributes and capabilities of and expertise in people leadership. This requires an insight and appreciation of the psychological drivers of the individual and an ability to leverage this knowledge to create cohesion, allegience and motivation for the benefit of the organisational community.

Strong resistance and outright rejection of the centrality of people in achieving optimal performance is inevitable, this for a number of reasons:

- The present generation of leaders perceive that they have succeeded in their careers on the basis of a "hard", pragmatic, masculine approach to leadership based upon direction, obedience, structure, procedure and process.
- Already there is a new cadre of aspiring leaders who have been imbued in the "masculine" principles of leadership by business schools and organisational training courses.
- The people centric approach is a "soft" feminine style of leadership, which appears inconsistent with the embedded profile of a leader.

Some readers might feel uncomfortable with the way that this book is going. They might argue that we are looking at the business organisation, an entity whose ultimate purpose is geared towards productivity and performance, rather than one whose primary purpose is directed at achieving more beneficial social objectives of, for instance, making people happier, more content, comfortable and self-fulfilled. This book does not disagree with the ultimate objectives of business, merely with the prevailing perceptions and emphasis regarding the means and priorities by which these objectives are achieved. I would term my proposals as practical, hard-headed and pragmatic, yet soft-hearted. However, I would not regard the results of taking a more people centric approach as being any "nicer" or "kinder" than the prevailing "masculine" approach. Where someone fails to perform to the standards required to optimise performance in the interests of the organisational and wider community, where the leader has applied the values, perspectives and priorities of the "quiet leader", then established guidance, appraisal and discipline processes should be applied, albeit in a people-focused manner, applying the principles and cognitive mental processes of practical and collaborative wisdom. Ultimately, the application of practical and collaborative wisdom dictates that if the individual or group are recognised and their actions widely interpreted as self-serving and/or not supporting the vision and objectives which will optimise the community of stakeholders' requirements and expectations then they will be invited to join another community where their perspectives and priorities are more compatible. This is not communism, utopianism or any other "ism". It is the wise, smart, practical and pragmatic approach to achieve optimal operational effectiveness and long-term optimal performance, as the most effective means to ensure that stakeholders continue to voluntarily offer their optimal levels of allegience, dedication, motivation and energy, acting as advocates of the values, principles, culture, objectives and vision of the organisation.

Effective Management of Acculturation Through Clarity and Consistency

The application of practical and collaborative wisdom within the operational business context is an intricate and complex one. However, at its most basic, it is essentially concerned with consistently resolving issues and taking decisions by viewing them through the people lens. On the basis of this critical process effective assimilation of staff is achieved through persuading them of a compatibility of values, perspectives and practices. Acculturation, which involves the acceptance and adoption of the principles, perspectives and priorities of the organisation by all employees is a critical component in achieving optimal long-term performance. It is therefore critical that the leadership of any organisation take active steps to ensure that effective acculturation has been achieved and take action to remedy any acculturation issues, particularly during periods of merger, acquisition or joint venture. The management of acculturation is equally important during those business episodes when the dominant coalition decides to implement policies related to organisational restructuring and refocus, which requires a reorientation by employees in respect of core perspectives, priorities and practices. An inability to effectively manage acculturation leads to diminishing levels of motivation, commitment, allegience, cooperation, resulting in increased turnover, lower productivity and a dramatic deterioration in organisational performance.

Organisations consistently fail to optimise productivity because their leadership does not recognise the force of three words, clarity, comfort and confidence and the resultant levels of distrust, trepidation, apprehension and anxiety which develop on the part of stakeholder groups where these are not in evidence. This is particularly pertinent during periods of substantial change, such as during mergers and acquisitions, but also during periods of organisational restructuring. However, they can also be a persistent drag on stakeholders, but particularly employee motivation, even where such episodes are not taking place. Putting aside monetary compensation stakeholders require from organisational leadership to be satisfied in a number of key areas, namely:

CRITICAL INTANGIBLE REQUIREMENTS FOR EFFECTIVE PEOPLE LEADERSHIP

- **Clarity of direction**: confidence that the organisation has a long-term vision which has been split into operational objectives. Also that each individual stakeholder has a specific role in this vision, and most importantly, that it has been clearly communicated to each individual.
- **Respect**: policy and strategic decisions taken have clearly taken into account the requirements and expectations of individuals and stakeholder groups. Also that appropriate consultation has been undertaken to clarify objectives and to exhibit an understanding of any individual and/or stakeholder group doubts and worries in order to maintain and enhance personal self-esteem and motivation.
- **Security and stability**: an expectation that events will not occur which dramatically impact upon a sense of understanding the framework within which decisions and events are likely to take place, and an ability to anticipate their personal implications.

In respect of the above, employees would not expect to suddenly receive a non-personalised email announcing a drop in salary of 30%, mass redundancy or plant closure. Similarly, shareholders would not expect to find that their share value had dropped by 50 per cen overnight, the organisation was moving the majority of its focus and resources into a radically new market sector or that the board and/or executive team were resigning en masse. Such situations do indeed occur and the impact upon comfort and confidence and the subconscious faith in organisational leadership is profound, having a dramatic effect on cohesion, dedication and motivation, ultimately productivity, even amongst those not directly affected.

A similar impact on clarity, comfort and confidence occurs in respect of a merger or acquisition, where the perceived framework within which issues are resolved and action taken appears to stakeholders to be subject to radical change, thereby generating feelings of anxiety and distrust. In such scenarios Very, Lubatkin and Calori contend that individual staff make judgements and respond on the basis of the answers to three questions:

QUESTIONS ASKED BY STAKEHOLDER GROUPS IN TIMES OF RADICAL CHANGE

- Are our personal circumstances as favourable and just, as someone else's circumstances to whom we relate?
- Are they as favourable and just as our past ones?
- Will our future be as favourable and just as our present?

Source: adapted from Very, Lubatkin and Calori (1996).

In respect of their assessment of the answers to these questions employees may individually or in groups decide that in fact they are better off (acculturative attraction) within the new organisational culture, or not, as the case may be, with the attendant impact on loyalty, dedication, motivation, productivity and overall organisational performance. It is therefore critical that not only the organisational dominant coalition but the whole leadership cadre down to the subunit, acknowledge and understand this decision-making process and take it into account in the planned operational process of assimilation, in order to achieve effective control whilst optimising performance over the long term. This is achieved by:

- Directly acknowledging and addressing the issue of acculturation.
- Convincing staff of the continuing compatibility in personal and organisational values, perspectives and practices.
- The acceptance by stakeholders of the ability of the changed organisational vision to continue to contribute to the attainment of personal requirements and aspirations.
- Recognition of their continuing inclusion as active, contributing and welcome members of the organisational community.

This process is acknowledged as intrinsic to effective operational leadership in the following quote,

If you acquire an organisation, get deeply involved in management of the organisation, to understand it, cannot afford to leave it on a long lead; assess the quality of the people, keep good ones, bring them into your family, give opportunity in the wider Group ... inculcating key HSBC principles is a key element of integration process, yet first there has to be a belief, sense that there is a compatibility in values, perspectives and practices otherwise making change is very difficult, has to be a desire to integrate, a motivation to mix ideas (Interviewee B).

Acculturation is defined in the *Oxford English Dictionary* as "the assimilation or adoption of the values of a different culture". It is effectively the process by which individuals accept the values, principles and priorities of the dominant coalition, becoming assimilated in respect of its widely held operational perspectives and generally applied practices. Whilst it might reasonably be included under the heading of people centricity it is considered an issue of such importance in effective leadership and optimal performance and of some complexity, to justify a separate section within this chapter on gaining credibility and trust. Inevitably, whether you are:

- A new entrant to business employment;
- Someone recruited to or currently employed within the organisation during your career path; or
- Part of the employees within an acquired or merged organisation.

there is a requirement and mental process by which you gain an insight into and accept the core principles, priorities and practices of the organiational dominant logic. Through a process of acceptance and inculation you become a member of that community and thereby feel loyal, motivated and energised by the organisation, in order that you generate optimal productivity for the organisation. Given the importance of effective acculturation for organisational performance it is wise that leaders register, acknowlege and understand its importance in their conscious operational management perspectives and practices, as part of the people centric mindset.

The following quote from a senior executive of HSBC Holdings plc, although lengthy, clearly describes the critical reflection, cognitive mental processes, priorities and practices of wise leaders during a period of integration and assimilation, subsequent to an organisational acquisition. It clearly indicates that operational decision-making schema, whilst taking into account organisational and social cultures, are primarily based at the level of the individual, satisfying their requirements, expectations and aspirations. This is in order to tap into and leverage their skills, experience, aptitudes and knowledge as the prime drivers of continuing performance. It also indicates an holistic, long-term business view (HSBC typically makes a 25-year market assessment prior to any acquisitions). It further indicates a patient, sympathetic approach and open-minded perspective, an appreciation that assimilation does not occur overnight. However, it also indicates a clarity of purpose and pragmatic, hard-headed determination that ultimately the organisational community of stakeholders takes precedence over any individual. Therefore that appropriate action will be taken to ensure that integration and assimilation occurs amongst the management and senior executive cadre within a timescale appropriate to achieving overall group business objectives,

People who work for a company tend to assume its identity, to release that identity takes time, and this is understood and accepted, recognised; companies acquired some time ago one can still recognise a strong sense of the old culture; equally there is no discomfort in working with the HSBC culture, there is a hierarchy of organisational cultures within any organisation. As an example, when HSBC took a significant share in (omitted for reasons of confidentiality) there was first a series of meetings, events between senior management to present, discuss, different organisational practices, so that they knew each other better. The second step was to have significant transfers between staff ... to understand perspectives and practices. If people resisted change and were unable to adapt then changes were necessary; not everyone can make the transition comfortably ... the philosophy of collegiate, collective management requires understanding and open mindedness ... and if people are not open to change and new ideas then they have no place in the organisation (Interviewee B).

HSBC management appreciate the need for staff to be part of a clear and greater vision, where their role is clearly defined and provides them with pride, self-respect and self-esteem,

That reminds me of the janitor who worked for NASA at the time of the space programme in the 60s. He was asked what he did. He didn't say he swept the floor. He said "I'm helping to put a man on the moon" (Sir John Bond, 2000a, p. 3).

During his research the author was allowed to converse at random with staff of HSBC in Mexico and the GCC states and gained the impression that employment by HSBC was regarded by both staff and their families as carrying substantial status. There was an eager and spontaneous desire to become assimilated and inculcated in the fundamental logic and culture of the organisation, to be recognised within the individual's in-groups as a member of the organisational community for the benefit which accrues to self-esteem and credibility. This perspective prevailed to the extent that they would wear the "badges" (e.g. ties, scarves, bags, name badges) of membership of this organisation to social events outside of the work context. On the basis of my personal experience in these regions this action was not widely representative of staff within other global and regional banks. There was a belief that HSBC is part of something more than providing global financial services for profit. This is often what attracts and motivates high-quality recruits to initially decide to join and remain with the organisation. Such a level of acculturation and assimilation provides a core competence impossible to emulate, except in the long term. This was reflected in the perspectives of senior management regarding the type of organisation of which they wished to be a part,

I wanted a company that I could be proud to work for. Being part of something which is worthwhile is important ... To be proud of a company means finding one that treats all its constituents with respect and care ... my job today is to create an environment where good people will want to work (Sir Bond, 2000a, p. 3).

This pride and feeling of communal membership was primarily due to the fact that the reputation and global status of HSBC enhanced the self-esteem of individuals. In addition, the reputation for fairness, integrity, staff development, remuneration on merit, professionalism, efficiency was considered by interviewees to often make membership of this organisational community far more attractive than membership of their previous organisation, reflecting the values of a broader society of which they would wish to be a part.

Whilst acculturation is an ongoing issue within the effectively led organisation, inevitably the primary focus by scholars and practitioners has fallen on the process of acculturation which occurs immediately following an acquisition or merger and has been of particular concern within the cross-cultural context. Cartwright and Cooper (1993) estimated that the cost of "culture collisions", resulting from poor integration, may typically be as high as 20–30% of the performance of the acquired organisation. This certainly makes effective acculturation of equal, if not greater, importance than "strategic fit". In this respect Very, Lubatkin and Calori (1996) have investigated the critical issue of "acculturative stress", which encapsulates the response and decision-making process of staff when they are confronted by the requirement to respond to a new organisational cultural context, which can occur as a result of an acquisition or merger, but equally when the dominant coalition of an organisation implement a radical restructuring and refocusing. The resultant disruptive tension, which may be brief, require ongoing remedial action or ultimately destroy the organisation, is associated with low levels of motivation, commitment, cooperation, obstructive practices, increased staff turnover, resulting in low productivity and performance.

As already alluded to, Geringer and Herbert (1989) encourage a practical and selective or "context-oriented" perspective in respect of management control, taking into account different organisational or societal cultures, achieving corporate objectives through gaining and maintaining the loyalty and motivation of "acquired" staff,

> This suggests that the exercise of effective control should emphasise selective control over those dimensions which a parent perceives as critical, rather than attempting to control the entire range of the IJV's activities. This notion of selective control efforts raises the prospect of a split control IJV, one in which the parent firm may exercise dominant control over a few dimensions of the venture (Geringer and Herbert, 1989, p. 240).

Given the proposed importance of a loyal and motivated staff the decision as to what control strategy to implement should to a significant degree be dependent upon a consideration and analysis of the reaction of staff within the merged/acquired company during the various stages in the integration process, who may:

- Reject and resist the proposed integration process, finding that it does not satisfy their tangible and intangible requirements, expectations and aspirations.
- Decide that overall the proposed benefits of the integration process satisfy their requirements and aspirations in a manner superior to the previous employment situation. They will therefore transfer their allegiance to this new employment situation and apply their talents, expertise, experience and energy to the new organisational vision.
- Find that at first glance there is little difference in pre- and post-integration benefits. Staff might therefore see how things go before deciding to accept or reject their new situation. The result is that they do not provide total commitment, motivation and energy to the integration process and may consider and communicate exit strategies within the organisational community, with the impact this can have on allegiance and dedication.

Cartwright and Cooper produced an *"Acculturation Model"* which encapsulates the options and results of the extent of acquired/merged staff assimilation.

THE ACCULTURATION MODEL

Options	Scenario and Results
Assimilation	Occurs when acquired staff willingly relinquish their existing culture, adopt and become absorbed in acquirer culture. Resistors are displaced
Deculturation	Occurs when members of acquired organisation are dissatisfied with existing culture but remain unconvinced as to the attractiveness of acquirer culture; acquired employees experience confusion and alienation
Integration	Occurs when interaction and adaptation occurs between two cultures, which results in the potential for the evolution of a new organisational culture, but may result in culture collisions and potential fragmentation
Separation	Occurs when significant members (in respect of numbers and/or levels of influence) of acquired organisation resist assimilation and/or adaptation, resulting in the emergence of separate cultures within an organisation. This results in a lack of common vision and direction, cohesion, cooperation and ultimately results in paralysis of decision making and the potential for separation

Source: adapted from Cartwright and Cooper (1993).

Hard-headed, pragmatic, yet soft-hearted leadership acknowledges the benefits of taking into consideration the requirements to achieve effective acculturation, but within the context of achieving corporate objectives in respect of a merger, acquisition or joint venture. The balancing of these two priority management issues to achieve optimal long-term performance dictates the type and extent of control by the dominant coalition. It requires practically wise leaders, able to understand the importance to the organisational community of addressing the views and concerns of staff in order that the vision of the organisation is seen to be consistent with the aspirations and expectations of stakeholder groups and individuals.

In this respect Cartwright and Cooper distinguish between three merger and control scenarios:

SELECTIVE CONTROL SCENARIOS

- **Extension mergers**: where business is conducted in a "hands off" manner and local management perspectives and practices are preserved. This type of control is undertaken since it is viewed that such an approach will optimise performance through leveraging local intellectual capital and tacit knowledge and also as a means of maximising employee motivation, allegience, loyalty and thereby productivity.
- **Collaborative mergers**: where exchanges of expertise or technology are at the root of the collaboration and where differences in tacit knowledge add value, whilst maintaining the self-esteem of both groups of employees, thereby ensuring optimal cooperation, energy and productivity.

- **Redesign mergers**: where the majority partner intends to introduce radical changes, impacting upon prevailing embedded perspectives and practices, in order to leverage competitive advantages or core competences of the junior partner organisation. This is a scenario which requires deft leadership skills, since there is a likelihood that there will be levels of resistance which will negate the perceived logic of the strategic fit between the two organisations.

Source: adapted from Cartwright and Cooper (1993).

Acculturation is therefore optimised when individuals consider that membership of the organisational community enhances credibility, self-esteem and self-respect within the broader societal community, rather than when the individual extends his/her labour to optimise personal and organisational material benefit. Cross and colleagues (2003) conclude that people are energised, excited and motivated when they feel that they are involved, contribute and are fully engaged and individually responsible for the achievement of a "community" vision, over and above their personal material and psychological aspirations. It is therefore the responsibility of the dominant coalition to satisfy this requirement in their leadership practices in order to optimise organisational performance,

> It is my job to create a work environment that attracts and retains the best people. People don't work just for money, important though that is. I want people to be proud to work for HSBC. We aim to treat all our constituencies with respect and care. For me this means a company with concern for its customers, its staff and its shareholders, that does its share in the community (Sir Bond, 2000c, p. 6).

In so stating, Bond acknowledges that effective business leadership is not merely a matter of "*painting by the numbers*". It is is rather a complex "build" process of consistently applying key principles and perspectives, to continually energise both staff and senior executives in order to optimise productivity and performance over the long term, the fundamental objectives of operational management. The process of management begins, not ends, when the "technical" table stakes issues are considered under control. The practice of wise leadership revolves around the psychological and physiological rather than the technical and administrative, concerning itself with the confidence, cohesion, motivation and allegience and advocacy of individuals, translated into proactive, clear operational perspectives and priorities, communicated and implemented on a day to day basis. Wise operational leadership revolves around the centrality of people management in the mindset of the decision maker. The key words which dominate in considering solutions for issue resolution are therefore energise, motivate, collaborate, cohesion, confidence, comfort, clarity, listen and persuade, this within the context of consistently applying the organisational dominant logic to achieve the organisation's long-term vision.

Rely on Expert Intuition in the Face of Doubt and Uncertainty

Credibility and trust develop and are reinforced when leadership is recognised and acknowledged to be able to take optimal decisions where issues have to be resolved and action taken with the minimum of confusion, anxiety, hesitation and undue delay. Due to the speed at which the resolution of issues is required within the business organisation, expert intuition rather than rational, analytical reasoning is utilised in a high proportion, probably the majority of cases. Expert intuition is therefore a critical component in the cognitive mental process of the practically wise leader. However, due to the ambivalent view of people leadership as a profession, expertise in this critical area is rarely developed and supported in a structured manner as an attribute and capability to be engendered from the early stages of a leader's career. The result is that expert intuition is therefore rarely available to be applied, with the result that the resolution of issues with a high people content is likely to be defective and/ or laboured over an extensive period of a leader's career . Research indicates that expertise is achieved through experience and structured learning and only marginally based on innate capabilities. A state of expertise requires a minimum of 10 years of dedicated, structured, intensive and deliberate practice. The development of people leadership attributes and capabilities must therefore be a priority feature of leadership education and development from the early stages of career development.

Intuition may be described as "knowing without thinking". It is arriving at a solution or decision without going through a rational analysis of the required information and knowledge.

DEFINITIONS OF INTUITION

Intuition is knowledge gained without rational thought. It comes from some stratum of awareness just below the conscious level and is slippery and elusive. Intuition comes with a feeling of "almost" but not quite knowing (Rowan, 1986, p. 96).

Intuition is a capacity for attaining direct knowledge or understanding without the apparent intrusion of rational thought or logical inference (Sadler-Smith and Shefy, 2004, p. 77).

Intuition involves awareness of things perceived below the threshold of conscious perception (Westcott, 1968).

Intuition is the mental faculty which allows you to instinctively step aside as a truck mounts the pavement behind you; to turn around as someone is about to pick your pocket; to conclude from limited information that someone is defrauding the corporation or stealing from customers. These are examples from my personal experience and I am sure that the reader can readily relate to the concept from their own personal experience. Scholars would contend that intuition is an "ancient biological wisdom" (Myers, 2002), an inherited, genetic, essential capability required for survival. It results from an ability to use the senses, accumulated knowledge and experience, allowing the individual, in an instant, to anticipate danger in the immediate environment, or through an insightful reading of the expression in animals and/or humans.

Intuition is not always right, but research has concluded that the intuition of "experts" in a field is frequently and indeed consistently correct (Simon, 1997). This is achieved on the basis of what has been termed "pattern matching" (Simon, 1996). It is an ability to react to stimuli rather than processing information. This is achieved by applying, in a fleeting moment, one's repository of experience, knowledge, insight, principles, perspectives and priorities to a given situation or issue, assessing its similarity to previous situations or issues, in order to reach an optimal decision, without a lengthy process of analytical reasoning. It is for this reason that non-experts are unable to effectively apply their intuition to situations, since they lack the required repository of knowledge, experience and insight. The majority of situations and issues are therefore for the inexpert too unfamiliar to effectively apply intuitive capabilities in order to facilitate optimal decision making.

Intuition is a critical component in the cognitive mental process of the practically wise leader within the operational business context. If the truth were but openly acknowledged, due to the speed and frequency by which decisions are required, there is neither the time nor the energy to go through a rational process of information and knowledge gathering and analysis in order to come to an optimal solution. In reality, one is expected, as an experienced leader and manager, to apply embedded knowledge, insight and analystical powers to arrive at a "satisficing" solution, which is predominantly correct and can be refined during the ongoing management process.

If, however, leadership is essentially about managing the behaviour of people, but few people, if any, in an organisation are "experts" or professionals in this field, then intuitive solutions and decisions are likely in this critical area to be less than satisfactory, requiring continuous ongoing refinement to reach a satisfactory rather than optimal result. Given the proposed importance of people in effective operational leadership and the optimal performance of the organisation, the lack of experts to apply optimal intuitive solutions within the operational leadership context is likely to have negative implications and impact on individuals, thereby significantly diminishing confidence, credibility, trust and respect for organisational leadership, resulting in diminishing motivation, cohesion, suboptimal productivity and performance.

Research into expert leadership indicates that the accumulation of expertise is conscious, intentional, deliberate and intensive, both on the part of the individual and his/her mentors and superiors within the organisation. It is not the intention of this book to investigate expertise per se but rather to gain insight into the requirements to create a cadre of leaders of people within the organisation with the attributes and capabilities of practical and collaborative wisdom. In this respect McCall and Hollenbeck (2008) have produced a concise list of eight conclusions on the factors which have most influence on leadership expertise.

KEY FACTORS IN THE DEVELOPMENT OF LEADERSHIP EXPERTISE

- Expertise is learned.
- Expertise is domain specific.
- Expertise is based on knowledge and how it is organised.
- Expertise requires more than just knowledge.
- Expertise requires more than just experience.
- Other people matter in becoming an expert.
- Expertise is intentional.
- Expertise is personal.

Source: McCall and Hollenbeck (2008).

Research indicates that expert leaders are not born with the required innate capabilities, which have been found to contribute to expert performance to only a small, perhaps negligible extent (Ericksson and Lehmann, 1996). They are rather developed through experience (Chase and Simon, 1973; de Groot, 1978) and structured development and learning (Ericsson, Prietula and Cokely, 2007). They do not develop by themselves, requiring extensive support from significant others, both personal and organisational. Research into expert leadership indicates that to attain an expertise level in any area requires a minimum of 10 years of dedicated, structured, intensive and deliberate practice (Ross, 2006).

By deliberate practice we do not mean dealing with people issues during operational work activities, which is how the majority of individuals hone their people management skills. Rather we are referring to intensive experiences where the individual can gain an insight into the critical aspects of the issue and mentors can view response and offer specific advice in order to achieve incremental improvement. Some might respond that bespoke people situations do not arise to order. However, in addition to specific training a number of organisations will appoint individuals to particular roles in order to gain deliberate practice in a specific area of leadership and upon which specific mentoring will occur. As an example, as part of a career development programme, an individual might be appointed as head of HR, followed by head of sales, followed by responsibility for implementing a successful acquisition, all primarily with a view to incremental improvement in people leadership capabilities through enhanced individual experience, knowledge and insight, supported by mentoring and appraisal in that specific area.

The absence of a recognition of the leadership of people as a dedicated area of expertise and professionalism ensures that very few people ever attain the required level of expertise. McCall and Hollenbeck concisely describe the situation of the inexpert leader,

We are surprised at how often companies expect executives to perform as expert leaders with little, if any, purposeful development. Instead managers are thrown into challenging assignments ... and are left to sink or swim; or worse, they are left in the swamp without the competence to carry out the mission". (McCall and Hollenbeck, 2008, p. 22).

Since people leadership is an expertise required throughout the organisation, the negative implications of the inability to undertake expert intuitive decision making on effective operational leadership and optimal organisational performance are substantial. The development of expert intuition in respect of people leadership therefore requires long-term investment on the part of the organisation. The attainment of leadership expertise requires a long-term commitment and understanding of its value, on the part of both the individual and the organisation's dominant coalition. This is the case since it entails the constant expenditure of substantial physical and mental energy, resilience and determination by individuals over a protracted period and an ongoing recognition of the value of this commitment and focus by their immediate superiors and the dominant coalition within the organisation. The key point is that if an organisation recognises the value of people leadership as a specific area of expertise then it can achieve great benefit from the creation of an environment which fosters such attributes and capabilities in its management cadre. This will be achieved through initiating a process early in an individual's career, of structured training, but more particularly in the development of incremental insight and judgement through a planned process of experience gathering during an individual's career. It is very much similar to the manner by which a parent might develop expertise in a specific area in his/her child who may not have innate capabilities in that field but has an aptitude and willingness to learn.

This understanding and long-term, structured commitment to create expertise by an organisation is clearly shown in relation to parenting in the following quotes,

> *The vast majority of exceptional adult performers were never child prodigies, but instead they started instruction early and increased their performance due to a sustained high level of training (Bloom, 1985).*

> *The role of early instruction and maximal parental support appears to be much more important than innate talent and there are many examples of parents of exceptional performers who successfully designed optimal environments for their children without any concern about innate talent (see Ericsson, Krampe and Tesch-Romer, 1993 and Howe, 1990). (Ericcson and Charness, 1994, p. 729).*

Only by making such an investment will an organisation be able to exhibit the quantity and quality of expert intuitive skills to achieve optimal performance over the long term. Interestingly, Hayashi (2001) has found that as individuals pass from middle to senior management roles they struggle to utilise their intuitive capabilities effectively, where the issues increasingly require a less technical and quantitative expertise and perspective and a more holistic, organisation wide perspective, which is likely to require greater experience and knowledge of and insight into people leadership.

If, as appears to be the case, intuition is a fundamental leadership capability to maintain the pace of operational decision making in the twenty-first century, then, in addition to a focus on people management, it is necessary to provide leaders, no matter the stage in their careers, at a minimum, with an appropriate framework of principles, perspectives and priorities upon which they can base their expert intuitive deductions. In addition, it is critical that the organisation provides leaders with changing business situations and leadership roles in order to build up their knowledge, experience and leadership skills. Thereby they will be able to fine tune their intuitive capabilities to pattern match an increasing range of situations and issues.

Exercises

1. Name three individuals from your personal experience whom you regard as expert people leaders. What do you consider are the five most important attributes and capabilities of these individuals which persuaded you to nominate them as expert people leaders and what was your personal response to their management style?
2. You have been a leader within an organisation for 10 years when you read in the newspaper that it is to be acquired by a multinational competitor. Consider your immediate response and how it impacts on your attitude towards your executive team and organisation. What would be the issues which you would discuss with friends and relations regarding future employment in the acquired organisation?
3. You have received notification that you have been appointed chief executive of a global organisation making bottom line profits of $10 billions for the last 3 years, employing 300,000 within 35 countries. Write down in order of priority what will be the six key issues to discuss with your executive team on day one.
4. Consider an important decision which you have recently taken in your personal or working life which had significant implications and impact on other individuals. To what extent was your decision based upon rational evaluation or intuitive thinking? If it was significantly or wholly based upon intuitive thinking can you say with confidence that it was supported by the required levels of embedded expertise and deliberate practice in the area(s) of the decision?

4 *Practically Wise Operational Leadership: Fundamental Principles and Perspectives*

Practically wise decision-making and issue resolution within the business organisation requires:

- The recognition and application of key values and principles.
- Their translation into operationally effective perspectives, priorities and practices.
- Utilising a cognitive mental process which considers and utilises the required knowledge, experience and powers of insight and judgement.

The absence of any of these ingredients will ultimately negate the optimal attainment of objectives which ensure the survival and prosperity of the organisation over the long term. This is primarily due to the disintegration of stakeholder clarity of purpose, cohesion, allegiance and energy expenditure on behalf of the organisation.

This chapter therefore focuses upon the existence, manner of development, clear definition, effective communication and consistent application of organisational values, principles and perspectives, which have a critical impact on operational leadership characteristics and outcome.

A dominant logic, based upon universally accepted values creates clarity of purpose and a sense of cohesion, dedication and allegiance amongst the leadership cadre and the broader stakeholder base. In addition, it facilitates effective assimilation and inculcation of key employee groups and the development of a cohesive leadership cadre who view their roles as a vocation geared to the benefit of the community, rather than the individual. The resultant low confusion and conflict environment is fundamental to effective organisational leadership.

Dangerous, Confusing and Operationally Unnecessary?

Effective organisational leadership and optimal performance requires that the principles and perspectives upon which senior executives take policy decisions pervade the whole organisation. By this means the organisation achieves a clarity, consistency, confidence and cohesion in policy, strategic and operational decision-making and resultant issue resolution. This is an issue of such importance for effective organisational management that the leadership cadre, particularly the dominant leadership coalition, must be proactive in managing this process and "realigning" individuals who consciously or subconsciously apply what are, for the organisation, deviant principles and practices.

If you were to ask an employee of most business organisations to describe the four core principles or perspectives by which their organisation is managed, how many could provide an answer? Some might refer you to the mission statement in a document which they had noticed recently or could recollect. Others might, in their defence, suggest that to be aware of such matters is not really important in respect of completing their operational, day to day duties. Would these responses differ as you questioned employees with greater longevity within the organisation or further up the leadership hierarchy? Probably only to the extent that they had a better idea of where the mission statements are located in the organisation's publications, or the extent to which they have been able to glean an impression of underlying principles and perspectives on the basis of their interpretation of decisions taken over time.

This confusion, it must be said, may in many instances be intentional. The practical problems for organisational leaders of clearly and prominently communicating core organisational principles and perspectives to their staff, employees and other stakeholders are significant. Indeed, such clear communication is perceived by many leaders to be a splendid way of putting a noose around their necks when they find them being recited back to them by such groups as shareholders, staff representatives, analysts and media commentators. It is also perceived to simultaneously restrict the operational freedom of action of decision makers to deal with practical, context-based issues in a speedy, experience-based and intuitive manner. There are therefore, on the surface, good, practical and personal reasons why the definition and clear communication of a framework of values, perspectives and priorities is not utilised as a fundamental leadership instrument to provide clarity of purpose, direction and a sense of cohesion in the operational management of the organisation.

However, this perspective and approach to the robust communication of core organisational principles and perspectives, much less their consistent application, is not only cowardly, shallow and indolent on the part of individual leaders and the dominant coalition but, more importantly, practically unwise and operationally flawed in respect of effective operational leadership and optimal long-term performance. Operational leadership, be it a unit, a department or a division is increasingly complex and confusing. This complexity and confusion will be significantly diminished by analysing issues and taking decisions on the basis of a defined foundation of principles and perspectives which are recognised, understood, widely acknowledged and understood as appropriate and consistently applied organisation wide by all staff and indeed other stakeholder groups. It will also simplify the resolution of the increasing number of cross-functional issues which in the twenty-first century requires consensual sign-off by peer group leaders, rather than the direct intervention and decision making by a single senior executive. Such latter individuals tend to act as one of a small number of gatekeepers of the organisation's values and principles, exposing them only fleetingly to the broader light of scrutiny in extreme circumstances.

In many, if not the majority, of business organisations there appears to be a disconnect between the embedded, core organisational principles and perspectives by which the dominant coalition take policy decisions and the operational, day to day tasks carried out by other leaders and employees. It is as if there is a view amongst senior executives that such matters will only worry, confuse and distract staff from their operational duties and that the definition and clarification of such principles and perspectives are unnecessary for the completion of an employee's operational duties and tasks. This is redolent of the perceived narrow, production line mentality of employees as human resources to complete tasks and mass produce items within a repetitive and minimal thinking working environment, based upon operations and methods. That era ended in the developed economies sometime in the 1970/80s with improved educational attainment and the knowledge economy. Yet conscious or subconscious attitudes amongst leaders of the required mindset of the perceptions, perspectives and cognitive abilities of employees remain largely rooted in a bygone age.

Without wishing to be too blunt this is why the Neanderthals disappeared from the face of the Earth. It reflects the continuing application of principles, perspectives, priorities and practices applied by leaders when they were in their prime, 10, 20, sometimes 30 years ago. These have been embedded in their psyche by business schools, the pronouncements of dominant coalitions and peer group leaders within business organisations in the formative years of their careers, when promotion was often the result of emulation rather than challenge and change, allied to the consistent and effective application of systems, processes, procedures and formulae. In this respect I am reminded of the quote by Bartlett and Ghoshal (2002) who recommended a synchronisation of management strategy and management mindset, this in order to achieve both effective operational leadership and optimal organisational performance in a rapidly changing market context.

However hard it is to change the organisation, it is even harder to change the orientation of its senior management. Hence today's managers are trying to implement third generation strategies (continuous self-renewal) through second generation organisations (sustainable competitive advantage) with first generation management (defensible product-market positions) (Bartlett and Ghoshal, 2002, p. 35).

How then can one effectively lead an organisation in a cohesive, coordinated and consistent manner towards optimal performance when different individuals and groups within the organisation are taking decisions based upon the principles and perspectives which they consider appropriate, this on the basis of their personal experience, principles,, perspectives, or those which they assume perhaps/possibly/probably reflect what the dominant coalition might approve of or expect?

The absence of adequate definition and direction in respect of values, principles and priorities, in addition to its adverse impact on performance, encourages unethical behaviour. This is due to a lack of a compass which clearly defines values, principles, perspectives to be consistently applied during the daily process of decision-making and issue resolution. In contrast, we are faced with a business environment where there are tangible, recognised operational pressures in relation to defined costs, revenues, profits and other target responsibilities which, in the absence of clearly defined principles and perspectives, appear to be the ultimate priorities and therefore dominate the thought processes and focus of operational leaders. The effect of the absence of a clearly defined logic of values, perspectives and priorities is that operational leaders seek to avoid addressing issues where principles and perspectives are concerned. This is achieved by focusing upon and highlighting the purely technical and tangible components and responsibilities of one's role (e.g. sales, revenues, costs, expenditures, profits), leaving other issues to fester until they become critical. It is at this stage that senior executives consider it imperative to become involved, when they apply whatever principles, perspectives and priorities by which the organisation is managed and which are clear to only a limited group of gatekeepers within the dominant coalition.

When I refer to organisational principles and perspectives I do not however refer primarily or specifically to issues of ethical codes of conduct and morality, upon which there has been much debate and text recently, due to the perceived corruption, greed and cronyism which lies at the core of the prevailing financial and economic crisis. I refer rather to those more fundamental business and leadership principles and perspectives upon which decisions are taken in order to achieve effective ongoing operational management and optimise long-term performance, with which ethical principles and practices are wholly consistent, but merely a natural by-product and reflection. Whilst it is not the specific subject of this book, any efforts to address unethical business practices and inculcate future generations of business leaders with an appropriate framework of ethical principles and perspectives will ultimately fail unless the values, principles and perspectives to which we will refer in this and subsequent chapters are deeply embedded throughout the organisational psyche.

What we propose in this chapter is to clarify the benefits of joined-up thinking by the dominant leadership coalition in the knowledge economy. This comprises of a process by which the embedded values, principles and perspectives upon which senior executives take policy decisions permeate the organisation in order to be directly and consistently reflected in operational leadership perspectives and priorities, which will in turn be reflected and recognised in decisions and issues resolved. This structured cascade process is illustrated by the boxed text below:

THE OPERATIONAL TANGIBILISATION OF ORGANISATIONAL PRINCIPLES AND PERSPECTIVES

- Agreeing the values, principles and leadership perspectives upon which policy, strategic and operational decisions will be based.
- Clearly and consistently communicating and emphasising these values, principles and perspectives and, most importantly, stressing that these should be utilised as the foundation for all decision-making and issue resolution within all aspects and at all levels of organisational leadership.
- Being seen in practice to consistently apply this dictum and "realigning", in a people focused manner, those leaders and other employees who appear to be applying alternative values, principles and/or perspectives.
- Developing training and staff development programmes for leaders to evaluate issues and take decisions based upon the consistent application of a core set of values, principles and perspectives.

The practical and operational benefits of applying such an approach are substantial and pervade not only within the leadership cadre and employees, but within the broader stakeholder community and comprise of the 4Cs:

THE OPERATIONAL BENEFITS OF COMMUNICATING AND APPLYING A FRAMEWORK OF PRINCIPLES

- Clarity
- Consistency
- Confidence
- Cohesion.

We will expound on these headings in greater detail within the chapter.

This chapter sets out the foundation stones for consistently delivering wise and effective organisational leadership and optimal long-term performance. There will, of course, be other stones to build onto these foundation stones in order to optimise leadership effectiveness and optimal organisational performance, dependent upon specific context. However, it is the contention of this book that these foundation stones have universal application; without them confused and lacklustre leadership, mediocre performance and ultimate failure is assured, since they act as an anchor for clear, consistent and, most importantly, optimal decision making. This chapter therefore focuses on those leadership values, principles, perspectives and practices which are required as a universal foundation to ensure that there is the opportunity to optimise performance. Subsequent chapters will build on this foundation to introduce further perspectives and priorities to enhance the probability of consistently achieving optimal performance. As with all "recipes", whether in relation to baking a cake or leading a global organisation, the foundational ingredients are surprisingly simple to understand but less so to consistently apply. As we all know, even boiling an egg can be fraught with difficulties in the absence of an understanding of the fundamentals of boiling foodstuffs, for example:

- Whether you should boil the water first and then put the eggs in or boil the water with the eggs in.
- Whether you should put salt into the water to prevent cracking.
- How long to boil the eggs for soft/hard requirements.
- How best to cool and peel the eggs in order not to leave large parts with the discarded shells.

These are not even the totality of principles which are required to make an egg sandwich! This perhaps banal example, hopefully, clearly emphasises the critical requirement to consistently base effective leadership on a clear understanding of core principles rather than assumption, instinct and inexpert intuition.

Whilst I am unable to authoritatively pronounce on the key principles of effective egg boiling I have condensed what I consider to be the key principles, perspectives and priorities of effective organisational management into six foundational building blocks. These principles, perspectives and priorities have the ability to develop a business organisational community which have the attributes of the 4Cs as noted above, which thereby create the foundations for consistent long-term optimal performance. These are shown in the boxed text entitled "Fundamental Ingredients for Effective Organisational Leadership"

The key point which I wish to emphasise from this list of building blocks is that effective organisational leadership requires the acknowledgement, understanding, definition and consistent application of core principles. In addition, their translation into perspectives, priorities and practices which are recognised as relevant to operational functions, tasks and responsibilities in which individuals consider themselves involved and responsible, for example:

STRATEGIC

- Market penetration
- Acquisition and integration
- Initiatives and development programmes to optimise assimilation and inculcation
- Development of leadership cadre.

OPERATIONAL

- Product development
- Advertising
- Balance sheet management
- Systems development
- Customer service quality
- Sales quality
- Remuneration criteria
- Appraisal
- Risk management.

In essence, the application of the building blocks in the boxed text below ensures that everyone is on both the right and also the same page.

FUNDAMENTAL BUILDING BLOCKS FOR EFFECTIVE ORGANISATIONAL LEADERSHIP

- Base all policy, strategic and operational decisions on a set of universal values which are acknowledged, understood and accepted by all staff within the organisation as those which they would wish to be the basis of any community of which they were a part.
- Translate and embed these values into a dominant organisational logic of core principles, perspectives and priorities which provides a compass and anchor, and facilitates consistent and clear decision making, no matter the function within the organisation, the organisational or social context.
- The provision of key leadership principles which are consistent with universal values encourages and facilitates the development of a cadre of long-term executives who have clarity of perspective and purpose and a pride in their organisation.
- This cadre are mentored, developed, monitored, and progressively promoted to senior leadership positions in respect of policy, strategy and operational responsibility. This creates a highly experienced and cohesive "bench" which consistently translates and

implements a single dominant logic within the organisation in respect of issues arising, resulting in sustained success over the long term.

- Where it is found necessary to recruit from outside the organisation do not appoint to senior leadership positions with substantial delegated authority until they have exhibited inculcation and commitment to the organisational dominant logic.
- Invoke in this leadership cadre a sense of vocation and self-sacrifice to the organisational community. A recognition that they must sacrifice their own well-being and those of significant others to the ultimate benefit of the organisational community.

Regrettably, these operational management priorities are not magic dust, to be sprinkled on any organisation to quickly enable it to become operationally effective and thereby optimise performance. These should rather be regarded as fundamental, without which no other aspects or tools of leadership and management will be optimally effective, therefore taking longer to embed into the organisational psyche and substantively impact on its performance. It is essentially creating the premium mix of soil to allow the best chance for the optimal crop, but which may not significantly enhance the crop for a number of seasons. These building blocks are of a higher priority and are more effective over the long term in achieving optimal performance than a focus on recruiting and developing for technical and systems expertise and/or the application of programmes, such as TQM, balanced scorecard, Six Sigma. These latter management tools and practices are essentially concerned with short-term, limited and shallow applications of the perspectives and practices of these building blocks, without the requirement to take the pain and cost of recognising and embedding the underlying values and principles across the organisation. Such an approach leads to a failure to achieve the required embedded long-term change and therefore any significant enhanced capability for long-term performance improvement. In the short term any perceived performance improvement cloaks an increase in confusion, disharmony and a diminution in operational productivity which will resonate into the long term.

Effective implementation of the foundational building blocks requires clarity of purpose, determination and resilience and, most of all, time to achieve effective acceptance, inculcation and embedding in the psyche of the organisational mindset. The best idea is therefore to start today, since tangible benefits are likely to take 5+ years and optimal benefits between 10–20 years. In response to the horror which this timescale might evoke amongst readers I would ask, which banking and other organisation would you prefer to work for, HSBC Holdings plc, an organisation which has survived, prospered and grown over the last 150 years, or Washington Mutual, Wachovia, Bear Stearns, RBS, HBOS, Lehman Brothers, AIG, Enron or WorldCom, whose crashes have reverberated throughout the global business community and diminished the credibility of the Western capitalist model and all the implications that this has for the remaining tenure of Western economic and social dominance? This horror is in many respects also a reflection of the inculcation of readers in respect of the principles and perspectives of short-term performance. In contrast, this book proposes values, principles, perspectives and priorities which, whilst achieving enhanced clarity of purpose, cohesion and credible short-term performance, also put in place the building blocks for optimal long-term performance.

It must be admitted that, on first reading the contents of this chapter, the implications of the operational implementation of these building blocks for the individual are a little scary. It gives the impression of some mindless bonding of "Borg-like" creatures and lemmings, trained and developed for synchronised thought and action for the benefit of the "collective". However, as we will see in this and subsequent chapters, having created a foundational set of principles and perspectives which enhances the 4Cs we are then able to:

- Create an environment of effective leadership based upon the principles, logic, attributes and capabilities of practical and collaborative wisdom.
- Which optimises performance through expert, context-related leadership.
- Firmly based upon the centrality of people leadership.
- Satisfying individual requirements and aspirations.
- Consistent with the paramountcy of the organisational and wider community.

Practical Wisdom and the Application of Universal Values

This section seeks to dispel a number of misperceptions which create unnecessary complexity and confusion in the mind of the operational business leader during the decision-making process. In so doing it expounds the validity and benefits of applying a universalist approach to the application of organisational values and principles. Such values are not consistent with the prevalent ideology of the primacy of the market and individual, but rather the rights of the individual within the overriding requirement for a healthy organisational community and societal framework, delivering effective leadership and optimal performance and benefit over the long term. This section therefore invites operational leaders to evaluate issues and take decisions with a "universalist" eye rather than determining options and solutions within a narrower individual and organisational perspective. By this means solutions and actions which are of optimal long-term value to the organisation will consistently predominate throughout the organisation.

PHILOSOPHY AND THE PRACTICE OF OPERATIONAL BUSINESS LEADERSHIP: A DIRECT LINK

It would be true to say that leaders rarely justify their decisions on the basis of citing from philosophical text. Moreover, it is unlikely that operational leaders consider philosophical treatise when they are evaluating practical solutions to prevailing day to day issues. Philosophy has become disconnected from organisational leadership for the same reasons that wisdom is considered less than relevant. Philosophy ranks with the spiritual, the religious, the intangible, the woolly rather than the practical and pragmatic requirements of operational leadership. However, when it is boiled down, philosophy entails a description of the values and principles by which a society or community can be effectively led. Where leaders seek to take decisions in the absence of a common foundation of values and principles or where values and principles applied change on the basis of expediency confusion, chaos and collapse is the inevitable result.

It is therefore the contention of this section that there is a substantive, indeed direct link between, at one extreme, established philosophical thought and, on the other, the principles, operational perspectives, practices and priorities of business leadership. Further, that no matter which groups of "philosophies" or principles one investigates, be they emanating from:

- Established and widely recognised philosophers;
- Religious or cultural philosophies (e.g. Christianity, Islam, Judaism, Confucianism);
- The plethora of management "philosophers "or gurus;
- Analysing the dominant logic of organisations which have survived over the long term, through many business cycles.

there is frequently exposed, embedded, often hidden between the lines of the writing or in the subconscious responses of leadership coalitions, a universal framework of principles, priorities and perspectives.

These clearly define the direction, decision-making and operational practices of those "communities" (be they empires, nations, societies, families or businesses) which have consistently achieved optimal performance over the long term. As we noted in Part One practical wisdom is based upon the consistent application of a foundation of values and principles. Similarly, in practice, effective organisational leaders recognise, whether consciously or subconsciously, that optimal decision making and action is founded upon the application of an appropriate framework of values and principles which consistently achieve effective operational management of the organisation and optimal long-term performance. In this respect this section proposes and discusses the relevance and value of a "universal" framework of values which are recognised, understood and consistently applied by all individuals, no matter their social, geographic, cultural, religious, gender, educational or occupational profile. This is despite the layer of prevailing espoused social, cultural "values" and ideology which so often complicate, confuse, obstruct and obscure their application.

LOOK TO THE WOOD RATHER THAN THE TREES

There are undoubtedly contextual differences which must be addressed by the organisational leader when making operational decisions. However, the importance of adaptability to context has recently become of such paramount amongst both scholars and practitioners that the issue of differences rather than constants has increasingly taken prominence when addressing the key variables which influence effective operational leadership. In this section we propose a refocus, from an analysis of the trees, to the value of recognition of the fundamental attributes of the wood. In this regard we refer to an acknowledgement and understanding of the foundation stones upon which effective leadership is built, rather than a focus on the ideal type of doors and window frames to utilise for a specific building or business context.

This chapter therefore seeks to provide clarity and direction for practicing business leaders in order to enhance the quality of day to day operational management and leadership. In seeking to articulate a universal leadership philosophy we reject the requirement for any distinct and unique body of thought dedicated to the philosophy of business leadership. Such a body of thought merely serves to complicate rather than clarify the fundamental principles, priorities, perspectives and practices of effective organisational leadership. By taking this approach we seek to:

- Get to the root of effective business leadership.
- Dispel the complexity and confusion created by the multiplicity of leadership and management theories.
- Dispel the ambiguity in the minds of leaders regarding what appear to be contrasting frameworks of values and principles of which they become aware, through contact with or membership of different branches of society and through reading and digesting texts on a variety of contrasting theories and concepts related to organisations and leadership, not necessarily related to business management.

We do not reject the relevance and value of the plethora of management philosophies, theories and concepts outright. However, we contend that in the absence of an acknowledgement by business scholars of a defined set of values, which apply universally within all "branches" of society, in such a situation these theories tend to "float", lacking an anchor of universal logic and resonance. Operational business leaders are therefore just as likely to accept and seek to apply the next, most recent theory, system or process espoused by advocates as a solution to a prevailing leadership issue, as they were to the previous "flavour" of the time. Such solutions fail to acknowledge that there exists a more fundamental and universal root and solution not apparent due to a narrow view of the context of the issue and therefore a limited appreciation of possible solutions. The result is confusion, unnecessary complexity, inconsistency and ultimately a diminishing confidence in leadership evaluation and decision-making capabilities amongst key stakeholder groups. Only those management/leadership theories which advocate values and principles which have universal application are therefore of value in providing business leadership with the requisite sound foundational values and principles, levels of clarity and direction, to achieve effective and consistent decision making. Ultimately effective operational leadership requires willing, believing and committed followers. The absence of the application of values to which stakeholders can relate and ascribe diminishes the credibility of, allegiance and dedication to individual and organisational leadership with a consequent impact on energy expended and individual and group productivity.

EFFECTIVE LEADERSHIP DEVELOPS FROM UNIVERSAL ROOTS

The first step in effective people leadership, which revolves around credibility, confidence, coordination and cohesion, is therefore to be seen to be consistently applying a set of values to which all individuals relate. These are values which are recognised, respected applied and, more importantly, expected to be applied at the interface between individuals, irrespective of geographic location, social or economic standing, political or religious complexion.

These universal values are fundamental to the development and maintenance of any community or society, or part thereof, of which the business sector and individual business organisations are but a component part. The development of bodies of thought described as organisational behaviour, business leadership or other spheres of business management obscure a more fundamental and relevant body of thought which examines universal values and leadership traits, which transcend both cultural and organisational values,

The world's religions and philosophies deal with morality and ethics. Whilst there are many differences often rooted in ethnicity, ideology, historicity and geography which gives rise to different cultural constructions of ethics, nonetheless the similarities are striking in the shared concerns for applying ethical standards to all matters dealing with human interaction (Gould, 1995, p. 63).

This perspective, of the existence of universal values, principles and priorities is supported by the views of senior executives within HSBC Holdings plc and its antecedents. Charles Addis, an early leader of HSBC (Senior Manager and Chairman of the London Committee of HSBC in 1922) believed that the principles of good business were rooted in universal values which applied in all people leadership contexts,

...and somehow I think we always finish up with the belief strengthened that folks with (pig) tails are very like those without and that a strong chain of human sympathy binds together the children of one father ... He believed that all great religions share a common truth (Dayer, 1983, p. 18).

Taking a somewhat less colonial and condescending perspective which is perhaps reminiscent of the perspectives of the late nineteenth and early twentieth century Sir John Bond, in 1999 reiterated this belief in universal values,

Values can, and should, have universal application. I believe that there are some values that are universally recognised ... And I believe that it is both perfectly possible, and desirable, to be multicultural in outlook, and at the same time to hold a set of universal values (Sir Bond, 1999, p. 2).

A number of management and business authors have alluded to the possibility of some principles and practices which are perceived to be culturally bound in fact being consistent with another culture's values. This is either because that other culture has been influenced by the *"home"* culture (Ogbor and Williams, 2003; Reed A.M., 2002; Reed D., 2002) or, more pertinently for this study, because many cultures encompass the same core, universal values,

When you dig deeply enough and scrape away all the trappings, the real ethical solid building blocks or principles of most cultures are the same (Tarantino, 1998, p. 560).

Table 4.1, indicates an issue of significant relevance to this study. This is the apparent substantial similarities in Islamic, Sinic and Japanese values, principles and perspectives. All appear to have their foundations built on the importance of the community, of harmony, cooperation, consensus and the centrality of relationships, respect for individuals and a willingness to sacrifice personal interests and beliefs for the benefit of the communal "group" to whom one relates and/or owes allegiance. This similarity in fundamental values and principles suggests that all communities seek to satisfy core requirements and expectations. Given that so many societal cultures ascribe to such values and principles we might reasonably assume that they reflect critical reflection within a holistic context and therefore might be termed "wise" in respect of their universal application. Therefore, a business organisation, as a part of such a society or number of societies cannot expect to succeed over the long term unless its stakeholders consider that it is clearly seen to subscribe to such values, principles and perspectives in both thought and action. The difficulties arise where some stakeholder groups deviate from universal values, causing the organisation's operational leadership to merely reflect the perspectives and priorities of these stakeholder groups in their evaluations, decision-making and issue resolution.

Table 4.1   Universal Values and Priorities of Contrasting Social Cultures

Chinese Cultural Values and Practices	Japanese Cultural Values and Practices	Islamic Values and Priorities
Importance of connections, relationships, interdependence and reciprocity to cope with crises	Long-term oriented time horizon	Priority is prosperity of community through "harmony"
Morality above all	Soft and flexible organisational structure	Efficiency and performance based on social harmony and cohesiveness
Group orientation – people, community and relationship oriented, downplaying notion of self	Lifetime employment based on development of competitive levels of tacit knowledge	Conformist – sacrificial of own interests, need structure and rules
Reliance on accumulated knowledge, holistic thinking and experience	Stakeholder contract based on respect for people and paternalistic social welfare	Socio-centric – affiliation and little concern for wealth
Face and high power distance	Balancing of multiple goals whilst maintaining respect for stakeholders	Flexible guidelines to maintain consensus and community. Decisions and actions relationship and context specific
High uncertainty avoidance	Decisions reached by consensus ("ringi")	Relationships (e.g. employee relations) based on societal framework of honour, fairness, loyalty, certainty, clarity, openness, generosity and equity for all
Performance based on reliance on cultural rules of social order – loyalty, obedience, harmony, teamwork rather than competition and rules/codes	Decisions based on "situationalism" or "contextualism"	Importance of individual, within context of cohesiveness of community
Low trust in individuals outside of "group"	Choose company/group beliefs and/or interest over personal interest/beliefs	Property and natural resources held in private ownership in trust and conditional upon, secondary to the interests of the community
Paternalistic headship – focus on order, stability, social harmony, compliance, considerateness and moral leadership		Organisational objective may not be profit maximisation or cost-efficiency, given community responsibilities

Sources: compiled and adapted from Ali, 1995, 1996; Ali and Amirshahi, 2002; Ali and Camp, 1995; Al-Kazemi and Zajac, 1999; Clegg and Kono, 2002; Fan, 2002; Hempel and Chang, 2002; Metwally, 1997; Montagu-Pollock, 1991; Nakano, 1997; Naughton and Naughton, 2000; Parnell, Shwiff, Yalin and Langford, 2003; Tayeb, 1997; Westwood, 1997.

Sustained success in business leadership is based upon clarity and simplicity. This is based upon consistent decision making, based upon a blueprint of business principles and priorities which are themselves based upon a framework of universal values, accepted by all stakeholder groups as appropriate to the achievement of both individual and group objectives. Such a scenario facilitates contextual adaptability where considered appropriate, this in order to optimise motivation, cohesion, allegiance, productivity and performance at the local level,

> *Each HSBC is a local bank, exhibiting local traits but based on a universal business blueprint. HSBC is now an All Terrain Vehicle, after so many years in different local cultures and organisational cultures (Interviewee D).*

The consistent application of a single dominant logic based upon universal values in a manner sympathetic to the local business context as epitomised by the HSBC Group clearly illustrates the application of practical and collaborative wisdom within the business context and its ability to achieve long-term survival and optimal performance.

THE BENEFITS ACCRUING FROM THE APPLICATION OF UNIVERSAL VALUES

Hongkong and Shanghai Banking Corporation (HSBC) was established in March 1865 in Hong Kong, primarily as a provider of trade, import/export finance and commercial banking, moving its headquarters to London in the 1990s. It now provides financial services to over 105 million individuals and self-employed customers, with employees in excess of 300,000, in 62 countries. It has a substantial footprint in the Far East and China, India, the UK, North and South America and the Middle East. HSBC utilises its management template, based upon universally accepted values, to consistently and effectively grow its global footprint. It thereby achieved, within a relatively short period of time (1–3 years), levels of allegiance, loyalty and dedication amongst new employees within a variety of societal contexts which enables it to embed the requisite technical standards, systems, processes, perspectives, priorities and practices, ensuring that they are in a position to achieve acquisition performance objectives. As just a number of examples, since the beginning of the financial crisis in 2007, HSBC has taken a significant stake in a Vietnamese bank, established a bank in rural China, taken a 51% share of Korea Exchange Bank, established a retail branch network in Peru, acquired 94% of a mortgage brokerage in India and 89% of a bank in Indonesia.

The present economic and financial crisis is only one of many crises overcome by HSBC since its foundation in the nineteenth century. HSBC has a natural advantage in penetrating new markets over its competitors since amongst key local stakeholder groups (e.g. local leaders and shareholders of targeted organisations, regulatory bodies, government ministries, analysts and commentators, potential employees, clients and customers) its embedded values and business principles are acknowledged as not predatory but rather as a preferred partner, working for the benefit of the wider economic and social stakeholder community. HSBC is recognised as an organisation which is both willing and able to substantively contribute to the development of the expertise, employment, wealth, confidence and credibility of the socio-economic community. The consistent application of these values by the dominant coalition over the last 150 years has allowed HSBC to survive, expand and diversify from a bank with local and then regional representation in the Far East to one with a substantial global footprint across the spectrum of available financial services. This has been achieved in the face of climatic catastrophe, civil war, revolution, economic and financial collapse, even the imprisonment and execution of senior executives, in part at least as a result of the internal cohesion and wide stakeholder support engendered by the application of universally accepted values.

EFFECTIVE LEADERSHIP IS FOUNDED ON SATISFYING UNIVERSAL MOTIVATIONS

Once senior executives have acknowledged the importance of a core set of universal values in the organisational management process the next important step is to anchor operational leadership decision-making, issue resolution to these values. This is undertaken to provide clarity, to optimise energy expended on behalf of the organisation, to enhance motivation, allegiance, dedication and advocacy amongst its stakeholder community. These universal values reflect the motivations and values upon which each individual carries on interpersonal relationships on a day to day basis, responding and reacting to their requirements and the actions and communications of other individuals and groups. A study by Schwartz and Bilsky (1987) was built around the basis of the theoretical assumption that values develop as a result of the individual need to satisfy three universal pre-existing human requirements:

UNIVERSAL HUMAN REQUIREMENTS

- The biological requirements of any organism (e.g. the ability to provide heat, shelter, food).
- The requirement of social interaction in order to regulate and coordinate interpersonal interaction.
- The requirements defined by the creation of institutions within society in order to ensure consistent community security, survival, well-being and development.

Through the individual and group development of perspectives, perceptions, awareness and judgement these universal human requirements are moulded into specific values, which have proven through time and practice to satisfy individual and group motivations and goals,

> *These three universal requirements pre-exist any individual; to cope with reality, individuals must recognise, think about, and plan responses to all three requirements ... Therefore, in building a typology of the content domains of values, we theorized that values could be derived from the universal human requirements reflected in needs (organism), social motives (interaction), and social institutional demands (Schwartz and Bilsky, 1987, p. 551).*

Empirical analysis supported the theoretical claim that people's behaviour and responses are therefore moulded by a universal framework of seven motivations from which core values have developed.

Values are cognitive representations of the important human goals or motivations about which people must communicate in order to coordinate their behaviour. The content that distinguishes one value most significantly from another is the type of motivation or goal that it represents (Bilsky and Schwartz, 1994, p. 164).

Whilst the studies of Schwartz and his colleagues were not focused specifically upon business organisations, as one form of society or community, it is appropriate and logical to appreciate the importance of the application of what they term their "motivational value domains" (Schwartz, 1992, 1994a, 1994b; Schwartz and Bilsky, 1987, 1990; Schwartz and Melech, 2001) to the leadership, decision-making and day to day operational management perspectives and priorities of the successful business organisation. These,

universal and distinctive motivational domains of values (Schwartz and Bilsky, 1987, p. 551).

which have derived from the above core motivations, are briefly described below:

MOTIVATIONAL VALUE DOMAINS

- **Prosocial/benevolence domain**: a positive and proactive concern for the welfare of others and the collective social context.
- **Restrictive conformity domain**: a propensity to control behaviours and actions which would cause distress and harm to others and the violation of accepted and expected institutionalised social or communal norms.
- **Tradition domain**: a motivation to create rites and modes of behaviour as symbols of group solidarity, imposing a requirement on the individual to respect, conform to and accept their role as a unit within a larger community.
- **Security domain**: mental and physical security. In respect of the business environment this relates to a respect for the integrity of the individual, rather than as merely a resource.
- **Achievement domain**: a perception of individual competence, progressive success and achievement, through the development of skills and talents and an acceptance that the organisation will facilitate this individual requirement.
- **Power domain**: a desire to achieve status and prestige in exchange for loyalty, motivation and advocacy.
- **Maturity/universalism domain**: the achievement of personal goals as a result of experience, understanding, appreciation and to protect the welfare of all individuals in a holistic manner given the interdependency between personal and group welfare.
- **Self-direction domain**: the desire and ability to control events which are considered important to one's well-being and those of in-groups.
- **Stimulation domain**: the requirement to be actively excited and to seek out challenge and novelty, linked to self-direction domain.

> - **Enjoyment (hedonism) domain**: individual emotional and sensuous gratification which are consistent with aspirations for a comfortable life, happiness and pleasure within a community context.
>
> *Source*: adapted from Schwartz, 1992, 1994a; Schwartz and Bilsky, 1987, 1990; Schwartz and Melech, 2001.

The results of the Schwartz (1992) research and a replication by Burgess, Schwartz and Blackwell (1993) confirmed the validity of the above value domains, indicating a nearly universally acknowledged set of motivational value domains.

It is therefore clear that the principles and perspectives upon which the leaders of organisations make decisions and how they are operationalised will dramatically impact upon these domains and affect the attitudes, allegiance and dedication of stakeholders towards the leadership cadre, the organisation, which will ultimately significantly impact on its long-term performance. In this respect it is critical that operational leaders acknowledge, understand and, most importantly, operationally take into account as fundamental considerations in their cognitive mental processes during the decision-making process, the fundamental motivations, expectations and aspirations of subordinates, peers and superiors

Whilst HSBC Group's values and principles, which reflect an understanding of universal human motivations, continue to be most effectively communicated and reinforced by actions and deliberations in resolving operational business issues, HSBC Group has also, as we have already noted, in the interests of consistent management practice across all global entities, produced a Group Standards Manual. This is in itself not unusual or unique. What is less unique is that it is neither a backside covering instrument nor something assigned to the bottom drawer. Senior Group executives and the Managing Directors of business units across the globe must confirm, annually in writing, that they are taking formal steps to ensure that their unit and all areas under their orbit are complying with the "Core Business Principles and Key Business Values". The researcher recalls receiving a terse annual memorandum on two occasions from separate managing directors to confirm that my function was so complying. Patently, receiving these reminders every year for 10–20+ years throughout one's career will have a reinforcing effect on key perspectives and priorities applied in the decision-making process, particularly if one is ambitious and has invested/sacrificed much to optimise the chances of career advancement.

The ability of an organisation to ensure that universal values are applied through the consistent application of a single dominant logic is circumscribed by the recruitment of technically talented leaders from outside the organisation. Such individuals have not been assimilated and inculcated to spontaneously and intuitively base their evaluation of issues, decision making and actions on the application of a dominant logic based upon universal values,

> *These are not unique to HSBC but more of how they are introduced and equally strengthened by action and application by the executive core and because executives have worked for a long period in the Group they have assimilated these core values and espoused them very well … more difficult to consistently apply in organisations where there are executive "musical chairs",*

with people coming in from other organisations where they have been inculcated by different
values, perspectives and practices (Interviewee A).

This is a point which we will expand upon in the next chapter section but it is appropriate
to raise in connection with the requirement to consistently apply a universal framework
of values.

It is the Key Business Values which provide the greatest insight into the operational
decision-making process of each individual leadership cadre within the HSBC Group of
global business entities. These values acted, as one respondent termed them, as a set of
"anchor points". They were a regular reminder to rein back on any creeping deviations
from embedded values, principles and practices, acting as a source of clarity, structure,
consistency and confidence, facilitating effective operational management. They ensure no
"sudden shocks" which might alarm key stakeholder groups and undermine a reputation
built up during a century and a half. This is a critical point to be recognised, emphasising
the requirement to manage the organisation at the psychological and physiological
level, to ensure consistent long-term organisational effectiveness and performance,
by maintaining the confidence and allegiance of stakeholders, through being seen to
apply universally acknowledged values. The result of ongoing confidence based on the
application of universal values is that stakeholders are happy to elect for optimal long-
term profit rather than maximising short-term profit. Stakeholders ultimately prefer to
see the sun come up every morning and the moon at night than to admire shooting stars.
This mindset is achieved through recognition of the consistent application of appropriate
values and principles by organisational operational leadership which they perceive to be
geared to their long-term requirements and expectations.

> *Ultimately, success in business depends on confidence ... confidence is about ... how well*
> *your company performs, how responsibly you behave, and how well-trained your colleagues*
> *are around the world. So that you can rely on them to look after your customers when you are*
> *asleep (Sir Bond, 2001, p. 4).*

Interviewees C and D explained very succinctly the success of HSBC on a global
scale as achieving the capability of an "all terrain vehicle", through the application of
values and principles which had universal resonance. HSBC had merged the consistent
application of a set of global values and principles with a management ability to listen,
adapt and be flexible within the context of the local business environment. By this means
HSBC was able to leverage local tacit knowledge and become accepted and "legitimate"
amongst local stakeholders (e.g. local management, shareholders, staff, regulators and
other government bodies) within all markets where they had representation. They are
thereby able to optimise business opportunities within all market contexts in which
they are represented. The following quotes encapsulate the management approach of
HSBC, consistently applying a single dominant logic based upon universal values, this in
a manner "sympathetic" to local practices. At the same time it provides an insight into its
consistent and spectacular expansion globally, relative to its peers,

> *Each HSBC is a local bank, exhibiting local traits but based on a universal business blueprint.*
> *HSBC is now an All Terrain Vehicle, after so many years in different local cultures and*
> *organisational cultures (Interviewee D).*

HSBC's business philosophy is based on achieving value and benefit through a long term investment ... this requires sensitivity, adaptability openness to ideas which will create an effective organisation. As long as the universal business blueprint is implemented HSBC sees the value in being culturally sensitive, it's pragmatic business sense (Interviewee C).

Practically wise leadership essentially therefore comprises of:

THE PRINCIPLES AND PROCESS OF PRACTICALLY WISE LEADERSHIP

- Acknowledging the existence of universal values and their importance to the individual and community and therefore their contribution to achieving sustained operational effectiveness and optimal performance.
- Translating these values into an organisational dominant logic comprised of principles, perspectives, priorities and standards which are considered by stakeholders as operationally relevant and applicable in issue resolution on a day to day basis.
- Considering relevant information in both an analytical and affective manner in order to reach optimal decisions.
- Implementing decisions taken in a manner which takes into account the people element at front of mind.
- This in a manner appropriate to and consistent with the local business context.

THE UNIVERSALIST VALUES UNDERPINNING CAPITALISM

The Western "capitalist", apparently individual, materially focused philosophy or ideology is in fact considered by a number of Western philosophers to inherently harbour universalist, community focused motivations, values and perspectives which underpin the majority of other global societal "cultures". Whilst it is not the intention of this book to delve deeply into the foundations and ethics of capitalism it is important, within the context of distinguishing the wood from the trees, to be aware that long-term successful global business organisations, primarily headquartered in Western "capitalist" societies, are not thereby necessarily driven by values rooted in the ideology perceived to prevail within the Anglo-American culture. This is generally considered to be based upon the primacy of market forces, individualism and self-interest. In this respect it is necessary to look beyond the prevalent societal ideology in order to gain an understanding of the fundamental universalist values, principles, perspectives and objectives upon which capitalism was founded.

The capitalism as espoused by Adam Smith is an example of efforts to aid the individual and social community to satisfy core universal values, this in response to a developing, undesirable social phenomenon of the time, which is encapsulated in the following brief quote,

People of the same trade seldom meet together, even for merriment and diversion, but the conversation ends in a conspiracy against the public, or in some contrivance to raise prices (Adam Smith, The Wealth of Nations, 1776).

It sought to combat the power of mercantilist groups of the time, rather than espousing the benefit of the individual over that of the community. As Bassiry and Jones describe Smith's views,

The political economy Smith was advocating was thus based on maximising consumer/citizen choice in both economic and political spheres. Smith's paradigm shifted the institutional emphasis from centralised to decentralised structures, from authoritarianism to representative democracy, from monopoly to competitive markets ... from producer appropriation of the societal surplus to consumer sovereignty (Bassiry and Jones, 1993, pp. 622–623).

In the view of Adam Smith the absence of dominant power in the hands of a few would create a situation where the "small" individual and by an "invisible hand" the needs of society, would be satisfied (Klein, 2003).

The key point to be highlighted is that Western "capitalist" philosophy essentially acknowledges the role and rights of the individual, but this *within* the societal framework and the existence of a set of values which are considered universally applicable within all communities. Moving this debate into the twentieth century, a number of Western philosophers have openly questioned the logic of individualism and economic, material reward as the basis for any society. They stress instead the importance of universal, community values. Durkheim, in his review of Schaffle's *Bau und Leben des Socialen Korpers*[1] agrees when Schaffle states,

Society is not simply an aggregate of individuals, but is a being which has existed prior to those who today compose it, and which will survive them; which influences them more than they influence it, and which has its own life, consciousness, its own interests and destiny (quoted in Giddens, 1970, p. 67).

Stanfield supports this position when he states,

The process of production and consumption is not an end in itself. It becomes so only in modern society, when, instead of economy being embedded in social relations, social relations become embedded in the economic system. The market is imperialist in that it tends to extend into all facets of social life; production and consumption become ends in themselves, or at least self-justifying (Stanfield, 1980, p. 600).

Of the classical liberalists of the twentieth century perhaps Friedrich A. Hayek has most to say concerning the existence of a fundamental set of universal values which act as guiding principles in the management and development of all units within society. His view is that societies develop most effectively by allowing individuals to develop, think and act within the context of a limited and general/universal set of social values and rules. These change through the evolutionary advancement of knowledge in a

---

1   Durkheim, E. (1885) Review of Albert Schaffle: *Bau und Leben des Socialen Korpers* (2nd ed.) RP, vol. 19.

continuously changing context. Hayek therefore seeks to reconcile the individualist/collectivist dichotomy by defining the rights of individual independence of thought and action within a broader objective of social cohesion and advancement,

> *The individualist concludes that the individuals should be allowed, within defined limits, to follow their own values and preferences rather than somebody else's, that within these spheres the individual's system of ends should be supreme and not subject to dictation by others ... This view does not, of course exclude the recognition of social ends, or rather a coincidence of individual ends which makes it advisable for men to combine for their pursuit (Hayek, 1944, p. 44).*

Hayek focuses less on the existence of universal values per se but rather on the requirement to respect a set of values, principles and practices which would have evolved and been found successful by the passage of time in benefiting the individual and sustaining the community. He stresses the requirement to resist the temptation to accept and adapt to prevailing ideologies and perspectives, which may be inconsistent or indeed conflict with evolved fundamental values and principles.

It is therefore important for the organisational business leader within the Western capitalist context to look beyond the transient and superficial values, principles and perspectives of prevailing societal ideologies, which pervade the cultures of a substantial number of organisations. Such ideologies tend to dominate the priorities of those individuals or stakeholder groups who are not ultimately concerned with the long-term survival of the organisation, lacking the capacity or inclination to consider such matters in great depth. Successful organisations accept that they are merely a "branch" of society and that ultimately long-term optimal performance is dependent upon the ongoing active support, commitment and productivity of all stakeholder groups. This is ensured and achieved through a confidence and belief by the broader stakeholder community that the leadership cadre will consistently satisfy their requirements and expectations through the translation of universal values into operational perspectives, priorities and practices and their operational application during the process of decision-making and issue resolution.

In many respects these latter propositions are central to the theme of practical and collaborative wisdom. The prevailing ideology which pervades many stakeholders groups within the Western business sector is fundamentally at odds with the application of the framework of wise leadership as detailed in Part One of this book. The prevailing and dominant stakeholder mindset would contend that the nature and dynamics of the business sector demands that perspectives and priorities should focus upon maximum short-term benefit and minimal short-term commitment to any organisational community as fundamental axioms of individual stakeholder group behaviour. However, such a perspective is self-defeating, as greater numbers of stakeholder groups abandon the community perspective in a rush to preserve what remains of what has, in their view, now become their respective "rights" and "privileges", resulting in the prevailing economic collapse and diminishing social cohesion. There is therefore a requirement to acknowledge and understand that the application of appropriate values and principles by the leadership cadre within organisations is of fundamental importance to the survival and performance of the organisation but also to the society or societies of which it is a part. These "anchor" perspectives and priorities are fundamental to the application of practical and collaborative wisdom.

This book is neither a philosophical nor a political treatise. Its primary objective is narrow, practical and focused on business leadership; to create a framework of understandable, inter-related propositions which ensure effective operational leadership and optimal organisational performance over the long term. However, in seeking to develop a framework of wise and effective operational leadership for optimal organisational performance it concludes that it is critical to develop and consistently apply perspectives in the day to day decision-making process which recognise the intrinsic link between the interests of the organisation, its broad stakeholder constituency and those of the society in which they exist and operate. This is clear headed, broad-minded, practical, pragmatic, hard headed and smart thinking in the face of twenty-first century business and organisational realities. Dominant leadership coalitions who fail to consider the implications of the link in such interests may succeed in the short term, receiving tumultuous plaudits and accolades, but will ultimately fail, with detrimental effects on the stakeholder constituency and society as a whole. These are not matters best left to the unwise amongst stakeholders, who elect to maximise profit now and move on quickly on the basis of perspectives which are not consistent with universal values. The practically wise leadership cadre should not therefore be considered a nice to have, but rather a fundamental prerequisite for survival and optimal performance, which must pervade not only the business organisation and sector but all sectors which comprise the societal community. Given the increasing interdependency between sectors within society, the suboptimal performance of one organisation or sector due to the absence of practical and collaborative wisdom within its leadership cadre is likely to resonate adversely across multiple sectors and organisations.

REJECT THE APPLICATION OF "HOST" OR "HOME" PRINCIPLES AND PERSPECTIVES

The universalist application of values and principles similarly has relevance and operational implications for merger and acquisition activity, particularly, but not exclusively, within a cross/multicultural context. The fundamental attainment of long-term success is dependent less on effective plans and strategies and more on the knowledge, experience, attributes and capabilities of those leaders responsible at the operational level for the implementation of acquisition and integration strategies. Whilst different societies appear on the surface to favour different perspectives, priorities and practices, the same values and principles underpin the underlying cognitive behaviour, decision making and actions of individuals in all societies. Leaders are therefore advised to base their approach to organisational management on the universal framework of values, no matter the business context.

This book therefore rejects the concept of long-term, cross-border success based on adaptation to local societal and/or organisational culture, which is in practice confusing, complex, counterproductive and unnecessary. A consistent finding of the interviews undertaken by the author during field research amongst Executive Committee members was that whilst interviewees recognised that there may indeed be differences in local business perspectives, they saw no justification in significantly adapting the institution's dominant logic. This was based upon a blueprint of universal values and business principles which had been tried and tested over decades. Rather they would apply these values and principles in a manner sympathetic to the local business (rather than cultural) context. It is important to recognise that issues are not viewed by business managers at the "cultural" dimension, but rather from the operational "business" dimension. It is the practically wise leader who can effectively and consistently balance these potentially conflicting requirements during the cognitive mental process to optimise organisational performance. Recent research looking into the reasons why cross border market penetrations sub-optimise and fail takes a more comprehensive view beyond the often cited issue of cultural distance. Increasingly there is a realisation that there are a range of "institutional" dimensions which inhibit and complicate effective operational leadership. Berry, Guillen and Zhou (2010) elucidate on these dimensions, for instance, in terms of differences in the state and nature of economic, financial, political, cultural and demographic profile, all of which must be considered in order to lead effectively within different business contexts.

It is not necessary to go into these dimensions in depth. Rather the point of relevance is that in order to consider and balance these complex dimensions within specific market and business contexts, to achieve optimal effectiveness and performance, requires no less than:

- A cadre of practically wise operational leaders who have been inculcated in the relevance and application of appropriate values and principles.
- The ability to assess facts and information in a practically wise manner as proposed in Chapter 2.
- The attributes and capabilities of the wise leader, which we will discuss at a later stage in this book.

Anything less is most likely to result in significant issues with key stakeholder groups, diminished energy and motivation and suboptimal organisational performance, no matter the inspired plans and strategies for effective market penetration and organisational integration. In this respect we return to the ability to analyse a range of complex issues and take optimal decisions based upon the people dimension rather than the technical, administrative or numerical.

Evidence from the author's research reinforces the perspective that global organisations which are considered successful over the long term contain a leadership cadre which is not hidebound by principles and perspectives which reflect a "home" societal culture, which would inhibit employee acculturation. Rather, they consistently apply universal values which are fundamental to the effective management of every community. There is a significant tendency on the part of acquiring business organisations and dominant coalitions to apply a default setting and continue to apply the business principles, perspectives and priorities of the "home" organisation, which are themselves predominantly based upon those of the "home" societal context.

In contrast, global business organisations, such as HSBC Holdings, may be said to be independent of such "home" tendencies, not circumscribed by any dominant cultural, institutional or industrial norms. This characteristic is particularly important in respect of the application of practical and collaborative wisdom. A lack of attachment to any single societal framework facilitates pragmatic and objective management, encouraging acculturative attraction amongst staff of the organisations acquired. Staff will therefore have no negative preconceptions or fears that their prevailing organisational and/or societal perspectives and practices will be dismissed, threatened or subsumed out of hand,

> *HSBC does not have a national home culture ... from our roots in the Far East we had developed a culture of sorts, based on fast decisions, running the bank on a military style approach ... Blended into the national cultures are the strategic norms of the Group and the main culture which is embedded in all of us ... integrity, speed to market, putting bank before self, integrity, integrity, integrity (Interviewee A).*

The dominant business logic of such organisations is built upon a foundational set of shared community-based values which are universally acknowledged, understood and applied by individuals, irrespective of specific geographic location, personal wealth, political or religious complexion. An already cited quote is relevant within this context,

> *Values can, and should, have universal application. I believe that there are some values that are universally recognised ... And I believe that it is both perfectly possible, and desirable, to be multicultural in outlook, and at the same time to hold a set of universal values (Sir Bond, 1999, p. 3).*

In this statement Bond was supported by John Weinberg, Chairman of the Management Committee, Goldman Sachs & Co, 1976–1990 when commenting on shared values,

> *It's the glue that holds the firm together so that we can all work together (Ellis, 2008, p. 304).*

The issue of applying "home" or "host" principles, perspectives and priorities has direct resonance for the author who, after a career spanning some 25 years in the UK and Ireland took up a general management role in the Arabian Gulf. To say that the application of previously successful "home" management principles, perspectives, priorities and practices failed would be an understatement. My initial interpretation of a lack of leadership success was that there must exist, unique principles, perspectives and priorities pertinent to the local cultural context. Once I thought that I had recognised these attributes I sought to embed them into my leadership perspectives and priorities, and consistently apply them in day to day leadership practices. In fact, the organisation for whom I was employed was respected by local stakeholders for its consistent application of universal values, in a manner sympathetic to the local business context, at the level of practices. Those organisations which fail to succeed within the cross-cultural context (and this applies whether you are expanding within a single society across organisational cultures or across societies) do so due to the absence of a framework of universal values driving their decision making, rather than an inability to adapt to the local context. The mark of the effective leader and "global" organisation is the ability to apply universal values in a manner which are appropriate to the local cultural context. This thereby overcomes the spontaneous and instinctive expectation from local stakeholders to see major adaptation in organisational dominant logic to reflect local perspectives and priorities. In my own case, adaptability to local context improved but did not optimise my leadership performance.What then is the importance and relevance of all of these philosophical and conceptual ruminations in relation to the practical issues with which the operational leader is faced on a day to day basis? An acknowledgement and understanding of the existence and nature of universal, globally applicable values has implications of critical importance for the operational business leader. Practical wisdom requires a clear framework of values and principles as the basis of effective evaluation and consistent decision making. The existence of a framework of universal values provides both clarity and simplicity. It reduces any confusion and doubt as regards the appropriate values and principles to apply, the absence of which causes the decision-making process to be based upon inconsistent value schema or, in many cases the absence of any clear framework of fundamental values whatsoever. This mental confusion is the direct cause within the operational, day to day leadership context of substantial wasted time, effort and energy, doubt, conflict and diminished productivity, on the part of both leaders and staff. Equally important, confidence in and the credibility of individual leaders and the leadership cadre is significantly diminished, which has a significant impact on allegiance to the organisation and individual/group motivation.

Business organisations which have been consistently successful over the long term are not guided by superficial, transient, home or host "local" values and principles but rather consistently apply values, principles and priorities which have universal logic and resonance. Consciously or subconsciously leaders take decisions on a day to day basis (e.g. best way to increase sales, cut costs, evaluate staff, interpretation of standards and regulations) based upon what they regard as appropriate values, principles and priorities. In my experience the predominant priorities as a leader within Western organisations tends to focus on such issues as market share, sales, revenue, promotion, salary increment and bonus, reflecting short term stakeholder perspectives. In many respects these priorities reflect the dominant values and principles upon which operational issues are evaluated and decisions made in respect of the manner by which objectives are set and achieved. Such values and principles are inconsistent with universal values which optimise performance through a primary focus on a "marathon" approach to building organisational capability and optimal performance through maximising the motivation, allegiance, dedication and cohesion of organisational stakeholders.

The Importance of the Consistent Application of a Single Dominant Logic

"What is bred in the bones comes out in the flesh"
Ancient Chinese proverb (Whitson, 2001)

Optimal long-term performance is dependent upon the pervasive and consistent application throughout the organisation of a single dominant logic, founded on universal values. Such an approach delivers the key attributes of clarity and simplicity to support effective operational leadership, confidence and comfort to ensure continuing stakeholder allegiance, dedication and advocacy. Critically, the application of the appropriate dominant logic must be based upon a soft-hearted, hard-headed approach which seeks to consistently apply the core values and principles of the dominant logic in a manner sympathetic to the local context in order to optimise the benefit of local stakeholder knowledge, expertise and support for the organisation.

WHAT IS A DOMINANT LOGIC?

An issue which is pivotal to the operational application of practical and collaborative wisdom is that propounded by Prahalad and Bettis (1986) in respect of what they term "Dominant Logic", to which we have already referred in passing in previous sections. They stress the nature of the evolution of the senior executive group's perspective and priorities and also their approach to issues and decision making as being probably the most important factor in both an organisation's early failures and its long-term success. This dominant logic tends to be developed and implemented by a dominant coalition of executives who control the allocation of material, human and knowledge resources. Over time they develop a decision-making framework and process on the basis of shared experience and embedded views in respect of those principles, perspectives, priorities, rules, behaviours and practices, which, in their view, have resulted in consistent personal and organisational "success" to date.

This dominant logic, once developed and tested during the initial phases of the organisation's life is "handed down" to successive dominant coalitions for operational interpretation, implementation and evolutionary amendment by the prevailing leadership cadre. It is fundamentally not focused narrowly on how to efficiently produce and sell the organisation's "widgets", but more holistically on how to most effectively manage the organisation's resources in order to optimise operational effectiveness, productivity and long-term performance. Within the context of managing people within the organisation the existence and consistent operational application of such a dominant logic at all levels and across all functions of the organisation provides clarity of purpose and direction, facilitating stakeholder cohesion and confidence.

THE DYNAMIC APPLICATION OF AN ORGANISATION'S DOMINANT LOGIC

Organisations which are successful in the long term require a dominant logic which is dynamic rather than sclerotic. Such frameworks of logic must include patterns and paradigms which encompass a sense of excitement, dynamism, anticipation, insight, adaptability and flexibility. Also the capability to quickly test new schema, whilst not destroying proven schema in the dominant logic, in order to continue to succeed in the constantly changing business environment,

> An organisation with the flexibility and competitive edge of a kid playing a video game rather than the analytical consistency of a grand master trying to hang on in a three day chess match (Bartlett and Ghoshal, 1998, p. 35).

Such a capability requires leaders with substantial experience, insight, intuition and judgement to make decisions on the subtle balance between change and maintenance of the core values, principles and priorities which are to form the pervasive foundation of evaluation and decision making throughout the organisation into the future.

The consistent application of a dominant logic, to be effective, must pervade every aspect and function of the organisation, influencing and affecting every operational decision and action. The prevailing crisis, predominantly within the Anglo-American financial service sector is likely to reflect those organisations where:

FINANCIAL SECTOR CRISIS–WEAKNESSES IN THE APPLICATION OF A DOMINANT LOGIC

- A dominant logic was not embedded and pervasive throughout the organisation and amongst its stakeholders; and/or
- Decisions and actions taken were considered by stakeholder groups as inconsistent with perceptions of established principles, perspectives and priorities, creating a lack of strategic and operational clarity, thereby diminishing cohesion, motivation, credibility and trust amongst both leaders and employees; and/or
- Changes to the dominant logic were not considered on the basis of the long-term optimal performance of the organisation and the benefit of the broad community of stakeholder groups.

Such organisations took advantage of prevailing market opportunities, created particularly by new financial instruments, but failed to recognise the impact on the perceptions and behaviour of stakeholder groups. The leadership approach undertaken is much akin to fitting a turbocharger onto an engine without taking into account the implications for other aspects of driving, such as the suspension, brakes, steering and the overall driver/passenger experience, a narrow rather than holistic perspective towards organisational leadership.

This ultimately has a negative impact on the credibility of and confidence in the leadership of the organisation, initially resulting in a lack of cohesion, motivation and loyalty, and finally abandonment, in the form of:

- Resignation by key and aspiring members of the leadership.
- A lack of total commitment and allegiance within the leadership cadre when key decisions and actions are required.
- Substantial diminution in motivation, dedication and energy amongst employees.
- Disinvestment and retrenchment by investors, customers/clients and suppliers.

This at a stage when continuing commitment by stakeholders might have ensured survival.

It is often in economic or other crises when those business organisations with a dominant and dynamic logic which is attuned to stakeholder requirements and optimal performance are revealed. These organisations survive and indeed are able to take advantage of opportunities arising with the continuing support and confidence of their stakeholders. HSBC Group has not been immune from market calamity. This included exclusion from its primary market in China following the end of the Second World War and also from Persia in the early 1950s, where it had opened in 1889 and had become the state bank (Imperial Bank of Persia) issuing banknotes. The bank was, however, able to adapt its business focus and strategy to survive in response to this latter crisis, pioneering banking in the Gulf states to support the development of the oil industry during the 1940s, resulting in the development of a multiregional business perspective. This is further evidence of a dominant logic comprising of universal values and principles which allow the organisation to quickly and successfully adapt, because they have the support and confidence of the broad community of stakeholders. The consistent operational application of a dominant logic based on universal values provides key benefits, as illustrated in the boxed text below:

KEY BENEFITS OF A DOMINANT LOGIC FOUNDED ON UNIVERSAL VALUES

- An ability to quickly generate confidence and enthusiastic support amongst new stakeholder groups. These groups acknowledge and understand that the organisation wishes to be a partner rather than a master and equitably distribute the benefits of association amongst the wider stakeholder base, rather than imposing "home" principles and priorities, and restricting the benefits to a narrow stakeholder base.
- An ability to anticipate the need for change in dominant logic and to adapt rather than discard the fundamental values, principles and perspectives of the dominant logic. This is achieved through the collegiate and collaborative nature of the stakeholder relationship and the desire to work for the benefit of the organisational "community".
- An ability to coordinate and implement new business strategy and move forward as if such situations were part of the business mix for which those running the organisation must be prepared.
- An ability to effectively adapt to the changing business context, whilst continuing to base decisions on a proven logic of foundational values and principles.

The importance (and perhaps complexity) of gradually adapting an organisation's dominant logic in a structured and holistic manner as the fundamental business context changes, whilst simultaneously applying this changing logic in a contextually appropriate manner at the operational level, is clearly illustrated by the dramatic changes within the UK banking sector over the last 50 years. Specifically the acquisition, ruin or demise, with few exceptions, of pretty much every major brand within the banking sector (e.g. Midland Bank, National Westminster Bank, Bank of Scotland, Royal Bank of Scotland, Halifax, Abbey National, Bradford and Bingley and Northern Rock), many established during the nineteenth century. As Sir John Bond states,

> You're looking at a firm believer that every company should have a board member who is responsible for "corporate insecurity" … that is his job: to remind people that a quarter of the FTSE 100 from 20 years ago have gone, and that if the 141 year old bank does not keep changing it could face the same fate (Kellaway, 2006, p. 10).

In many cases the collapse of these institutions of long standing occurred when an organisation's dominant logic, largely based upon prudent banking principles and/or narrow expertise, was overwhelmed by the rapidly changing perspectives and priorities of an existing or new dominant coalition. This group became convinced, in the absence of the expert intuition to which we have already referred, by developing market opportunities (e.g. buildings and savings banks competing across the range of retail and commercial banking products with clearing banks; expansion and utilisation of and exposure to derivatives, hedging, securitisation instruments) of the requirement for the rapid introduction of a new dominant logic (comprised of principles, perspectives, priorities and practices) which had previously taken decades or longer to become embedded in the psyche of stakeholders. Existing stakeholders were therefore not familiar with and convinced/confident that they were consistent with their personal requirements and aspirations. The result was a negative impact on comprehension, energy expended on behalf of the organisation, cohesion, dedication and motivation. This dominant coalition sought to convert the core organisational focus without appreciating that stakeholder groups were still committed to the embedded dominant logic, resulting in a distancing of the leadership coalition from key stakeholder groups in respect of key principles, perspectives and priorities. Insufficient attention was given to the requirement for acculturation and the satisfaction of stakeholder requirements and expectations, blinded by the glare of market opportunity, glory and self-aggrandisement.

The response of many readers might be that you must with alacrity adapt to rapidly changing market situations, particularly new opportunities to survive and prosper. My response is that the leadership cadre of a few financial institutions in the UK (e.g. Barclays, Lloyds TSB, HSBC Group, Nationwide and Co-operative Bank) undertook what we might recognise as a practically wise cognitive mental process. They recognised and anticipated the implications for their organisations, taking into account their short and long-term capabilities and desire to respond to market opportunities. In some cases organisations took steps to enhance capabilities and clearly communicate a changing dominant logic in respect of perspectives, priorities and practices, in a manner geared to maintain the allegiance, commitment and confidence of stakeholders. In others the decision was that they could continue to prosper on the basis of the prevailing dominant logic and areas of business focus. These organisations did not frenetically throw the existing dominant logic of principles, perspectives and priorities which had led to their success to date over their shoulders in order to quickly jump on the new train, fearful that if they did not get on it quickly they would miss the benefits. It is interesting to note that the cited institutions might be considered to have a deeply embedded dominant logic of key principles and perspectives in which its leadership cadre had been inculcated over an extended period. We will return to the issue of inculcation at a later stage in the book.

Effective organisational leadership is therefore dependent upon the existence of and dynamic management of the evolution of a single dominant logic in order to optimise performance by adapting to changing and variable business contexts. It emphasises a framework of embedded leadership schema, comprising principles, perspectives and priorities which have been translated into organisation wide leadership capabilities and expertise at the day to day, operational level.

THE INFLUENCE OF A SINGLE DOMINANT LOGIC ON OPERATIONAL LEADERSHIP

The importance of the application of a single dominant logic lies not only in everyone "singing from the same hymn sheet", providing clarity, simplicity and a sense of purpose. Critically, if the single dominant logic is the appropriate blueprint of embedded leadership values, principles, perspectives and priorities, based upon universal values it will lead to optimal levels of motivation, confidence, allegiance, dedication and cohesion amongst stakeholders, with a direct, sustained and substantial impact on productivity and performance. The benefits of the application of a single dominant logic provide an indicator of how the dominant coalition intends to interact with and deal with stakeholder groups (e.g. employees, shareholders, suppliers, customers/clients, regulators) and the wider social environment. The consistent application of a dominant logic therefore provides two critical benefits in effective leadership, as noted in the boxed text "Key Benefits of the Consistent Application of a Single Dominant Logic" below:

KEY BENEFITS OF THE CONSISTENT APPLICATION OF A SINGLE DOMINANT LOGIC

- **Clarity and simplicity**: it provides organisational leaders with anchor points and a compass upon which to base decisions on the multitude of operational issues which they must face on a daily basis. This has the advantages of speeding up decision making but also automatically ensuring that there is a consistency of decision making throughout the organisation, allowing a light and deft leadership approach. Also an ability to delegate authority to enhance confidence and encourage the utilisation of tacit knowledge and intuition, confident in the knowledge that there will be no major deviations from core principles, perspectives, standards and practices.
- **Confidence and comfort**: no organisation is in control of their environment and therefore is prone to the effects of factors out of their control. In such circumstances those organisations which consistently apply a single dominant logic which is effectively communicated, understood and based upon values accepted by stakeholders are less likely to experience the severe negative effects of such sudden shocks. This is due to the fact that stakeholders are aware of the principles and priorities of the dominant coalition and are therefore confident of the manner in which the dominant coalition will respond and comfortable that, for instance, they will not blatantly "burn" the majority of stakeholder groups to ensure the survival and benefit of a limited group.

The results are tangibly and financially significant for the organisation, in the form of share price levels and oscillations, credit rating, availability of credit, take up of rights issues, labour unrest and adverse media comment. Perhaps equally, if not more significant, is an ongoing confidence and positive attitude towards and belief in the pronouncements and actions of the dominant coalition within the organisation. This is of substantial and tangible value to the operational leadership cadre as they take day to day decisions, confident of the continuing support, allegiance and motivation of the workforce in the attainment of tasks and targets.

It is important to not merely blindly accept the benefits to the organisation of the consistent application of a single dominant logic, taking it for granted. The reality is that most dominant coalitions within business organisations lack the embedded, inherited knowledge, experience, insight, intuition, judgement, the cumulative practical wisdom, to appropriately develop and manage the organisation's dominant logic. The effective application of an organisation's dominant logic is the epitome of "joined-up thinking" since it impacts upon every aspect of the organisation's operations. The effective implementation of an appropriate dominant logic requires the application of the principles and cognitive mental processes of practical wisdom, to which we have referred in Part One. An inability/unwillingness to implement each stage in the development, communication and implementation of an appropriate dominant logic has a knock on effect on clarity of purpose, motivation and productivity.

THE MISAPPLICATION OF DOMINANT LOGIC

Organisations which are Incapable of Optimal Long-Term Performance

- Do not recognise the importance of consistently applying such logic.
- If they do, they apply inappropriate principles, perspectives and priorities which fail to gain acceptance by stakeholders in order to gain the optimal benefit from their application through optimal confidence, comfort, allegiance, dedication, motivation and advocacy.
- Fail to understand the operational management implications of their consistent application with regard, in particular, to such issues as recruitment, leadership development, assimilation, inculcation and promotion to senior executive positions (these are points which we will discuss later in greater depth).
- Fail to effectively communicate and translate the values and principles upon which the dominant logic is founded, ensuring that these are privy only to the dominant coalition, as an elitist badge of clarity and insight. This ensures that it does not become "owned" by operational leadership, precluding consistent decision making throughout the organisation based upon an anchor of logic. The dominant coalition, thereby miss the opportunity to make it an asset in the development and maintenance of stakeholder cohesion and allegiance.
- Fail to appreciate how the absence of effective communication of core principles and perspectives, or alternatively the communication of aberrant principles and perspectives, impacts adversely on the decision-making schema and issue resolution by leaders within operational units such as finance, marketing, risk, product development, sales, customer service, distribution channels and HR.

In order to make the above comments tangible and real it is appropriate to include a brief case study which briefly details the development of an organisation's dominant logic, whilst at the same time emphasising the importance of taking into account the prevailing realities of the specific business context to its development and composition.

HSBC GROUP: THE DEVELOPMENT OF AN OPTIMAL DOMINANT LOGIC

The geopolitical context of the period when the bank was founded created a high risk/high reward business dynamic,

The failure of so many Eastern banks had taught the need for sound banking at the same time as the consequent relative lack of competition made such banking practices enforceable (King, 1983, p. 47).

The founding bank therefore applied a management blueprint whose foundations were largely but not exclusively based upon the consistent application of a core set of business principles which are even today termed "Scottish Presbyterian",

"But it appeared to me that, if a suitable opportunity occurred, one of the very simplest things in the world would be to start a bank in China more or less founded upon Scottish principles" Thomas Sutherland, P&O agent and one of founders (quoted in King, 1969, p. 7).

This encompassed decision-making schema which might be considered conservative, prudent, efficient, moralistic, based upon devotion to duty and a comprehensive assessment of all risk issues, rather than a risk aversion. It required an emphasis upon maintaining close control over issues which related to financial, credit, political and operational risk. This perspective rests upon the development, understanding and implementation of a long-term vision and clear definition of the role and contribution of each business unit and individual within the organisation.

To these were added what might be considered merchant "Empire" characteristics of speedy decision making, high levels of integrity, a responsibility to the "natives" and an acceptance of personal sacrifice for the greater good of the in-group and community to which they related, namely Hongkong and Shanghai Banking Corporation. This created a philosophy and personal characteristics rich in righteousness, direction, confidence, certainty, sympathy and security, which, from the recent interviews with senior executives remains core to their perspectives, priorities and decision making into the twenty-first century,

Addis's life was to demonstrate the advantages which such a heritage bequeathed – its certainty, confidence, optimism and faith in the ultimate triumph of righteousness and goodness instilled a sense of purpose, gave security and direction to life which future generations could regard with both envy and wonder (Dayer, 1983, p. 14).

HSBC does not feel compelled to show stellar performances in the short term and is accepted by major institutions as a consistent and long-term performer due to innate core competences,

We are not managing for the next reporting period, we are managing an organisation that has survived and prospered for almost 140 years and is running a marathon, not a series of sprints (Whitson, 2001, p. 5)

In major statements Sir John Bond expressed the core characteristics of the Group, which have ensured its survival and development into the pre-eminent if not now the only global "universal" bank (Sir Bond, 1998, 2000b).

- **International**: from its inception in Hong Kong, it had an international business perspective, with German, Indian, American, Norwegian, Scottish and English board members.
1. **Conservative**: international experience of political, economic and natural storms created justification for a conservative balance sheet, the view that *"a little hay collected every day is better than one good crop"* and that a long-term plan which creates consistent growth, although dull, is better than a plan which provides a cyclical growth pattern and, on balance, is preferred by key stakeholder groups.
2. **Opportunistic**: once appropriate prudent and conservative frameworks are in place to assess credit and operational risk, HSBC is opportunistic in its approach to the acquisition of businesses throughout the world which are likely to enhance stakeholder value over the long term.
3. **Pioneering**: linked to its opportunistic and conservative characteristics, HSBC has been pioneering, for example, founding banking systems in Thailand, Japan and the Gulf states, whilst more recently entering Armenia, Azerbaijan, Kazakhstan and Iraq.
4. **Independent**: HSBC is not circumscribed by cultural, institutional or industry norms. Rather it adapts on the basis of business context, initially to reflect the realities of business in Asia and being subservient to the perspectives and practices of the London banking fraternity.

Source: adapted from Park (2006).

The final characteristic in the above case study, Independence, is particularly important in relation to this study and is one to which we have already alluded in the previous section of this chapter. As we have already mentioned, a lack of attachment to any single societal framework facilitates a global leadership capability based upon pragmatic, objective and sympathetic management, encouraging acculturative attraction amongst staff of the organisations acquired. To emphasise this important point it is appropriate to cite once more the following quote from a senior executive interviewed by the author.

> *HSBC does not have a national home culture ... from our roots in the Far East we had developed a culture of sorts, based on fast decisions, running the bank on a military style approach which has evolved into various types of cultures with large banks in various parts ... Chinese style culture in Asia, in Europe, blend, US and Mexican cultures ... Blended into the national cultures are the strategic norms of the Group and the main culture which is embedded in all of us ... integrity, speed to market, putting bank before self, integrity, integrity, integrity (Interviewee A).*

The important point is that whilst many of the principles and perspectives may have developed within the business context of a bygone age, these have been translated and adapted into a single dominant logic which corresponds with present day business contexts, because fundamentally the embedded logic and cognitive schema upon which universal values are based continue to deliver leadership attributes and capabilities which optimise organisational performance.

THE NATURE OF DOMINANT LOGIC – SOFT HEART, HARD HEAD

Goldman Sachs & Co has, like HSBC, developed and consistently applied a dominant logic from the early days of its foundation. Despite the recent substantial adverse comment over recent years from a number of sections of society on the values, principles and priorities upon which Goldman Sachs & Co is presently led there is no doubt that its leadership cadre consciously and consistently formulated and operationalised a dominant logic based upon satisfying the requirements and aspirations of the community of stakeholders to which it was and continues to be affiliated. Goldman Sachs & Co has historically exhibited in leadership decision-making and issue resolution the principles, attributes and cognitive mental processes characteristic of practical and collaborative wisdom.

Charles D. Ellis (2008) and Lisa Endlich (2007a) in their books on the history of Goldman, Sachs & Co, since its foundation in 1869, encapsulate much of what is contained within this chapter with respect to issues of dominant logic and the key principles and perspectives of the operational leadership of the successful organisation over the long term. The key area of impact resides in how the dominant logic influences operational leadership perspectives, priorities and practices. This drives the complexion of the process of evaluation, decision-making and issue resolution, particularly in respect of the interaction between individuals and stakeholder groups, which lies at the root of consistently optimising organisational performance.

In the case of Goldman Sachs & Co the key perspectives and priorities which have during its history influenced operational leadership are detailed in the table below:

GOLDMAN SACHS & CO – DOMINANT PERSPECTIVES AND PRIORITIES

- "Servant leaders" who stay with the organisation over the long term, seeing it as their primary role to serve the organisation, rather than themselves and significant others.
- A willingness to share the management and benefits of the organisation in a collegiate, collaborative and meritocratic manner.
- A pre-eminent and dominant focus on customer focus as a primary means of long-term success, often to the detriment of short-term personal and organisational benefit.
- Professional and ethical standards which are distinctive within those financial services sectors within which they operate.
- An organisational culture which emphasises a work ethic and professional standards of excellence and competency.
- A single organisational culture, with consistent long-term values and operational practices across all geographic and business entities.

Source: adapted from Ellis (2008) and Endlich (2007a).

Fundamentally, the success of Goldman Sachs & Co has been based upon an acceptance by all stakeholder groups of shared values and teamwork. The view of senior executives within Goldman Sachs & Co was that the key requirements for success over the long term were primarily "soft" qualitative, people-focused attributes, this in a market where everyone had ready access to the key table stakes of communication and information,

There are only four ways to gain and keep significant advantage: more effective recruiting, a stronger culture, a better strategy, and a greater intensity of commitment (Ellis, 2008, p. 554).

This has had a dramatic effect on the key principles, perspectives and priorities which are the foundation of the organisation's dominant logic, based upon engendering and actively managing the commitment, loyalty, dedication and motivation of both leaders and employees. This intensity of commitment, loyalty and dedication persisted amongst senior executives due to the maintenance of the partnership model, this at a time when other Wall Street firms had gone public in an effort to raise capital, to provide financial flexibility in order to grow in both asset size and value and to support ever larger M&A transactions. The partnership model means that the partners own the firm, taking both the risks and the profits. Taking decisions where your own money is involved keeps the mind a little more focused than if you consider it someone else's. In 1999 Goldman Sachs & Co did have an IPO, but offered only a small proportion to the public (12 per cent). Given the prevailing credibility travails of Goldman Sachs & Co it may be that the recent change in the ownership structure, from being predominantly a partnership to public ownership (approximately 70 per cent is now owned by institutions), may have caused fundamental perspectives and priorities within the dominant coalition to have been significantly altered.

However, winding back from more recent times, in order to maintain the firm's unique culture, as success dictated a growing and more complex organisation, it was considered critical to its continuing growth and success to translate these general principles into a clear code, to be communicated and reinforced consistently. John Whitehead (co-senior partner and co-chairman from 1976–84) contended that the core question is,

How can we get the message to all those individuals who were new to GS in such a way that they would understand our core values, come to believe in them, and make the firm's values their values in everything they did every day? (Ellis, 2008, p. 184).

In response Whitehead developed "Our Business Principles" during the latter half of the 1970s, (to which we have already alluded),

But when I think of my major contribution to building Goldman Sachs, I don't think so much of the new business I helped develop, or the sales techniques I tried to implement. Rather, I believe the most important thing I did was to set down in writing what Goldman Sachs stood for (Whitehead, 2005).

These were a set of values and priorities which focused upon directing and influencing the perspectives, priorities, attitudes, behaviours and emotions of individuals in order to create an energised and motivated community of stakeholders with a clear and common purpose and vision. These 14 principles were printed and sent to all employees and their families at their home address, referred to frequently and featured in every year's annual review and annual report since their publication as:

- The foundation stones upon which the organisation is to be led.
- The anchor and compass for the resolution of all business issues.

DOMINANT LOGIC AND GLOBAL LEADERSHIP CAPABILITIES

The resolution of the continuing mystery surrounding the fundamentals of long-term, practically wise and effective leadership essentially revolves around:

- The blanket application of a framework of management principles and standards; versus.
- An ability and willingness by the organisation and individual leaders to appropriately and contextually effect the subtle and pragmatic application of the organisation's dominant logic through a cognitive mental process characterised by the practically wise leader. This is achieved on the basis of the development within the leadership cadre of the appropriate perspectives, attributes and capabilities to exhibit expert intuition, insight and judgement in order to take optimal decisions no matter the business context. In this respect we have already discussed those organisations which may be termed "all terrain".

Flexibility and adaptability within consistently successful business organisations occurs predominantly at the level of local practices and processes, rather than fundamental principles and perspectives. Optimal long-term performance requires the consistent application of a dominant logic of "global" leadership values, perspectives and priorities. As we have already quoted,

> HSBC has a framework of technical, management standards and principles which are applied universally. Such practices are not considered rooted in any single national culture and to that extent are considered understandable and agreeable within any local cultural context. These principles are largely non-negotiable but in other respects HSBC is willing to adapt to comply with local customs and practices (Interviewee D).

In many respects the line between effective and defective individual and organisational leadership is drawn by the manner in which an organisation's dominant logic is implemented in order to leverage both its benefits and those of the local assets. Effective operational leadership requires innate and intuitive judgement, returning us to the attributes and capabilities of the practically wise leader. This is based upon substantial experience, expertise, insight and intuition, to decide when it is in the interests of optimal organisational performance to be sympathetic to the perspectives, priorities and practices of the local context, this without jeopardising proven organisational values and principles,

> HSBC put people into acquired companies specifically with a view to a transfer of culture and standards; that said there remains significant diversity ... practices and perspectives may change but changes in values must be strongly justified due to the fact that their validity has been proven in the fire of international business over a hundred and forty years (Interviewee B).

The extent to which this approach is highly complex and problematic to apply in practice, when bereft of the application of the required universal values, leadership perspectives and extensive people management experience, is reflected in a quote from a dominant coalition interviewee of an organisation which has only relatively recently (i.e. in the last two decades) embarked upon intensive, focused, cross-border acquisition. This organisation lacked the "global" dominant logic based on universal values and management insight and experience to apply appropriate operational management perspectives and practices in order to overcome the significant institutional distance which is common during periods of market expansion, organisational acquisition and integration. It sought to apply the dominant logic which had consistently proven successful in its home market. The result was a lack of credibility, respect, relatedness and legitimacy amongst key local stakeholders in the new markets which they sought to penetrate. This led to conflict, friction, and the absence of cooperation on the part of local stakeholders within the acquiring organisation, particularly the leadership cadre tasked with effective implementation. The result was a lack of allegiance to and cohesion within the organisation and frequent changes in senior management, leading to substantial financial loss over a sustained period,

> Overall (X Group) sought to transfer their (home) business standards to cross-border acquisitions on the assumption that these are universally appropriate and they had the upper hand as acquirers of distressed banks in developing economies. (This approach) initially failed due to a lack of appropriate advocates and opposition from socio-political institutions (Interviewee I).

Failure to effectively acquire and integrate an organisation therefore lies in:

THE ROOTS OF FAILURE IN ORGANISATIONAL INTEGRATION

- The absence of a "global" dominant logic based upon universal values recognised, accepted and understood by the new stakeholder groups.
- The absence of leaders with the appropriate experience, insight, intuition and judgement to communicate and apply the organisation's dominant logic in a manner sympathetic to the local business context.
- A fundamental lack of appreciation of, capability in and focus on the importance of innate soft management capabilities, principles and perspectives.

These factors, rather than the fact that the "numbers" (e.g. sales, revenue, cost savings) projected prior to acquisition or merger did not materialise lie at the heart of suboptimal performance and the failure of the majority of merger/acquisitions,

> Bear in mind the (X) Group is essentially a (F societal culture) based Group, only recently expanded into Central Europe; whilst easy to quickly acquire assets and increase headcount in significant markets, much more difficult to change from local, regional to truly European, international perspective; not yet reflected in any significant way in character, nature of (X) Group (Interviewee G).

The implications of a short-sighted, mechanistic rather than "global" and holistic view of the required leadership perspectives, priorities, attributes, capabilities and experience during the acquisition assessment stage is a substantial expenditure of management resources on conflict resolution and an internal organisational rather than external market focus. This results in a lack of allegiance, cohesion and a stunted transfer of tacit knowledge and suboptimal performance for a protracted period, The implications are critical inefficiencies, stakeholder conflict, enhanced costs, sub-optimal revenues and often market exit and retrenchment to home market in confusion and self-doubt.

> *With hindsight this may have been regarded as imprudent and impulsive and no doubt created management problems (Interviewee F).*

In this respect the key point to take from this chapter section on "global" leadership and the application of a single dominant logic is that in the excitement of a proposed merger or acquisition it is critical that the dominant coalition consider more than the financial, technical and systems implications, which are ultimately merely the table stakes for efficient rather than effective implementation. Long-term success is rather dependent upon a global dominant logic, founded on universal values, delivered on the basis of practical and collaborative wisdom. This in turn results in a leadership cadre whose perspectives, attributes and capabilities allow it to evaluate, critically reflect upon and resolve situations and issues in a contextually sympathetic and therefore optimal manner, within the operational, day to day context,this on the basis of hard-headed yet soft-hearted perspectives, priorities and practices.

Practical Wisdom: The Development and Maintenance of an Inculcated Leadership Cadre

A critical component in and also benefit from the application of a single dominant logic founded on universal values is the development of an assimilated, inculcated leadership cadre. Such a cadre has a uniform business and leadership cognitive mental process which aids collegiate decision-making and effective implementation. Consistent with this dynamic is the application of a policy of minimal external recruitment and the careful consideration of any proposed mergers and acquisitions in order to minimise "contamination" of the organisational dominant logic.

MAINTENANCE OF THE DOMINANT LOGIC THROUGH OPTIMAL LEADERSHIP PERSPECTIVES

In this and the following section of this chapter, we stress that the substantial benefits of consistently applying a single dominant logic based upon universally accepted values do not accrue through a process of osmosis, through the very fact that such a logic exists in the mind of one, some or all of the members of the dominant coalition within an organisation. Rather, it is critical that the dominant coalition put in place policies to appropriately reflect this logic at the operational, "shop floor" level. A key facet in this respect, which radiates the dominant logic throughout the organisation, is to develop, mould and actively manage, without constraining, the mindset of the leadership cadre. This is undertaken to ensure, as we intimated in the previous section, that they consistently and intuitively evaluate operational issues on the basis of the appropriate framework of principles, perspectives and priorities. Once this has been achieved and is reflected in the ongoing manner of issue resolution, decision making and responses to stakeholder groups (e.g. employees, shareholders, customers, suppliers, regulatory bodies) the benefits of a single dominant logic will continue to consistently accrue over the long term. It is therefore of value to spend some time discussing the manner of the inculcation of the organisation's leadership cadre.

In order to maintain and indeed leverage the benefits of the consistent application of a single dominant logic there is a fundamental requirement not to allow the development of an environment where there are contrasting, competing or indeed conflicting logics vying for supremacy. This dilution of the positive impact of a single dominant logic can occur due to the absence of clear policies in respect of recruitment and leadership development, for instance:

- **Where much of the recruitment for leadership positions is open to external candidates, who naturally introduce dominant logics from other organisations with whom they have been employed.**
  If optimal leadership and organisational performance is indeed highly dependent upon a cohesive, collegiate leadership cadre then we must carefully consider the optimal balance between the priority of attracting those individuals with the epitome of technical excellence and the creation of a team of organisational leaders who know, trust, are loyal to, familiar with, confident in and can anticipate the responses and actions of each other, who have over time grown to rely on each other through a series of personal and organisational "situations".

- **Where there is no proactive, conscious and determined policy to assimilate and inculcate new and existing staff in the core principles, perspectives and priorities of the organisation's dominant logic.**
  This may be considered contrary to current views on the benefit to organisations of allowing staff to optimally contribute through not restricting their scope of thought. However, whilst there is little doubt that the highly educated and sophisticated employees and leaders of the twenty-first century do not wish to be forcibly assimilated and inculcated into a rigid framework of principles and priorities which dictate their every action, "Borg-like", they do have both an operational desire and requirement to be aware of the framework of organisational norms in respect of core principles, perspectives and priorities. This is important in order to be confident and comfortable in taking decisions and undertaking actions on behalf of the organisation. In operational terms, much time and energy continues to be wasted by employees with a mindset operating in an apprehensive and indecisive mode in respect of the basis upon which issues should be evaluated, decisions taken and action undertaken.

Such perspectives must however in practice be applied with balance, pragmatism and common sense as we will see a little later in the manner by which HSBC appoints individuals to senior executive and leadership roles. We must highlight the desirability of distinguishing between leaders and technicians, even at the Executive Committee level. Whilst it would be the ideal to have senior executives as heads of legal, risk, finance and IT who have been home grown within the organisation there is a logic in recruiting more on technical capabilities and expertise in appointment to such positions, as long as appointment to such a senior "management" role does not automatically convey leadership responsibility and authority. Such individuals can only be allocated leadership responsibility and authority once and only once they have been realigned and observed to subscribe in thought and actions the principles, perspectives, priorities and practices of the organisational dominant logic. Long-term successful organisations will also ensure that such individuals exhibit a people focus within the context of the consistent application of practical and collaborative wisdom.

The provision and ongoing reinforcement of a clearly defined framework of key leadership principles and priorities, encapsulated within a single dominant logic, which are consistent with universal values, through:

- Effective recruitment
- Dedicated training
- On the ground development and experience gathering
- Peer/superior example and sustained, focused mentoring.

encourages and facilitates a cadre of executives who have clarity of perspective, purpose and pride in their organisation. This cadre are mentored, developed, monitored and promoted to senior positions within the organisation, creating a highly experienced, collegiate and cohesive leadership "bench",

> The succession reflects HSBC's emphasis on management continuity and on promoting long term executives from within the (constituent) banks (Croft and Larsen, 2005, p. 1).

This cadre consistently translates and implements a single dominant logic within the organisation with respect to contextual issues which might arise. This clarity of thought and cohesion amongst the leadership cadre pervades the organisation, minimising conflict, enhancing productivity and optimising long-term organisational performance.

The collegiate principle and people-focused, collaborative and collegiate approach to management of the organisation, allied to promotion from within to leadership positions, as a reward for performance, loyalty and self-sacrifice (which we will discuss in greater detail at a later juncture), was historically and continues to be considered an important aspect of the sustained organisational survival and continuing success of HSBC,

> The top 50 people in HSBC have been here 1,000 years. We know each other extraordinarily well, which is what makes teamwork possible (Kellaway, 2006, p. 10).

This leadership dynamic, based upon inculcation and cohesion saves a lot of time and nervous energy on internal issues, particularly during times of crisis and turmoil.

To date, the majority of leaders within HSBC Group have been primarily selected from amongst a cadre of "International Officers", although this term is no longer used. Typically, individuals would be recruited in their early 20s and would spend 3-year terms in different markets and/or divisions in order to gain experience, insight and maturity over a period of 20+ years, before they might be considered for a "minor" CEO/MD position (e.g. Oman, Armenia, Malta, Jordan), always tested and retrained/redeveloped, to develop and hone both technical and leadership skills, attributes, capabilities and perspectives. The best would be appointed to such territories as India, Singapore, Malaysia, Brazil, Argentina, Middle East and Saudi Arabia. The very best would ultimately be appointed to MD positions in Hong Kong, North America and UK or group divisions (with global responsibility for such divisions as personal and commercial banking, on the one hand, or with responsibility for regional markets, South and Central America, North America, Europe, Middle East, Far East), with the best of the very best selected for ultimate promotion to Group CEO and Group Executive Chairman. In this respect I would like to cite from a News Release of HSBC Holdings plc in respect of Sandy Flockhart, recently retired from that organisation.

SANDY FLOCKHART RETIRES AFTER 37 YEARS – REMAINS ON BOARD AS NON-EXECUTIVE DIRECTOR

Sandy Flockhart is retiring as an Executive Director of HSBC Holdings plc, with effect from 30 April 2012, after a distinguished career spanning 37 years … Sandy will also retain his positions as Chairman of HSBC Bank plc, the Group's principal UK and European subsidiary, as Chairman of HSBC Latin America Holdings (UK) Ltd and as a Director of HSBC Middle East Ltd.

Sandy Flockhart joined HSBC in 1974 and began his international career in the Middle East, going on to hold many of the most senior positions in every region in which HSBC operates. Currently Chairman of HSBC's operations in Europe, the Middle East and Africa, Sandy previously served as Chief Executive Officer of the Hongkong and Shanghai Banking Corporation and was President and Group Managing Director with responsibility for Latin America and the Caribbean. In a career that saw service in eight countries, Sandy also served as Chief Executive Officer in Mexico, Managing Director in Saudi Arabia, Chief Executive Officer in Thailand and Chairman of HSBC Malaysia, as well as undertaking further senior roles in the United States of America, Qatar and the United Arab Emirates (HSBC News Release: 5 April 2012).

This is in marked contrast to many financial services organisations who, particularly over the last decade, have increasingly recruited for senior leadership positions from amongst competitors and in some cases from outside the industry, often resulting in conflicts and clashes in dominant logic, with a detrimental ripple effect on stakeholder confidence, leadership credibility and organisational performance.

Over the last 10–15 years there have increasingly been exceptions by HSBC Group to this approach of inculcating a cadre of leaders for gradual promotion to positions of increasing seniority. This change very much reflects the attributes of practical and collaborative wisdom, signifying a willingness to adapt dominant logic on the basis of an acknowledgement of a change in long-term circumstances and context. In order to gain and maintain "legitimacy", in line with the changing global complexion of independence, education and national self-belief HSBC has appointed "local" individuals who do not have the historically substantial and varied leadership experience specifically within HSBC Group (e.g. Latin America, Middle East and China). However, nationals appointed to CEO and MD positions must first clearly exhibit total "assimilation" and dedication to

HSBC business and leadership principles before authority is vested in them (e.g. Emilson Alonso, Head of Latin America and Piraye Antika, CEO HSBC Turkey). Only in extremis, particularly in areas of technical support and excellence will HSBC recruit "outsiders", but invariably with an experienced and inculcated HSBC cadre member as their superior and/or mentor, to ensure decisions are consistent with HSBC principles and perspectives, and that the recruit is effectively assimilated and inculcated in the foundational schema upon which the dominant logic is based,

> *Among the strategic reasons for HSBC's acquisition of Household International were obtaining world-class talent in consumer finance in all its forms, in areas like data mining, point-of-sale technology, marketing and experience dealing with consumer education and consumer activist organisations (Sir Bond, 2004, p. 3).*

It is interesting to note the results of one recent instance where these leadership development principles and perspectives were not followed by HSBC Holdings plc. Following the acquisition of Household International in USA in 2003, a consumer finance business operating primarily within the subprime segment, primarily due to the perceived lack of technical and market expertise in subprime products within the HSBC leadership cadre, management and strategic/operational decision making was left primarily in the hands of the existing Household leadership. However, following the collapse of Household Mortgage Corporation during the onset of the prevailing global financial and economic crisis and a subsequent increase in its reserves for bad loans in 2007 to $10.56 billion, HSBC Group sent in a cadre of assimilated and inculcated executives with extensive global experience of leading HSBC businesses to lead the organisation, with the Group CEO and Finance Director taking personal responsibility for policy decisions.

On the basis of the author's research into HSBC and Goldman Sachs & Co, where each organisation did find it necessary to go outside to fill a position, usually where the organisation was entering a new business sector or lacked specific technical/support skills, it was considered critical that the successful candidate should be seen to be adapting to the organisational culture. If they did not then their career prospects were bleak and short-lived,

> *When, as we rarely did, we decided to go outside the firm for talent ... we would identify the very best people, get to know them well, and bring them over individually. These new individuals would learn the Goldman Sachs culture and either blend into the firm or they would not make it at Goldman Sachs (Ellis, 2008, p.179).*

The process of adaptation and acculturation with respect to external hires, particularly in key and/or senior positions is resource and energy intensive, both on the part of the hired and, importantly, on the part of other employees. It is therefore one of the reasons why these two long-term successful organisations prefer to train, mentor and promote from within. A wrong hire taken on in a hurry due to market developments can lead to significant organisational disruption and resistance, resulting in a dramatic impact on productivity and bottom line performance. Existing employees, who feel threatened by a potentially, or perceived to be, alien culture, principles, perspectives and practices may resist by restricting communication, tacit knowledge and support, the lifeblood of a successful organisation in the twenty-first century,

It stood to reason that those organisations with the least amount of friction in the flow of information would find the greatest success. Friction resulted from cultures in which employees were not used to a contiguous dialogue and in which their efforts to communicate among themselves were neither encouraged nor rewarded. This facet of the firm's culture ... allowed it to move away from the pack in the early part of the 1990s (Endlich, 2007(a), p. 278).

This is particularly detrimental to an organisation whose success is based upon a team-based, collegiate approach and the free flow of knowledge and experienced insight. As a banking partner of Goldman Sachs & Co says,

When you are growing too rapidly to develop all your own people, and start hiring people laterally, you will make mistakes ... Those people can become the organisation's enemy within ... people other people don't want to help, do want to avoid, will even risk hurting the firm just to penalise the bad guy ... The odds go up again when they come as strong individuals to a culture that depends upon teamwork and interchangeability to the group ... to we, not me (Ellis, 2008, p. 398).

I have personally experienced the dramatic impact on a cohesive, motivated and operationally highly productive management cadre of the recruitment of individuals primarily on the basis of technical excellence, without the concomitant focus on leadership in an open-minded, collegiate and collaborative manner. The requirement for rapid issue resolution in such a scenario is much akin to preventing the destructive power of a runaway train.

The key points here are an acknowledgement and understanding, during the cognitive mental process, by the organisational leadership cadre, of the benefits of internal versus external hire to key positions and the potentially substantial negative impact on the ability of the single dominant logic to support effective operational leadership and optimal long-term performance. In this respect, most important is an understanding that the organisation is a living organism made up of many interdependent parts, composed of individuals whose productivity ultimately depends upon how they feel about the organisation. Therefore, hiring does not merely impact on the psyche of an isolated unit, department or division but larger swathes, if not the whole organisation. Senior executives must therefore consider the psychological and physiological aspects of leadership as a priority and viewing the management of the organisation in a holistic manner if the optimal operational management of the organisation is to be achieved.

In a similar vein, the loss of experienced, assimilated employees from the organisational "bench" can be very disruptive, not only in the loss of tacit knowledge but breaking the delicate network of trust and communication which makes an effective team spirit, which in turn leads to enhanced long-term organisational performance,

No matter how skilled the individual performers, an all star team is never as strong as an excellent experienced team ... Losses of strong people are very disruptive ... partly in the interrupted relationships with clients, but even more seriously in the internal loss of closeness, trust and superb teamwork and coordination that characterise the best performing firms (Ellis, 2008, p. 546).

THE BENEFITS OF A COLLEGIATE LEADERSHIP CADRE DURING THE ACQUISITION AND INTEGRATION PROCESS

In order to benefit over the long term from its inculcation and collaborative, collegiate philosophy in its ongoing acquisition process, HSBC has developed a strong "bench" of experienced and inculcated senior executives, ready to support acquisitions or crises (e.g. Household Mortgage Corporation, acquisitions in Brazil and Argentina) who are importantly guaranteed the support of all of their peers, without question. This is due to the fact that they are like-minded, trained, inculcated and assimilated in a single dominant logic. This cohesion is reinforced by the fact that they have known, supported and depended upon each other on their way up the experience and leadership ladder. This is an embedded core competence which those who assess acquisition opportunities on the basis of capital adequacy and other accounting ratios fail to recognise, with increasingly negative and predictable consequences,

> *Globalisation is no longer a popular word among bankers. Too many have lost money in ill-conceived ventures in remote parts of the globe. Japanese, American and British banks that once claimed the world as their market have now limped home to tend battered balance sheets. Yet globalisation has lost none of its allure for HSBC Holdings (Economist, 1992, p. 12).*

It became evident whilst interviewing one of the senior executives responsible for assessing acquisition opportunities that even for an organisation with a substantial pool of leadership experience and expertise, the existence of sufficient senior management and technical staffing to ensure effective control and management was a high priority in the ultimate desirability and decision to make an acquisition. Even where HSBC Group has the capital to make an acquisition, if they consider that they do not have the required "spare" Group leadership resources to embed technical standards and dominant logic within the requisite timescales (varies, but around 2–4 years), the acquisition is effectively stalled and the subject of further detailed consideration and analysis with respect to justification, operational implementation and the practical reality of achieving primary objectives.

An acquisition might often require the appointment of Group "bench" executives to the CEO/COO/CFO and Heads of Treasury/Risk/ Corporate and/or the secondment of appropriate "technical" middle ranking executives for a sustained period, this in order to achieve the requisite selective control and the embedding of core Group dominant logic. HSBC would not be in a hurry to replace these "Group" staff with local executives until they were confident of appropriate levels of inculcation in respect of management principles and business standards. In extremis, HSBC has sent in up to 200–300 technical and leadership staff into an acquired organisation for short to medium-term periods (1–5 years), assessing the benefits of such a transfer of management/leadership principles and technical competency against the costs of their absence from other businesses within the Group. This emphasises the existence of a holistic approach by HSBC, focusing the embedded knowledge and expertise where it will have greatest positive impact on Group performance over the long term.

Ultimately it is accepted that optimal performance will be achieved from each business unit through delegation of responsibility and authority to management on the ground (with the assured support and availability of Group technical resources and expertise), confident in the fact that, once effectively inculcated, they will not deviate from the established framework of values, principles, priorities and standards which comprise the organisation's dominant logic. It is appropriate to reiterate the quote from Sir John Bond,

> *Ultimately, success in business depends on confidence ... confidence is about ... how well your company performs, how responsibly you behave, and how well-trained your colleagues are around the world. So that you can rely on them to look after your customers when you are asleep (Sir Bond, 2001, p. 4).*

THE IMPORTANCE OF THE CONSIDERATION OF DOMINANT LOGIC WHEN CONSIDERING MERGERS

Within the same context of maintaining the organisational dominant logic and the cohesion of the leadership cadre, Goldman Sachs & Co rarely acquired or merged with another organisation and for long would not become involved in its M&A business with hostile takeovers. Both HSBC and Goldman Sachs & Co recognised, understood and prioritised the people-centred complexities of M&A compared with organic growth, seeing them in a broader and holistic context in relation to technical, structural, systems and financial considerations. As a senior executive in Goldman Sachs & Co stated,

> *From my M&A experience, I knew that mergers are always hard and often don't work out. It's not that they actually fail financially, but they underperform and disappoint relative to expectations because the organisational cultures don't fit together. Conflicts and tensions are so easy to have and cultures are so hard to integrate (Ellis, 2008, p. 260).*

This perspective is reinforced when it is understood that Sandy Weill, the then Chief Executive of Travelers Group (Later CEO of CitiGroup following its merger with Travelers), prior to the merger with investment bank Salomon Inc, in late 1997 approached Jon S. Corzine, the then Chief Executive of Goldman Sachs proposing a buyout, to create what Weill termed a "match made in heaven". Corzine replied that Goldman Sachs was doing just fine on its own (Spiro and Reed, 1997). This focus more on enhancing the product range to attract a wider range of market segments rather than an understanding of the ultimate market impact of a compatible and consistent dominant logic throughout the organisation may explain the dramatic differences in performance and financial health of each institution during the recent financial crisis, with the part nationalisation of CitiGroup, whilst Goldman Sachs & Co, with its performance stunted and credibility tarnished, continues to maintain the confidence of its clients,

> *Many investors concluded that Goldman Sachs retains underlying strength, despite serious questions about whether it can be as profitable as it once was. Goldman, which transformed itself into a bank holding company ... can no longer take the risks it once did and faces far greater regulatory oversight (White, 2008, p. B4).*

Similarly, Henry "Hank" Paulson (latterly United States Secretary of the Treasury until January 2009), when running Goldman Sachs & Co, seriously considered a merger with JPMorgan, but pulled out at the last moment, fearful that the combination would negatively impact the close-knit culture of Goldman Sachs & Co, (Economist, 2008). This, like the other examples reinforces the perceived value amongst leaders within long-term, optimal performing business organisations of maintaining, indeed reinforcing, the "purity" and resilience of a single organisational dominant logic. Also an appreciation of the "soft" people dependent factors which dramatically influence long-term performance and are fundamental to the operational application of practical and collaborative wisdom.

Individual Self-Sacrifice for the Benefit of the Organisational Community

> The effective and consistent application of a single dominant logic, based on universal values and geared to the benefit of the organisation, as a branch of society, requires a sense of sacrifice and vocation on the part of the leadership cadre. The benefits of a sense of vocation are a feeling of making a valuable contribution to the development of communities and societies, rather than spending a life with a narrow self and significant others focus. This perspective is fundamental to the application of practical and collaborative wisdom. The downside is a potentially dysfunctional personal life. Going forward, changes in personal perspectives and priorities may limit the number of individuals willing to make such sacrifices for the greater good.

In a similar way to the terms assimilation and inculcation, the terms self-sacrifice and vocation have fallen out of favour in the lexicon of organisational management, sometime during the latter half of the twentieth century. Such terms are more reminiscent of the priesthood or military of yesteryear than with working in a business of the twenty-first century. However, many of the most long-term successful business organisations were founded on such a philosophy and culture of self-sacrifice and a sense of vocation,

> *In those days especially, there were many similarities between working for the bank and being in the army. In return for looking after its expatriate workers the Hong Kong Bank demanded their total loyalty and exercised large control over their lives. Officers lived in bachelor quarters ... marriage to a non-European was frowned upon and could end the chances of promotion ... In the matter of transfers, officers went where they were told without question (Redding, 1983, p. 625).*

In contrast to the perceived core characteristics of senior executives within global financial services and other business organisations during the ongoing financial and economic crisis as greedy, self-serving and egotistical, to rise to the senior ranks within either HSBC or Goldman Sachs & Co continues to require an abrogation of the cult of the self. You are expected, indeed required, to sacrifice your own life (in some cases both figuratively and metaphorically) and those close to you for the greater good and long-term survival of the organisational community. Self-sacrifice was, from the foundation of HSBC, until the present day, a requirement for advancement amongst the expatriate cadre from amongst whom senior leadership positions were filled. Salaries were generally set on the assumption of a bachelor life, based upon the principles of prudence, cost-efficiency and minimal distraction from the primary objective, the benefit of the organisational community. Employment in HSBC was and indeed continues to be for those who wish to advance, a vocation rather than a career. How many readers would today wince and sit with trepidation and surprise if such expectations were openly expressed by an interview board today?

However, one of the constant themes in my research with leaders within long-term successful organisations is acceptance of the requirement to sacrifice their personal well-being and that of their nearest and dearest over the term of their 30+ year career for the survival, growth and ongoing performance of the organisational community. There is within such individuals, due to such sacrifice, a sense of achievement, of being part of a greater good, through a broad, holistic focus on the organisation, indeed on the wider society, rather than a primary focus on personal benefit and that of a small group of significant others,

> *I have spent the whole of my career with one company ... that had a deeply imbued and long standing belief that in order to fulfil our duties to society, we had to be a force for good in the wider community ... we recognise that no company can succeed in a failed world. So every successful company ... has a responsibility to contribute to the development of the community. To give something back (Sir Bond, 2005, p. 2).*

Rather than individuals regarding their work as personally defining, as reflecting their talents, capabilities and character, in some organisations individuals regard their role and membership as more than personally defining, it defines the meaning of their very life, indeed it is their life,

> *At Morgan Stanley ... people saw their work as personally defining ... it was what they could do and did do ... but at Goldman Sachs, it was much more, it was life (Ellis, 2008, p. 397).*

In this respect we do not refer to individuals who require the badge of membership of a successful and renowned organisation to bolster their ego and self-esteem. We rather refer to those who exhibit talent pertinent to and have interests outside the organisation, but who find personal fulfilment in a total dedication to the well-being and development of the organisation. On the basis of my practitioner experience, allied to my scholarly research, few substantial business organisations possess a dominant logic of values, principles, perspectives and priorities which will attract and retain individuals who have a propensity to make a vocation out of a job.

Cynics and sceptics would counter that in reality this sacrifice is in most cases limited in extent and time, until you have convinced the organisation that you have "made your bones" and you are committed to the benefit of the organisation, at which time you then convert to maximum individual remuneration and career benefit. These individuals might work late for a decade, not attend their kid's ballet and rugby classes, and miss out on social gatherings. However, those individuals who regard their role as a vocation put their children in boarding school from the age of seven, do not see their wives for months, have no permanent home, live a transient life, are unavailable for the acute sickness or indeed death of loved ones, are dedicated to the benefit of, show unswerving allegiance to the organisation over all other pressing matters. Put bluntly, if you were to ask such an individual to justify such a perspective they might respond that looking objectively it is wholly logical that the greater good of the organisation and its many stakeholders, plus the significant contribution to social development and economic growth, must be more important and take precedence over the well-being of an individual and a family unit. This perspective of self-sacrifice and unswerving dedication to the organisation and the greater good is encapsulated in a quote by a senior executive in Goldman Sachs & Co, who bluntly states,

> To function around here ... you really have to work hard and give up a lot of your outside activities, even frankly, your family life to some extent. To do that you have to be ambitious and hard driving. Everybody works hard around here. If they don't, they have to leave (Ellis, 2008, p. 207).

The point which is important is that the executive feels comfortable to make this statement because it is the accepted culture of the organisation, whereas in other organisations it may be the reality but it is not the accepted culture, such that it is openly expressed without some embarrassment.

I recall speaking to the wife of a senior executive of a global bank who said that her life was exciting and personally highly rewarding, except for the constant guilt. The guilt of not being available to tend ailing relatives; of entertaining board members instead of tending to a teenage son who was recovering from and acute illness and was flying back to his boarding school alone; of wondering how her other children were coping in a variety of boarding schools 4,000 miles away. The motivation to endure such hardship on the part of self and others close to you can only be based upon a sense of vocation and self-sacrifice, for a greater "community" good, which is based upon an intense belief in and commitment to a dominant logic founded on universally acknowledged and understood universal values. This is reflected in the fundamental values and principles considered during the cognitive mental process of the "phronimos".

In many respects it is not a sacrifice, this due to a sense of achievement, of being part of and contributing to the benefit of a greater whole than the self and the lives of an individual family. This is a contentious point. From personal experience, the sense of being part of and making a contribution to the success of a global organisation, whilst also considering that you are contributing to the economic and social development of states, is indeed heady. However, only a strong sense of vocation can sustain you in the face of the prospects of a potentially dysfunctional personal life and the reality that such dedication and sacrifice facilitates but does not guarantee a successful career. Some readers may by now be thinking that the author has entered never-never land with his views on business executives willing to sacrifice themselves and their nearest and dearest for the benefit of the organisational community. In some sense these thoughts are a reflection of the prevailing embedded ideology of the importance of immediate and clearly evident individual material gain and gratification; a logic which is now regarded by many as self-evident, as if there is no tangible alternative.

In reality, in the business organisation of the twenty-first century self-sacrifice comes at a significant price to the organisation, insofar as there is general acceptance that one is commensurately materially recompensed for one's total devotion and dedication, the expending of one's talent and experience exclusively for one organisation during one's career. Whilst the remuneration of executives within Goldman Sachs & Co is considered by many during recent years as excessive in both absolute and relative terms, beyond even what one might expect for the self-sacrifice which we are discussing (Lloyd Blankfein, whilst CEO of Goldman Sachs Group in 2007, earned a total compensation of

$53,965,418, which included a base salary of $600,000 and a cash bonus of $26,985,474, plus stocks granted of $15,542,756 and options granted of $10,453,031). In contrast, executive directors at HSBC, managing a global operation of 300,000 staff and in excess of 100 million customers earned in 2011 the following:

Table 4.2   A Balance between Self-Sacrifice and Material Benefit

Name	Remuneration
Douglas Flint Executive Group Chairman of Board	Salary £845,000 Bonus £1,805,000
Stuart Gulliver Group Chief Executive	Salary £800,000 Bonus £2,934,000
Alexander Flockhart Chairman, Europe, Middle East, Africa, Latin America, Commercial Banking and Chairman HSBC Bank plc	Salary £820,000 Bonus £1,385,000

Source: HSBC Holdings plc website – Company Profile – Officers; accessed 27 January 2012.

Perhaps, in reality, the point is less well made on the basis of a focus on the compensation of members of the Executive Committee. It rather revolves around the large number of members of the operational leadership cadre willing to sacrifice much without the guarantees of lumps of money arriving in the foreseeable future, or ever. Those who recognise that they are not going to hit the heights, yet see the personal value of their efforts within the context of contributing to the benefit of a greater community of stakeholders. Whilst many might find this statement incredulous, with considerable discomfort, responding in terms corresponding with a lack of realism and pragmatism, others might accept its underlying practical logic in terms of long-term personal satisfaction and organisational survival and optimal productivity.

Practical and collaborative wisdom lies at the heart of this individual allegiance and dedication to the organisational community. The ability to persuade talented individuals to accept long-term self-sacrifice and an unyielding dedication of effort for the organisation is based upon the operation of an often unwritten, yet clearly communicated covenant (Pava, 2001). In this respect the Goldman Sachs & Co culture looks to people, their knowledge, their intellect, their drive and determination to succeed, for themselves and their community, as the primary driver and skill required for sustained success. In exchange for dedication and motivated, hard work in the long term interests of the organisation, people are rewarded on a meritocratic and equitable basis. Remuneration packages will be structured to ensure that there are no unnecessary distractions from the primary focus (e.g. comprehensive health cover for the family, private education allowance, status accommodation, membership of social and sports facilities for self and family).

This does not mean that people are paid equally, but everyone recognises the justification for any differentiation in the interests of the overall, long-term benefit of the organisation. Goldman Sachs & Co is a modern "tribe", with roles and responsibilities to ensure the ongoing development and well-being of the individual, towards the long-term survival and flourishing of the community. Individuals have specific roles and responsibilities in the attainment of the common vision. There are chiefs who are trusted as wise, experienced, looking to the interests of the community. There are clerks who also have a defined and acknowledged role, value, and satisfaction in contributing to the attainment of that common vision.

If you are in the tribe and have exhibited your unswerving loyalty, you are looked after as a member, coached, sponsored and protected. However, once you are out you are very much an outsider, like everyone else not in the in-group, and quickly forgotten. Once you express doubts and/or disloyalty to the interests of the community or you are considered to have broken the covenant of "*loyalty up, loyalty down*" (Ellis, 2008), you are stigmatised and effectively expelled from the community. This perspective applies, no matter the senior executive position and contribution which you had previously made to that community over an extended period. The attitude towards those who abandon Goldman Sachs & Co in its hour of need, who are seen to prioritise individual over "tribal" benefit (of which there have been a few during its history) is neatly expressed thus,

> *As one partner listed the names of those who had left, he was interrupted by an angry colleague,* "*Enough talk about those guys; those guys are dead*" *(Endlich, 2007a, p. 337).*

In many respects Goldman Sachs may be described more like a single organism than a community of individuals, with every part of the organism playing its evolved part. Apart from the two or three top executives, all other individuals are anonymous to the outside world, parts of a body, operating unseen, sacrificing themselves and their families to the common good. Asked what would derail the firm's strategy Robert Rubin (spent 26 years with Goldman Sachs & Co and was co-senior partner with Stephen Friedman from 1990–1992; subsequently United States Treasury Secretary and Director, Senior Counsel and Chairman of Citigroup) replied,

> *Ego, arrogance, a sense of importance. If you allow them to develop that's when you fall off the track (Ellis, 2008, p. 200).*

The bywords of Goldman Sachs & Co are anonymity, modesty, sacrifice, long-term profit and work, more work and even more work. Goldman Sachs & Co believed in people working very hard, constantly accepting "stretch goals" (Kerr, 2004). The logic was that the harder you worked and the more learning, experience and knowledge you attained would lead to a higher level of individual and organisational performance and better prospects for promotion.

Perhaps the evolving social perspectives and priorities within the developed regions of the world will limit the number of individuals willing to make such a level of personal commitment and go on such risky long-term career and personal life adventures,

> *If you are looking for challenge, adventure, responsibility, authority, variety, then IM (international management cadre) is for you. Perhaps this is not so attractive now since people can travel in their gap year to exotic areas and then come home after a couple of months (Interviewee A).*

"HSBC has a framework of technical, management standards and principles which are applied universally. Such practices are not considered rooted in any single national culture and to that extent are considered understandable and agreeable within any local cultural context. These principles are largely non-negotiable but in other respects HSBC is willing to adapt to comply with local customs and practices" (Interviewee D)

Operational Leadership
Principles & Perspectives

Principles & Practices – Make the Link

1. Clarity
2. Consistency
3. Confidence
4. Cohesion

The Application of Universal Values

1. Acknowledge & understand the primacy of universal values as the foundation of effective leadership.
2. Optimise cohesion, allegiance, motivation & productivity through satisfying universal individual motivations.
3. Translate universal values into operational perspectives, priorities and practices.
4. Reject the application of "home" or "host" principles & perspectives in favour of global leadership attributes.

The Consistent Application of a Single Dominant Logic

1. Ensure that prevailing dominant logic is founded on universal values.
2. Single dominant logic acts as both an anchor and compass, ensuring consistency and clarity of leadership direction.
3. Single dominant logic creates an environment of no sudden shocks amongst stakeholders, engendering confidence and comfort.
4. Dominant logic schema include a capability for dynamic evolution and contextual application.
5. Dominant logic translates into operational perspectives, priorities and practices with a focus on "soft" qualitative attributes.
6. Ensure dominant logic pervades all key operational evaluations, decisions and strategies, particularly in relation to leadership development.

A Sense of Self-Sacrifice & Vocation within the Leadership Cadre

1. Primary focus on benefit of wider stakeholder community.
2. Greater sense of personal achievement and contribution.
3. Individuals not only have a role but acknowledged and defined value and and contribution to the organisation.
4. Membership of "tribe" who look after their own.
5. Future prospects of maintaining a sense of self-sacrifice within leadership cadre?

Development & Maintenance of an Inculcated Leadership Cadre

1. Maintenance of Dominant Logic through effective inculcation of leadership cadre.
2. Minimal external recruitment, promotion from within.
3. Development of cohesive, collegiate leadership cadre.
4. Priority consideration of conflict in dominant logic in acquisition assessment.

Figure 4.1   The Route to Effective Operational Leadership

However, perhaps the economic and financial crisis of the first decade of the twenty-first century will realign such developing social perspectives and priorities amongst sectors of this working population, to expect a less comfortable and predictable lifestyle in order to attain life aspirations. More likely, those organisation which seek to support the consistent operational implementation of their dominant logic through a leadership cadre of individuals willing to sacrifice their private lives for a greater good may become increasingly dependent upon talented recruits from the developing regions, who retain a sense of contribution to the broader "tribe" and community. This is a prime example of an area critical to sustained optimal long-term performance which requires practical and collaborative wisdom in order to make appropriate amendments to the application of the dominant logic, even to the dominant logic itself, in the face of factors in the environment of which the organisation is a part and on which it is dependent and over which the dominant coalition has no control.

This chapter has been a lengthy one, containing many important themes and perspectives in illustrating many of the key principles, perspectives, processes and practices in the application of practical and collaborative wisdom within the context of operational leadership. Therefore, for the purposes of clarity of understanding I have encompassed the crux of what is contained in Chapter 4 within the Figure 4.1.

Exercises

1. Compile what you consider to be a comprehensive list which represents the core principles, perspectives and priorities of two organisations in which you are or have been personally involved as an employee, student or active participant.
2. Provide reasons if you feel strongly that there are fundamental flaws in founding operational business leadership on a set of universal values and/or a single organisational dominant logic.
3. Put forward the names of two multinational and/or "global" organisations which you consider failed in their espoused objectives due to the absence of a dominant logic based upon universal values. Explain why you consider this to be the case.
4. Put forward the names of three multinational and/or "global" organisations which you consider apply a dominant logic which ensures the consistent success of acquisitions. Provide five principles, perspectives or priorities which you consider have been fundamental to this success.
5. Put forward the names of two organisations, business or otherwise, whom you would be willing to make substantial self-sacrifice in your personal life. Explain the reasons why you would be willing to make such a sacrifice.
6. Put forward two individuals from your personal experience whom you consider made substantial sacrifices and/or their significant others for the long-term benefit of a business organisation or other community. Provide examples of the manner by which they made such sacrifices and put forward reasons why they considered it appropriate.

5 *Operational Leadership Imperatives*

Previous chapters have primarily focused upon those values and principles underpinning practical and collaborative wisdom which form the foundation for effective operational leadership. This and subsequent chapters will take the next steps in the journey to translate these "wise" principles into operationally recognisable and relevant leadership imperatives which directly influence the resolution of issues faced by operational leaders on a day to day basis. It will illustrate those required perspectives, attributes, capabilities and practices which will create an effective operational environment and determine the nature of day to day decisions and the manner of issue resolution.

A prerequisite for effective operational leadership is to recognise that your primary role is one of people leadership, rather than as a manager of a technical area or function. On the basis of my experience to date it is my conclusion that many individuals in leadership positions are loathe to and incapable of taking on that mantle. This is primarily due to the fact that they recognise that it requires a deeper more complex and complicated, less scientific, less determinate, more fluid, adaptable, insightful, judgmental approach to each task and their functional role within the organisation. A more holistic appreciation of the operation of the organisation and, most worryingly, a requirement to develop and consistently apply expert people management skills, which few possess or indeed have been encouraged to develop.

This latter capability in particular requires a depth and breadth of insight, judgement and wisdom which many individuals in leadership positions actively avoid (due to perceptions of the added complexity which this brings to their role and responsibility), or of which they are generally unaware and for which they are therefore unprepared. This is due primarily to the prevailing perspectives, priorities and objectives of the dominant coalition, which are translated into an organisational culture and management development programmes which encourage and celebrate technical expertise and continues to view operational people leadership skills as a nice to have in the process of optimal organisational performance.

The present and subsequent chapters seek to address this imbalance by highlighting those operational leadership perspectives, attributes, capabilities and practices which reorientate and enhance the breadth and depth of insight, judgement and wisdom of those individuals in operational leadership roles. In this chapter we assume that you have attained the levels of technical expertise required to achieve the "widgets" targets of your management role, be it in respect of sales, product development, production, balance sheet management, systems development, procedures, processes or other operational outputs. We will therefore seek to address those operational leadership foundation stones which will begin to create perspectives and priorities which will result in enhanced insight and judgement and ultimately a leadership capability for practical, but more particularly, collaborative wisdom. This entails an acknowledgement and understanding of the importance of the people dynamic in the achievement of optimal performance. It entails a collegiate, collaborative and consultative leadership approach to decision-making and issue resolution, allied to a "quiet" approach to leadership, in the form of decisiveness supported by a persuasive, listening, open-minded perspective.

Raise Your Gaze from the Desk

The first step in the operational implementation of the foundation of values, principles and perspectives previously cited is to be prepared to fundamentally change your embedded leadership perspectives and priorities, rather than merely receive a tool or process which you can "plug and play" to modify their application and output on the surface. Also to look beyond your pressing technical role and responsibilities in which you are by now expert. To view your leadership role as fundamentally involved in directing, in a collegiate manner with other members of the leadership cadre, the organic body of individuals which make up the organisation, towards achieving the communal vision. This is not BS. It first requires a change in perspectives and priorities which will ultimately simplify rather than complicate your leadership role, by creating both an anchor and compass for leadership issue evaluation and decision making.

As I have mentioned in earlier parts of the book, the primary objective of this book is not to provide a programme, a system, a toolbox to improve operational leadership capabilities, in the form of TQM, balanced scorecard, Six Sigma and other "plug and play" solutions and supports which give the impression of fundamental performance enhancement. The objective is rather to change the perspectives and mindset of the operational leader, to provide a foundation of values, principles and priorities and to facilitate the development of appropriate attributes and capabilities for sustained, effective leadership. This will allow the operational leader to respond appropriately and effectively to any issue which arises on a day to day, minute by minute basis. The above and many other "plug and play" management solutions are in many respects short-term stop gap solutions in the absence of appropriate embedded organisational values, principles, perspectives and priorities which require a longer term development and sustained organisational commitment. Previous chapters have focused primarily on the required foundation of values and principles, which, whilst important, do not really hit the spot for the operational leader, who is looking for points which he can directly relate and apply to daily issues and tasks. This and following chapters are therefore intended to bring the values and principles to the level of the workplace, in the form of operational leadership perspectives, priorities and practices to develop and enhance appropriate leadership aptitudes, attributes and capabilities.

My wife always used to say to me (she has given up now) that in order to get on you have to raise your gaze from the desk, to pick up what is happening around you, to appreciate the macro action, pick up the vibes, the bigger organisational picture, if you will. This is an important but perhaps not immediately clear point so let me seek to provide greater clarity by providing a personal example. In my own case I was for many years a leader with a technical perspective. I sought to achieve my personal and departmental/divisional objectives and enhance my career prospects through a focus upon the "mechanical", technical aspects of my roles and responsibilities, for instance, in respect of new product development, advertising, remote banking (e.g. call centre, internet, mobile phone, remote teller banking), market research, CRM, sales and service quality management, product pricing, credit scoring, risk management, compliance, Islamic and Expatriate banking. Whilst my wife's primary focus in making these often acidic remarks was my elevation in the organisational hierarchy, this perspective applies equally in respect of the attainment of a state of wise and effective operational leadership. Reading this book would be largely wasted if the reader did not gain an understanding that the attainment of expertise in a technical area is merely the achievement of the table stakes in their role as an organisational leader. It is therefore necessary that heads of units, sections, departments and divisions raise their gaze from the desk or the confines of their office and technical responsibilities, to consider their leadership role and responsibilities within a broader context, taking, as I have previously mentioned, an holistic mindset which clarifies, focuses, defines and determines their role, context and priorities as operational leaders within a business organisation. The reality of their situation is that they are leading an organisation made up of motivated, enthusiastic, energised (or not) individuals who have come together to attain both individual and organisational objectives, who ultimately will be the primary factor in determining the survival and performance of the organisation. This occurs within a greater socio-economic context of which the organisation is but a dependent, minor but organic part.

The truth is that "technical" roles and responsibilities are optimally achieved through taking a primary focus and placing a priority on the holistic and people perspective. Ultimately you are dependent upon other functions, fundamentally the responses of others to optimise your own performance. Therefore an organisation wide insight and expertise in people direction, persuasion, influencing and nurturing through and interest in and understanding of people motivation and expectations is of equal if not more value to you and the organisation than expertise in technical fields and functions. If you are in a leadership position but lack the necessary people leadership focus, attributes and capabilities, then you will not/cannot optimise your contribution to the organisation's long-term performance. Your operational focus, direction and momentum will be continuously distracted by unresolved people issues which will frequently impact on your career prospects on the basis of "silent whispers", this as a result of a limited, amateur understanding and approach to people management.

This new, enhanced, collaborative leadership mindset is achieved through a collegiate and coordinated rather than isolated functional approach to organisational leadership. It can only be achieved through the understanding and translation, for the purposes of operational application, of universal values and principles, which create and maintain a vibrant and energetic organisational "organic" community, rather than merely a well-oiled machine. The sections within this and subsequent chapters will therefore pinpoint the translation and interpretation of the recommended values, principles which are fundamental to the application of practical and collaborative wisdom into operational leadership imperatives, in the form of perspectives, attributes, capabilities and practices. This is necessary if the individual leader and the leadership cadre are to make an optimal contribution to the effective operational management and long-term performance of the organisation.

How Not to Manage a Change in an Organisation's Dominant Logic

A radical change in dominant logic has the potential to radically impact on stakeholder perspectives and relationships. The result is frequently confusion and conflict, resulting in operational crisis, ensuring that the desired organisational objectives resulting from the change in dominant logic fail to materialise. A focus on the "numbers" in these circumstances must, at the very least, be balanced by a focus on and considerations of the "soft" implications.

As a junior and middle-ranking leader in a number of organisations I was always fascinated to gain insights into the logic and motivations behind the policy and strategic decisions taken by executive leaders and board members in respect of such issues as mergers, acquisitions, market expansion and conversions in corporate status. I had the good fortune to be employed by two mutual financial services organisations, where it occurred to me that there appeared to be a more effective harmony and balance between the interests of key stakeholder groups, in the form of customers, staff, management and board members (trustees) than in a number of public limited companies within which I have been employed.

The perceived problem within mutual financial services organisations was that the profit margin was not in the same league as those financial institutions run as public limited companies. There were also concerns regarding liquidity, capital adequacy and governance. As social ideologies changed mutual organisations were increasingly regarded as institutions reminiscent of an earlier age and inappropriate in the age of the individual who is educated and capable of looking after him/herself, without the aid of mutual or communal institutions. The result was pressure and influence from external stakeholders, such as governments and regulatory bodies, who were having enough problems regulating financial institutions under the plc legal framework, without having another significantly different legal framework with which to wrestle.

On the basis of my own experience in these institutions a decision to de-mutualise had a dramatic effect on the prevailing values, principles, perspectives and priorities within the senior leadership cadre of such institutions. On the one hand, existing leadership might be replaced by executives from financial institutions which were already limited companies, with share and bondholders, board members, who then sought to apply a dominant logic template based upon the principles, perspectives and priorities of the "home" organisation with whom they had previously been employed for the last 10, 20 or 30 years. The result was confusion, trepidation and fear, amongst the existing stakeholder groups, primarily in the form of customers and staff, creating conflict, a collapse in cohesion, allegiance, motivation and productivity. This led to:

- The voluntary or involuntary exit of experienced leaders.
- The exit of other long-term employees with valued tacit knowledge.
- The exit of customers who preferred the relationship-based service embedded in the mutual business proposition.
- The voluntary or involuntary exit of the leaders initially brought in to embed more market than community-related principles, perspectives and priorities, Who failed to anticipate the nature and level of stakeholder resistance and its impact on business policy, objectives and performance.

Once the dominant coalition had taken the decision to go the plc route the only option considered appropriate to achieve the required rapid transformation to enhanced profit dynamics was to destroy the existing dominant logic, with the concomitant danger of the disintegration of the unique bond of trust and community between staff, customers and the organisation, which had been the underlying key survival/success factor and source of "profit" generation for such institutions. The result was that the numbers never came up to expectations because there was little appreciation or understanding or indeed interest in the "soft" impact on the changing relationship between and attitudes of key stakeholder groups and the resultant impact on productivity, sales, revenue and profitability.

On the other hand, where all or some of the existing dominant coalition were retained, this was on the basis that these executives appeared willing to adapt their perspectives, priorities, perhaps also principles and values, in the interests of the maximum profit/cost efficiency doctrine. In many respects they also saw the opportunity to make dramatic (positive) changes in personal status and remuneration, from the CEO, COO, CFO, CIO, CMO positions of a mutual to a similar position within a "universal banking" or "bancassurance" financial services plc. Even if they only lasted 1, 3 or 5 years and as long as the result was not outright catastrophe they would likely receive a tasty redundancy package and retire early, acting in a consultancy capacity for the organisation for a few years, whilst improving their golf handicap.

I make these points and comments not out of some malevolence or taking a political or philosophical stance but to highlight a key theme in this book for effective operational leadership. This is that where you as a leader are taking or implementing a strategic or policy decision which will have a dramatic and long-term impact on the existing dominant logic of the organisation, do not take a perspective and focus on priorities which are short sighted (e.g. cost/income ratios, enhanced profitability, share price, dividends, enhanced salaries and bonuses) and fail to take into account the "soft" responses of key stakeholder groups if you are to have any chance of achieving the medium to long-term objectives of your strategic or policy initiative. Many executives will counter that this was indeed a consideration. However, in reality, it was a consideration within the context of the glory and other material benefits of a quick hike in profits and other tangible measures of success which would accrue from "sweating" the assets of the mutual organisation, including the "captive" customer base.

The soft-hearted, hard-headed, pragmatic approach required to apply practical and collaborative wisdom requires a holistic and long-term perspective, to manage the evolution of the dominant logic and gradually change the perspectives of key stakeholder groups. However, this will not occur if the underlying values and principles of the initiative are inconsistent with universal values. The business attractiveness of de-mutualisation lay primarily in the potential which existed for substantial cross-sales to a predominantly loyal, captive and unsophisticated customer base and the opportunity for substantial cost efficiencies. This without any clear perceptions of the responses and reaction of customers and staff in respect of loyalty, allegiance and motivation to the policies undertaken to achieve these objectives. This short-term, "cash cow" approach is banal, since the result is to diminish levels of allegiance and dedication amongst key stakeholder groups, which had been your organisation's competitive advantage, to the levels of competitor institutions whose success was based upon alternative areas of core competence and competitive advantage.

It is appropriate to point out that the outcome (indeed one must presume the primary objective of the dominant coalition) of the above two de-mutualisations in which I was involved was a merger with another financial institution which was already a public limited company, to create a larger financial institution, thereby creating a larger market share and lower cost base, larger profits, remuneration packages and peer group status for the dominant coalitions. Sad to relate, both enlarged financial institutions collapsed in the present financial crisis and have been largely or totally nationalised. Not, however, before their long-term relationship with key stakeholder groups, which had constituted their USP, had been irreparably damaged.

Regrettably the policies developed to ensure a rapid privatisation are similar to those which brought them to collapse. A focus on the numbers and the rapid implementation of a dramatic change in dominant logic, hard-headed, "pragmatic" leadership, but lacking insight, judgement and wisdom in respect of the organisation as an organism rather than a machine. A perspective and priority geared towards the short-term fix, with a change in focus from satisfying the requirements of a broad stakeholder base to one based on the ultimate benefit of a narrow stakeholder base, to the detriment of the community/society of which the organisation is a part.

In the case of these two de-mutualisations, the result was the voluntary exit of many talented staff who sought something more than the material benefit offered in the short term, with uncertain employment prospects over the medium to long term. Customers who experienced shell shocked front office staff, where before they had been faced by motivated organisational advocates declined cross sales offers or transferred their banking custom elsewhere. The result was a continuous slimming down of the organisation to achieve the promised numbers in the face of a diminishing transfer of tacit knowledge, insight, loyalty and staff motivation and customer loyalty and advocacy. Again, I feel it necessary to state that there are no hidden philosophical or political agendas in the perspectives and propositions which I put forward. As a practicing operational leader over four decades I must conclude from the results that the mechanical, numerical leadership approach, devoid of the people dynamic is not wise but more importantly does not deliver in the form of long term organisational performance and ultimate survival. Perhaps this is no longer the primary objective of the dominant coalitions of business organisations and this is the weak link in the book's overall conclusions. If this is the case we must question the logic, desirability and inevitability of this "smash and grab" perspective.

Putting aside this somewhat apocalyptic possibility, this chapter therefore seeks to highlight those operational leadership perspectives, attributes and capabilities which will optimise the opportunities for the long-term survival and continuing prosperity of the organisation in the face of crises which periodically sweep across an economy and society, and which cast aside those organisations which are "hollow" inside. The leadership of these "hollow" organisations has ultimately failed to develop and maintain the allegiance and loyalty of key stakeholder groups, who had consciously or subconsciously delivered suboptimal levels of commitment and productivity over an extended period, as they became aware that the organisation's objectives were not consistent with their requirements and expectations. However, during this intermediate period the organisation was able to successfully project a successful veneer to the outside world. However, these stakeholder groups ultimately withdrew their commitment, allegiance and dedication when the organisation faced imminent collapse, when it most needed the support of the community of stakeholders. Such a situation must be the antithesis of the application of the principles and process of practical and collaborative wisdom.

This chapter section is written to highlight the operational requirements and implications of the absence of practically wise leadership. It requires the application of appropriate operational leadership perspectives, priorities and practices, the development of key attributes and capabilities and cognitive mental processes to support optimal decision-making and issue resolution. This process allows the leader to define and consider the important data and information in an analytical and affective manner in order to reach the optimal solution, applying individual and collective intellect, practical knowledge, experience, insight, intuition and judgement to reach a wise and courageous conclusion in the interests of the continuing survival and optimal long term performance of the organisational community. Also in the face of aberrant perspectives and motivations which are inconsistent with "wise" principles and priorities. The following sections therefore highlight a framework of operational leadership imperatives, in the form of perspectives, priorities and practices which facilitate the process of practically wise decision-making and issue resolution.

Operational Leadership Imperative One: Recognise You Are Running a Marathon

An acknowledgement by the organisation's dominant coalition that they are running a marathon rather than a sprint has a dramatic effect on the perspectives and priorities of operational leadership and the resultant relationship between stakeholder groups. This in turn has a positive effect on the stability, survival and long-term performance of the organisation. Such a conclusion is consistent with both the logic and cognitive mental process of practical and collaborative wisdom,

We are not managing for the next reporting period, we are managing an organisation that has survived and prospered for almost 140 years and is running a marathon, not a series of sprints (Whitson, 2001, p. 3).

The above quote was made by Keith Whitson, the then Group Chief Executive of HSBC Group in a speech to the Institute of Directors in 2001. It succinctly encapsulates the fundamental perspectives and priorities of the organisation's dominant coalition. This emphasises an embedded management vision, perspective, capability and expertise geared to long-term survival and sustained performance. More importantly it lies at the heart of a practically and collaboratively wise leadership mindset. Such a perspective at the senior executive level has a direct impact on operational leadership perspectives, decision making, issue resolution and the day to day management and allocation of resources within the organisation.

This awareness and resultant perspective lies at the heart of this book, as it seeks to expose the key attributes and capabilities of organisations which succeed during periods of crisis, when others crash and burn and in particular, the perspectives and practices of their leadership cadres. The very fact of an organisation surviving and growing over a period of 150 years to become the dominant global player within its sector indicates the existence of fundamental management attributes likely to reflect practical and collaborative wisdom. Therefore, attributes which other organisations must examine and emulate within their dominant logic and their own business context if indeed their focus is upon long-term performance and survival.

Whilst I would not propound what appears to be the blueprint for sustained success of HSBC as the universal blueprint to be applied by all organisations (nor do its senior executives), it may be of value to pick out a few dominant perspectives for consideration by the reader as we discuss those principles and priorities underpinning the attributes and capabilities of practical and collaborative wisdom. These are set out in the text box "The Psychology of Running a Business Marathon" below, which portrays a framework of principles, perspectives and priorities which can only effectively be developed and applied on the basis of a leadership mindset which looks to the long term.

HSBC – THE PSYCHOLOGY OF RUNNING A BUSINESS MARATHON

International experience of political, economic and natural storms created justification for a conservative balance sheet, the view that a little hay collected every day is better than one good crop. A long-term plan which creates consistent growth, although dull, is better than a plan which provides a cyclical growth pattern and, on balance, is preferred by key stakeholder groups who, as stated previously seek confidence and comfort. This is achieved by a high degree of predictability and reassurance regarding the basis and direction of leadership decision making. HSBC does not feel compelled to show stellar performances in the short term and is accepted by major institutional investors as a consistent and long-term performer due to innate core competencies.

The founding bank therefore applied a management blueprint or dominant logic whose foundations were largely but not exclusively based upon the consistent application of a core set of business principles which are even today termed **"Scottish Presbyterian"**,

> But it appeared to me that, if a suitable opportunity occurred, one of the simplest things in the world would be to start a bank in China more or less founded upon Scottish principles (Thomas Sutherland, P&O agent and one of founders, quoted in King, 1969, p. 7).

This dominant logic encompassed a decision-making schema which may be considered conservative, prudent, efficient, moralistic, based upon devotion to duty and a comprehensive assessment of all risk issues, rather than a risk aversion. It required an emphasis upon maintaining close control over issues which related to financial, credit, political and operational risk. This perspective rests upon the development, understanding and implementation of a long-term vision and clear definition of the role and contribution of each business unit and individual within the organisation. To these were added what might today be considered merchant "Empire" characteristics of speedy decision making, high levels of integrity, a responsibility to the "natives" and, as already stated, an acceptance of personal sacrifice for the greater good of the in-group and community to which they related, namely Hongkong and Shanghai Banking Corporation. This created a philosophy and personal characteristics rich in righteousness, direction, confidence, certainty, sympathy and security, which, from the recent interviews with senior executives remains core to their perspectives and decisions into the twenty-first century.

Source: adapted from Park (2006).

We can therefore appreciate from the brief details of the principles and priorities of the dominant logic of HSBC from its foundation that effective management of the organisation for long-term success is based upon the key logic, values, principles, perspectives and practices which are required to build a house to stand for a hundred years, rather than with a short term "until I've sold it and made my profit" perspective. Such a framework of principles and priorities inevitably impacts upon the perspectives and practices of operational leadership in respect of day to day decision-making and issue resolution. This inevitably impacts upon the attitude towards staff and in turn, staff perspectives and attitudes in respect of their perceptions of the purpose, nature and priorities of the organisation,

> *HSBC's business philosophy is based on achieving value and benefit through a long term investment ... this requires sensitivity, adaptability openness to ideas which will create an effective organisation (Interviewee C).*

This dominant logic which has generated a long-term perspective is encapsulated by the quote below, which indicates that unless you consistently apply the requisite universal values, principles, perspectives and priorities, organisational success and acclamation is fated to be short lived,

> *Today you're a rooster, tomorrow, you're a feather duster (Sir Bond, 2000a, p. 5).*

An organisation with a dominant coalition which has this perspective embedded in their psyche starts at least from the right end of the stick. Many banks, particularly throughout the developing world have over recent decades been set up to maximise profitability and assets in the short term, for sale/acquisition/merger and the ultimate benefit of a small cadre of shareholders and senior management. Whilst perhaps not considered by some to be laudable, these are nevertheless logical and understandable objectives within the context of the prevailing ideology of the broader societal environment and the objectives of the dominant stakeholder groups within those societies. The result is a view of the organisation as a cash cow over the short term, most importantly with no cognisance of a requirement to understand its psychology and physiology, to nurture staff and develop tacit knowledge. Such a leadership perspective does not require the perspectives, attributes and capabilities of wisdom, merely intelligence, appropriate technical experience and an astute insight of the short-term market opportunity.

The problem arises when the organisation is unable to achieve its short-term objectives due to a changing market context. Albeit, too late, the dominant coalition recognises that it leads a hollow organisation with no common purpose or cohesion amongst its key stakeholders or allegiance to the organisation. The key organisational resources for remedial action, cohesion, loyalty, dedication, confidence, energy and advocacy, are therefore out of the effective control of management, unable to adapt to the drivers of the new business context with the required confidence, purpose and alacrity. Lacking the confidence and dedication of key stakeholder groups they find that whilst continuing to be in control of the steering wheel and accelerator is now of little value since it has become disconnected from the engine. Such a scenario reflects an organisation lacking in direction, cohesion and energy, populated by a despondent and disloyal management and staff, who await (or indeed conspire towards) the acquisition or ultimate collapse of the organisation. This is perhaps the profile of a significant number of financial institutions which have recently collapsed or which have required substantial government support during the prevailing financial and economic crisis. Such organisations and their dominant coalitions rode the market wave, but lacked, on the one hand, the required operational leadership expertise, perspectives, priorities attributes and capabilities and, on the other, the embedded loyalty, dedication of key stakeholder groups who ultimately recognised that their requirements and expectations were not an organisational priority.

This study seeks to look beyond the symptoms which have attracted the financial and business press, to investigate whether there are any similarities in leadership principles, perspectives and priorities in organisations which can justifiably be termed consistently "successful" over the long term. It looks beyond/beneath such issues as capital adequacy, cost/income, P/E and risk ratios, which tend to confound rather than clarify. Many organisations today spend substantial management resources monitoring and adjusting these and many other ratios, rather than reflecting on the fundamental and more complex issue of effective organisational leadership, which is founded upon the "marathon" approach, based upon providing the capability for the "soft" development and nurturing of primary organisational assets, that is, people. This latter focus ensures that the foundation is in place to create an internal environment and synergy with the external environment where profits are optimised over both the short and long term and many of the disparate elements of risk and costs are minimised, without excessive focus, attention and monitoring. This is because aware, motivated, dedicated and loyal stakeholders are energetically and proactively looking out for the interests of an organisational community of which they feel an intrinsic part, which is aligned with their interests, requirements and aspirations, rather than such risks and costs being the specific responsibility of technical functions.

Senior executives and board members in financial services organisations (indeed stakeholders within the majority of industrial sectors, including institutional and private investors) have become accustomed to operate at the level and perspective of the "trader", managing the organisation by focusing on product, credit risk, Basle II/III compliance, profit and loss, and the balance sheet because it appears to work within the context of a "there is no such thing as the long term in business" perspective. This is a statement often times heard by the author when making presentations to senior executives, reflecting not only a prevalent business but societal perspective.

There is ample evidence to indicate that this primary focus on numbers for decision making, particularly when considering mergers and acquisitions, has proven short sighted and ultimately value destroying in the medium to long term. Research by Altunbas and Molyneuex. (1997) indicate that the repercussions of the recent plethora of "shotgun weddings" between banks during the financial and economic crisis, based upon expediency, desperation and no small degree of opportunism, allied to what was thought to be a close examination of "the numbers", between organisations with disparate dominant logics (e.g. J.P. Morgan and Bear Stearns, J. P. Morgan and Washington Mutual (WaMu), Bank of America and Merrill Lynch, Wachovia and CitiGroup/Wells Fargo, Lloyds TSB Group and HBOS), are not in the interests of long-term survival and stakeholder value creation. A study by Barth and Caprio (2004) reinforces this primary focus on tangible, hard factors when assessing the condition of a market and institutions for entry and acquisition, rather than any cognisance of the importance of "soft" people and organisational attributes during the consideration of organisational acquisition or merger. Barth and

Caprio conclude that the following factors bear primary consideration when studying the dynamics, characteristics and the performance of banks within host countries. What is immediately evident is the impetus on the part of senior executives during the initial assessment of market opportunity to concentrate on the largely *"institutional"* related and driven context of local markets when considering acquisitions:

- Total bank assets as a percentage of GDP
- Percentage of bank assets government owned
- Percentage of bank assets foreign owned
- Gross national income per capita
- Permissible banking activities and restrictions
- Structure, scope and independence of bank supervision
- Implementation of banking supervision
- Nature of deposit insurance schemes
- Corporate governance index.

The successful, pragmatic senior executive recognises (consciously or subconsciously) that they are leading and directing a living, breathing community of people, no less. Ultimately, therefore, success requires not a primary focus by leaders and senior management upon managing issues such as risk, compliance, legal, treasury, balance sheet management, profit and loss, and other organisational "table stakes" requirements. This is the approach of the "mechanic", who has a piecemeal understanding of the organisation, whose purpose is to make a living by keeping it running through ongoing repair and replacement. Rather it requires a long-term "marathon" perspective, with a primary focus upon the conscious, effective and dynamic leadership, and development of people and the organisational "community". This ensures that individuals within the organisation consider the organisation's values, principles, vision and objectives to be consistent with their aspirations and that they are respected as valued and knowledgeable contributors, rather than resources. Also that the organisation is recognised by key stakeholder groups as contributing within the wider "community" within which it operates, upon which it ultimately depends and within which its staff live. This ensures high levels of energy, dedication, loyalty, motivation, advocacy, teamwork and the free flow of enhanced levels of tacit knowledge, resulting in competitive advantage and levels of productivity and profitability impossible to emulate over the long term by those taking a more mechanistic approach to organisational leadership. Such leaders are "Engineers", for whom management of the organisation is a vocation, life itself, whose purpose is to optimise long-term performance, to continuously build and improve through committed, energised and dynamic adaptation and innovation within a community of which they consider themselves an intrinsic part.

In this regard and in the present economic, financial and increasingly social crisis it is apposite to quote Abraham Maslow,[1]

We are in an interregnum between old value systems that have not worked and new ones not yet born ... we need a validated, usable system of human values, values that we can believe in

---

1   Maslow, A. H., *Religions, Values, and Peak Experiences*, Penguin Books, USA

and devote ourselves to because they are true, rather than because we are exhorted to believe and have faith (quoted in Primeaux and Vega, 2002, p. 97).

Increasingly the values and principles upon which prevailing cultures and ideologies within society are based are being questioned, this due to the detrimental effect of the prevailing economic crisis on substantial numbers of individuals and societal groups. Similarly, operational leaders within business organisations, which are a part of society and reflect its fundamental principles and perspectives, must similarly review those values, principles and priorities which are the foundation of the organisation's dominant logic and long-term survival. Many readers might respond that operational leaders look after operational issues and leave such matters to the people on the top floor. This would be the ideal, except that effluent as well as water runs down hills. It is therefore necessary that all members are aware, willing and able to contribute to the resolution of such issues, whether they are encouraged to do so or not. Ultimately aberrant perspectives and priorities will both impact and reflect upon the individual as a leader and as an individual. Complicit rather than culpable can in practice result in similar if not more detrimental implications for the individual. If you abrogate responsibility then how can you be a leader of people and expect their allegiance and energy? Conviction and courage are fundamental to those leaders who apply practical and collaborative wisdom. We will return to the effective management of this dilemma in Chapter 8.

The "marathon" approach to business leadership is logical and similar to the requirements for success in respect of any other "branch" of society or indeed society itself. Empires have blossomed when all stakeholders considered that they had a stake in its prosperity. Empires collapsed when they were hijacked by a limited group of stakeholders who sought to maximise short-term benefit for themselves, leaving them exposed to external predators who sought to take advantage of weaknesses in social cohesion. Similarly, those totalitarian states run for the benefit of narrow cliques will sub-optimise their potential and performance, and be prone to instability and collapse because the universal values are not in place to achieve stakeholder cohesion, allegiance and motivation (e.g. Idi Amin in Uganda, Saddam Hussein in Iraq, Muammar Gadaffi in Libya, Robert Mugabe in Zimbabwe, N. Korea, Myanmar and Syria). The recent crisis within the financial services sector, the recent demise of so many totalitarian leaders and their regimes and the continuing instability and collapse of their economies and societies is a clear message regarding the requirement for leadership imperatives less narrowly focused and short term, more attuned to the long-term requirements and aspirations of a broader stakeholder community, to ensure both personal and organisational survival.

Readers are therefore encouraged to key in "marathon" on each page of their electronic diary for the next year in order to embed and engender a key perspective which results in a range of practices towards achieving practical and collaborative wisdom and effective operational leadership.

Operational Leadership Imperative Two: A Holistic Leadership Approach

The presence of an organisational dominant logic which takes a long-term, holistic perspective translates directly into operational leadership perspectives, priorities, perspectives, attributes and capabilities more attuned to effective people management. It creates an organisation more consistent with the achievement of individual aspirations, creating enhanced levels of cohesion, allegiance, dedication and advocacy, which in turn have a positive impact on long-term productivity and performance.

The recognition of the logic of a long-term perspective has a number of significant implications for the operational leadership of the organisation. A key benefit is that it allows leaders to breathe, to take a holistic view of issues, to take in the bigger picture, rather than seeking immediate, short-term solutions to issues which arise in order to respond to short-term objectives, such as profits, share price, dividends and bonuses. Once you have convinced stakeholders of the individual and organisational benefits of a long-term and holistic perspective and they have developed a confidence and faith in leadership principles and perspectives, a new leadership mindset, a way of viewing, operating, directing the organisation, of better understanding and taking advantage of market opportunities and changes in global power becomes both apparent and achievable. Perhaps most importantly it is possible to approach people management and the utilisation of human resources in a new and more effective manner towards achieving optimal long-term performance.

It is perhaps difficult to appreciate with clarity the impact of the long-term, holistic leadership perspective versus the short-term approach to issues resolution unless we provide examples. Text box "Operational Implications and Applications of a Long-Term Holistic Perspective" overleaf therefore seeks to provide examples from the HSBC leadership perspective. These impact on a number of leadership areas, some to which we have already referred, in order to gain an understanding of the broader and deeper insight which benefits operational leadership evaluation and decision making, through taking a holistic perspective.

OPERATIONAL IMPLICATIONS AND APPLICATIONS OF A LONG-TERM HOLISTIC PERSPECTIVE

An ability see the broader and changing global picture: an acknowledgement that things change, that those people, organisations, countries and cultures who are today in the ascendant will not always be so. Therefore, a sense of superiority, self-importance and arrogance on the part of the "successful" individual and/or organisation is not appropriate or desirable over the long term if survival and optimal long-term performance are primary objectives. Sir John Bond places this perspective within the context of the British expatriate in leadership positions within developing countries, benefiting from gaining broader insights and perspectives rather than taking a superior attitude,

Being an expatriate gives you the opportunity to absorb and relish the fascinating customs, cultures, languages of other countries. This is something that I have spent most of my adult life doing ... Living in these countries was enormous fun and educational. It taught me three fundamental lessons.

- *That being British gives me, as an individual, no intrinsic moral superiority;*
- *That we all inhabit a relative universe and that, on every issue, there is usually another, if not opposite point of view;*
- *And, perhaps most importantly of all, that Britain is only one small piece in a much larger jigsaw puzzle.*

(Sir Bond, 1996, p. 3).

It is therefore necessary to have an open-minded and dynamic appreciation of the ebb and flow of business sources, as economies rise and fall over decades and centuries,

For most of recorded history China was the world's largest economy. In 1820, China and India had about half of the world's population and the world's income. In the West we sometimes view history from a rather myopic perspective ... Today, China is the world's manufacturer ... by not managing this process, we would be abrogating our responsibilities to our customers and shareholders (Green, 2004, p. 1).

Due to its long international history HSBC is therefore aware of the importance of a diversity of perspective, taking into account differing opinions of people and cultures in order to maximise business opportunities, to accommodate the culture of the individual with that of the community,

China has both a tradition of Buddhism – which promotes the growth of the individual – and of Confucianism – which places the well being of the family and society above any individual's needs. This ability to live with ambiguity is a trait often found in Asia, less so in the West (Sir Bond, 2003, p. 3).

- **An ability to be both prudent and opportunistic**: once appropriate prudent and conservative frameworks are in place to assess credit and operational risk, HSBC is opportunistic in its approach to the acquisition of businesses throughout the world which are likely to enhance stakeholder value over the long term.
- **An ability to be pioneering**: linked to its opportunistic and conservative characteristics, HSBC has been pioneering, on the basis of a long-term holistic

perspective, for example, founding banking systems in Thailand, Japan and the Gulf states, whilst more recently entering Armenia, Azerbaijan, Kazakhstan and Iraq.

- **Development of a local leadership cadre**: HSBC acknowledges and understands the long-term benefits which accrue in respect of more effective operational management of the organisation and long-term productivity and profitability, through the leadership of an organisation by local staff. In this respect it will invest over a sustained period, extending to 10–20 years, to raise the quality of local leadership to global standards in those local staff identified as capable of senior leadership roles. This will be achieved by secondment to Group technical functions for 1–2 years, followed by appointment to senior management positions (e.g. head of department or general manager) in their home market, followed by their appointment to Chief Executive position in adjacent markets, to gain broader insight, experience and judgement and to be tested to assess their capabilities as international calibre managers. This is a calculated but high risk, high cost strategy, based upon enhancing local and overall Group leadership and technical capabilities with a view to optimal long term performance.
- **Effective assimilation and inculcation of leadership cadre**: this is a process to which we have already referred in some detail. However, within the context of the long-term and holistic perspective it is appropriate to reinforce the considerable investment in cash, time, monitoring and mentoring by functional management and line leadership in order to ensure that this critical process is successfully achieved to the high levels required to maintain the benefits of an organisation wide dominant logic. Such a sustained initiative can only be achieved where the dominant coalition is committed to the long-term, holistic perspective. We have already noted the substantial costs in terms of sustained losses, leadership and stakeholder conflict which accrued to a bank which expanded into Central and Eastern Europe when it failed to acknowledge, understand and prioritise this issue from the initial stages of the integration process.

The long-term, holistic perspective provides the capability to evaluate issues, options and, most importantly, people, in a patient and considered manner in order to arrive at the optimal solution for all stakeholder groups. The result is cohesion, a committed and dedicated and loyal employee base, which is rare in organisations whose focus is on short-term performance and benefit. Once again it is probably true to say that the importance and impact on leadership perspectives, attributes and capabilities is not adequately appreciated by the reader merely by making the point. Rather than go into detail in respect of key attributes and capabilities, Figure 5.1 provides a graphic representation of how the long-term, holistic perspective translates into operational leadership traits which create a profile of the mindset of effective leaders. In particular, we see a more confident, relaxed individual, better able to consider all pertinent factors in order to undertake an evaluation and take decisions which optimise performance. Able to translate experience into insight, judgement and wisdom, thereby better able to gain the respect, confidence and allegiance of stakeholders and deliver on business objectives which others might regard as unattainable. Some of the key terms within Figure 5.1 which reflect enhanced, one might say superior, leadership capability, insight, judgment and practical wisdom are empathy, sensitivity, flexibility, consistency, empower and persuade.

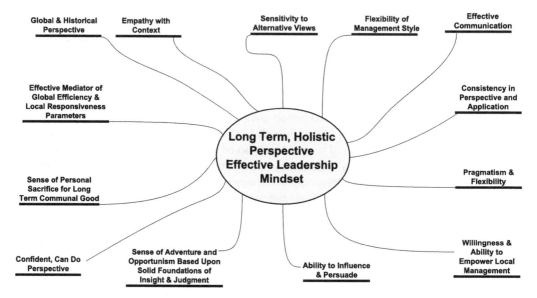

Figure 5.1 **Holistic Leadership: Attributes Fundamental to Practical and Collaborative Wisdom**

Operational Leadership Imperative Three: Re-Prioritise Profitability

The recognition of profit as an objective rather than merely one indicator of success have should this not be has? a detrimental impact on operational leadership perspectives and priorities. The result is an organisation which fails to focus on the people aspiration and motivation "buttons", with a resultant detrimental impact on operational cohesion, employee allegiance, productivity and performance.

An important implication of the long-term, holistic leadership perspective and the resultant change in priorities and the manner of operational management, is the fundamental re-prioritisation and reinterpretation of profit. Profit is a result, an indicator, a function of success; it is not an objective in itself. Indeed there is some doubt whether such financial measures are effective indicators of performance or excellence,

> *Essentially, this debate concerns the appropriateness of traditional financial measures (for example ROI, growth) as providing a unique measure of performance, versus the relevance of other indicators (such as maximising shareholders' wealth; qualitative returns to non-financial stakeholders, such as customer satisfaction) (Glaister and Buckley, 1998, p. 92).*

or are able to discriminate between successful and mediocre organisations,

> *Chakravarthy (1989) showed that traditional accounting measures, including profitability figures, are unable to statistically discern excellent from ordinary firms (Geringer and Herbert, 1989, p. 251).*

The long-term successful organisation has put profit in its place. The problem about making such a statement is that it appears to many, if not the majority, of readers to be outlandish, unrealistic, "soft" and naive. This is due primarily to the inculcation of generations of aspiring and practicing business leaders, that profit is the ultimate product of organisational and individual success, and therefore maximum profit is the primary and ultimate objective, the central focus of the effective operational leader. Many might argue that this is not the case, it is market share, revenue, sales, productivity, but ultimately we are talking about the amount of cash in the bank at the end of the year. Due to the inculcation of generations, to promote an alternative leadership perspective, to make individuals change their operational business practices is a hard sell. However, it is a critical component in the operational application of practical and collaborative wisdom and the attainment of consistently effective leadership practices and optimal long-term organisational performance.

It is important to re-emphasise what we are specifically talking about here. We are talking about what should be the perspectives and central, front of mind priorities of operational leaders who have the operational responsibility for those organisational units, be they sections, departments or divisions whose efforts ultimately deliver the goods and/ or services and achieve the objectives of the organisation. We have deliberated in this book about the development of a dominant logic determined by the dominant coalition. This is primarily with a view to the inculcation of the operational leadership cadre in the appropriate practically wise values and principles, and their ability to tangibilise these into appropriate practically wise perspectives and priorities, attributes and capabilities in order to resolve issues and take decisions in a practically wise manner which optimises the performance of the organisational community.

We are talking here about a balance, getting the right balance of emphasis in the operational leadership of a business organisation between the numbers and the people, between the "hard" and the "soft", terms which, like the terms masculine and feminine are generally misinterpreted in the business context. In my view the continuing emphasis on product and profit is a throwback to the production line mentality where employees were regarded as of limited education, insight and comprehension and who did not therefore need to understand much more than their immediate and narrow task, be it manual or administrative. The objective of operational leadership was therefore to simplify a narrow set of priorities in order to minimise confusion and distraction from the immediate task at hand. However, in the knowledge age, where success depends upon educated, intelligent, sophisticated staff who? populate the workstations of the modern organisation, hard financial indicators of success cannot be the drivers and motivators which sustain dedication, motivation, productivity and performance over the long term,

Achieving return on equity does not, as a goal, mobilise the most noble forces of our soul (quoted in Senge, 1990, p. 12).

Whilst this may seem "soft" and "feminine" operational leaders need to recognise early in their careers that businesses fail at the stage at which senior executives see the organisation merely as a product and moneymaking machine, rather than as a community of individuals who have come together to satisfy a range of personal requirements and objectives, through the production of product and profit (Geus de, 1997). This is nothing thing to do with socialism, psychology, sociology or any other "ology". This is practical, pragmatic, realistic, most importantly, insightful, hard-headed business management, focussed on how best to lead effectively and optimise performance It is primarily achieved by energising and motivating stakeholders to optimise organisational performance. Ultimately decisions on the distribution of the fruits of this performance achieved through the operational application of practical and collaborative wisdom are decided by the dominant coalition. An aberrant and inequitable distribution will ultimately be reflected in the mindset of the operational leadership cadre and the resultant energy, motivation and allegiance of stakeholder groups, threatening the optimal performance and survival of the organisation. In the past it was probably true that you could fool most of the people most of the time. However, today, with social change, experience and talent is increasingly confident and mobile and you are most likely in such a scenario to be left with the moderately capable to achieve organisational objectives.

Some might respond that the emphasis on interpersonal skills and management style in appraisals, the increasing application of balanced scorecards, indicates that a more holistic and people-focused approach is becoming embedded in organisations. To be fair, I believe that there is a subconscious if not conscious recognition of the value of such an approach for long-term performance, particularly in those developing industries whose success is highly dependent upon intellect and innovation. Regrettably, when the organisation is up against the wall (as it always seems to be) and dominant coalitions and operational leaders need to deliver, they revert to type, with an emphasis on product and profit. Long-term, holistic, people focused leadership attributes and capabilities quickly become nice to haves rather than need to haves.

Operational leaders within organisations are not welfare or social workers and it is their responsibility to optimise return on resources invested. This book seeks to provide a foundation, a compass, an anchor, which provides a clarity and consistency of direction, perspective, focus and priority which facilitates effective evaluation, decision making and action during the process of operational leadership in order to ultimately and consistently achieve this objective. Optimal performance is not maximum profit. It is rather focused upon a broad stakeholder approach and active management of the individual's requirements and expectations. This is not rocket science. There are a large number of sports clubs, be they soccer, rugby, baseball, American football, who have sought to buy success and consistently fallen when it mattered to those who were better able to balance cohesion and teamwork with optimal bottom line performance.

It is ultimately about achieving a balance in the satisfaction of stakeholder requirements and expectations, rather than excelling in technical areas and leading in a mechanical rather than intuitive manner. Many leaders might respond that they instinctively and intuitively acknowledge and understand the need for such a balance and consciously or subconsciously seek its achievement. Regrettably the fundamental values, principles, perspectives and priorities which constitute the dominant logic of many organisations make such a balance unattainable in practical and operational terms.

Part, but not all, of the achievement of stakeholder requirements and expectations requires the generation of product and profit. Hayek, to whom we have already referred, pronounces on an issue which tends to dominate the conversation when discussing the management of organisations. This is the relative priority and importance of economic and psychological factors in optimising the productivity of individuals. He contends that the economic motive is merely a means to achieving ultimate ends, be they material or spiritual,

The ultimate ends of the activities of reasonable beings are never economic. Strictly speaking there is no "economic motive" but only economic factors conditioning our striving for other ends ... If we strive for money it is because it offers us the widest choice in enjoying the fruits of our efforts (Hayek, 1944, p. 67).

It is the role of the operational leader to deliver on both the material and psychological requirements and expectations of the diverse range of stakeholder groups. If the appropriate balance is not achieved the result is a diminution in commitment, allegiance and application by stakeholder groups. If these stakeholders are the staff, operational leadership and/or customers then the impact on the organisation is more insidious but ultimately more dramatic than if it was shareholders and senior leadership.

Ultimately it is a question of which is the chicken and which is the egg. A primary leadership focus on people, based upon universal values results in optimal stakeholder cohesion, allegiance, dedication, motivation, productivity, resulting in optimal long-term performance, of which profit is but one component. A primary leadership focus on product and profit may destroy the commitment and cohesion of stakeholders, which limits the ability of the organisation to optimise profit over the long term. The re-prioritisation of profit in the "onion skin" (for further insight into the "onion skin" issue see Chapter 7: Resolving the Onion Skin Issue) of organisational leadership is not an interesting scholarly or theoretical proposition to broaden the mind. It is rather a fundamental practical requirement in the mindset of the operational leader within the changed organisational mix of the twenty-first century society and marketplace in order to survive and optimise long-term performance. It is not a topic for discussion when you run out of conversation at boring social events, or a nice to have once in a while to raise the motivation of individuals during presentations, recruitment drives or appraisals. It is rather a need to have as the basis for everyday leadership evaluations, decision-making and issue resolution.

My recommendation, to tangibilise the place of profit within the leadership psyche of the organisation, as a first step, is to inform those operational leaders who are responsible for large numbers of employees or other stakeholders (e.g. production, distribution, sales, call centres) that there is a recognition that their primary (although not sole) responsibility and therefore core personal attributes and capabilities must revolve around consistent optimal motivation and energising of their staff in order to optimise productivity. Leave the issue of profit, revenue and costs to the technically proficient and focused. My point is that operational leaders must be advocates for people motivation, energy, allegiance and dedication, must understand the direct link with productivity and performance. Of course they must include cost into their calculations but as a subsidiary consideration. It is the role of the technicians to prioritise costs and revenues, but this within an organisational culture where the dominant coalition acknowledge, understand and clearly communicate to and inculcate in the leadership cadre the priority of and direct link between optimal employee and stakeholder energy and optimal long-term performance. Operational leadership is very complex and hidebound by prevailing dominant perspectives, priorities and practices which prevail throughout the organisation. Perhaps in this respect the above proposition is, in practice, a leap too far for the present. However, essentially what I propose is a change of emphasis during the day to day consideration of the best means of addressing issues which arise for resolution.

In this regard the next entry in the reader's electronic diary should therefore read: people = performance. This in order to encourage the required evolutionary change in operational leadership perspectives and practices, on the basis of a recognition of the impact on operational efficiency and organisational performance of changes in the process of decision making and issue resolution at the point of "production".

Operational Leadership Imperative Four: Soft-Hearted Pragmatism – The Development of the Organisational Community

Long-term optimal performance is based upon the operational application of an unwritten covenant between organisational leadership and other stakeholder groups which has at its core the application of universal values. The inability or unwillingness to apply such a covenant due to a dominant logic deficient in appropriate values and principles results in a "hollow" organisation where individuals are unwilling to invest their optimal energy and enthusiasm. The result is that in times of organisational hardship and crisis key stakeholder groups consider that their allegiance is no longer appropriate and they abandon the organisational community, in mind if not always in body,

> *There is no charity for charity's sake in our handling of the company's money or in our asking the company's people to ask of their time. P&Gs support of civic campaigns is now and always will be limited to what we believe represents the enlightened self-interest of the business ... The future earnings of this company rest first and foremost on our ability to attract and hold bright, capable, dedicated and concerned people as our employees ... it serves the interests of the stockholders for us to support soundly conceived efforts to maintain and enhance this community as a good place to live and raise families (Snoeyenbos, Almeder and Humber, 2001, pp. 125–126).*

I have put this quote from a corporate policy statement of Proctor & Gamble at the beginning of this section because, on the one hand, it clearly sets out the hard-headed, pragmatic perspective and priority which is required in business leadership. Equally, it encapsulates the equally pragmatic, "soft-hearted" perspective and priority to support the society or societies within which the organisation operates in the "enlightened self-interest of the business". One must contribute to society and certainly not undertake policies and practices which threaten the survival, development and growth of the society and economy, this in the interests of the primary priority of the business leader, the survival and optimal performance of the organisational community. It is the contention of this book that it is the ability to acknowledge and understand, and to consistently and effectively balance this complex operational perspective in its application which ultimately distinguishes superior and practically wise from mediocre operational leadership. This capability is the primary source of operational effectiveness and optimal long-term organisational performance.

In this book HSBC Holdings plc is not offered or indeed viewed as a management panacea of corporate excellence, to which all other business organisations should aspire. Indeed there was no evidence from the interviewees (two of whom subsequently became Group Managing Directors) that they viewed their organisation as having developed the ultimate management "recipe" for a successful, large, global and complex organisation.

Rather they regarded it as one which was considered to have consistently satisfied the requirements and expectations of all key stakeholder groups. It was this facet of the operational management of the organisation which they considered to have been fundamental to long-term survival and sustained performance, as they expanded to become a global organisation, dependent upon both:

- An allegiance to group principles from all the constituent businesses.
- A willingness by local management to apply their local tacit knowledge for the benefit of the organisation.

This is due to an acknowledgement and understanding by the HSBC Group management cadre that they regarded the satisfaction of and investment in the aspirations of the individual and the wider community as fundamentally consistent with the overall vision and optimal performance of the organisation.

It would not be an exaggeration to suggest that the prevailing and dominant leadership and management theories, certainly operational management perspectives and practices continue to be underpinned by a "Western" individualist performance and reward orientation (Littrell, 2002). It is however debatable whether, in practice, the successful business organisation, over the long term, does anything but pay lip service to an approach which is fundamentally inconsistent with universal values, as elucidated above. Voluntary or not, there is occurring a gradual shift from well-being based on personal self-interest to one based upon the individual's rights, within the context of society's long-term well-being and the individual's societal duties (Chang and Ha, 2001). A number of authors conclude that this is due to the onset of the technology and information age. This reinforces the relevance of speed of response and therefore of people, through the better utilisation of their experience, knowledge and business insights, rather than a strategy and capital focused management approach. Speed is dependent upon the existence of the required repository and free flow of tacit knowledge within the organisation or relevant group of stakeholders; also the ability to leverage it across the organisation, thereby creating a competitive advantage difficult to replicate.

This is a proposition originally espoused by Perlmutter (1969), which he terms "geocentric". Every individual within the organisation is incentivised to work towards the benefit of the whole organisation, through communication, consultation, respect and remuneration. There is a common vision, common management perspectives and practices throughout the group (subject to local "massaging", but rarely radical change). These focus on activities and actions which support the operational efficiency and long-term performance of the whole organisation, rather than the short-term benefit of the local or group operations and/or specific individuals or stakeholders,

> The most crucial task of transnational managers is to encourage a shared vision and personal commitment to integrate the organisation at the fundamental level of individual members (Korbin, 1994, p. 500).

This is achieved by not only effectively communicating a vision which satisfies the objectives of the organisation, but equally important, those of individual stakeholders. Further, in order to achieve cohesion and motivation it is necessary to take the time and effort to explain to individuals what is their specific role in the achievement of the overall vision. To offer them a sense of responsibility and participation in the achievement of the communal vision, for which everyone feels a subconscious need to strive and a recognition that they are moving forward as a team to together achieve community objectives,

> *People are energised by interactions in which a compelling vision is created ... people are energised by interaction in which they can contribute meaningfully ... People are energised when participants are fully engaged in an interaction ... people are energised in interactions marked by progress ... People are energised in interactions when hope becomes part of the equation (Cross, Baker and Parker, 2003, pp. 54–55).*

If there is one word which describes the environment, the culture of the long term successful organisation it is "energetic". There is a dynamic energy, an excitement, a sense of optimism and achievement at all levels which is absent in organisations which have a dominant logic geared to short term objectives and performance.

Perlmutter concluded in 1969 that no company had achieved a totally geocentric mindset. It was rather that in the case of a few companies the appropriate and optimal path had been selected and the point already reached along that path which was of particular significance. I must admit that for the first two decades of my career I regarded staff as a means of getting the job done, as a resource. The priority in respect of people management was to clearly communicate and explain their task and monitor its effective achievement, usually by memorandum or telephone. Sometimes by tightly managed meetings whose purpose was to delegate responsibility on the basis of decisions already taken, rather than discuss options and collaboratively take decisions. In contrast, at later stages in my career I recognised that optimum productivity and performance was best achieved by clarifying an individual's responsibility, but also appreciating their contribution in achieving an organisational objective or its overall vision, whilst persuading them that these objectives and the manner by which they were to be achieved were consistent with their personal values, priorities, objectives and aspirations. At the end of the day effective leadership concerns itself with optimising the productivity of the organisational community, made up of singles and groups of individuals. People primacy is the most effective leadership mindset to achieve that fundamental objective.

Chang and Ha (2001) and Grant (1996) contend that, in contrast to Western leaders' apparent struggle to adapt to the new global paradigm of the twenty-first century, East Asian corporations are intrinsically more adaptable, growing out of societal, welfare-based cultural values, which look to the interests of a wider set of stakeholders (e.g. shareholders, management, staff, suppliers the broader community), on the basis of Kyosei, translated as a sense of living together for the benefit of both the individual and the community (Goodpaster, 2003). In particular, they have "naturally" recognised that the retention and nurturing of key staff, suppliers and other stakeholders over the long term creates a repository of intellectual and social capital and an environment for learning, knowledge creation and innovation (Swan, Newell et al., 1999). This has the effect of increasing the size of the cake rather than that of the share of a particular stakeholder group. Simultaneously it creates a core organisational competitive advantage difficult to emulate, except over the long term, through a redefinition of core leadership principles, perspectives, priorities and operational practices.

Those organisations which base their success on the dominant logic of short-term efficiency, cost-cutting, process re-engineering and "shareholder value" will ultimately become "hollow", devoid of energy, enthusiasm and cohesion, this in the absence of changes in management perspectives, priorities, processes and procedures (Prahalad and Oosterveld, 1999). Such organisations impress to deceive, declaring consistent growth in terms of sales, revenue and profits, but only through destroying those "soft" attributes which ensure long-term survival and optimal performance. This short-term, shallow, mechanistic and formulaic management perspective is replaced by a flat organisation, with strong relationships, easy communication, trust, obligation, cooperation, security, motivation, excitement and challenge, resulting in collective action (Nahapiet and Ghoshal, 1998; Tsai and Ghoshal, 1998). This is not "soft" management based upon a welfare or communistic philosophy. It is rather a warm-hearted, yet cold-headed, pragmatic approach, attuned to the requirement to gain the trust, allegiance, confidence and dedication of those who hold the key tacit knowledge necessary to optimise the prospects for organisational survival and profitability over the long term,

Leadership is a combination of personal behaviours which focus on the soft stuff which enables the leader to gain the allegiance and dedication of others. Leaders demonstrate integrity, generate trust and communicate vision and values. By this means they create energy and motivation in their staff and employees (Bennis and O'Toole, 2000, p. 172).

The cognitive mental processes which support practically wise and effective operational leadership are in practice not complicated. You first base decisions on actions which you consider will best achieve defined objectives for which you are personally responsible. My experience strongly indicates that this is optimally achieved through the people = performance formula. Regrettably, due to the absence of the structured development and inculcation of appropriate principles, perspectives and priorities and development of key attributes and capabilities throughout my career, the application and onward communication of this logic has been haphazard, limited, late, ultimately reflecting practical insight and judgment rather than practical wisdom on the part of myself and many of those organisations with whom I have been employed.

In the new age of education, confidence and knowledge, the prevailing financial crisis has and will continue to act as a spur to weed out those financial and other institutions which have reneged on a predominantly unwritten covenant (Pava, 2001) of equity and respect for staff and other stakeholder groups. Even if some investors and governments consider it beneficial/appropriate to invest to ensure the survival of an organisation, employees, in particular amongst the stakeholder groups, whilst continuing to take the remuneration in the short to medium term, will not invest their energy, their enthusiasm and their lives for an organisation which does not recognise their value nor applies a dominant logic based upon universally acceptable values. Operational implementation of such a covenant by the individual operational leader is not complicated, rather it is first necessary to accept the features of the covenant as fundamental to effective organisational management and ongoing optimal performance and to be aware of, consider and apply them on a day to day basis as you undertake your operational leadership tasks.

The text box "Soft-Hearted, Pragmatic Leadership Perspectives and Attributes" below sets out the key leadership perspectives and attributes which constitute the unwritten covenant between leaders and "followers" and which should act as the foundation for operational issue resolution and task implementation. Every leadership decision involves directing, persuading and motivating individuals, be they subordinates, peers, but also superiors, who equally require reinforcement in respect of the terms of the covenant. On the surface an operational issue may appear to revolve around a decision in respect of a technical area, the development of a process, system, procedure or the achievement of a "number" in terms of sales, revenue, profits or costs. However, fundamentally, effective decision making and particularly the resolution of an issue and the effective implementation of an action plan, requires the dedicated commitment of people, many of whom you may have no direct leadership influence over, who are motivated to act primarily for the benefit of their respective function, themselves and/or due to their allegiance and dedication to the overall benefit of the organisational community. Therefore, the primary focus, expertise and competence of the operational leader must revolve around people. Too often the issue of resolving table stakes issues and reaching the optimal technical solution and its technical implementation takes precedence and centre stage over the terms of the covenant which ensure the long-term survival and effective operation of the organisation.

SOFT-HEARTED, PRAGMATIC LEADERSHIP PERSPECTIVES AND ATTRIBUTES

- **Provide predictability of employment**: do not implement business strategies which indicate that security of tenure and employment is not a fundamental principle. Exhibit in your operational leadership practices and actions which reinforce your commitment to predictability of employment and that such a perspective and priority will only be compromised in exceptional circumstances.
- **Clarity of purpose and direction**: ensure that time is regularly taken to inform and update individuals (particularly when there is no time to do it) on the objectives and vision of the organisation, progress made and reiterate and clarify the responsibilities and contribution which individuals have and are expected to make.
- **Continuously exhibit respect**: treat each individual as you would wish to be treated yourself at all times no matter their status and/or capabilities. Respect them as valuable members of the organisational community and assume their allegiance and dedication unless there is incontrovertible evidence to the contrary.
- **Dignity and self-esteem**: take proactive steps to maintain and enhance the dignity and self-esteem of individuals. If in doubt, stroke, if only mildly. Understand the benefit to organisational productivity of an energised individual. However, be sure to avoid any tendencies for unjustified preference.
- **Consult, inform and discuss**: anticipate when individuals will expect to be consulted and/or informed in respect of their roles and responsibilities with regard to ongoing organisational developments. Seek to over rather than under consult in order to stress the value of their contribution in the achievement of organisational objectives and the overall organisational vision. In this respect we return to some of the requirements for effective management to which we have already referred, open-minded discussion, patience and sympathetic consideration. This requirement is succinctly elucidated by Tom Styer, a partner when Robert Rubin was co-senior partner at Goldman Sachs,

Bob Rubin was my best boss ever ... Whether Bob agreed with you or not, he made it so clear that he really understood the point you'd made or the view you held that you didn't feel any personal loss if he made a different decision, because you knew he knew all you knew ... and must know more (Ellis, 2008, p. 377).

- **Aspirations**: understand the nature of individual aspirations, both material and psychological. If you are not sure what their aspirations are, ask them, in order that they are aware that you are interested in them personally and wish to relate to them as individuals, not as units of output or production. The impact on energy and allegiance to individual leaders who apply such a practice is tangible and long term.
- **Equitable remuneration**: avoid the false economy of penny pinching on remuneration. Be honest in your evaluation of an individual's worth, whether it is below or above an individual's perceptions, clearly explaining the objective criteria utilised in the case of all individuals when considering remuneration issues. Be honest regarding your ability to deliver on your evaluation of their worth given that you may not be the final arbiter. In this respect be seen to be making tangible efforts to deliver an equitable compensation for the individual in relation to their absolute and relative contribution to the organisation's objectives. Be seen to be consistent in your treatment of all your direct reports.

In the case of HSBC a number of factors were active at its foundation in creating a soft-hearted, hard-headed pragmatic leadership perspective, directed to the benefit of the organisational community, instead of the individual. Perhaps, most importantly, the fact that the bank was owned and run by expatriate businessmen who, being pragmatic in the interests of long-term revenue generation, realised that as "outsiders" they had to develop a dominant logic and decision-making schema which revolved around open-mindedness, flexibility and adaptability, give and take, as regards operational practices. This was required in order to gain "legitimacy" and acceptance amongst local stakeholder groups (e.g. local traders and merchants, governments and "compradors", that is those individuals who managed within the organisation at the interface between the expatriate leadership cadre and local management, staff and other local stakeholders) if the bank was to survive and prosper in an "alien" environment. This latter factor created a tight-knit management community and collegiate approach to management. Everyone was working for the benefit of the Hongkong and Shanghai Banking Corporation community and culture, within an alien environment, accepting the logic of a defined schema of "HSBC" values, principles, standards and practices, grounded on a reputation for integrity, reliability, trust and professionalism.

Those who take the time and make the effort to manage the organisation as a long-term living, "organic" entity made up of people, rather than a short-term balance sheet will focus on the psychology and physiology of the organisation as part of the local and global community. The tangible value of investing substantial leadership time, resources and energy into prioritising the creation of a community of individuals with common values, principles, perspectives and priorities is an environment where conflict and friction is minimised, teamwork is maximised and where intellectual capital and tacit knowledge are free flowing.

The impact upon effective operational management and optimal performance, compared with organisations where an organisational community is not in evidence is evident almost immediately to those working within it,

> *It stood to reason that those organisations with the least amount of friction in the flow of information would find the greatest success. Friction resulted from cultures in which employees were not used to a contiguous dialogue and in which their efforts to communicate ... were neither encouraged nor rewarded. This facet of the firm's culture ... allowed it to move away from the pack (Endlich, 2007a, p. 278)*

In an organisational environment where staff have been assimilated to consistently apply universally accepted values for the ultimate benefit of the organisational community decisions can with confidence be delegated to the points of actual business (be it New York, Los Angeles, London or Tokyo) and local executives made accountable for the achievement of targets and objectives, based on their judgement, experience and local tacit knowledge. In the case of Goldman Sachs & Co, if a difficult business or management issue arises the principles are utilised as an anchor or compass to arrive at a solution which is consistent with the overall, long-term business vision. In this manner executives feel that they are involved and are actively contributing to the achievement of corporate objectives, without the senior leadership cadre ever delegating its final authority.

We should not, however, be under any illusions. The individual who exhibits the attributes and capabilities to lead in a soft-hearted, hard-headed manner on the basis of acknowledging the pre-eminence of the organisational community potentially, but not assuredly achieves for him/herself great material and psychological benefits. However, the personal cost, the complexity and stress of managing so many apparently conflicting priorities is substantial, despite the fact that you are supported by a like-minded cadre of inculcated leaders. My experience of long-term successful leaders, no matter their hierarchical position, is that earning $1, 5, 10 or 20 million and having power and authority is not unimportant. However, more important, is the self-esteem and respect of others from making a major contribution to and being a member of a vibrant and successful organisational community in the face of the ups and downs of the business cycle. As discussed in Part One, those who lack the values, principles, priorities, attributes and capabilities of practical and collaborative wisdom continue to look and recognise success in terms of short-term personal attainment rather than seeing them as part of the organisational and wider community.

Unlike many organisations, Goldman Sachs embeds in the psyche of their staff, particularly their leaders the requirement, indeed the responsibility to support the organisation by continuously expending time and effort to support the enhancement of knowledge, insight and judgement of the organisational team, this in order to sustain the organisation over the long term,

> *You must want success so badly you can taste it, but never dare to look overly ambitious. You must make time, real time, to advise and guide those coming up behind you, even if you feel you barely have a minute to breathe. You must pretend not to notice that although you work for the most valuable securities firm ever, the furniture is battered, the carpets are worn, and little about the décor has been updated in a quarter of a century. You will become wealthy beyond*

your wildest dreams, but you must not be seen using this money in a flashy or ostentatious manner (Endlich, 2007b, p. 78).

Wise and effective operational leadership is both highly complex and time-consuming in the absence of expert intuitive evaluation and decision making in not only technical areas of competence but equally if not more importantly in the area of the leadership of people. Just as the technically competent make the necessary intuitive decisions in order to keep pace with the rapidly developing operational business context, equally leaders require appropriate principles, perspectives, expertise, insight and judgement to take intuitive evaluations, decisions and actions in respect of the people arena in order to maintain the commitment, motivation and energy which sustains the organisational community. The consistent application of the operational leadership imperatives discussed within this chapter facilitate expert intuition and support a decision making process and issue resolution consistent the cognitive mental process of practical and collaborative wisdom. The absence of intuitive people leadership skills in this critical area, building an allegiance, dedication and optimal energy levels for the benefit of the organic organisational body, will result in slow, ponderous, flat-footed, inept decision making. Ultimately, it will lead to levels of dissatisfaction and conflict which will sub-optimise both productivity and performance over the long term, continuously placing its long-term survival in jeopardy, no matter its performance in terms of tangible indicators of success such as sales, profits and cost efficiency.

Exercises

1. You have been called into the Group Chief Executive's London office to be informed that you are to be appointed CEO to the newly acquired operations in Vietnam. You know nothing about the acquired company but he asks you to consider: what are the top eight operational leadership issues which you consider should be your primary focus in order to ensure survival and optimal long-term performance. You have 20 minutes to draw up your list before you discuss them with members of the Group Executive Committee.
2. On the basis of your knowledge of the collapse of a major corporation (e.g. Lehman Brothers, Bear Stearns, Enron, WorldCom, Arthur Andersen, RBS) consider the relevance of a dominant logic which bases its operational leadership perspectives and priorities on running the organisation as if it was engaged in a marathon rather than a series of sprints.
3. On the basis of your personal experience and/or knowledge of the performance of specific business organisations, consider for 15 minutes why profit measures are/are not an effective discriminator of the excellent from the ordinary business organisation.
4. Consider whether/why there is no such thing as the long term in business and the implications which this has for leadership perspectives and priorities.
5. Consider an organisation for whom you have great respect for the manner in which it has been led over a sustained period (e.g. 2/3 decades). Draw up a list of six leadership perspectives, priorities and attributes which describe why you have such a view.

6. Taking a pragmatic, hard-headed realistic perspective, consider for 15 minutes whether and why it is important in terms of effective operational leadership and optimal long-term productivity and performance to consistently expend scarce management time and energy to develop and maintain the cohesion, allegiance, dedication, advocacy and motivation of the organisation's employees. Is it a nice to have or a need to have? In your view what percentage of a leader's daily time should be proactively and consciously dedicated to this task?

3
Practical and Collaborative Wisdom within a Global Leadership Context

So now, enough of the focus on philosophy, paradigms, concepts, theories and quotations from business and scholarly worthies. Time now to boil all of the preceding down to key operational, practical bullet points which are of value in developing a clear, understandable and relevant framework of perspectives, personal attributes and capabilities, of direct relevance to supporting real, live day to day decision-making and issue resolution by you as operational leaders. In Part Three we see how, in practical, operational situations, leaders have applied the principles, priorities and processes of practical and collaborative wisdom as encompassed by what we have termed global leadership.

Part Three will clearly illustrate why technical proficiency, whilst important as a table stake capability, must be recognised as a given; also why effective operational leadership requires a broader, holistic, communal, organic perspective of the organisation and its context, resulting in the centrality of proactive and dynamic people management in the cognitive mental processing of the operational leader. It takes into consideration a range of the most pertinent leadership theories and concepts cited in Part Two and merges them into an operational leadership approach that reflects the multifaceted issues, perspectives and priorities which must be simultaneously considered in an instinctive and intuitive manner on a daily basis in order to maintain the pace required by the demands of the business context.

We will illustrate how collaborative and practical leadership directs the leadership mindset in the effective analysis and resolution of every single daily issue and decision as it becomes a subconscious, instinctive and intuitive capability. In Part Three we bridge the apparently yawning gap between scholarly concepts and everyday leadership practice through the use of interesting if somewhat offbeat examples. By this means we also clearly demonstrate that collaborative and practical wisdom, which we translate into foundational leadership attributes, capabilities, perspectives, priorities and practices utilised in business leadership, are not unique to that sector, but are similarly exhibited and required in many if not all other branches of society. We translate and interpret the principles, perspectives, attributes and capabilities of practical and collaborative wisdom into ideas which are recognisable within the mindset of the aspiring or established business leader on the basis of their knowledge, practical experiences, cognition and understanding of reality.

The majority of readers will relate to working in an organisation where it seems impossible to agree upon, much less achieve tasks and projects. This is usually because every individual appears to have differing perspectives and priorities, and often lacks an organisational "community" focus, preferring to act in the interests of themselves and/

or groups to whom they personally relate, within and/or without the organisation. In this age of multifunctional projects and matrix management such increasingly complex operational leadership situations are only resolved when an individual has not only the responsibility and authority but comprehends the value of and makes the effort to clearly define and communicate the scope, parameters, priorities and timescales of a task or project. Equally importantly, when the individual operational leader is both willing and able to link these to the requirements and aspirations of each individual involved in its optimal completion.

The downside of such an individual leadership approach to wise and effective leadership is that this process most often has to be repeated for each organisational function, initiative or project, requiring each unit leader to individually attain the mind of the "engineer" in a self-developed, haphazard and uncoordinated manner. How much easier it would be if this process was not required, if individuals started with common perspectives and priorities, and the benefit of an organisational community with common purpose and direction. Although few readers may have experienced working in organisations where this is the common practice some may have caught glimpses or episodes where it occurred for a short period in their organisations, usually during periods of organisational crisis, where everyone sought its survival to minimise the threat to their personal well-being. However, in a few business organisations this uniformity of mindset amongst the leadership cadre is a fundamental principle and priority within the organisation's dominant logic.

We have shown in Part Two a number of organisations where individuals are convinced of organisational and personal benefits of the consistent application by all of a common framework of values, principles, perspectives and priorities. Part Three will expose what are considered to be the practical and operational leadership attributes and characteristics of this mindset. It is a bit like learning maths; consistently effective leadership starts with understanding and acknowledging the fundamentals and which end of the stick is up and thereafter consistently resolving all issues upon these foundations. If these have not been embedded or are not clearly understood then confusion, errors and a laborious mental process ensues. The result is diminishing self-esteem, credibility and productivity (I know because I missed 2 years of the learning blocks of mathematics in my teenage years). The majority of aspiring leaders do not begin their careers with a grounding in or repository of fundamental people leadership values, principles, perspectives and priorities, which provide clarity and direction from the outset of the leadership journey, unless imbued by parents, mentors during childhood or adolescence or, as we have described in Part One, as a result of personal crisis.

If you start your career from a pretty much "blank page" position, from thereon there is rarely the opportunity to stop peddling frenetically, to draw breath to consider such matters as optimal leadership principles. You are intently focusing on delivering on tasks, projects and targets within the daily, operational context. You therefore tend to construct your leadership mindset (if at all) on the hoof, in a haphazard, uncoordinated, instinctive manner, dictated primarily by day to day experiences and the example of leadership styles of peers and superiors, rather than with the added benefit of a foundational logic allied to reflection, insight and judgement.

The value of receiving and embedding the foundational principles, perspectives and priorities whilst clarifying which end of the stick is up prior to or at the outset of a career in operational business leadership is admirably portrayed in the quote below. This is by the grandfather and mentor of Donaldson Brown, contained in a family document which he treasured, entitled "A Letter From A Father to His Sons". Brown, the originator of ROI, was a senior executive within General Motors (GM) in the early twentieth century and an architect of its management structure. He is also reputed to have developed and implemented many of the ideas for which Alfred Sloan was subsequently credited. Whilst the quote is lengthy it portrays the situation of the individual about to enter employment and seeks to provide clear direction and embed a mindset and logic for wise analysis, decision-making and issue resolution. Whilst somewhat dated in its terminology and emphasis it admirably sets the tone for the specific points contained within Part Three,

You are now blessed with a spotless character, a reputable ancestry, and under the whole canopy of heaven have in right and in trust no superior. Preserve your name and character through life as pure and virtuous as it now is. Be plain, uniform and unassuming in your manners, - habits and dress. Learn to respect the manly good sense which always resides in the mass of the people – cherish a habitual sentiment of benevolence for mankind, of patriotism for your country, and of reverence for your Creator, through faith in the Christian religion. Assume a lofty and manly mode of thinking and acting – affect superiority over no one and acknowledge no superior – let your outward manners be modest and gentle, but let your heart be fearless and resolute. Be just and fear not. Meet your fellowmen in all the transactions of life, face to face – do justice to him and compel him to do justice to you. Never for an instant, nor for the sake of temporary advantages swerve in the least from the direct line of honor and integrity. Do nothing which will lessen you in your own esteem, for your own consciousness of your own rectitude is of far more importance to you than the approbation of the world (Dale, Greenwood and Greenwood, 1980, pp. 119–120).

The quote, in common with Parts Three and Four focuses upon the attributes of "quiet" leadership, confidence, integrity, enhancing the self-esteem and respect of others, honesty, frankness. It takes a practical, objective, broad and insightful view of issues, based upon the application of the sum total of your knowledge, insight and judgment. This has been gained from the full breadth of personal experiences and influences to date, towards achieving a state of practical and collaborative wisdom in your present and future roles as an effective operational leader.

6 *Global Leadership Perspectives and Capabilities*

Blackburn Needs Global Leaders! – Consistently Apply the Global Leadership Mindset

The attributes of global leadership apply no matter the context, not only in roles which have global, international or even national responsibilities. When addressing an individual operational leadership issue start your analysis and assessment by applying global leadership principles, perspectives and priorities. This will act as an anchor to furnish you with foundations of an optimal solution, which can be refined by contextual considerations. The absence of such an approach leads to inconsistent and ad hoc decision making, which fails to deliver the fundamental leadership attributes of clarity and direction.

No matter where or what you are leading, there exists a foundation of perspectives, priorities, attributes and capabilities which are fundamental to effective leadership. Whilst undoubtedly there are contextual considerations which will affect the ultimate decision and action, the process and issues for consideration, the values, principles, perspectives and priorities, individual attitudes, attributes and capabilities for wise decision making, as detailed in Parts One and Two remain consistent as the foundations for optimal long-term performance. Any differences in approach and issue resolution lie in the operational practices at the contextual level rather than the logic and mindset to be applied. In this respect the application of global leadership perspectives is not restricted to the management of large and/or multinational corporations.

I use the example of Blackburn to illustrate this point because I was employed around there as an enthusiastic young banking executive in my early thirties. Blackburn is a significant town in east Lancashire, in England, some 27 miles northwest of the city of Manchester. During the mid-eighteenth to early twentieth century it evolved from a small market town to become the weaving capital of the world and one of the first industrialised towns in the world, its population rising from less than 5,000 to over 130,000 during that period. Those of you who are interested in the history of the British Industrial Revolution will be conversant with such surrounding towns as Burnley, Accrington, Darwen, Barnoldswick, Oswaldtwistle, Nelson, Colne and Clitheroe, all towns closely involved in the burgeoning cotton spinning industry in Lancashire of the nineteenth century (James Hargreaves, inventor of the spinning jenny was a weaver in Blackburn). Since the mid-twentieth century Blackburn's textile industry, upon which the region's economy was so dependent, has fallen into terminal decline, facing de-industrialisation, economic deprivation, immigration and housing issues. As an example of the dramatic decline, in 1976 there were 2,100 looms still operating, compared with 79,000 in 1907, with a decline in population to approximately 100,000.

I arrived in Nelson and Colne in 1986 as a 34-year-old rising star, having received Nelson and surrounding branches as a result of winning a national competition as the best branch manager in the bank that year. After a month, afflicted by a swollen head, pride and self-importance; reality rushed in. I had in fact been parachuted in as a last desperate resort by the bank to quench an already well-established forest fire which had already defeated the more experienced and pragmatic, who had either retired or elected to take up positions as far away as possible:

- Deposits were haemorrhaging from the branches, as high net worth and commercial customers exited the area.
- Bad debts were escalating as individuals became unemployed and businesses struggled or went out of business.
- Capable staff were exiting to take up positions down the motorway in Manchester, due to a lack of promotion and bonus prospects. Remaining staff were demotivated and resistant to change.
- Fraud and embezzlement were a constant and escalating issue as managers desperately sought business from increasingly slim pickings.
- There existed an undercurrent of racial discrimination, if not outright belligerence and hatred as a result of a substantial influx of immigrants from the Indian subcontinent into the local manufacturing industries, recruited as a means of maintaining a competitive cost base.

Wise, global leadership was therefore of critical value in a local backwater in the shadow of the dynamic economic and business centre which was Manchester. Resolution of these "global" business issues was left in the hands of a callow, naive, adventurous, enthusiastic and inexperienced candidate from amongst the organisation's leadership cadre, after only a relatively few years in business and even fewer in leadership positions. In later years of my career I established retail banking operations in developing societies, where there was an economic boom, a rapidly changing society, excitement, adventure and a pervading sense of energy, hope and purpose, but where a banking infrastructure and retail banking market had barely developed. In both contexts similar leadership issues of limited staff and management expertise/skills/motivation, vision, direction and infrastructure existed. Leadership attributes and capabilities which we have discussed in Part Two, such as:

- Personal confidence, but with an ability to be open and consider alternative views;
- To listen;
- To persuade;
- To convince;
- To analyse, taking into consideration both tangible and emotional issues; and
- To see the business in a holistic manner and within the context of the socio-economic context.

all were essential in both scenarios in order to engender an effective operational context, by creating direction, hope, purpose, allegiance and advocacy amongst all stakeholder groups, in order to optimise long-term performance.

In a similar vein, I have a neighbour who was the sales and marketing director (now chairman) of a disposable paper company (e.g. kitchen towels, toilet paper) and also a family friend who owns and is the managing director of a company which produces crisps (potato chips) of many varieties. Both products are not likely to be headline grabbing, yet require the attributes of practical and collaborative wisdom and global leadership to compete with multinationals in order to optimise limited opportunities and performance. However, can you imagine the leadership issues related to persuading, convincing and motivating a variety of stakeholder groups in respect of a proposal to produce and sell a range of crisps in China, when you are sitting in an office on the outskirts of Dublin, Ireland; or the persuasive capabilities required to convince conservative stakeholders to invest in a herd of bison (the company had just introduced bison-flavoured crisps) and a theme park in order to project and extend the brand in Ireland, whilst diversifying revenue streams? My family friend eventually persuaded a disbelieving board of directors, executive committee, staff, local planning authority and government bodies to support all three initiatives, even though the bison-flavoured crisps were quickly discontinued.

Therefore, the core point which I wish to make is that no matter your role within the organisation, the product or service offered by your organisation, the geographic scope or complexity of your organisation, the requirement to address leadership issues in a collaboratively and practically wise manner persists in respect of the appropriate values, principles, perspectives and priorities, the personal attributes and capabilities and the issues to be considered in the decision making process. Therefore, the perspectives, priorities and insights which we will discuss in this chapter apply to you, no matter your individual, operational, leadership context and will facilitate the development of the attributes and capabilities of collaborative and practical wisdom which are critical to global leadership. So sign up now and read on with an open mind.

What Happened to the Hittites? – Have a Sense of Global and Historical Perspective

Individual and organisational success, influence and power are, by their very nature, transient. Success must be continuously reinvented through the application of a practically wise mindset which consistently applies a clear vision based upon the consistent application of a foundation of values, principles, perspectives and priorities within a constantly changing context. Many individuals and organisations fail to recognise that they can no longer justify their existence within a context which is constantly changing. The wise leader, no matter his role or seniority within the organisation, must constantly question his own ability to lead effectively and the relevance and core competencies of his unit and organisation within this constantly changing context. Not to do so ensures inevitable collapse and failure.

I have selected the Hittite civilisation to make this point because it more clearly reflects the typical life of the organisation and/or the individual leader. Unlike the Roman, Hellenic, Persian, Chinese, British and other great empires or civilisations, the Hittites came and they went almost without leaving a sign of their existence or lasting impact on history. In this respect I am reminded of the already cited Chinese quote, *Today you are a rooster, tomorrow you are a feather duster.*

It is important for organisational leaders to understand and acknowledge a number of realities in order to ensure operational efficiency and the survival and optimal performance of their organisation:

- **The transience of success, influence and power**: whilst it is important to have a clear vision and direction, to be confident in your own abilities and the long-term success of the organisation, nothing remains constant, omnipotence is transient. The power, influence and credibility of individuals, organisations, countries, empires, civilisations and economic blocks are here today, gone tomorrow. Just when you think that ongoing success and prosperity is a given and you can therefore relax your vigilance, intuitive senses, your clarity of purpose, drive and determination towards achieving a vision, the context changes and you are suddenly a feather duster. We are increasingly recognising this fact in the first decade of the twenty-first century, with the waning influence of "Western" economic, political and cultural influence and the rise of Chinese, Indian and Middle Eastern influence, particularly within the economic, business and investment sectors. This point is made not to deflate enthusiasm, exuberance and confidence, but rather to dent self-serving arrogance and a narrow, short-term perspective that today's good times will persist because of a divine right or that was the way it was meant to be.

  Some readers might respond that they fully understand and appreciate this point. However, practical wisdom requires a proactive consideration of this reality within the context of each leader's individual direct functional responsibilities and global leadership obligations to the organisational community, with respect to such issues as
  - Markets
  - Products and services
  - Competitors
  - Suppliers
  - Processes
  - Technology and systems
  - Economic, political and financial developments
  all foundation stones upon which the organisation depends for survival and performance.
- **Justify the existence of the organisation and your role**: entities, be they individuals, business organisations, states, empires, civilisations, cultures persist because they have substance, because the reason for their existence, the vision which drives them, the values, principles and priorities are understood, acknowledged and accepted by all stakeholders as consistent with their personal values and aspirations. They are not merely the creation and creature of an individual but have meaning and utility for many stakeholder groups who are willing to strive and sacrifice to ensure its survival, growth and continuing success. Leaders must therefore continuously question and justify to all (not a limited group of) stakeholder groups the purpose and substance of their own role, their function, their organisation, its products or services within the markets and societies upon which it is dependent. Many organisations have ultimately failed because their leaders have failed to recognise that key stakeholder groups, whilst remaining with them in body (e.g. shareholders, board members, suppliers, staff and customers) have disengaged in allegiance, motivation and dedication.

- **Nokia will always be at the forefront of mobile phone innovation**: organisational longevity is similarly dependent upon the ability of its leaders to take stock of the changing environment within which the organisation operates and to adapt their dominant logic and operational perspectives, priorities and practices to the changing context. This is no guarantee of success and optimal performance, but may ensure survival. A cursory glance at the members of the FTSE 100, S&P over the last 50 years is testament to this point.

What this means is the requirement for every leader, no matter the role or level within the organisation (so this means you), to look beyond their "knitting", their technical role, beyond the organisation, the immediate market, to the societies within which they are represented, for the implications to their specific role and working context, of macro, global developments. This perspective will not only prevent a sense of the invincible, the omnipotent in the "successful" and much admired organisations which we hear daily on Reuters, Bloomberg, CNBC and other business media outlets, but instil a sense of the long-term reality for survival and sustained success. I stress that it is a responsibility for each and every operational leader within the organisation, to see the bigger, holistic picture, to think outside the box, to anticipate and prepare for and, if possible, prevent impending organisational "community" crises. This will be achieved by proactively considering, developing, effectively communicating and ultimately contributing to the implementation of solutions. These may, at first glance, be considered to be outside of your immediate area of responsibility, but will have a dramatic effect on you and those who are dependent upon and put their trust in your leadership capabilities.

As a leader of people, be it one, ten, a hundred, a thousand, a hundred thousand or more, you have a primary responsibility beyond the production of product units, completion of a process or procedure or achievement of a revenue target. You have a covenant with those who depend upon you for your qualities of experience, insight, judgment, decision-making and issue resolution in respect of their requirements and aspirations. If you are unable or unwilling to undertake this complex pre-emptive and pro-active thought and action process, potentially dangerous to a budding career, preferring to leave this to others then, despite your lofty title, you are merely a follower, unknowing and unprepared. You thereby expose yourself and those for whom you are responsible within the organisation, leaving you and them prey to the often aberrant perspectives, priorities and decisions of the dominant coalition, as well as peer groups external to the organisation, whose priorities are likely to have a substantial impact on the survival, much less long-term performance of the organisation. As an individual you must question those employers who resist such a holistic, dynamic and proactive approach to leadership, their leadership capabilities, their attitude towards stakeholders and ultimately their ability and interest in organisational longevity. Many amongst you may be thinking that what is proposed is a guaranteed means of ensuring that one's developing career quickly crashes and burns as you are faced by those who wish to keep you in your box and feel uncomfortable and threatened by such holistic thinking and assertive, confident communication. The reality is that we are entering a new era in business and leadership where the speed of response and knowledge requirements compels leaders to encourage more open and "flat" communication and the ongoing and proactive consideration of alternative, novel views and solutions. If you find that your superiors do not take an open-minded and nurturing approach to your interest and proactivity in the broader issues of the organisation then you must actively question whether this is an appropriate environment upon which to develop your leadership experience, insight and judgment. In the interim, Part Four of this book addresses your possible strategies and options, dependent upon your prevailing role within the organisation, personal attributes and characteristics and the nature of your commitment to practically wise, global leadership principles and perspectives.

I am stunned by individuals who wonder how various civilisations just disappeared without a trace, all of a sudden. We have only recently seen New Orleans, the tsunami and Fukushima disasters, which, without the global aid and support available in the twenty-first century would likely have resulted in a depopulation of these areas and the extinction of a number of societies and communities, markets, industries, organisations, divisions, departments, sections, families and individuals within them. Many national and global events and situations cannot be prevented, but they can be anticipated, delayed, prepared for, in order to mitigate any catastrophic impact.

Every operational leader must therefore raise their gaze from the desk, from their immediate and pressing responsibilities to anticipate, prepare for developments within the broader business context which will ultimately impact upon them personally and those for whom they are responsible. It is the role and responsibility of every operational leader, no matter their role or position within the hierarchy, if they are practically wise and therefore have the interests of the organisational community uppermost, to exhibit and dynamically utilise this global perspective. A brief study of the Hittites illustrates many of the points within this section.

THE RALLYING CALL OF THE HITTITE EMPERORS – FOLLOW ME, I'VE GOT A CHARIOT

The Hittites were a Bronze Age people of Anatolia (today's Turkey) who established a kingdom with their capital initially located in north-central Anatolia circa the eighteenth century BC. The Hittite empire reached its zenith around the fourteenth century BC, encompassing large parts of Anatolia, north-west Syria, as far south as the mouth of the Litani River (in southern Lebanon) and eastward into upper Mesopotamia (Iraq). Hittite power fell into obscurity in fifteenth century BC but re-emerged circa 1400 BC and under Suppiluliuma I and Mursili II, the Empire was extended so that by 1300 BC they bordered on the Egyptian sphere of influence in Canaan and Judea, resulting in the battle of Kadesh with Ramesses II, Pharaoh of Egypt, in 1274 BC for influence within the Levant and Near East.

The Hittite Empire was ultimately dependent upon the warlike capabilities of its rulers and, it is postulated, the introduction of the chariot in battle, rather than any embedded and intrinsic values and principles. Its leaders failed to create and effectively communicate a long-term vision, a cohesive society or an ability to adapt to rapid change in this fast developing and fertile region. Therefore, barely a hundred years after the Battle of Kadesh, as a result of civil war, rival claims to the throne and external threat from the Sea People (whose origins are disputed and lost in the mists of history) the Empire collapsed into petty vassal kingdoms under Assyrian rule, with their languages lingering into Persian times before being extinguished by the spread of Hellenism in the wake of Alexander the Great.

Does this ring any bells amongst business organisations with which you are familiar?

Sources: various websites.

It is the exception rather than the norm that empires and civilisations stand the test of time. Yet, in their time, I am sure that their rulers and dominant coalitions could not envisage their eclipse, until too late. So it is with the leaders within the majority of business organisations. Only in a few does the dominant coalition or operational leadership cadre have a sense of global and historical perspective, which facilitates survival and growth beyond the normal life cycle, in the manner of global civilisations and cultures which have in one form or another survived epochs and millennia.

Those readers, who might be saying that this perspective has nothing to do with their understanding of their role and responsibilities and the expectations of their superiors, as an operational business manager, would be correct. However, it is a fundamental primary focus, perspective, remit and responsibility of the effective "global" leader within the organisation. Each individual must make their choice. Is it in their interests and that of the organisation, that they be a manager and follower, lacking control and a broad, holistic insight. Alternatively they can be a leader, with foresight, capabilities and furnished with a greater knowledge and insight of critical events and therefore options, thereby better able to act with judgement and wisdom no matter their leadership role within the organisation, for the long-term benefit of that organisation (and themselves, plus significant others).

On the basis of your prevailing principles, perspectives, priorities, attributes and capabilities do you consider yourself a follower, a manager or global leader, exhibiting the above traits of practical and collaborative wisdom?

Who was Magellan? – Eagerly Go Where You Have Never Gone Before

Ultimately the success of the global leader in optimising long-term organisational performance requires a sense of adventure and excitement in the face of adversity, a willingness, indeed eagerness to be challenged and stretched. Also the ability to stretch and take others with you, through clear direction, decisiveness in the face of crisis, with an emphasis on cohesion, consensus and collaborative decision making. By this means, ends are attained previously considered beyond reach. The success of Magellan, where others had previously failed, ultimately reflects a cognitive mental process which illustrates the attributes and capabilities of practical and collaborative wisdom.

As someone who has spent some 25 per cent of my career as an expatriate I have always been surprised by employers who have tended to reject such individuals at the first cut, primarily because they have had no experience of the "home" market over the recent past. These are individuals who, for a variety of reasons, have decided to leave their country of birth, and/or schooling and employment, which have had to:

- Adapt to one or more different societal cultural contexts;
- Overcome significant difficulties understanding differing approaches and perspectives;

and

- Have had to listen and balance contrasting perspectives and reach difficult decisions which might meet with entrenched resistance based upon embedded differing cultural values and principles.

Similarly, they may have had to compromise in their private life, with children perhaps educated abroad, spouses forever travelling to visit ailing relatives. These are individuals who are most likely to have worked in Central and Eastern Europe, the Arabian Gulf, Africa, South America and the Far East, and have had to adapt to increasing levels of cultural assertiveness. Whilst many of such individuals are forced to take up expatriate roles due to prevailing employment opportunities many others select expatriate life because it better suits their personal characteristics, perhaps due to their parental family context and/or appetite for risk, responsibility, sense of adventure and excitement. Whilst I am admittedly somewhat biased, it appears to me that these individuals have been forced to consider, to analyse across multiple parameters, to adapt, compromise, take hard decisions, to an extent which will develop a deep insight and a confidence in their own beliefs, whilst understanding and acknowledging that their beliefs, perspectives and priorities are unique, rather than universally applicable.

I utilise the example of the expatriate merely to make the point that a sense of adventure, of the calculated risk, not at the "mechanical" level but rather at the holistic leadership level is an intrinsic capability in the application of practical wisdom. This is a fundamental capability of the global leader, who has to leverage the benefits of the consistent application of Group values, principles and standards, but in a manner which is sympathetic to the local context, in order to benefit from local tacit knowledge and advocacy,

> In order to survive and prosper in the new global competition companies are embracing global integration and coordination, but at the same time they must push for local flexibility and speed ... To succeed in global competition requires an open and empowered organisational climate but also a tightly focused global competitive culture (Pucik, 1997, p. 163).

Global leadership facilitates the creation of a *"mental map"*, allowing managers to predict and anticipate positive and negative developments across a much wider and deeper spectrum than is necessary for leaders who manage within a less complex operational context (Black and Gregerson, 2000; McLelland, 1994). I do believe that the expatriate and cross/multinational leadership role facilitates the development of practical wisdom, due to the constant requirement to analyse and take decisions across multiple, complex and conflicting dimensions. However, as someone who has also worked within a number of organisations within the same "home" culture yet within different subcultures (i.e. Scotland, Manchester, London and Dublin) and within differing organisational life stages (e.g. mergers, acquisitions, market repositioning, restructuring), it is quite feasible to develop practical wisdom when confronted by "crisis" issues, to which we have referred in Part One, within the context of personal and/or business leadership contexts, without being a globetrotting leader. Global leadership requires willingness, a confidence, an eagerness to be challenged by issues, problems and situations with which one is not remotely familiar. By this means one gains knowledge and experience, but more importantly, enhanced insight and judgement in order to take optimal decisions in the broad array of leadership contexts.

Gregerson and Morrison (1998) have proposed that today's global leaders have much in common with explorers, such as Vasco da Gama and Magellan. Like explorers they are excited by opportunities, adventure and uncertainty, exhibiting unbridled curiosity and inquisitiveness, and a capacity for managing and tolerating uncertainty/ambiguity and unfamiliar contexts. Such individuals have, through experience, recognised that in situations of high risk and uncertainty cohesion is a key attribute. Also that a collaborative and collegiate approach to decision making, whilst retaining the final say in the face of a lack of consensus, leads to effective and optimal decision making, because you are accessing the knowledge and insight of all of those who will be affected. They therefore have open minds, are willing to listen to alternative views, to listen and compromise according to circumstances and context,

> *Global leaders have exceptionally open minds, respect how things are different and can imagine why these things are different. Global managers are incisive as well as generous and patient (Ghoshal and Bartlett, 1995)*

> *They have an understanding of their own roots, are sensitive and adaptable to global issues/ cultures and are adaptable to new things (Brake et al 1995) (Stanek, 2000, p. 233).*

They view diversity as opportunity, are open to change, listening, challenging accepted assumptions, attitudes and practices. Their management philosophy is based on a soft, people-focused approach, supplemented by hard structural, procedural planning, not vice versa. They have a high perceived value of cross-cultural teams and accept the importance of global assignments in order to develop the required *"savvy"* (Paul, 2000) in terms of:

- The characteristics of global leadership.
- The development of strength and insight through chaos and personal crisis.
- A sense of adventure, courage, tenacity and confidence.
- An ability to persuade and adapt.
- To take decisions which impact adversely, often severely on some individuals (including self), for the attainment of the long-term vision and well-being of the community to which the global leader relates and owes and/or gives allegiance.

These reflect the hard-headed, pragmatic, yet soft-hearted approach which is fundamental to the operational application of practical and collaborative wisdom, and are admirably illustrated in the character and achievements of Ferdinand de Magellan, as described overleaf.

FERDINAND DE MAGELLAN – EXPLORER AND GLOBAL LEADER?

Ferdinand de Magellan, born 1480, a Portuguese, captained the first circumnavigation of the Earth (although he did not complete the entire voyage, having been killed during the Battle of Mactan in the Philippines), on behalf of King Charles I of Spain, in the face of active obstruction, indeed the military aggression of King Manuel of Portugal.

Both of Magellan's parents died when he was 10 years of age. In 1505, at the age of 25 he enlisted in the fleet which hosted the first viceroy of Portuguese India, remaining in Goa, Cochin and Quilon for 8 years, participating in several battles, in one of which he was wounded. He later sailed in the first Portuguese ambassadorial mission to Malacca (one of the earliest Malay sultanates), where he earned honours and promotion due to his cool head and swift action.

After taking leave without permission, he fell out of favour and received no further offers of employment. After a quarrel with King Manuel of Portugal in 1517 he left for Spain, married, had two children. Both children died at a young age and his wife died in 1521.

In October 1517 Magellan and his business partner Rui Faleiro presented their project to Charles I of Spain to open the "spice route" without further damaging already fraught relations with the Portuguese. In March 1518 the Spanish Crown agreed to largely fund an expedition in search of the Spice Islands to begin in July of that year. Major problems arose during the preparation of the expedition, a lack of the funds as promised, the King of Portugal placing obstructions in their way, the suspicion of the Spaniards towards Magellan and his fellow Portuguese and the arrogance and self-importance of Faleiro (who withdrew prior to boarding). However, the tenacity, can do confidence and powers of persuasion of Magellan ensured that the expedition was finally ready. Their goal was to find a sea passage around the Americas and continue on to the East Indies. This was an adventure of supreme proportions; the equivalent in terms of entry into the unknown to the landing on the moon. Contemporary knowledge was comprised of vague conjecture and it was assumed that it was only a short distance beyond the shores of South America across the Pacific Ocean to the Spice Islands. The journey took 3 years, requiring attributes and capabilities of raw leadership rarely experienced even in wartime in the twentieth century, dealing with starvation, disease, mutiny, execution and desertion.

The fleet commanded by Magellan comprised of five ships made up of a crew of about 270 men from several nationalities, including Spaniards, Portuguese Italians, Germans, Flemish, Greeks, English and French, requiring persuasive and "quiet" leadership qualities even in those days of strict discipline, corporal and capital punishment. In this respect on 2 April 1520 a mutiny involving two of the ship's captains broke out but failed due to the loyalty of the majority of crew towards Magellan. As a result, Magellan sanctioned the execution of one captain, whilst another captain and a priest were left marooned, to live or die by their own devices. Difficult decisions when replacements were in short supply. Magellan continued to face resistance from his senior management when, having discovered the passage between Atlantic to Pacific (now named the Strait of Magellan), the captain of the San Antonio deserted and returned to Spain.

However, Magellan persuaded the crew of the remaining ships to continue and on 28 November they entered what Magellan named Mar Pacifico because of its still waters. The depleted fleet headed north-west and reached Guam and the Marianas around the equator and the Philippines in March 1521 with the remaining 150 crew, where he traded gifts with the Rajah and baptized him and his wife as Christians. Magellan hoped to trade with and baptize the ruler of an adjoining island, Mactan, but was refused. He led a small attack force to effect more aggressive persuasive tactics but he was stabbed with a spear and butchered,

they killed our mirror, our light, our comfort and true guide (Eyewitness to History, 2001, p. 1).

and his body was never recovered.

Only one ship, the Victoria, survived the voyage, arriving in Spain almost 3 years after they had departed, with 26 tons of spices and 18 men, having circumnavigated the world, a distance of 60,440 km or 37,560 miles.

Sources: adapted from various websites.

That Bill Gates is Just a Geek – Leaders Must See Entrepreneurial Opportunities in Innovative Ideas

Ultimately the organisational leader is responsible for balancing the often conflicting objectives of operational effectiveness and optimal performance with the application of innovative ideas. The attainment of these first two leadership responsibilities require both a willingness and an ability to continuously consider and assess innovative ideas, within the context of market requirements and organisational capabilities and is an intrinsic capability in the cognitive mental process of the practically wise leader. The leadership capability to accommodate innovation must also include considerations revolving around ethics, people management and operational stability.

I have got to admit that once you have peeled away my general management veneer you will find a bit of a nerd. At heart, I have always had a fascination for developing and tinkering with financial products. It was not just an interesting job, it was a vocation. In many ways it reflected my life's perspectives and priorities. I can still taste the bile in my mouth from when the Product and Pricing Committees of a range of banks rejected the majority of my proposals on the basis of cost, revenue, systems capabilities, market penetration or a range of other terms used to communicate a negative response, which I interpreted as a lack of insight, courage, business acumen, or just plain risk aversion. I grimaced as I saw, over time, their launch by more aggressive and entrepreneurial institutions, which were in the main at the market entry life stage. I therefore relate to the frustrations of such "nerds" or "geeks", perceived as individuals who do not fit in, disrupt the stability and cost efficiency of the operation, whilst appearing to add nothing to organisational performance.

In reality, whilst short term success largely revolves around sticking to your knitting, doing well what you already know, long term survival and optimal performance is more about utilising leadership insight and judgement to consider, encourage and invest in innovative ideas, primarily in the form of people who are able to create or take advantage of changing market requirements, expectations and opportunities as a result of changing tastes, technologies and systems. This requires leadership attributes and capabilities in excess of those which keep the organisation on a steady course and speed. The attributes of the practically wise and effective leader require that when assessing and appraising the attributes, capabilities, the value of the individual to the organisation, you must utilise your judgement beyond the obvious personal characteristics. Many individuals may indeed be at a "nerd" stage in their personal and career development due to their present personal focus, interests and influences, stage of personal development and opportunities to date. They may however, also have the insight and capability to create or reinvent a business and strong long-term revenue flow from an idea.

At a certain stage in my career development I started putting the development of new products and product quality within a broader business mindset, of a framework of "front-end" key success factors, such as distribution channels, service levels, staff training and motivation, market positioning and market image and, I must admit, the pragmatic, hard-headed revenue versus risk calculation required in order to satisfy stakeholder imperatives and expectations. However, I never lost my understanding of the leadership requirement to always take the time to listen to new ideas, be it in respect of products/services, distribution or sales and service quality, since one idea might create the ability for the organisation to survive and/or move into a new business paradigm or, potentially equally important, improve operational effectiveness and team cohesion.

There have been many books written about the entrepreneur or innovator who has a novel idea or solution for a product, process, distribution channel, an operation or some other key aspect of the value chain. He/she stakes all on setting up an organisation which is tremendously successful, growing exponentially and throwing off mega profits. The primary issue subsequently becomes continuing to leverage the innovation by managing the organisation effectively. This requires that individuals with excellent operational management credentials are recruited and frequently gain effective control of the organisation. As a result, in many organisations innovation and the entrepreneurial spirit gradually (or quickly) diminishes in importance within the organisational dominant logic, dependent upon the prevailing power and influence of the original entrepreneur and/or innovator to mould the organisational culture within the context of continuing market developments. It is this balance of managing innovation and change whilst maintaining operational stability in order to maintain confidence, cohesion and allegiance amongst stakeholders, which challenges the capabilities of individual leaders and the organisational leadership cadre. Such is the mark of the global leader who possesses the attributes, characteristics and cognitive mental processes of practical and collaborative wisdom.

Over recent years the free market emphasis by governments on economic growth in the face of limited opportunities within Western economies for GNP growth beyond 1–3 per cent has led to a "flexibility" in the application of regulatory controls of those industries which could exhibit high growth potential and the resultant positive impact on short-term taxes, employment, personal wealth, economic stimulation and political survival. In the case of the financial services sector the result has been entrepreneurial activity in the development of such services as securitisation, subprime mortgages, hedging, derivatives and credit default swaps, which have ballooned under ineffective statutory regulation and which, many would argue, has ultimately adversely affected the standards and quality of life of generations to come and threatens the survival of the Western economic system. The drive to encourage entrepreneurial opportunities must therefore be tempered by tying them back to universal values, principles and priorities. This issue has been a prevalent theme within the burgeoning hardware and software industries over recent decades in respect of the creation of monopoly positions and contravention of patents. These industries are therefore an ideal case to view the existence or lack of global leadership and practically wise attributes and characteristics.

The life and times of Bill Gates and Microsoft are a classic example of the successful nurturing and subsequently the effective management of innovation in a sector where the majority of innovative ideas have failed to survive to create value over the long term, due to the absence of appropriate leadership perspectives, attributes and capabilities. It is now evident that the "geek" has subsequently developed, to expose substantial capabilities in respect of business insight and judgement in innovation management to maintain optimal performance. Gates may also have developed personal values and principles which reflect the subsidiary and "servant" role of business within the wider community. This, however, requires a longer term assessment of his vision, purpose, objectives and motivations.

BILL GATES: SOMETIME GEEK TO LEADER AND GLOBAL MAGNATE?

William Henry "Bill" Gates III, or Bill Gates, could during the early stages of his life have been described as a geek. Today he is reputed to be the richest person in the world (net worth estimated at approx. $60 billion in 2011, briefly surpassing $100 billion in 1999), competing for this role on an annual basis with Carlos Slim. He is Chairman of Microsoft, a friend of heads of state and pop stars, welcomed at the World Economic Forum in Davos for his views on global economic development and a philanthropist surpassing the deeds of the American tycoons of the late nineteenth and early twentieth century. Acknowledged, on the one hand, as one of, if not the, best known pioneer and entrepreneur of the personal computer revolution, he has also been increasingly criticised for sharp, anti-competitive business tactics and an abrasive leadership style and gave up full-time operational responsibilities within Microsoft in 2008.

Gates became interested in computer programming in his early teens when at Lakeside preparatory school he was given access to a terminal and a block of computer time on a General Electric computer. Gates, along with four other Lakeside students (including Paul Allen with whom he set up Microsoft) at an early age exhibited business acumen and an ability to leverage their increasing programming knowledge for benefit, initially by finding bugs in the operating systems of Computer Center Corporation in exchange for computer time. This was followed by these four school students writing a payroll programme in COBOL for Information Sciences Inc in exchange for computer time and royalties. Gates (at 17) and Allen then went on to set up Traf-O-Data to make traffic counters software. Scoring 1590 out of 1600 on the SAT Gates briefly entered Harvard in 1973. However in 1974, based upon ongoing hardware developments, particularly the Intel 8080 CPU, Gates and Allen decided to set up their own computer software company as a partnership, initially named Micro-Soft but in November 1976 the trade name "Microsoft" was registered in the State of New Mexico with the objective of developing Microsoft's BASIC.

A key point in the success of Gates and Allen up to this time was that established computer companies recognised that these "geeks" had ideas which would enhance the value of their products. However, Gates and Allen were exiting their "geek" stage. Gates and Allen single-mindedly utilised their developing contacts within the industry and the hardware platforms of their partners to develop and refine their software, and to gain knowledge and experience of operating systems in order to create a unique product capability. To this technical knowledge they added their developing business acumen.

In 1980 Microsoft was approached by IBM to find an acceptable operating system for its upcoming personal computer. Gates found an appropriate operating system offered by Seattle Computer Products (SCP), making a deal to be its exclusive licensing agent and later full owner of 86-DOS. After adapting the operating system for use within a PC Microsoft delivered it to IBM for a onetime fee of $50,000, but did not transfer the copyright on the operating system because Gates correctly deduced that other hardware manufacturers would clone IBM's system. The resultant sales of what became MS-DOS created a new innovative and entrepreneurial force within an industry which was subsequently to change pretty much every aspect of our working and personal life. In November 1985 Microsoft launched its first retail version of Microsoft Windows.

Bill Gates turned from a chrysalis to a butterfly, but with attitude, purpose and a vision. Whilst companies utilised his technical and computer brilliance to support their own, perhaps limited vision of the industry's future, in the end Gates used these companies, including IBM as stepping stones towards the achievement of his more expansive vision of the industry, leaving them in his wake. If Gates had merely been a geek and a nerd he might now be working for IBM and it would be a very different organisation. Yet Gates was also a highly talented entrepreneur and businessman who could not be accommodated within what had previously been regarded as an entrepreneurial and innovative organisation.

Gates, however, failed in the collaborative and practical wisdom stakes, lacking the ability to listen, persuade and take into account the views and perspectives of his colleagues and the requirements and expectations of the wider societal community. Steve Ballmer, whom Gates met at Harvard, joined Microsoft in 1980 and was its first business manager. He is now CEO of Microsoft. He is perhaps more typical of the operational business leader who follows the entrepreneur and innovator, seeking to maintain the culture of innovation and entrepreneurship within a more formal and structured business environment in order to sustain operational effectiveness and efficiency over the long term whilst continuously assessing the value of business innovations.

Sources: adapted from various websites.

When we talk of entrepreneurship and innovation in the same breathe technology companies such as Microsoft, Apple, Yahoo, Google, Intel, and Dell spring to mind, primarily because there is an obvious link to tangible "products". However, India is increasingly viewed as offering a wide variety of examples of entrepreneurship and innovation which straddles not only products, but also processes, operations and distribution channels which have challenged fundamental principles of business strategy and operational business management. These bleeding edge operational developments within existing industries are perhaps more resonant and relevant to the majority of readers and leaders within business organisations than the examples of the resultant creation of new industries. They perhaps better emphasise the need to be open to the wider range of entrepreneurial ideas and opportunities within the operational context which can create new market opportunities.

Indian entrepreneurs face a massive latent market for a wide range of products and services, within both the urban and rural context. In Western terms, however, much of this market is too impoverished to merit the development of products and services. However, entrepreneurs in India take a different perspective. Develop products and services which are affordable and make a small amount of money from a large number of sales with the minimum of capital. Take a "basic" car which might cost $8,000 dollars in the West and re-engineer the component parts to sell a car for $2,000. Similarly, re-engineer medical procedures to cost $30–50, compared with $100s and $1,000s in the West. Make radios, televisions, computers, mobile phones affordable to the rural poor. These products are now increasingly achieving market opportunities in other developing but also developed markets. Perhaps a prime example of this entrepreneurial paradigm shift and a redefinition in operational business leadership perspectives and business dynamics is the case of Bharti Airtel, as cited by Prahalad and Mashelkar (2010), a company which has been able to charge 1 cent per minute of talk time, compared with 2 cents in China and 8 cents in the USA.

BHARTI AIRTEL – TURNING ESTABLISHED BUSINESS LOGIC ON ITS HEAD

Bharti Airtel Limited, founded in 1995, is the market leader in mobile telephony in India, with approximately 172 million subscribers. It is also the fifth largest mobile operator in the world in terms of subscriber base (approx. 230 million subscribers), operating in 20 countries, predominantly in the Indian subcontinent (India, Bangladesh and Sri Lanka) and 16 African countries. It has approximately 23,000 employees and made a net profit of approximately $2 billion at end 2010. It has succeeded primarily as a result of questioning established business logic and innovating business principles and practices in order to optimise opportunities within its market context.

In an effort to recoup the high front-end costs of a successful government tender in 1985 to provide mobile phone telecommunications in Delhi, Bharti Airtel had followed a strategy of charging a high price to subscribers. However, in the face of a resultant low subscriber base, high set up and fixed costs, funded primarily through debt, funds were quickly running out as new players entered the market. A strategy to radically increase its subscriber base was required through a more entrepreneurial approach to business generation. The following are a few of the innovative perspectives which led to a turnaround in Bharti Airtel's fortunes:

- Bharti Airtel abandoned the average revenue per user metric which is the key metric applied by every mobile phone company as an appropriate indicator of customer attractiveness and value. Given the size of the potential market, Bharti moved away from segment to total market. The metric focus thereby moved to gross rather than customer profitability and changed its key dashboard measures to gross revenue and profit, the ratio of operating expenses to gross revenue and ratio of revenue to capital expenditure.

• In an effort to minimise capital requirements it outsourced all functions except customer management, people motivation, financial management, regulatory affairs, brand management and strategy creation. Bharti Airtel even outsourced its IT services to IBM on the basis of paying them a percentage of monthly revenues, with a minimum monthly payment. By this means it incentivised the provider to maintain excellent quality of service in order to optimise customer satisfaction and revenue streams.

• Bharti Airtel similarly decided not to pay for software applications up front but rather on the basis of the revenue which is created by the value-added services.

• In an effort to quickly expand its distribution channels it utilised existing established channels (e.g. Unilever and Godrej), providing approx. 10,000 distributors with specific, dedicated territories who paid Bharti up front but provided retailers with credit, allowing some 2 million retailers to offer Airtel pre- and post-paid telecom cards by 2012.

• To make inroads into rural India, Bharti teamed up with SKS, India's largest microfinance institution. This allows customers to borrow and then to purchase a Nokia 1650 and repay the cost over 25 months.

As a result of these and other entrepreneurial ideas Bharti Airtel is now debt free, its operating margins increased from -2.25% in 2003 to 28.3% in 2008, it achieved a 43% growth in revenues 2004–2008 and a 27% return on capital employed in 2009, this with an ARPU of $5.95 compared with one of $50 in the USA.

Source: adapted from Prahalad and Mashelkar (2010) and other sources.

The ability to be open to entrepreneurial opportunities in new ideas and indeed to effectively realise and operationalise these within a complex organisational context, in a constantly and rapidly changing market environment, is a fundamental capability of the global leader. The long term leveraging of such innovations over the long term in operational terms is ultimately down to the intrinsic principles, perspectives and cognitive mental process of practical and collaborative wisdom. The ability to consider all relevant information in respect of a new idea in a practically wise cognitive mental process, within the context of organisational capabilities and market dynamics, and thereby from a holistic perspective to take the optimal calculated risk, is fundamental to optimising organisational performance over the long term.

This section highlights three key points in the process of effective operational leadership:

• The wise and effective leadership requirement, no matter the role or seniority, to take a holistic perspective, recognising and nurturing the developing attributes and capabilities of individuals who have the ability to create a paradigm shift in the capabilities, effectiveness and performance of the organisation. This requires a primary people emphasis and focus, to motivate and nurture in order to harness individual potential for the optimal performance of the organisational community.

- A recognition that innovative ideas which can result in a paradigm shift for the organisation or significant enhancement in performance can occur within any part of the organisational dynamic. It is therefore the responsibility of every operational leader to create an appropriate environment to stimulate, encourage and assess innovative thinking and ideas within their area of direct responsibility.
- Wise and effective leaders must have a mindset and capability to accommodate innovation and change within the context of a stable, operationally focused, organisational environment. This is necessary in order to maintain confidence, cohesion and allegiance amongst the stakeholder community, who may be less open-minded to innovations which potentially create instability in performance in the absence of wise and effective global leadership.

Is The Earth Really Spherical? – Sensitivity to Alternative Views

Operational business leaders must be sensitive to and effectively manage the changes in the framework of fundamental beliefs and knowledge, within the context of effectively managing the organisation towards optimal performance. Leaders must manage on the assumption that existing knowledge is not foundational, but rather transitional. The leader's role is therefore to utilise their insight and judgement to introduce and embed new knowledge, through a process of practical and collaborative wisdom, utilising the attributes of quiet leadership in order to maintain the focus and vision of the organisation and the energy, motivation and cohesion of its employees,

For centuries, mankind knew all there was to know about the shape of the Earth. It was a flat planet, shaped roughly like a circle, with lots of pointy things hanging down from the underside. On the comparatively smooth topside, Europe sat in the middle of the circle, with the other continents scattered about the fringes, and parts of Africa hanging over the edge. The oceans lapped against the sides of the Earth, and in places ran over, creating currents that would pull over the edge ships that ventured too far out to sea.

The Flat Earth Society: "deprogramming the masses since 1547",
first sentence of Mission Statement.

As a child of the early 1950s I have always eaten a lot of carrots and have continued to do so, even after I became short-sighted at the early age of 11. This was because my parents convinced, indeed ingrained in my mindset, that carrots were good for my eyesight, a myth propagated by the British Government during the Second World War to encourage people to eat the most easily available vegetables for their nutritional benefits. This is a belief which is now ingrained in the psyche of millions of British people of that era and probably many of their children and grandchildren, as they continued to propagate the myth, which in any event, has no detrimental results.

The above is a somewhat light hearted example of a very serious issue. This is that Man is still at the amoeba stage in the pursuit of knowledge and therefore the unquestioned and obvious truths of today are the absurdities of tomorrow or, in business terms, suboptimal perspectives and practices at best, at worst, principles and beliefs destructive of value and organisational survival. The previous section pretty much proves this point. Those, for instance, who became accustomed to horse-drawn carriages and buggies, and considered that locomotives and automobiles would never catch on. Many knowledgeable people scoffed at the potential market for personal computers and, more recently, the longevity of the tablet (Stan Shih, Chairman and CEO of Acer Group). As we have already noted, Bharti Airtel questioned and re-engineered what had become recognised as fundamental business beliefs, perceptions, principles and presumptions.

Having said this, it is impractical to be questioning every belief and practice all of the time; otherwise no progress will be made. However, the practically wise global leader will question, during the cognitive mental process, those facts, beliefs and practices whose validity are considered critical to success or failure, but which at the end of the day are insufficiently substantiated. The prevailing financial crisis is an example of a belief in the continuing validity of many of the existing institutional structures, principles, beliefs, norms and standards, when in fact the economic, financial and technological environment had changed so radically as, when challenged and tested by developing crisis, to make them ineffective and redundant. It is much easier just to go with the flow, living and working within an environment based upon a framework of accepted "truths"– facts, perspectives, priorities, standards, relationships and practices, not causing waves uncomfortable to the stability and comfort of self and others. That approach might be perceived to be the best option for career longevity by many, if not the majority, but a leader, much less a global leader, you are not.

The fundamental point which this section makes is that to be a global leader you need to question. Equally you must be open to views which are divergent from the norms, beliefs, perspectives and frameworks which form a path followed by the majority. There are always (and must always be) a small number of "crusaders" in an organisation who question norms and propose alternative perspectives and solutions. These individuals may be 100 per cent right, but even if what they say is 10 per cent, 20 per cent or 30 per cent right the implications need to be considered and assessed for practical validity and implementation.

This practice is intuitive in the wise, global leader, if only to ensure that the organisational dominant logic is not applied on tram lines with an inability to change perspectives and priorities. I believe that most individuals prefer to continue to apply principles, perspectives and practices to which they have become accustomed and comfortable. This is human nature, until danger or crisis arises, preferring to continue to apply that which has always worked for the organisation in the past. The role of the global leader is to assess the requirement to change the business dynamic and embedded principles and perspectives on the basis of important changes in the business context. Part of this intuitive skill is to be aware of alternative views which forewarn and facilitate appropriate change before the requirement becomes altogether clear to the competition and/or the situation becomes critical.

In this respect, whilst I am pretty sure that the world is spherical, I remain only 95 per cent convinced. I remain open to alternative views because in 300 BC the majority thought that it was flat, but even then there were a few plaintive voices saying that there was evidence to suggest that it was spherical. Throughout history there have been similar fundamental truths, ingrained beliefs and perspectives, for which there was apparently ample supporting evidence:

• The Divine Right of Kings;

- Only the landed/educated should have the vote;
- Women should not have the vote because they decide on an emotional basis;
- Black/brown are intellectually inferior to white people;
- The Malthusian theory of population; and
- The sun will never set on Western economic prosperity and hegemony.

These fundamental truths and many others have all been debunked and cast aside as a result of enhanced knowledge, experience and insight, allied to changes in perspectives and power. Equally, the twentieth century has witnessed the introduction of many business principles and practices by both business and scholarly luminaries which were hailed as inspired, only to be found wanting through operational application or made redundant by changing business contexts and/or enhanced leadership understanding, experience, insight and judgement in respect of the market and organisational dynamic. As mentioned in Part One, in assessing information and opinions it is always wise to be aware of and consider the motivations of those putting those ideas forward, both propounding maintenance of the status quo or a radical reappraisal of generally accepted, principles, perspectives, standards and practices.

An interesting finding whilst undertaking initial investigations into the flat versus spherical Earth issue is the fallacy that the discovery or conclusion that the Earth is in fact spherical occurred around the time and as a result of the voyages of Christopher Columbus in the sixteenth century. In fact Pythagoras in the sixth century BC proposed a spherical Earth and Aristotle in the third century BC supported this position on empirical grounds. Whilst the delineation of supporters of flat versus spherical is generally based upon education and literacy up to and during the Middle Ages, many venerated theologians continued thereafter to support a "flattist" approach following the letter of the Old Testament. Others followed the spherical approach but with doubts and misgivings, including Basil, Ambrose and Augustine. The point is that to be ahead of the curve you must be able and willing to listen to and consider the plaintive voices as well as the established "truth" accepted by the majority. Also to distinguish those hailed as the bringers of knowledge who may be charlatans and self-promoters, seeking out those who possess the fundamental knowledge and logic. Such insight and commitment reflects the attributes of the practically wise cognitive mental process described in detail in Chapter 2.

This flat/spherical Earth issue is utilised for illustration purposes only and I will therefore not go into any further detail on its history and the continuing discussion into the twenty-first century, as illustrated by the quotation at the beginning of this chapter section. It is used as a somewhat outlandish example to illustrate a point of significance in the required attributes and capabilities of the global leader, since we all, of course recognise and agree that the Earth is spherical, don't we? It reflects the process and manner by which business and leadership principles and perspectives change and take root within an organisation, which is a critical consideration for operational leaders.

Rather than everyone agreeing to the logic of a single perspective, organisations tend to split into influential groupings, often unrelated by educational level and/or seniority, taking divergent positions. Some continue to advocate and apply what are perceived by many to be "Dark Age" perspectives which are considered by "New Age", forward thinking individuals within any organisation to have been disproven by "scientific" analysis and evidence. Such "Dark Age" proponents are often perceived to employ guerrilla tactics and make indefensible last stands in support of their embedded, hard-coded beliefs.

I must admit to having been a bit of a Luddite or flat Earther in respect of the introduction of desktop computers at the office desk, TQM and matrix management and other new business and organisation management ideas, this even though I was often selected to introduce and embed such new ideas, perspectives and practices within the operational business context.

This is perhaps where the wisdom of the global operational leader is critical. Having decided that changes in the dominant logic, perspectives, priorities and practices are justified and required in order to optimise performance, he/she must:

- First, consider the implications of such change from a holistic rather than a narrow functional perspective.
- Second, apply attributes of open-mindedness, persuasion, nurturing and compromise to achieve coordinated and structured change.
- Third, succeed in maintaining or renewing cohesion, allegiance, motivation and advocacy amongst stakeholder groups behind a new business dynamic.

The key issue to keep in mind is that these points are not primarily directed at the Executive Committee of the organisation but to the swathe of operational leaders who are really in control of operational efficiency and performance. Every leader within the organisation has the responsibility to challenge prevailing perspectives, priorities and practices, propose, initiate and engineer radical change at the holistic and functionally specific change.

An example might be appropriate to justify such a controversial point. As the individual responsible for the marketing function in a number of financial institutions I considered what should be its role and purpose in the achievement of organisational objectives, within the context of increasing competition, customer sophistication and market complexity. I decided that marketing, rather than focusing on technical capability, on such issues as advertising, promotions, direct marketing, should instead act as the champion, focal point and owner of market penetration and market development. In this respect the function's scope should be expanded to encompass such matters as competitor, market and customer research, product development and management, distribution channel development (i.e. branches, ATMs, call centres, internet and mobile phone banking) customer service, CRM, sales and service quality, and new market development initiatives (e.g. expatriate and Islamic banking). The marketing function was to become a dynamic and pro-active centre of excellence for creating an organisational capability for market penetration, rather than merely a centre of functional marketing excellence. Once an enhanced operational capability had been created for market penetration (e.g. call centre, internet banking, CRM, Islamic Banking) then it could subsequently be transferred to those with long-term operational rather than development management capability.

Convincing senior management of the logic was the easy part. Resistance came from those who perceived diminishing levels of responsibility and authority. Also the organisational benefits of radically changing from an operational leadership focus and emphasis to which they had become familiar and comfortable to one focused on development. Success was achieved on the basis that the development role is high risk and complex, and the majority of functional heads were experts in the operations of tried and tested functionality, preferring to take over initiatives once all the bugs had been identified and the chances of long-term success and enhanced credibility were optimised.

Was Alexander So Great? – Common Vision and Long-Term Perspective

Charismatic leaders regularly fail to sustain performance due to the fact that their perspectives and capabilities are geared to short-term achievements. As a result they fail to value and prioritise buy-in by employees to the organisational vision, thereby failing to institute practices which engender optimal energy, motivation, dedication and allegiance. The consequence is frequently suboptimal performance and the collapse of the organisation in the face of adverse market conditions and/or internal conflict over the medium to long term, once the power of the charismatic leader has declined. Alexander the Great failed to exhibit the principles, perspectives and cognitive mental process of global leadership and practical and collaborative wisdom.

Alexander the Great is much admired as a great commander and a charismatic and inspirational leader. There are many parallels in modern business leadership folklore. Yet it is highly debatable whether many, if any, were characterised by practical and collaborative wisdom. Many failed to achieve buy-in to a common vision and therefore failed to achieve optimal performance and in many cases, the survival of their "empires".

ALEXANDER THE GREAT – EXPERT IN MERGERS AND ACQUISITIONS?

The reign of Alexander the Great, a mere 13 years, (336–323BC) reminds one of the old adage, which has resonance equally within business organisations that it is easier to conquer than to reign. By the age of 30 he had created one of the largest empires in history, spanning from the Aegean to the Himalayas, with titles including Hegemon of the Hellenistic League, Shahanshah of Persia and Pharaoh of Egypt.

It is possible to achieve much in the short term by dint of charisma, force of character, personality, generating excitement, euphoria and momentum. The critical part is to realise the benefits for everyone involved over the long term, to keep the "empire" going through persuasion, the effective communication of a common vision, which people understand and to which they relate. By this means one engenders enthusiasm, motivation, cohesion and allegiance. To achieve this over the long term you require the patience and capabilities of the global, "quiet" leader to deliver on the vision and objectives over a sustained period.

Alexander, despite his historical veneration, succeeded as a conqueror, but failed as a ruler. The career of Alexander the Great has numerous parallels in business. He was held in awe due to his continuous success in conquests (this might be paralleled with the success of businessmen in M&A or being appointed to increasingly broader responsibilities within the organisation). However, his ultimate personal ambition and vision, to reach the "ends of the world and the Great Outer Sea" was not fundamentally shared by his subordinates. This was primarily due to the resultant hardship experienced, perceived role in and ownership of achievements, compared with the nature and significance of the rewards.

The result, during a reign dominated by a rash, impulsive nature and a focus on self, latterly turning into megalomania, paranoia, delusions of grandeur (which perhaps has parallels and resonance in many branches of society, including business) and a disregard for the well-being and reward of those whom he led was:

- Disaffection
- Conspiracy
- Plots on his life
- Mutiny.

This was followed by 40 years of civil war and the disintegration of his empire upon his untimely death. Fundamentally this was due to the absence of a buy-in to his vision and the inability or effort of Alexander to undertake operational, day to day efforts to embed the vision amongst his followers, to persuade and consult in order to achieve long-term buy-in. One does not have to look far for parallels in business leadership in both the twentieth and early twenty-first century.

Sources: adapted from various websites.

As I have already mentioned, some years ago I was operationally and directly responsible for a number of diverse departments within a single division of a financial services organisation As one might expect, each head of department and its staff looked to achieve as the priority, their specific departmental objectives and targets. Due to the close interdependencies and interrelationships in, for example, the launch of a new product or service, there will be substantial resource support, cooperation, coordination required from business development, advertising, remote banking channels to achieve effective sales, service quality and market penetration. At the same time remote banking channels will have their own dedicated objectives, such as the rollout of internet banking or outbound calling for mutual funds, for which they are likely to feel greater commitment and ownership. In any single departmental initiative towards the achievement of what is ultimately an organisational objective, there is always therefore the potential for and likelihood of considerable disorganisation, chaos, conflict and recriminations. This is often likely to spill over to supporting divisions and functions, with the resultant loss in divisional leadership credibility and suboptimal performance within a multiplicity of functions within the organisation.

The prescribed solution to this suboptimal operational situation is to forestall any confusion by creating a cascade of Gantt charts during the annual and 3–5-year planning process of all the various initiatives at each business unit level (e.g. organisational, divisional, departmental) in order that everything is coordinated. However, as operational leaders well appreciate, after the first month these sophisticated coordination plans go into the bin, as the application of projects uncovers unthought of tasks, which causes unanticipated delays. New projects are added, some are cancelled, with the resultant impact on scheduled resource support between business units. Whilst the administrative process solution is to arrange meetings, reallocate interdepartmental resources, amend Gantt charts, in reality you can spend over 50 per cent of working hours on such unproductive work, to the detriment of project completion. Such a process rarely improves output, except in short-term spurts, until the next change in business project priority or objectives occurs.

Whilst there have been a wide variety of solutions put forward for this common organisational issue, including the inclusion of other divisions' and departments' initiatives as part of targets in order to achieve commitment and ownership, increasingly there is a realisation that this is insufficient to achieve the required levels of coordination and cohesion. Whilst it requires substantial levels of leadership capabilities and confidence, the solution lies in an appreciation by all staff that they are not members of a single departmental unit. Rather they are making specific contributions to the achievement of divisional objectives and to the long-term organisational vision, requiring an expansion of perceptions of the community to which they relate and owe allegiance.

I believe that most leaders lack the confidence to stand up and speak with conviction on such matters, believing that ultimately staff are only interested in completing their narrow, dedicated operational tasks in product development, customer service, call centre, advertising, cards operations, etc. without considering any "fluffy" intangible issues which only distract them from their work. However, this is a cop-out and aberration of reality and detrimentally affects optimal operational efficiency. It is demeaning to the increasingly intelligent and educated workforce, who benefit in respect of self-respect and esteem to feel that they are part of and contributing positively to a greater long-term vision in support of a broader community to which they relate and belong. In this respect I am reminded of the quote by Sir John Bond, to which we have already referred in Part Two,

That reminds me of the janitor who worked for NASA at the time of the space programme in the 60s. He was asked what he did. He didn't say he swept the floor. He said, "I'm helping put a man on the moon" (Sir Bond, 2000a, p. 3).

This is not only about ownership and responsibility; it is about sharing and being part of a common vision, enhancing commitment, motivation, allegiance and advocacy. The role of the product developer, call centre agent, advertising officer is much akin to the village blacksmith in medieval times shoeing horses, not for the groats or ducats with which he is paid, but an appreciation that the horses which he has shod help to generate the trade and defend the community, of which he is part and upon which he is dependent. This relationship, and the requirement for a common long-term vision in order to optimise performance has become obscured by the size and complexity of modern business organisations and the outdated mass production, narrow employee role perspectives of business management. The new leadership reality requires a constant focus on and communication of the people and community element for optimal long-term performance, rather than on the achievement of tasks and projects. This results in a requirement to educate staff not only in technical proficiency, project management and other operational matters, but in the holistic and community perspective and priority and its importance for operational effectiveness and long term performance. In this respect an ancient Chinese proverb has twenty-first century resonance,

If you are planning for a year, sow rice (implement targets). If you are planning for a decade plant trees (new markets, organisational structures, technical training). If you are planning for a generation, educate the people (in the common vision)

Note: words in brackets reflect my reinterpretation for the purposes of this point.

An organisation and its leadership coalition does not achieve optimal cohesion, motivation, allegiance and work rate by appearing to focus on a business plan spanning 12–18 months. This encourages staff to also think in the short term vis-à-vis their longevity with the firm. Only through a long-term leadership perspective can the required employee attributes of allegiance, dedication, cohesion, energy and easy transfer of tacit knowledge be achieved,

We are not managing for the next reporting period, we are managing an organisation that has survived and prospered for almost 140 years and is running a marathon, not a series of sprints (Whitson, 2001, p. 3).

So how is this applied in practice, in the heat of operational, day to day leadership, in order to achieve consistent operational effectiveness and optimal long-term performance? As a practitioner I offer a template of key points for adaptation and improvement by individual leaders according to knowledge, insight, context and personal characteristics.

ALIGNMENT OF UNIT OBJECTIVES: THE OPERATIONAL APPLICATION OF PRACTICAL AND COLLABORATIVE WISDOM

Key Steps

- Agreement of unit targets and objectives with superior (as a result of formulation by organisation of annual, 3–5-year plan).
- Compilation of draft Gantt chart encompassing all tasks/projects with respect to unit responsibilities/tasks, indicating the priority of each task/project, for discussion with heads of support units.
- This is followed by discussion with subordinates and their subordinates in order to engender initial ownership.
- Presentation (preferably only one) by unit head to all staff to explain the long-term vision and core objectives of the organisation and the unit's specific contribution in this regard. If the unit is in operational terms split into subunits explain the role of such units in terms of the contribution of the overall unit (e.g. department or division).
- Stress that subunits and individuals will be assessed on the basis of their contribution to the achievement of the unit's objectives, based on the priority of each objective in the achievement of the organisation's overall vision. Individual objectives set at the beginning of the year for the purposes of assessment will be on the basis of unit rather than individual prioritised objectives.
- Clarify that whilst if the unit of performance had been the individual, this means of assessment approach might appear imprecise and inequitable. However, the unit

> of performance is to be the divisional and organisational objective(s) rather than specific tasks for which the individual is responsible. The individual's focus must therefore be the success of those organisational community objectives in which the individual is involved and carries responsibility.
>
> - For example, if an internet banking facility is to be up and running in March but in fact only launches in November then everyone who was defined as involved and responsible will be penalised, because they did not as a group provide the enthusiasm, insight, experience and judgment to combine and coordinate to anticipate and resolve issues towards a launch on time. Inevitably, in reality, there will be one individual or group of individuals who screwed up, either in setting an unrealistic timescale or failing in their defined operational tasks. These individuals will feel the ire of superiors, peers and subordinates. If they fail to deliver on a range of unit objectives then they will receive an adverse assessment and appropriate action will be taken – whilst others will only be penalised on the basis of one project or task where otherwise their performance is considered satisfactory, or above.
> - The result of this "community" assessment approach is that individuals are compelled to perform due to the adverse impact on their colleagues, who are looking holistically at the dynamic achievement of unit and organisational objectives.
> - Ultimately individuals will be assessed and remunerated on the basis of a quantification of the unit's performance on objectives in which the individual was involved. Individuals will be clearly informed how/where their superior sees their career progressing over a 1–3 year projection, all things being equal, this in order that they have a clear understanding of their role, contribution, performance and value within the community over a sustained period.

On the basis of my personal experience with frameworks of appraisal and remuneration every equation causes heated argument, disagreement and consternation. Whilst technical experts in remuneration and benefits and other relevant areas might poke holes in this framework, it does serve to provide a foundation to indicate how the benefits to the organisation of a common long-term vision might be achieved in practical, operational terms, primarily by changing perspectives, priorities and, inevitably, terms of recompense. The first step in technical experts developing appropriate benchmarks is to clarify key organisational perspectives and priorities in terms of a community approach to individual output and effort.

Given the embedded nature of loyalty to and ownership of the targets and issues of the individual and the subunit within which the individual is directly employed, it is imperative that the head of department, division and whole organisation develop operational routines and practices to emphasise and reinforce the common vision perspective and priority to their direct staff. In my own case I changed the emphasis of regular meetings in line with a contribution to the broader objectives of the organisational community, rather than the achievement of tasks and projects for which individuals and subunits have personal responsibility:

- Weekly meetings, maximum 1 hour, with individual departmental heads to primarily discuss and emphasise progress in respect of their contribution to divisional key projects/objectives, rather than their individual task responsibilities. This approach emphasises their responsibility for achieving departmental tasks and projects since I am concerned with the contribution to the overall picture. Having said that, if there is a technical problem which requires discussion or intra/interdivisional issues which are stunting progress then these will also be discussed. In many respects it is likely that the same issues are discussed, it is the perspective, emphasis and context which has changed.

- Fortnightly meeting with all heads of departments of division, 1-hour maximum, to discuss issues relating to intradivisional coordination issues.
- Monthly meeting with all department heads and their immediate subordinates within the division, 90-minutes maximum, as an open forum where each individual raises issues of concern where he/she is unable to find a solution, inviting comments. This is structured on the basis of offering advice and guidance within the emphasis and context of supporting divisional and organisational objectives, utilising the experience of many heads to achieve divisional and organisational objectives.
- Quarterly meeting with other organisational divisions, 90-minutes maximum (but which might be repeated if items remain unresolved), with which my division has an interface, either as suppliers or consumers of services, to discuss issues which are obstructing the achievement of organisational objectives and long-term vision.
- Six monthly meeting with all staff down to junior manager within division, 90-minutes maximum, to discuss the contribution of the division to organisational objectives and long-term vision, raising issues which are stunting divisional progress and asking for ideas and solutions to issues for which they are not directly responsible, but emphasising that everyone has ownership of and responsibility for the division's progress and their experience and insight is a resource which the division wishes to and expects to be able to tap into. The objective of this meeting is to optimise coordination, cohesion and cooperation and embed/reinforce the common vision.

From the outside it is difficult to discern any obvious difference in the role of the operational leader, which tends to be crisis management within the function, inter-functional issues and dealing with strategy and policy issues. In fact the leader is effecting a culture change, by changing perspectives, priorities, attitudes which will enhance clarity of direction, motivation, cohesion, with a substantial impact on productivity and performance through the development of a common vision and commitment to the broader community objectives. In the absence of such an inclusive and communal approach to operational leadership you will be destined to be a shooting star perhaps in a number of organisations throughout your career, turning round one day to find that in reality you have no followers, most importantly in mind, if not in body.

Sell Soap: How Difficult Can It Be? – Global Effectiveness and Local Responsiveness

The possession of practical wisdom allows the global leader to accurately distinguish between tasks which are within and outside of the capabilities of him/herself as individuals and the organisational leadership cadre as a collaborative capability. Fundamental to the effective implementation of any management strategy is an intrinsic leadership ability to "balance" contrasting requirements and objectives. Such a balance is achieved through the development and conversion of core attributes and capabilities into appropriate perspectives and priorities. This, in turn, facilitates levels of insight and judgment, and ultimately wisdom, which consistently ensure optimal decision-making and issue resolution. Once global leadership attributes and capabilities, based upon practical and collaborative wisdom are more widely acknowledged and understood, they will increasingly be recognised as equally relevant and necessary within individual markets, which will be identified as comprising of distinct societal contexts.

One of the fundamental obstacles to wise and effective operational leadership is how you perceive an issue or a situation, whether it is perceived as complicated, requiring a type and level of knowledge and experience with which you are or are not familiar or capable. This view is, in turn, formulated by what you read or hear about the subject from peer group leaders and/or individuals whom you consider to have looked into the subject in great detail and therefore to have accumulated appropriate knowledge, experience, perspective, insight and judgment. Regrettably, perceptions are frequently at variance with reality in this regard and it is often the case that those without the requisite perspectives, attributes and capabilities who perceive issues as less complicated, thereby struggle in practice, resulting in suboptimal results. The above section title seeks to encompass these perceptual difficulties. It is in fact difficult to sell a bar of soap or a bottle of shampoo, particularly within different market contexts.

The maxim of global efficiency with local responsiveness, recently mooted as a formula to clarify the complicated process of multinational market penetration, whilst offering useful insights is:

- Neither the strategic leadership platform for global domination of the soap market;
- Nor of value creation only within the global context;

it is rather a simplistic, formulaic approach, obscuring the global leadership perspectives, insights, attributes and capabilities which are required for consistent optimal performance, no matter the market context. As Part One of this book indicated, wise decision making requires an ability to select and appropriately process that information, which will achieve the optimal solution within the context of the stakeholder requirements and the aspirations of the organisational community.

Many scholars and business gurus have made their reputations and a wide variety of dedicated theories have been developed on the premise that it is much more difficult or different to lead an organisation which has operations or representation in a multiplicity of countries, societies and markets (see "Blackburn Needs Global Leaders!") and this is why such maxims as global effectiveness with local responsiveness have been penned. Over the last four decades we have increasingly become familiar with such terms as multinational enterprise (MNE), international, multi-domestic, transnational and global business strategies. As someone who has been employed by multinational organisations, in dealing with, for example, differing:

- Consumer preferences
- Human resource practices
- Regulatory frameworks
- States of distribution channel development
- Attitudes towards customer service

- Attitudes towards work and loyalty to the organisation.

It is my experience that these do indeed result in a significant additional complexity to effective operational organisational management (rather than leadership). However, the differences have perhaps been over-egged to make the point and create a new body of management thought. This has had the detrimental effect of creating a sense of trepidation and mental blockage that multimarket leadership requires a breed of super leaders of enhanced intelligence, experience, insight and judgement to handle the multinational context. Not so, for two reasons:

- Many of the most difficult issues above are also increasingly experienced in operational leadership when expanding, merging or acquiring within a single market which comprise a variety of distinct societal groupings and sub-markets (e.g. USA, India, China, Russia, Spain, France, Belgium, the UK and Germany). In many respects the complexity of operational leadership arises in the appropriate and practical application of uniform laws, rules and standards where they are not considered by peer group leaders as appropriate and consistent with prevailing values, principles and practices of a distinct social/cultural grouping within a defined social context. Continuing and increasing migration on the basis of perceived economic and political necessity will further complicate operational leadership decision-making and issue resolution in order to maintain cohesion and allegiance within an organisational unit. In this respect leading an organisational unit in India, USA or France may require similar if not greater capabilities in global leadership than that required where you are responsible for a range of organisational units in say Saudi Arabia, Egypt, North Africa, Lebanon and Turkey.
- As we have already noted (and reinforced by the above), the capabilities of global leadership are not based upon geography, but are rather attitudinal, based upon perspectives and priorities, which can be effectively developed within a single market.

The much discussed issue of optimal performance through applying global efficiency with local responsiveness fundamentally applies equally if your head office is in Leeds, Northern England and you also have operations located in London, Belfast, Glasgow, Manchester, Dublin and Newcastle than if you have your head office in London and operations in New York, Mexico City, Berlin, Riyadh, Kuala Lumpur, Mumbai and Beijing. As a young, aspiring leader I was involved in the merger of eight loosely connected savings banks in the UK. Whilst, as the initial step towards merger, they had unified IT systems and other technical and administrative functions, each retained business and management autonomy, including differing product ranges, advertising plans, sales and business development strategies. One bank, whilst accepting the overall desirability of merger contended that their customers had financial requirements which required differences in the product range than that agreed by the other constituent banks. Whilst there were some doubts regarding the validity of this contention it was agreed that there might continue to be significant differences in the product range post-merger. Another bank was so resistant to merger at the fundamental level of not being directed by "foreigners" (even though located in the UK) from London that it decided to disconnect completely and become independent.

My point is that the skills, aptitudes, perspectives and priorities required of the multinational leader can be and frequently are possessed by the operational leader who has been operating within a "single" market. These are fundamentally global leadership skills, which apply equally to leaders within an operation in Birmingham or Nottingham in England as a leader who is responsible for managing operations in London, Berlin, Mumbai and Rio de Janeiro. I am sure that there will be a number of readers who will at this stage be if-ing and but-ing but, taking my own industry, financial services, if you are an effective divisional leader responsible for say, 3,000 branches in the UK, it is likely that your experience, knowledge, insight, judgement and wisdom would allow you to adapt to manage multinational operations in Europe, the Far East and/or Middle East, or indeed any other part of the globe. You can develop global leadership skills exclusively in one market due to your personal and business experience and knowledge. This provides an ability to assess and analyse, providing the perspectives, insight and judgement to take responsibility for multinational operations.

This section of Part Three takes the opportunity to utilise the maxim of global effectiveness with local responsiveness as a concept widely understood by readers as a means of further exposing and illustrating the attributes of the wise, global operational leader. The foundation of consistent optimal performance lies in the ability to take a balanced view, on the basis of the existence of individual and accumulated organisational leadership attributes and capabilities. This facilitates clarity of insight, resulting in sound judgement, which ultimately results in wise leadership (see Figure 6.1). This proposition is quickly written, but in practice slowly acknowledged, understood, accepted and achieved, and even then only by a few organisations. This is so because:

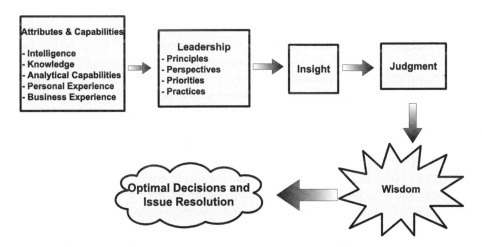

Figure 6.1　Key Attributes and Capabilities and the Process Towards Wise Leadership

- It takes substantial time to select and develop a critical mass of leaders within the organisation who are inculcated in the principles, perspectives and priorities of a single dominant logic founded on universal values.
- To thereby create an organisational repository of knowledge and experience which remains embedded in the organisation as the individual holders depart, primarily, in such organisations, at or near the end of their careers.
- In addition, there are few organisations whose dominant coalitions possess the "marathon" perspectives and priorities to which we have already referred, or the patience to nurture these leadership attributes, particularly in the face of stakeholder demands for "sprint" results in the form of maximum short-term returns.

Optimal performance is achieved by the most effective balance between global effectiveness and local responsiveness. This is achieved only by an organisation's operational leadership cadre being furnished with the above practically wise attributes and capabilities, no matter the extent of the market (be it local, regional, national, multinational or global). By this means they are furnished with the ability to take the optimal decisions to balance these apparently opposing priorities, in an intuitive rather than mechanical manner, representing an embedded, subconscious understanding of the drivers of effective leadership and optimal performance. Global effectiveness is not achieved by delivering global cost-efficiencies across all operating units. Global effectiveness is rather the application of a uniform vision based upon a single dominant logic of values and principles which are understood and acknowledged by all individual leaders and staff, and upon which all decisions are made, no matter the global location.

Global effectiveness is represented by a perspective rather than a numeric, although the results can be expressed both quantitatively and qualitatively. Local responsiveness is achieved by delegating those responsibilities which have maximum impact on the self-respect and esteem of local leaders and staff, without jeopardising a uniform vision and optimal organisational effectiveness. The result is optimal local productivity, this due to optimal access to the repository of local tacit knowledge, employee motivation, dedication, allegiance and advocacy. The result is that the organisation is regarded as part of and making a tangible contribution to the societal and economic community. This process is represented in Figure 6.2.

The critical point to appreciate is that this section is not directed at the scholar, the writer of organisational policy or strategy, or the members of the executive committee. It is primarily directed at you, the present or aspiring operational leader, be it of a local branch office with two staff, a regional or head office section, departmental or divisional head. In order that you might carry out your leadership role effectively, you must possess the attributes as described in Figure 6.1, to take operational decisions utilising optimal insight, judgement and wisdom. Utilising this capability allows you to achieve your primary objective of optimising performance through actively and continuously balancing the single dominant logic of the organisation, comprising universally acknowledged values with an appropriate delegation of responsibilities in order to leverage available local knowledge and insight and generate optimal motivation, dedication and allegiance. The role of the global leader revolves around the accumulation, effective communication and utilisation of the attributes and capabilities of practical and collaborative wisdom, not only by yourself, but by your peers and subordinates. As a result, we achieve an organisation-wide understanding of the important variables and the process of optimally balancing global effectiveness with local responsiveness, no matter whether you are leading a supermarket in Blackburn, north of Manchester, England or a global supermarket chain.

I have selected Procter & Gamble (P&G) as an appropriate example for the points made in this section since it appears from the evidence to be an organisation whose leadership cadre have been inculcated in a single dominant logic and who possess the embedded perspectives, attributes and capabilities of the global leader. The P&G leadership cadre have (consciously or subconsciously) undertaken a practically wise assessment based upon the cognitive mental process described in Part One. They have thereby developed an appropriate organisational structure and global framework of responsibility and authority which has created a balance between global effectiveness and local responsiveness, consistent with optimal operational efficiency and long-term performance within their selected market segments. There is little doubt, given the nature of the leadership structure that their dominant logic, global leadership principles, perspectives, priorities, attributes and capabilities are acknowledged, understood and consistently applied, no matter the level in the leadership hierarchy or the divisional/geographic location within the organisation.

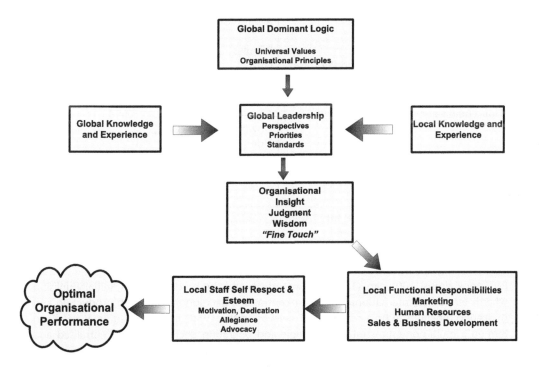

Figure 6.2   The Operational Process of Applying Global Leadership Attributes

PROCTER & GAMBLE (P&G): TRANSNATIONAL LEADERSHIP IN ACTION

P&G was founded in 1837 and has its headquarters in Cincinnati, Ohio, USA. As at 2011 it had approximately 140,000 employees worldwide and net sales of $83 billion. It is a global player with a portfolio of 250+ brands in three key segments of the consumer goods sector which is significantly impacted by many local variables, such as product content, distribution, pricing, packaging, branding and competition, which has a significant impact on the distribution of responsibility and authority within the organisational leadership cadre.

Table 6.1   P&G: Net Sales by Global Business Unit

Global Business Unit	Reportable Segment	Billion Dollar Brands	2011 Net Sales by GBU $billion
Beauty	Beauty	Head & Shoulders, Olay, Pantene, Wella	20.2
Grooming	Grooming	Braun, Fusion, Gillette, Mach3	8.0
Health	Health Care	Always, Crest, Oral-B	12.0
Well-Being	Snacks and Pet Care	Pringles Iams	3.2
Household Care	Fabric Care and Home Care	Ace, Ariel, Dawn, Downy, Duracell, Gain, Tide	24.8
	Baby Care and Family Care	Bounty, Chamin, Pampers	15.6

Source: adapted from P&G website: http://www.pg.com/en_US/company/global_structure_operations/corporate_structure.shtml

P&G took almost 100 years (1930) to expand beyond the borders of USA, initially utilising what is termed an international strategy (centraliised decision making with production and marketing functions in host countries). However, in the 1950s it introduced what has been termed a multi-domestic strategy (strategic and operating decisions are decentralised and delegated to strategic business units to allow decisions in such areas as products, distribution, marketing, sales management to be fine-tuned to the needs of the local market) specifically to penetrate the Chinese market. It was not until the 1980s that P&G implemented what is termed a transnational strategy (where a business organisation seeks to balance the double-edged objectives of global efficiency and local responsiveness) as it sought to respond more flexibly and "wisely" to penetrate a range of market contexts (e.g. emerging markets) and utilise the repository of operational leadership experience, knowledge and insight which had developed, particularly during the preceding 50 years, specifically in respect of the coordination of decision making for optimal global performance.

It is difficult to ascertain whether P&G applies the global leadership framework which is proposed by this book, this in the absence of in-depth research within the senior executive cadre of the organisation. However, it is evident from an analysis of their structure that they do have an in-depth understanding of the global efficiency and local responsiveness dynamic, combining:

- A central dominant logic and singular, uniform business vision.
- A central repository of knowledge, experience and resources.
- An appreciation of and focus on the local stakeholder dynamic.
- A leveraging of the experience, knowledge and insight of local staff in order to achieve an organisational and leadership structure conducive to creating a cohesive, collaborative, focused, motivated and energised global workforce which possesses the attributes, perspectives and priorities to achieve optimal long-term performance within those business sectors within which P&G is competing.

The organisational structure (see Figure 6.3), apart from lean corporate functions, comprises functions which do not differentiate between Group and local entities. It rather creates centres of responsibility and authority across the whole business, comprising of pertinent units at both the centre and locally, to optimise cohesion, coordination, focus, communication,

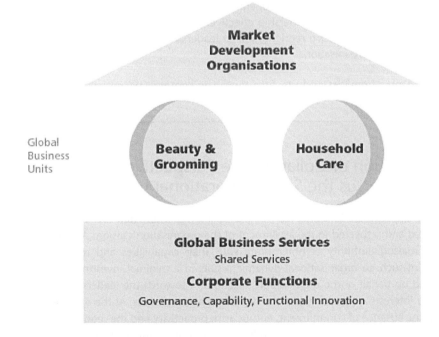

Figure 6.3 P&G Global Structures to Effect Optimal Long Term Performance

Source: P&G website: http://www.pg.com/en_US/company/global_structure_operations/corporate_structure.shtml

learning and the transfer of learning, knowledge and experience. This allows, for example, expertise in market development with respect to China but also the ability to cross– fertilise the experience and insight of those responsible for the market development of Japan who is also within the same organisational function.

P&G Global Structure: Roles and Responsibilities of Core Functions

- Global Business Units (GBUs) focus solely on consumers, brands and competitors around the world. They are responsible for the innovation pipeline, profitability and shareholder returns from their businesses.
- Market Development Organisations (MDOs) are charged with knowing consumers and retailers in each market where P&G competes and integrating the innovations flowing from the GBUs into business plans that work in each country.
- Global Business Services (GBS) utilises P&G talent and expert partners to provide best-in-class business support services at the lowest possible costs to leverage P&G's scale for a winning advantage.
- Lean corporate functions ensure ongoing functional innovation and capability improvement.

The evidence does indicate that P&G has ascended the global leadership learning curve over a protracted period (likely to be at least fifty years, although also likely to have been significantly influenced by the values and principles of its founders in early nineteenth century). By this means it has developed and gained, as an organisation, the attributes, capabilities, insight and judgement for wise decision making within the business sectors within which they have decided to operate over the long term. This has created a core competence for operational leadership effectiveness and optimal performance difficult to emulate without a long-term reorientation of leadership perspectives and priorities which must pervade the organisation.

Sources: adapted from P&G website: http://www.pg.com/en_US/company/global_structure_operations

The Application of Collaborative Perspectives and Attributes: The Dumb versus the Smart Operational Leader

Long-term optimal performance can only be achieved when staff feel that their views are considered and respected in the attainment of the organisation's vision. Also, that they have decision-making authority commensurate with their capabilities and responsibilities. The absence of such an organisational dynamic results in a minimal investment in and energy expended on behalf of the organisation, resentment towards the leadership and a concern that their interests are peripheral in the decision-making process. At the operational level the result is the absence of commitment, enthusiasm, proactivity and the requirement for step by step, micro-managing, which consistently produces operational inefficiency and suboptimal performance.

This section is very much linked to the previous section in expanding on the local responsiveness issue, looking at it as a more general and fundamental leadership attribute in respect of practical and collaborative wisdom. It looks at the organisational implications and substantial benefits of proactive delegation and empowerment. Empowerment within this context refers to:

- An acknowledgement amongst the dominant coalition of an organisation that there is a tangible logic and value in operational leaders and staff feeling that their views are considered and respected.
- Their recognition, by the dominant coalition, as an important part of the decision-making process.
- The tangible broad delegation of leadership responsibility and authority down and across the organisation, in terms of the achievement of the targets and objectives of the organisation.

Like so many children and adolescents (particularly males) I never experienced the pleasures of washing and ironing clothes, digging the garden, cutting the grass, painting and decorating, changing plugs and light bulbs, bits of DIY. My father wanted me to focus on my studies and he thought that there would be lots of time in the future to learn such mundane tasks. As it turns out I have been married 30 years and my wife tends to deal with all of these matters. I bring up this personal matter because if you do not learn and gain confidence you tend to avoid taking responsibility and becoming actively and spontaneously involved in such matters. If someone does not make the effort as an individual to take the time to teach, guide and advise, and ultimately to delegate and empower then you are not stretched, your perspectives and capabilities remain limited. You therefore feel unable to confidently take responsibility beyond your limited span of experience and thereby sub-optimise your contribution to your community, be it to your immediate family or the organisation within which you are a potential or present leader. Equally importantly, if you are indeed skilled in how to do a task yet are not invited to participate in that task but feel that you are confident to take wider responsibility and make a contribution, then this is likely to be regarded as a slight to your self-esteem and respect, with a resultant adverse impact on commitment, energy expended on behalf of, dedication, allegiance to and advocacy of the organisation.

As a leader it is dumb not to proactively develop, delegate and empower; dumb for both you, the individual and also for the organisation. Whilst at a point in time it may seem like sound judgment to do the job yourself or delegate it to people you can trust to get it completed fast and with certainty of quality, you miss the fundamental purpose of leadership. This is to optimise performance through developing, nurturing and managing the capabilities and perspectives of the community of people, be they subordinates, peers or superiors, through challenging, encouraging and nurturing. This smart versus dumb, short-term, short-sighted leadership approach brings me back to Bill Gates whom it is reputed would interrupt presentations with the retort, "That's the stupidest thing I've ever heard" (Isaacson, 1997) or when he became exasperated with someone would say, "I'll do it over the weekend" (Microsoft News Center, 1997).

I must admit to have often heard and also made comments similar to both quotes and to have preferred to do the work myself in the face of frequent short timeframes, believing that I could not trust anyone else to do the job. It is therefore an issue of which to be constantly aware and to actively personally manage. Leadership requires an appreciation of both the holistic and the specific. Rather than reacting to situations and throwing the available resources at it in some desperation, you must consider how such recurring situations might be resolved over the long term (if this is not clear refer to the "wise" cognitive mental process described in Chapter 2). Proactive responsibility for leadership development, inculcation, delegation and empowerment must be a central, front of mind perspective and priority of the operational leader, a task which is critical to effective operational management and consistent optimal performance of the organisation. This is a fundamental leadership perspective, priority and capability, not to be delegated or subordinated to the completion of technical responsibilities and tasks. If:

- You are not proactively involved in this process, unable and/or unwilling to accept this as a central responsibility, preferring to view it as an HR role and responsibility or not related to operational leadership responsibilities.
- You conclude that these are aspirational, nice to have, unrealistic words, written by someone removed from the operational coalface.

then you are responsible for and sentencing yourself and your organisation to mediocre rather than optimal operational effectiveness and performance over the long term and. In addition, regrettably, effective operational leadership , much less global leadership and the cognitive mental process of practical and collaborative wisdom are not for you.

In today's complex and increasingly global organisation no leader has all of the knowledge, experience and insight to take the optimal decision every time. This is why this book emphasises collaborative wisdom, based upon a collegiate approach to leadership. As an example of the need for delegation of empowerment, the global leader, despite his substantial knowledge and experience is unlikely to be sufficiently knowledgeable of the historical and prevailing institutional and ideological culture, the beliefs and perspectives of a specific organisation or social context, which have evolved over an extended period, to be able to understand the local context sufficiently to optimise the potential which exists. There is therefore a requirement to take advantage of and in many cases defer to, empower and entrust, the holders of "local" knowledge. The smart leader, through a proactive application of the perspectives and practices of development, delegation and empowerment therefore gains from a number of angles:

- He is able to focus his time, knowledge, experience and insight on his specific defined role.
- He is able to optimally leverage the knowledge, experience and insight of his staff to achieve the objectives of the unit and organisation.
- He is able to engender a feeling of ownership, personal contribution and identification with the organisation. This enhances productivity, creativity and entrepreneurship amongst staff with a significant impact on performance.

This enhanced performance is the result of proactive collaboration; an acknowledgment and understanding of the benefits which accrue to self, the organisation and the community of stakeholder groups involved in the organisation, tapping into willingness, indeed eagerness, amongst staff (and other stakeholders) to contribute to a community to which they closely relate. It is achieved through a primary focus on the active leadership of people to achieve organisational objectives, rather than managing and completing tasks, projects and achieving targets. Enhanced performance is primarily achieved through changes in leadership perspective and improvements in leadership capability, rather than by more efficient task and project process management. The difference in the two revolves around where you start from and the emphasis of your leadership effort.

Success comes through empowering rather than directing, from motivating and encouraging staff at all levels towards a reliance on self-discipline and self-direction, allied to organisational commitment, rather than formal control systems which often engender resentment, guerrilla tactics and obstruction. In many organisations there continues to be a "what do I do now?" culture. Due to the fact that leaders consider that staff do not have the knowledge, experience, insight and judgment and/or lack confidence in their people leadership capabilities they restrict and repress staff initiative and responsibility, closely controlling and monitoring actions, step by step, stifling creativity, initiative, ambition and entrepreneurship. In this respect I am reminded of a quote by Ghoshal and Bartlett,

> the leader looks down on order, symmetry, and uniformity – a neat step-by-step decomposition of the company's tasks and responsibilities. From the bottom, frontline managers look up at a phalanx of controllers whose demands soak up most of their energy and time. The result, as General Electric's chairman and CEO Jack Welch puts it, is an organisation with its face toward the CEO and its ass toward the customer (Ghoshal and Bartlett, 1995, p. 87).

Naturally, one of the roles of the leader of a unit within an organisation is to ensure that tasks and projects for which he is responsible are progressing towards completion, to agreed timescales and levels of professionalism and quality. However, these responsibilities are merely the table stakes and should not, as so often happens, be the central focus of the organisational leader. The role of the leader is about:

- Communicating and regularly and consistently reinforcing a vision and sense of organisational purpose.
- Engendering a sense of cooperation, of unity, of community, that the efforts of the organisation are consistent with the expectations of staff in respect of helping them to achieve their material and psychological aspirations.
- Creating a sense of trust rather than doubt in order to enhance self-esteem.
- Creating a sense of excitement, challenge, enthusiasm, dynamism, enjoyment even.
- Encourage a culture of creativity and entrepreneurship with regard to issue resolution.

I must admit that I have rarely met leaders who reflect and communicate a sense of excitement, enthusiasm and enjoyment for their role, even though many do indeed view their roles in this light. As I progressed in my career I only accepted or applied for positions which challenged, even scared me, but also excited and stretched me, where my superior stood back from micro-managing, effectively delegating responsibility and authority, thereby enhancing my confidence and self-esteem. There seems to be a view that it is more appropriate to project a serious aspect, of labouring under a heavy load, of gravitas and professionalism, perhaps to justify their stature and remuneration. This is counterproductive in the twenty-first century organisational context, where to achieve objectives whilst smiling is smart (and wise), because it is infectious. If a person in a leadership position cannot communicate and project technical proficiency, professionalism, a deep understanding of people motivation and aspirations and an excitement for the role and task then it is most unlikely that they have developed the perspectives, priorities, attributes and capabilities of global leadership and practical and collaborative wisdom.

Many readers may consider this leadership perspective and capability as a nice to have. Others might consider it aspirational, impractical, unrealistic and naive, borne of inexperience of the operational leadership environment within the business organisation. I am sympathetic to this view. In many if not the majority of organisations the foundations do not exist to apply this perspective, without substantial organisational investment and also personal risk:

- Staff and management are recruited largely on the basis of their technical skills, task orientation and dedication.
- The dominant logic of the organisation is not based upon universal values and principles to which individuals can relate and to which they can commit as being consistent with their own personal values.
- Little effort is made to inculcate staff in the values and principles of the organisational dominant logic. This creates a situation where leaders are loathe to delegate and empower because they are not confident that staff will take decisions and take action on the basis of fundamental organisational parameters in respect of principles, perspectives and priorities.
- The result is a repressive leadership style which fails to energise, excite relevant stakeholder groups and optimise creativity and productivity.

It would be true to say that leaders in an organisation have to work with what they have in respect of the prevailing dominant logic, perspectives, priorities and structures, the practices and available staff competencies and capabilities. Change can and must be slow and must be subtly implemented in order not to raise the awareness of the fearful, doubtful and outright obstructive. In my general management roles I applied a number of perspectives and priorities with regard to leading my staff in respect of the above issues:

- Where the dominant logic of the organisation was unclear I defined the principles, perspectives and priorities which would guide and define the decisions within the functional units under my direct responsibility. These would not be totally inconsistent with those of the organisation, since I would not work for an organisation whose values were inconsistent with my own.
- On the basis that I knew very little about the technical aspects of such issues as mobile phone banking, credit cards, Expatriate banking, Islamic Banking, for which I was personally responsible as general manager, I left the management of these areas to technical experts. I saw my role as rigorously questioning the logic of the technical decision-making process. In this respect I saw my key responsibility as ensuring that the decisions made were consistent with the divisional dominant logic, which I had defined and communicated (encompassing a primary focus on achieving objectives through effective people leadership), and attaining defined divisional targets and objectives as part of the achievement of the overall organisational vision.
- Once key milestones of divisional projects were agreed direct reports were made aware that they were empowered to, responsible for, but supported in their completion.

- Regular meetings to ascertain progress in respect of divisional objectives. The tone of these meetings was open, enthusiastic and inclusive regarding progress towards achieving divisional objectives and the organisation's vision, encouraging ideas, openly complimenting individuals and groups towards achievements, whilst highlighting issues in a constructive and solution-based manner.
- Appointment and promotion to leadership of units within the division was clearly recognised to be based primarily upon an ability to direct, guide, advise, persuade, enthuse, excite and persuade people (an assessment of relevant technical capability was also part of but a table stakes rather than predominant consideration).

The resultant benefits from a cohesive divisional community, where individuals are enthusiastic about communication in order to optimise the performance of an entity with whom they actively relate translates into a quantifiable enhancement in performance compared with that based upon individual material benefit within a fractured community where there was an absence of common logic and purpose.

In general, business organisations fail to recognise the value of clearly defining, communicating and regularly reinforcing the values and principles by which it is to be led. Whilst such communication can initially be in the form of a mission statement-type communication it will only become embedded through consistent example in the form of operational leadership decisions and actions. The problems arise in the communication of organisational values and principles:

- Where they are recognised as inconsistent with universal values;

and/or

- Where there is an inconsistency in avowed values and principles and operational leadership decisions and actions.

The result of an unwillingness or inability to effectively communicate the organisation's dominant logic is that the substantial benefits of inculcating the leadership cadre are not available. In the absence of inculcation the substantial benefits of empowerment cannot accrue, since the dominant coalition will regard it as too much of a risk, this in the absence of a generally agreed framework of principles, perspectives, priorities and standards within which analysis, assessment and decisions are taken. Optimal operational effectiveness and long-term performance is therefore only attainable if the dominant coalition is committed to what is a long-term investment in people, in terms of funds to train, operational resources to develop and mentor over the span of a career. Most of all, an operational leadership focus, time and dedication, in terms of a day to day process on moulding mindsets in respect of perspectives, priorities and practices. This is in contrast to short-term solutions towards the achievement of organisational objectives, in the form of a mindset which focuses on external recruitment, merger and/or acquisition, restructuring and cost-efficiencies, based on short-term perspectives, investment and commitment horizons.

So why be a dumb leader when you can be a smart leader. Actively collaborate with, enthuse and energise your subordinates, peers, even superiors (strangely enough many superiors welcome expressions of enthusiasm and energy, although it may not register on their faces due to the perceived requirement for gravitas and a weighty load of responsibility on their shoulders), thereby achieving objectives unimagined, with less conflict and aggravation. Such a scenario leaves more time and energy to look to the market, customers and other stakeholders, rather than looking inwards and forever watching your back. It starts from acknowledging, understanding and consistently applying the principles, cognitive mental processes, perspectives, priorities and practices which reflect practical and collaborative wisdom detailed in this and previous chapters.

Exercises

1. Consider an organisation of which you have significant knowledge and insight which has been successful within the context of a national or subnational market presence. To what extent do you consider that its management style and logic reflects the perspectives, attributes and capabilities of global leadership?
2. Consider two organisations with whom you have worked or know well on the basis of study and research. Assess their attitude towards entrepreneurial ideas and/or innovative ideas, not exclusively in respect of products but also processes, procedures, systems, structures and management approaches. Is there a correlation between their attitude in this respect and their performance over the last 10–20 years?
3. Consider two organisations with whom you have worked or know well on the basis of study and/or research. How clearly are the organisations' visions communicated and reinforced to their staff? To what extent do staff consider that they are a critical part in the attainment of the organisation's vision and thereby feel energised, motivated, dedicated to the organisation? Compare their comparative performance over a 10–15-year period.
4. Consider an organisation with whom you have worked or are familiar. To what extent do they expend energy and resources on developing staff to take responsibility for leadership and delegate tangible responsibility and authority for decision making to operational leadership? Consider the extent to which they have consistently achieved optimal performance over the last 10–15 years.

7 *Resolving the "Onion Skin" Issue*

I'm Leading – How Did That Happen?

Whilst one is appointed to a management role, the attainment of a leadership position frequently occurs by stealth, accident, more often by circumstance. This very often leaves individuals unprepared, initially responding instinctively and intuitively in the absence of a comprehension of the requirements and responsibilities of the role which they have acquired or had thrust upon them. This tends to result in the development of leadership perspectives, priorities, attributes and capabilities in a reactive, haphazard and unstructured manner, resulting in suboptimal organisational performance. Business and other relevant societal organisations and individual leaders must therefore initiate programmes of appropriate leadership logic and judgment, based upon the principles and cognitive mental process of practical and collaborative wisdom, which begin even prior to recruitment to the organisation.

This book's primary target market is those who aspire to leadership positions. They are either presently undertaking studies in this respect or are presently at the initial stages of their career. In practice, leadership responsibility tends to attack by stealth. One day, you are undertaking purely technical tasks, for instance, in finance, marketing, IT, production, R&D, with minimal direct influence on the activity of others. Next day you find that you are formally or informally influencing and/or responsible for the actions and output of two other individuals. As an example of this process, I have a son who is at the initial stages of a career in HR management. Due to his varied experience to date he finds peers asking him for advice not only in technical areas but also how to resolve operational issues which require a definition of appropriate principles, standards, perspectives and priorities for decision making. He is therefore providing clarity, direction, confidence and comfort, although, as yet, he fails to recognise this fact.

Soon you find that you are directly responsible for the output and performance of 6 individuals and informally influencing the actions of 10 others. This subsequently results in directly leading 20 and indirectly influencing 40 to 60 others. If you are considered to be achieving targets and objectives without causing any nasty, uncomfortable ripples for significant others, quite quickly you find yourself a section, departmental, division head and ultimately, perhaps, Chief Executive or a member of the Executive Committee. It would be true to say that an individual's leadership perspectives, style, whatever you might wish to term it, generally develops on the hoof, influenced by personal perspectives, capabilities, the influences of other individuals, institutions and social norms, and the perceived requirements of the immediate contextual circumstances. The result tends to be a leadership soup of indeterminate nature and quality, reflecting those perspectives, attributes and capabilities which appear to get the job done in a manner comparable and compatible with the leadership approach of those whom one regards as reference points.

I am not berating this process of the development of operational leadership perspectives and capabilities. It is based upon practical experience and the development of insight and judgement, intuitive and instinctive decision making, all critical for success in the fast moving, context-driven business context. My concern is that in the majority of individuals' cases this development process normally takes so long as to reach a state of leadership "wisdom" when one is closer to retirement than the beginning of one's career, with the resultant suboptimal impact on the contribution by each leader to organisational performance over the span of a leadership career. What appears to be missing in this process of the development of an appropriate leadership mindset from the early stages of a leader's career is a proactive and structured approach to embedding a single, uniform framework of principles, perspectives and priorities based upon universal values which will facilitate decisions based upon the principles and process of practical and collaborative wisdom. The introduction of this critical ingredient to the development process provides purpose, clarity, cohesion and confidence within the leadership cadre, throughout the career of nascent leaders.

Everyone accepts that it is logical that you should peel an onion from the outside; you can then deal with the layers of the onion in an orderly way and based upon your culinary requirements. If, however, you were to cut it in half and approach its dissection from the inside this results in a more confusing, complex and time-consuming task. It occurs to me that in the absence of the embedding of the foundations of global leadership, based upon the principles, perspectives, priorities and cognitive processes upon which collaborative and practical wisdom is founded, operational leaders are liable to continuously struggle to find and apply optimal leadership perspectives and priorities in the absence of an anchor or compass upon which to base decisions and resolve issues. They are peeling the decision-making onion from the inside. The result is inefficient, ineffective, confusing, inconsistent and altogether messy operational leadership and suboptimal organisational performance. Organisations which fail to inculcate the leadership cadre from the outset of their individual careers with appropriate leadership values, perspectives and priorities, leaving individual leaders to define their own leadership mindset, leave their organisational performance over the long-term hostage to conflict and a lack of cohesion and consistency in the decision-making process.

In essence, we are talking about three issues here:

- The inculcation of nascent leaders, at the onset of their careers, in a set of leadership perspectives and priorities which are based upon universal values and principles, understood and acknowledged by all staff as consistent with the manner in which they wish to lead their lives. By this means the organisation will benefit from optimal levels of allegiance, dedication, motivation and advocacy amongst stakeholders.
- The application of a single dominant logic to ensure consistent and cohesive operational decision making, resulting in optimal clarity of purpose and the expending of optimal energy amongst staff towards the organisational vision.
- The development of a cognitive mental process amongst the operational leadership cadre which is able to optimally define the priority of perspectives and priorities considered relevant for consideration, whilst analysing them in a manner which is both appropriately analytical and affective.

This will facilitate the optimal performance of leaders from the outset of their careers, possessed with the raw materials, the clarity of vision and purpose, the knowledge foundation and the overall mindset to make practically wise, operationally effective leadership decisions within the context of individual business issues.

But what are the practical steps to be taken by leaders in this respect? It must be emphasised that in reading the content of this chapter aspiring and existing leaders must translate, adapt and implement its contents to accommodate their particular leadership situation. This is a fundamental, practically wise, leadership requirement and capability. Whilst the text tends to view leadership from the perspective of embedding a uniform foundation of principles, perspectives and priorities, leaders of individual organisational units must translate and apply them within the context of their specific leadership role and context. In those organisations which are already operating on the basis of practical wisdom and global leadership attributes and capabilities, the role of the unit leader is primarily to act as a coordinator and reinforce where required in order to maintain clarity, confidence and cohesion. In those organisations where global leadership is interpreted as a term of geographic responsibility, this does not preclude the unit leader from applying the principles and process of practical and collaborative wisdom, taking responsibility for embedding a framework of global leadership perspectives, attributes and capabilities within the mindset of subordinates in their area of direct responsibility. In addition, the possession of practical and collaborative wisdom allows the operational leader to consciously, proactively and sensibly, subtly and delicately persuade and inculcate individuals throughout the organisation. The individual with global leadership attributes and capabilities consciously understands the logic of and perhaps subconsciously also accepts their responsibility to stretch themselves and take personal career risks to apply universal values in the form of appropriate principles, perspectives and priorities as far as their capabilities and position allow. This is due to the fact that they understand that the priority of the global leader in respect of achieving operational efficiency and long-term organisational performance is to optimise the benefit to the organisational community, rather than to individual stakeholder groups, themselves and significant others.

In order to clarify, tangibilise, and make practical the development of a global leadership perspective and capability within the operational context, rather than the development of isolated pockets throughout the organisation, I have set out in the boxed text "Key Steps Towards a Global Leadership Capability" below what I consider to be the seven key steps in the creation of an appropriate logic of perspectives, priorities and practices. Their consistent implementation will fundamentally change the mindset of the leadership cadre in respect of those fundamental principles, perspectives and priorities, leadership attributes and capabilities required to consistently achieve optimal operational effectiveness and long-term performance.

KEY STEPS TOWARDS A GLOBAL LEADERSHIP CAPABILITY

Step One: Pre-Career Embedding of Values and Principles

Rather than making students as a priority aware of prevailing management and leadership theories and concepts, and seeking to maximise their technical proficiency, universities, colleges and business schools must focus on inculcating in students universal values, principles and the cognitive mental process of practical and cognitive wisdom, undertaking the groundwork, in preparation for their operational application within the organisational context.

In this respect, the dominant coalitions within business organisations must emphasise to academic institutions that this embedded mindset is a fundamental prerequisite in the mindset and attributes of any students whom they recruit, rather than merely technical skills, which are the expected table stakes in all graduates. The role of scholarly institutions is one to which we have already referred in Part One.

Step Two: Translation into Operational Priorities and Standards

These universal values and principles must be translated into a set of operational priorities, standards and practices which are to act as the foundation for all decisions and actions undertaken by the leader during all stages of their career. It must be emphasised to new recruits that the dominant coalition consider that such perspectives, priorities and standards are wholly consistent with optimal long-term performance and will not be sacrificed as a means of achieving any short-term targets or objectives.

This is a controversial and contentious statement, particularly in the face of the background to the economic and financial crisis which presently faces the Western hemisphere. Leadership is neither for the faint-hearted nor the inexperienced. If it is possible to achieve both the priority short-term objectives of myopic leadership, primarily in the form of maximum profitability, plus long-term objectives in support of the organisational community, then it is incumbent on a leader to achieve both. However, ultimately the priority is optimal long-term performance for the benefit of the organisational community.

If an individual in a leadership role is unable or unwilling to take such a position with regard to universal values, principles and priorities, in the interests of the benefits to the organisation of stakeholder cohesion, allegiance, dedication and organisational advocacy then in effect they are acknowledging that their mindset is rather one of a manager and/or mechanic. Note that this is not meant to suggest a negative choice to an inferior role. It is rather horses for courses; a question of allocating individuals to roles for which their perspectives, competencies and capabilities are most suited, for the benefit of the organisational community. It is much akin to deciding to be a general practitioner or a brain surgeon. Whilst I would not wish a general practitioner to operate on my brain, nor would I wish a brain surgeon to pronounce on other medical matters which influenced my general health and well-being.

Step Three: Continuous Reinforcement

Reinforcement of these perspectives, priorities and standards should occur throughout a leader's career, through introducing measures to stress their importance such as regularly questioning individual leadership decisions on the basis of these standards and requesting written confirmation that the leader and staff are applying these standards during their operational, day to day duties. Similarly, appraisal structures and scores should emphasise the importance of applying these perspectives, priorities and standards in relation to career progression.

Operational leaders, of units, departments, divisions, have the primary responsibility to consistently emphasise the importance of these priorities in achieving the organisation's vision and key objectives, compared with an individual's technical achievements and capabilities in achieving organisational long-term objectives.

Step Four: Structured Leadership Development

The operational development plan, in respect of leadership experience must be:

- Based upon the accumulation of knowledge, experience, insight and judgement;
- Consistent with a collaborative and practical wisdom mindset;
- Built upon a dominant logic of universal values and principles;
- Translated into operational perspectives, priorities and standards.

This development of leadership capability will be undertaken hand in hand with any enhancement and broadening of technical capabilities required to carry out increasingly senior positions within the organisation.

Step Five: Training and Development Courses

Training and development courses, no matter their nature, whether technical or leadership related, should emphasise that any deliverables must be mindful of, consistent with and developed within the overall priority and context of consistently applying these operational leadership principles, perspectives, priorities and practices.

Step Six: Criteria for Appointment to a Leadership Position

Positions within the organisation which are highly dependent upon the continuing and effective operational management of people should be reserved for those who have exhibited the required understanding of the priority of the human dynamic, to ensure operational effectiveness and consistent organisational performance. Whilst displaying the required perspectives, attributes and capabilities to fulfil their role as a leader they must of course be technically proficient to carry out their role as a functional manager. However, these capabilities should be of secondary priority as selection criteria.

Step Seven: Criteria for Senior Leadership

Ultimately, progression to senior leadership positions should ideally be restricted to global leaders who exhibit collaborative and practical wisdom capabilities, with the required technical skills constituting table stakes for consideration in respect of a functional leadership role. All members of the Executive Committee should ideally exhibit a preponderance of global leadership insight, perspectives, attributes and capabilities, particularly an ability to listen, persuade, motivate, energise, rather than technical excellence (but see below: "I'm Confused – Where Do I Start?"). In this way such individuals are able to appropriately plan, develop and communicate the operational application of the inculcation process throughout the organisation, if not in many cases effect this task themselves.

Through the operational implementation of these steps you have created an organisational mindset where there is both an acknowledgement and understanding that the practice of effective people leadership must become the primary focus of the organisational leadership culture and the individual leadership operational priority, this in order to optimise organisational performance over the long term. It is no longer subordinate to the dominance of technical excellence as a prerequisite for advancement to senior leadership positions within the organisation. These are stages and steps in the development of the cognitive mental process where you have the greatest opportunity to influence operational leadership values, principles, perspectives and priorities and their interpretation and application during the decision-making and issue resolution process.

I'm Confused – Where Do I Start?

As discussed above, Executive Committee members facilitate the development of leadership perspectives, attributes and capabilities within the organisation. It is however not necessary (although desirable) that they are themselves leaders. Finely tuned leadership capabilities are however a prerequisite, a need to have, within the operational context of the organisation. As an operational leader, with a primary responsibility for directing, energising and motivating those who ultimately deliver on the objectives of the organisation, you must proactively develop and consistently implement a single dominant logic which is consistent with your own and the belief system of your staff and others within the organisation. Simultaneously you must balance the requirements of the local business context in a responsive and sympathetic manner.

It is a fundamental tenet of this book that much unneeded confusion and complexity prevails in the practice of operational leadership due to the fact that people think that individuals responsible for functions such as finance, or marketing, production or R&D all require different leadership attributes, capabilities, perspectives and priorities. This is an example of peeling the onion from the inside. This chapter section sets out a number of key steps comprising perspectives, priorities and practices, to provide direction and clarity for the aspiring leader regarding the foundation stones of effective decision-making and issue resolution in respect of effective operational leadership.

KEY CONSIDERATIONS FOR THE ASPIRING GLOBAL LEADER

Step One: Develop and Consistently Implement Your Dominant Logic

The first step to becoming a global leader is to understand and acknowledge that no matter your leadership role or level, there exists a core foundation of values, principles, perspectives and priorities which must always be consistently applied in order to ensure that one optimises the opportunity for optimal decision making. The consistent application of such values and principles ensures that leadership decisions are perhaps 80–90% optimal. That is, optimal leadership decisions are predominantly dependent upon the consistent application of such principles.

A fundamental problem of leadership is that followers and other leaders may not be convinced of the validity or relevance of the values and principles underlying individual decisions. This will be predominantly overcome by consistently applying values and principles which are understood and acknowledged as sustaining the growth of a cohesive community. These are universal values and principles, translated into a dominant logic which is specific to the achievement of an organisation's long-term vision. Leadership performance is suboptimal where:

- There is no recognition of universal values and principles by the organisation, certain groups or functions or by the individual leader as the foundation for decision making.
- The dominant logic of the organisation is inconsistent with universal values and principles.
- There is no identifiable organisational dominant logic

or

- where there is, it is not communicated beyond the dominant coalition

or

- in practice it is not consistently applied;

all of which result in operational confusion, conflict and a lack of focus and vision.

One, some, or all of these scenarios prevail within most organisations and are fundamental to suboptimal operational leadership effectiveness and organisational performance. In the face of this practical reality, of multiple logics operating within the organisation, individual leaders find themselves in a quandary, since effective leadership is fundamentally collaborative rather than solitary and undertaken in isolation, highly dependent upon the prevailing organisational culture and the perspectives and priorities of others.

Despite this, accept that you as a leader have personal beliefs on how to lead, based upon universal values and principles, which you must test, develop and apply as part of the process of improving your own and the organisation's leadership capabilities; also a responsibility to act as a global leader for the benefit of the organisation and those who look to you for guidance (who are often outside the orbit of your direct functional responsibility).

In this respect I would advise the following steps, cognisant of the fact that you are applying global leadership perspectives and attributes somewhat in isolation, therefore the organisation, or part of it, is on the road to but far from a leadership mindset which will achieve optimal performance. In this regard it is important that you keep in mind that the predominant purpose of your leadership role is to provide holistic (i.e. taking a broad perspective which takes a multiplicity of factors and issues into account) rather than technical direction, clarity, guidance and consistency, this in order to energise staff to achieve optimal cohesion, dedication, allegiance and advocacy in the interests of the organisational community:

- Decide and commit to the belief that the application of universal values and principles is the most appropriate and effective foundation for your leadership contribution to the organisation.
- As an individual leader, translate these into what you consider is a dominant logic of operational principles, perspectives, priorities and standards consistent with the manner by which you consider the organisation should be led. Where you consider

that this dominant logic is inconsistent with the manner in which the organisation is, in fact, led, communicate and consistently apply initially only within the orbit of your functional authority.

Communicate and explain what you consider is the organisational vision and its business objectives to your direct reports in a manner which reiterates and reinforces the universal values and your dominant logic.

Ensure that all of the decisions which you take as a leader are seen to be consistent with and based upon these values and principles.

When you or your unit staff are in contact with other functions' staff ensure that decisions and proposed actions are clearly explained and justified on the basis of the principles, perspectives and priorities of this dominant logic. By this means, where there is a vacuum vis-à-vis dominant logic, other leaders may acknowledge the logic and begin, gradually, to base their decisions and actions on this logic.

This may also expose leaders who have alternative logics which they are applying which, within the context of global leadership attributes, should be discussed in an open-minded manner with a view to the implementation of a uniform logic.

Where this is not possible or, for a variety of reasons, any logic which is not consistent with universal values is applied then you, as an individual and an operational leader, must consider your options, as we will discuss in greater detail in Part Four.

However, it is pertinent to mention at this juncture that the application of practical and collaborative wisdom is only possible where you are directing and seeking to energise individuals on the basis of a dominant logic of principles and priorities which are consistent with your personal set of beliefs, which are themselves based upon universal values. Where this is not the case you are unlikely to be optimally energised to motivate staff. In such circumstances your perspective becomes one of managing someone else's beliefs and therefore your contribution to the optimal performance of the organisation becomes significantly circumscribed.

Only once you have dealt with the issues of the development, embedding and operational application of a dominant logic within your leadership role will you be able to effectively progress to Step Two.

KEY CONSIDERATIONS FOR THE ASPIRING GLOBAL LEADER (CONTINUED)

Step Two: Consideration of Contextual Issues

The second step is consideration of contextual issues, which provides the final 10–20% for optimal decision making. Some would say that this percentage should be more, some less, but the point is that, as we have already mentioned in a previous section, local responsiveness is an important attribute of consistently effective operational leadership and optimal performance, but is not the primary factor in its achievement.

Some people will nod in agreement when they read this, but in the fire of the operational leadership context will revert to applying group policy, since it appears, on the surface, to be simpler and more straightforward, because it carries the weight of authority.

Alternatively, leaders may find it difficult to distinguish when local issues should prevail in decision making. The development of global leadership perspectives, attributes and capabilities, based upon practical and collaborative wisdom, will cultivate this critical "balance" capability and thereby enhance the confidence, support and advocacy of key stakeholder groups such as staff, shareholders, customers, suppliers and regulatory authorities. Such a capability will engender appropriate fine-tuning in decision making at the level of operational practices in respect of such issues as HR (e.g. recruitment, remuneration, and discipline), marketing, sales, customer service, distribution and product development and management, which have a substantial impact on stakeholder energy, commitment, motivation and dedication.

In respect of the onion skin analogy, it is important to recognise that you are a leader, not a missionary or a crusader. The art (or science) of effective leadership is to apply the "group" logic of values, principles, standards and priorities (which is itself based upon universal values) in an environment over which you do not in fact have total control, or anything like it. This is why the global leadership attributes of an open mind, acceptance of the value and active utilisation of local tacit knowledge, persuasion, compromise and adaptability are so important to organisational performance, through engendering collaboration and cohesion amongst stakeholders. They are a natural output of the process of cognition upon which practical and collaborative wisdom is founded.

The ability to implement the group dominant logic in a logical yet locally responsive and sympathetic manner is the optimal "balance" of which the global leader, applying the principles and cognitive mental process of practical and collaborative wisdom, is only capable.

KEY CONSIDERATIONS FOR THE ASPIRING GLOBAL LEADER (CONTINUED)

Step Three: The Optimal Process of Cognition – Affectively Analyse and Assess

Equally important, particularly in respect of the second step, is the process of decision making, which has been the subject of a major part of Part One, particularly the nature and type of contextual issue to be considered and the manner in which they are to be considered.

In this respect it is important to emphasise that, given the importance of the energy and motivation of the staff within the organisation, whilst the analysis and final decision must be seen to be based on logical analysis, we must not forget the importance of including affective (emotional) considerations. This latter consideration in leadership analysis and decision making is of critical importance when leading those who ultimately deliver on organisational performance.

Whilst we have already introduced the concept of acculturation, particularly within the context of the integration process during mergers and acquisitions, it is increasingly relevant across the spectrum of operational leadership situations in the fast moving business environment when plans, policies, strategies and processes are constantly changing. It is important that individual leaders are aware and take into consideration in their operational leadership approach and practices that within such a context stakeholders are continuously evaluating whether they are better or worse off, with the resultant impact on energy expended, allegiance, dedication and commitment towards the objectives of the organisation.

Effective leadership is achieved through a clear understanding of the interplay and interaction between the business vision and business environment, this in order to achieve the optimal balance between multiple and often conflicting pressures and options. This optimal balance is achieved by being confident in your own views on the basis of:

- Knowledge
- Experience
- A process of continuous personal development proactively sought and implemented by both the individual and organisation.

Such attributes foster a mental process which engenders sound insight and judgment, on the one hand, and an open-minded, collaborative perspective on the other. This enables the leader to gather all pertinent facts to achieve optimal issue resolution, whilst also optimising energy, motivation and dedication on behalf of the organisational community.

This is much easier said than done within the day to day realities of operational leadership, as you seek to achieve business targets through focus, coordination and cooperation in an environment fraught with conflicting visions, objectives, values, priorities and standards. This is why an understanding, acknowledgement and resolution of the onion skin dilemma, in providing clarity in respect of the anchor and compass of leadership principles, perspectives, priorities and practices, is an important step towards creating clarity of purpose, often hope, in the midst of an operational environment generally typified by confusion and the absence of consistent and significant levels of coordination, cooperation and cohesion. This operational state of continuous confusion and suboptimal coordination, cooperation, ongoing and underlying obstructiveness and guerrilla warfare, is a situation which many dominant coalitions, for good reason, refuse to openly acknowledge, whilst recognising in private. In the absence of the perspectives, priorities, attributes, capabilities and cognitive processes of practical and collaborative wisdom dominant coalitions, not perceiving of any alternatives, prefer to consider such a chaotic organisational environment the normal state of affairs and therefore an operational leadership reality and responsibility, to be actively managed in order to achieve targets.

Typically, the chaotic operational context and fragmented leadership coordination and focus is only effectively acknowledged and addressed during a period of organisational crisis, when sales, profits and/or share price have plummeted. Only then is there likely to be effective interaction and communication of a clear vision, direction, perspectives and priorities between the dominant coalition and the operational leadership cadre, down to subunits and the "shop floor", for the purposes of getting out of the hole. Once the crisis is over the interaction and communication drawbridge between the dominant coalition and operational leadership is typically drawn up with alacrity in order that one group can focus on policy, overall numbers and external stakeholders (e.g. shareholders, regulators, analysts and ratings agencies) and the other the operational management of the organisation and achievement of targets. This approach to and process of organisational leadership is the very antithesis of the application of practical and collaborative wisdom

Let's Play Find the Leader

But where is the leadership in this process? where and who are the individuals who are exhibiting the leadership perspectives, attributes and characteristics of collaborative wisdom within the organisation? This is a classic example of everyone managing their technical and narrowly defined responsibilities rather than truly leading an "organic" organisation. Readers are invited to look at their present organisations and those for whom they will be employed in the future to assess whether this Janus-like (two faces looking in opposite directions) prevails, where neither management group wishes to recognise or become involved in the complexities of the other, creating a barrier of comprehension and communication, resulting in confusion and chaos at the very heart of the organisation. This is less the fault of individuals but rather of the framework of pressures, priorities and allegiances which have evolved and developed in business organisations over recent decades as a result of those dominant principles, values, perspectives and practices which have prevailed within the broader environment within which the business organisation operates.

Effective leadership requires the peeling of the leadership onion from the outside in a progressive, structured, consistent manner, utilising the fine and subtle balance of perspectives, mental processes, attributes and capabilities achieved only by the application of practical and collaborative wisdom by all members of the leadership cadre, to consistently provide clarity of direction and purpose. This process is illustrated by Figure 7.1.

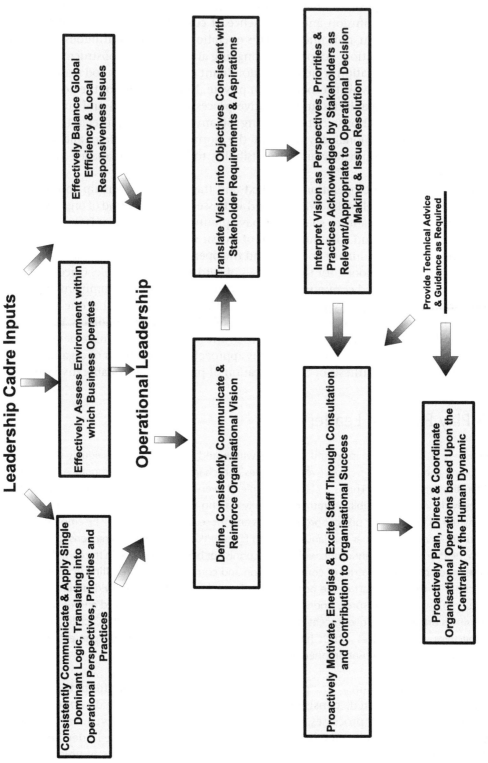

Figure 7.1   Effective Leadership Through Peeling the Onion from the Outside

If leadership is about directing, guiding, persuading, motivating people then the dominant coalition are, in practice, not proactively and consistently involved in the process. In practice, they are voluntarily or involuntarily isolated and insulated from communicating and interacting with the majority of those who require direction and leadership. Therefore, in realistic and practical terms, operational leaders must be the primary agents in this critical process. Except that they rarely or at best vaguely comprehend the organisation's dominant logic, or its long-term vision by which operational leaders can create and maintain a cohesive and motivated workforce.

So, in practice, no one individual or group is able to lead effectively within the organisation. No individual or group of individuals has the insight in respect of those key principles which direct decision making, the focus, perspective, attributes and capabilities and the opportunities for interaction required for effective organisational leadership. We give the executive committee members the epaulettes of leaders because they are ultimately responsible for achieving the numbers, they develop policy and deal with "important" external stakeholders. However, in operational terms their role is essentially one of management of the "dashboard", holding the levers of power, but unable to control them due to a remoteness, a reticence, an indifference and/or inability in respect of key perspectives, attributes and capabilities, to guide, motivate and energise staff, through the effective and consistent communication of a business vision and single dominant logic.

Some might respond that if the dominant coalition effectively communicate the single dominant logic to and guide, inspire and energise the operational leadership cadre, who are therefore the true leaders within the organisation, then this is an acceptable scenario in facilitating optimal organisational performance. It is therefore this latter group who must have the perspectives, attributes, capabilities, collaborative and practical wisdom of the global leader. My own experience suggests that this is likely in practice to be the optimal option for most business organisations. The problem arises where there is no dominant logic or it is not effectively communicated and reinforced by the dominant coalition to the operational leadership cadre, who are therefore unable to consistently translate, communicate and operationalise it to resolve day to day operational issues (e.g. in terms of issues related to sales, finance, production, R&D, HR, service quality and marketing). The result will be the development of a number of logics within the organisation, the outcome of translations of "signs" from the dominant coalition by individual operational leaders, leading to confusion, suboptimal coordination, cooperation, cohesion, energy, allegiance and advocacy in support of the organisation. It is a lot like driving in the fog to what you think is the destination which someone else has described to you as your objective. Even if you avoid one or a number of collisions, progress will be slow and laborious, undertaken with trepidation and misgivings. Ultimately you are likely to find that the destination achieved was not in fact that defined by the individual who has given you the direction to be reached. Great for motivation and commitment!

Effective communication and inculcation of the entire organisational leadership cadre in a single dominant logic is therefore a prerequisite in peeling the onion in a practically wise manner within the operational leadership context in order to achieve operational effectiveness and optimal long-term performance. Where this does not occur, which in reality is the majority of organisational cases, then it is the primary responsibility of those who operationally lead the people, rather than those whose primary responsibility, in practice, is to manage the plan and numbers, to apply the steps, detailed in this section and the operational leadership process detailed in Figure 7.1. This in order to ensure that there is some degree of operational clarity, purpose, energy and commitment towards achieving tangible targets and objectives.

The nature and location of leadership responsibility within the organisation is an important, indeed critical point upon which to ponder in order to attain clarity, since it allows for proactivity and decisiveness in decision-making and issue resolution. In effect, what we are saying is that substantial leadership (i.e. people management) insight and capabilities at the executive committee level is a nice to have, whilst it is a prerequisite, a need to have, at the operational leadership level. This is both a controversial and inconvenient truth. It perhaps explains why in practice highly developed leadership skills as we have defined, are not, in practice, a prerequisite for advancement to executive committee posts. What is required from such individuals is rather an acknowledgement of and support for the development of appropriate operational leadership perspectives, attributes and capabilities (based upon practical and collaborative wisdom), particularly within those operational functions which require high and constant levels of people interaction, direction and motivation.

The practical and operational reality is that if we continue to look upwards and wait for leadership direction then we will be waiting, in the majority of cases, for a long time. This is not an indictment of senior management, who are faced with the urgent and pressing complexities of twenty-first century business management; the vagaries of the market, analysts, commentators, regulatory and compliance issues, capital and other financial considerations. Nor is it how we might want it to be, but practical, operational leadership is about optimal performance within the realities of the business context. Operational leaders, those who are directly responsible for energising and motivating those who ultimately deliver the goods must therefore be proactive in creating the requisite operational framework as described within this section, to facilitate global leadership capabilities within the operational business context.

The application of practical and collaborative wisdom requires the acknowledgement and understanding of this role definition by all members of the organisational leadership cadre and, most importantly, the appropriate delegation of responsibility and authority. The primary obstacle to the application of this practical reality is an unwillingness to transfer effective authority and decision making to operational leadership. As far as the roles of leadership within the organisation's leadership cadre are concerned, it is the responsibility of the dominant coalition to:

- Define the values, principles, perspectives and priorities upon which the dominant logic is founded and therefore direct and guide operational leadership decision making.
- Effectively communicate and monitor the consistent application of the dominant logic by the operational leadership cadre.
- Facilitate the development of an operational leadership cadre which possesses the appropriate values, principles, perspectives and priorities, attributes, capabilities and cognitive processes to optimally direct, motivate and energise key stakeholder groups (e.g. staff, customers, suppliers, regulatory bodies, media).

It is therefore not necessary, and in many cases not desirable, that in practice the dominant coalition becomes involved in the operational process of leadership.

Some might seek to fudge the practical implications of this reality, due to the implications for perceived status and prevent any true clarity of understanding in respect of how leadership does/does not work in practice within business organisations. Others might respond that there are different forms of leadership. However, the practical and inconvenient reality persists that in order to be an effective leader you must have willing and enthusiastic followers, with whom you are in contact and communication, consistently providing clarity of direction and purpose, which satisfies their personal aspirations and expectations. This is not a role for which many of the members of the dominant coalition are equipped or prepared, due to operational, day to day priorities and personal perspectives, attributes and capabilities. This is an inconvenient truth which must be acknowledged and understood if significant progress is to be made in respect of enhancing operational leadership effectiveness and organisational performance.

Sounds Reasonable: But How Does it Work in the Context of My Present Role?

This section synthesises the key themes of the book to clearly describe their operational application within leadership contexts and situations which you have or will frequently experience during your career. It provides a template, replacing the doubt, complexity, stress, angst, controversy and conflict which are interminably a feature of leadership decision making. This is replaced by a mindset where clarity, confidence and cohesion predominates, facilitating effective, practically wise operational leadership.

Fundamentally, what we are saying is that no matter the leadership role, situation or context, the application of collaborative and practical wisdom rests on the consistent application of a defined foundation of principles, perspectives, priorities, the possession of specific attributes and capabilities and a specific decision-making process. Whilst the context may influence the final decision and individual actions, if you do not consistently apply the foundation and the process of what we have termed practical and collaborative wisdom then decisions will be considered confused and inconsistent by individual and groups of stakeholders and result in sub-optimal issue resolution and organisational performance. No matter if, as a leader you are dealing, for example, with:

- The acquisition and integration of another organisation;
- The merger or refocusing of an organisation, division or department;
- Taking over an existing leadership position;
- The implementation of a new system, process or procedure;
- The launch of a new product or service into the marketplace;
- The ongoing operational leadership of a sales force or back office function;
- The allocation of individuals to work stations;
- The development of a timetable for lunch hour cover.

you should apply the same foundation stones for effective and optimal decision making.

Consistent and effective leadership is about balance; recognising the relevance and priority of a wide range of principles, perspectives, priorities, standards, practices, views, facts, issues, which appear to justify consideration in coming to a decision which will have a significant impact on organisational efficiency and performance. This book has put forward a template for consistently providing solutions and taking leadership decisions in a collaboratively and practically wise manner by:

- Defining the nature of the analytical process for optimal decision making;
- Providing insight into the nature of appropriate values and principles;
- Clarifying the need to translate these values and principles into operationally relevant and understandable perspectives, priorities and standards;
- Defining the perspectives, priorities, attributes and capabilities of the global leader who consistently applies practical and collaborative wisdom within the operational leadership context on a daily basis.

Despite extensive knowledge and experience on the part of leadership it would be true to say that the majority of organisational decisions are made on a wing and a prayer, often based upon a desire to minimise short-term organisational and personal downside. This is primarily due to the nature of the perceived requirements and expectations of what are regarded as key stakeholder groups. However, it is also due to a lack of confidence and insight in respect of those key factors and issues for consideration in order to achieve the optimal solution. However, no matter the reasons, suboptimal performance is assured in the absence of the facets of practical and collaborative wisdom within the operational leadership cadre.

As a practitioner, I would not denigrate the relevance and value of intuition, insight and judgment, based upon knowledge and experience gained during 5, 10, 20 or 30 years, in a range of business contexts. The majority of practitioners would admit in moments of honesty that they take decisions in a void, grasping to create logic for decisions out of a multitude of points and issues for consideration whose relevance and priority could appear to change on a daily basis, undermining clarity, confidence and decisiveness. Within this void leadership decisions are taken in a context of angst, stress, doubt, complexity, controversy, conflict, resentment and other emotions, counterproductive in respect of optimal cohesion, teamwork and dedication to the objectives of the organisational community.

I THINK I'VE GOT IT – BUT GIVE ME AN EXAMPLE TO MAKE SURE

OK. This is really, excuse the expression, the "piss or get off the pot" moment in this book. So far you might have been reading and thinking:

- This is brilliant
- Sounds good
- Not sure I believe all/some is true/relevant/practical/possible
- Probably right but is it worth the hassle?
- Probably right, but will it cost me my job if I implement?

This is where we detail and combine operational leadership perspectives, priorities and practices, and propose the application of leadership attributes and capabilities which are at variance with those you are likely to have experienced or consider are applied in practice within the majority of business organisations. It will therefore test your belief, commitment and courage to be an operationally wise leader, willing to initiate change for the benefit of an organisation operating in the twenty-first century business environment. OK, let me put you in the hot seat.

Imagine, for the purposes of this example, that your organisation, head office based in Canada, has recently purchased 45 per cent of a successful business in Hungary, but has also agreed a rolling management contract which provides for a standard fee plus bonus to your company, based upon the extent of net profit enhancement. The existing CEO, a Hungarian has recently been confirmed to the post. You are an experienced leader within the Group organisation, having held senior positions in a variety of posts, (e.g. finance, marketing, sales, systems, production, corporate and strategic planning) in a number of markets (e.g. Canada, USA, UK, Japan, Saudi Arabia, Mexico) and are presently Chief Operating Officer of their operations in Armenia. You have been requested to attend a meeting in London chaired by the Group Head of European Operations, attended by other members of Group management and members of the Hungarian Executive Committee, to discuss plans for the effective integration of the Hungarian acquisition. You are not entirely clear on why you have been invited or what is to be your contribution, but you feel excited and pleased to have been invited.

You arrive at your hotel in London the night before the meeting and are handed an envelope at reception when checking in. Once you arrive in your room you get settled and then open the envelope. In the envelope you find a letter from the Group Head of Human Resources which informs you that you are seconded, with immediate effect, from your present duties for a term of 3 years and will from tomorrow be responsible for the effective integration of the Hungarian acquisition, reporting operationally to the Hungarian CEO but also to the Group Head of European Operations for the successful implementation of the plan. Attached to this letter is a hand-written note of congratulations from the Group Head of European Operations requesting that you put together a rough outline of what you consider to be the six to eight priorities in the integration process and give a 20-minute presentation the next day in order to provide structure and direction to the meeting (note: whilst this is not an autobiographical example, I have, like so many executives, frequently been faced with this "just knock off a 20–30-minute presentation for tomorrow" task).

Once you get over the shock, you take off your jacket, make yourself a strong pot of coffee (you might also delve into the mini-bar to look for something which will enhance your powers of focus and inspiration), take out your laptop and ponder on the top priorities, primarily on the basis of:

- Your understanding of your company's objectives in making the percentage acquisition and agreeing the management contract.
- The resultant relationship between Group and local stakeholders.

From the outset of this task you must peel the onion from the outside, to consider issues according to their priority and in the appropriate sequence, in a proactive, logical and affective manner, achieved on the basis of knowledge, experience and insight, rather than on the basis of pressures from specific groups and/or priorities which do not correspond to the optimal benefit of the organisation as a whole. I have therefore detailed below a synopsis of the approach which I believe should be taken on the basis of the key themes within this book, by translating and moulding them to reflect the specific operational business context. By this means we will seek to reach wise decisions in respect of this integration task which are based on the principles and process of practical and collaborative wisdom and reflect the perspectives, priorities, attributes and capabilities of the global leader. The presentation's primary objective will be clear, focused, practical, pragmatic and hard-headed. It will provide clarity and direction amongst attending stakeholders and by this means will optimise the chances of buy-in in respect of the operational leadership priorities and practices which will be applied and prevail to ensure effective integration and which will provide an anchor and compass in the resolution of complex and difficult people-related issues.

THE APPLICATION OF A PROCESS OF COLLABORATIVE AND PRACTICAL WISDOM TO A SPECIFIC LEADERSHIP ISSUE

Step One: Clearly Define Your Personal Leadership Perspectives and Priorities

The first step to recognise is that whilst the Hungarian integration is unique in its contextual detail you are likely to have experienced many of the leadership issues for consideration in previous postings, although perhaps in different guises. You must therefore acknowledge that you are not starting from scratch. On this basis you will consciously recognise and understand that, on the basis of your extensive and varied career to date you have the knowledge, experience and insight to deliver sound judgment and wise decisions, taking into consideration both "scientific" and affective information.

Your role is not technical, to integrate for example the marketing, IT or finance functions; it is holistic, to create an organisational environment and employee mindset which facilitates optimal efficiency and performance. Whilst this is likely to entail a number of significant technical issues in its implementation (e.g. putting in place appropriate accounting, HR, IT, sales, CROM processes and standards), these are not the central focus and priority of your role.

Similarly, whilst performance in numeric terms may in the minds of many stakeholders be the primary objectives, you as the individual responsible for effective integration, must recognise that these are merely reflections of leadership performance. If you focus on the key leadership priorities, optimal cost/benefit, revenue, net profit, ROI will be the output.

These perspectives and priorities are likely to be alien to all or most of your superiors, peers and subordinates and are therefore likely to meet with resistance and adversely affect your initial and ongoing credibility. It is therefore important to couch your fundamental perspectives and priorities in terms which will be acceptable to the audience, whilst not deviating in their application from the foundation stones of effective operational leadership. Once you are in situ you can decide whether there is value to the organisation in gradually apprising individuals or all of your audience(s) in the logic of your true perspectives and priorities. This is a pragmatic, hard-headed and smart "balance" intrinsic to the attributes and capabilities of the practically wise global leader.

Step Two: Develop a Clear and Exciting Vision

As we have already mentioned, the development of a vision creates clarity, direction, cohesion and excitement. The vision has to be achievable but ensure that all members of staff are stretched in their capabilities and contribution to the organisation. The vision has to be consistent with the requirements and expectations of key stakeholder groups, within both the Group and local context.

The vision, to achieve its objectives, must be seen to be relevant to operational business practices; all major decisions therefore have to be seen to tie back to the big picture vision. Let me tangibilise these points with an example in respect of this integration task. Given my background, let us say that the vision is to be recognised by the market as the premier provider of retail banking services in Hungary within 7 years. If, due to the market context this is not achievable due to an existing banking monopoly or duopoly then we must further define it to the premier bank within defined retail banking segments.

Whilst for many these visions are a bit vague they will be clarified by defined operational objectives in respect of, for instance, scores for customer service, retail deposits, insurance, investment and lending services, industry and regulatory accolades. The key value of an organisational vision is that it provides a general direction but, most importantly, that as a result of its clear definition, communication and reinforcement, staff consider that they are contributing to a long-term community objective, that the numeric target which they have been allocated to achieve is part of a bigger picture and that they, as individuals, are recognised as being important in its attainment (e.g. the cleaner who considered that he was contributing to putting a man on the Moon). The importance of a vision is its ability to direct, energise, to motivate, to excite, rather than to directly impact on target achievement.

Those organisations which decry the value of a vision or do not closely link operational decision making with a defined vision have a mindset which operates in the mass production rather than knowledge business environment, taking a management, mechanical, instead of holistic and leadership approach to business performance.

It is important to recognise that the issue of the organisational vision is important to the leader, no matter whether you are leading a unit, a department, a division or other organisational function. In the first instance it is your responsibility to clearly communicate and reinforce the organisational vision and the role which your function and each individual will have in its achievement.

Perhaps equally if not more importantly, particularly where there is no obvious organisational vision, is the development of your function's vision. As a leader within a subunit of the organisation, in achieving your defined objectives, you have a responsibility to define a clear vision for your function and its members, to provide clarity, purpose, cohesion and excitement. Rather than working on a treadmill of tasks, everyone within your function thereby feels that what they are, as individuals, undertaking is geared towards a common purpose. The results, in my experience, in terms of atmosphere, productivity and performance, when tasks are consistently tied back to a common vision by operational leadership, are substantial. However, they do require conscious attention, recognition and prioritisation of the leadership of people role, rather than the achievement of technical tasks.

In terms of the meeting tomorrow then it is important to project a vision which creates:

- Cohesion;
- A sense of common purpose which satisfies individual requirements and expectations and those of all stakeholder groups within the new organisational community;
- An excitement to be working together (i.e. Group and host organisation leaders and employees) towards a defined end, within a timescale which is just out of reach.

Step Three: Define the Nature of the Global Efficiency versus Local Effectiveness Balance

In practice, a number of issues generally define this relationship:

- The nature of the service provided to the market;
- The value of the core skills provided by each party in respect of the efficient provision of service and therefore to revenue/profit generation;
- The balance of power in the relationship between Group and local leadership.

In this situation we have a delicate relationship between Group and local stakeholders, with a minority stake held by Group but a management contract which provides broad powers of management autonomy. Presumably local stakeholders have agreed and welcomed partnership, particularly in respect of the management contract, not merely on the basis of a capital injection but an acceptance of levels of enhanced technical and leadership experience and professionalism which, it is recognised, will achieve significantly improved organisational performance.

At the meeting it is therefore a priority to clearly communicate the key aspects of how this will apply in the operational management of the organisation. The following are a few examples of how this clarity is achieved:

- State from the outset that the foundation of leadership decisions will not be based on "home" or "host" organisational cultures, but rather on an open-minded approach, in order to reach optimal solutions to specific issues. In this respect it is anticipated that decisions will be taken in a collegiate and consensual context, without anyone ceding individual responsibility and authority. This will be achieved on the basis of an agreed framework of principles, perspectives and priorities which will consistently be utilised to take leadership decisions. You state that you recognise that there will inevitably be some trepidation, if not resentment and antagonism, on the part of local management and this will be recognised and addressed from the outset. You will therefore clarify from the outset and ensure in operational practice that local knowledge, experience and insight is clearly seen to be fully taken into account and will be utilised to fine tune and optimise decision-making and issue resolution in order to enhance and optimise organisational performance.
- Clearly communicate the values, principles, perspectives, priorities and standards which are the foundation of Group dominant logic and which will represent the organisational mindset for strategic and operational decision making in respect of the individual decisions and the issues of integration process. This may cause initial irritation, resentment, if not anger amongst some within the audience. However it is important to emphasise that it is imperative that there is agreement on this foundation, to minimise any initial and ongoing conflict, obstruction and potential guerrilla warfare whilst thereby optimising cohesion, cooperation and coordination. Also emphasise that whilst this dominant logic has been developed

on the basis of consistently achieving the organisational vision and objectives it is open to amendment where it is clearly evident and agreed by the inculcated senior leadership cadre that such amendment will enhance performance. Operationally, the dominant logic will be applied on the basis of sympathy for the local business context, resulting in operational practices which are specific to context. Any dissension will be minimised when it becomes evident that the dominant logic is built upon universal values and principles and seeks the optimal benefit of the organisational community rather than the interests of home or host stakeholders.

- State from the outset that it is recognised that there will be apprehension and trepidation in respect of any radical changes and this will be a critical factor in the development of the strategy for effective integration. However, whilst every effort will therefore be made to persuade individuals to support the dominant logic over an acceptable period, where it is evident that this is not possible then members of the meeting will accept that the interests of the organisation must be the priority. Therefore, despite the valuable knowledge, technical and leadership attributes and capabilities of the individual, they must be released on mutually agreeable terms. This is in order that they might be employed within an organisation which is more compatible with their individual perspectives and priorities.

- The Group objective will be to control the key organisational components of risk and performance, without appearing to create a dominant leadership situation where local leadership feel bereft of authority and feel that they have no responsibility for and ownership of organisational performance.

- Where there is agreement in principle to the application of the single dominant logic then details will be provided in respect of its implementation in respect of the operational integration process, for example:
  - Those technical standards which will be transferred from Group and applied/ embedded within the local organisation (e.g. accounting, treasury, IT, systems, risk, product development, compliance, recruitment, disciplining, customer service). Reasonable timescales will be agreed to replace existing with proposed standards.
  - Those local positions which will be held by Group appointees, the period of such appointment and the steps which will be taken to train and develop local staff to subsequently take up these positions. This may include executive committee functions, heads of technical functions and/or the provision of technical expertise below head of function in order to embed standards, priorities and perspectives.
  - Agreement and clear communication of those functions which will be held by local leadership and where they will have both responsibility and authority to take operational decisions (although often within the context of the application of Group standards). These functions will generally be those where there is a high people contact and impact (e.g. HR, marketing, business development, customer service, distribution and sales, production and manufacturing) and those which require high levels of local knowledge (e.g. property/premises, purchasing, legal, compliance and contact with government and regulatory bodies). In this respect, given the definition of leadership which we have applied, effective leadership of the Hungarian organisation will predominantly be held in the hands of the local leadership cadre.
  - Most importantly, the necessity of/and process by which all leaders within the organisation will be inculcated in the single dominant logic of values,

principles, perspectives and priorities, this in order that decisions are taken on the basis of a common mindset. This mindset will be clearly and consistently communicated to all stakeholder groups. By this means the organisation will benefit from the provision of a common purpose, confidence and comfort in the minds of stakeholders that there will be no sudden surprises or that performance will be jeopardised and sub-optimised by internal conflict on the basis of fundamental differences between individuals and groups within the organisation.

Step Four: Effective Integration Requires Optimal Acculturation

At the meeting it is critical to emphasise that effective integration requires optimal acculturation, without which optimal organisational performance, reflected by any preferred numeric, will be illusory. Optimal acculturation indicates that leadership decisions are consistent with the requirements, expectations and aspirations of key stakeholders. This will ensure levels of motivation, energy, allegiance and dedication which will produce an optimal level of productivity per unit of resource expended. In this respect it is important to ensure that the vision, the organisational logic, the values, principles, perspectives and priorities and the manner of decision making described in steps 1–3 are clearly communicated and reinforced within all areas and levels of the organisation.

Staff and other key stakeholder groups must be convinced that the manner by which the organisation is led is the best possible option in the achievement of personal objectives and aspirations, optimising a sense of self-worth and esteem. The objective is acceptance and inclusion within the organisational and wider community in order to minimise obstruction and optimise motivation of all stakeholder groups towards optimising productivity and organisational performance.

Emphasise to meeting members that despite the tendency to focus on the numeric, such as sales, revenue, net profit, ROI during a merger, acquisition or joint venture process, when an organisation fails, ultimately it is due to a dissonance between the principles and/ or requirements and expectations of the dominant coalition and key stakeholders of the organisation. This results in a disillusionment and resultant withering of commitment, allegiance and dedication, particularly at times when the organisation requires optimal cohesion. Periods of change such as integration processes are just such occasions, when it is critical that the importance of the effective process of acculturation are acknowledged and appropriate plans effectively implemented. This subject must be communicated in terms which do not engender trepidation, antagonism, resistance and a diminution in credibility from the outset of your integration role; yet the point must be made and the importance of people leadership acknowledged and understood, utilising all of the attributes of practical and collaborative wisdom.

The above steps describe what the theme of this book considers to be the priority issues for consideration and application, in a light rather than heavy footed, yet focused, clear, pragmatic and hard-headed manner in the interests of the effective leadership of a process of integration. They stress the analytical and affective cognitive process which is the hallmark of practical and collaborative wisdom. There is a tendency in leadership decision-making processes, such as in the case of organisational integration, to focus on the hard issues, such as systems, accounting integration, performance monitoring, technical standards, senior and technical appointments, because this is supposed to be the nature of leadership, the hardnosed, tangible issues. In contrast, this list of priorities focuses on the people aspects of the organisational management of the integration process, which tend to be regarded as a nice to have (or alternatively are brushed under the carpet because those responsible for the effective attainment of such operational tasks do not consider themselves experienced or competent to describe much less implement such people focused initiatives). These people focused perspectives, priorities and practices are, in practice, fundamental to effective operational leadership and the long-term survival and optimal performance of the organisation during and post integration.

As with all books, there is a tendency for the reader to stand back as if the examples relate to someone else; superiors, subordinates, peers, even organisations outside of the reader's sphere of experience. This example of organisational integration may be outside the sphere of experience of the majority of readers. However, the steps and points are equally pertinent to day to day leadership decision making within your specific area of operations, today, tomorrow and each day thereafter as you address and make decisions in respect of individual operational issues within your remit. This is particularly the case regarding issues where you do not have total control (which tends to predominate in today's increasingly complex business organisation) and you therefore have to consider the priorities, requirements and expectations of other individuals and groups. Effective, wise leadership requires:

- A clear definition of a framework of values, principles, perspectives, priorities and standards to be consistently applied as the basis all decisions.
- Clarity in communication and reinforcement of vision and purpose.
- The inculcation of subordinates in this dominant logic to ensure consistency towards a defined destination.
- Decisive action in respect of embedding standards and practices; also decisive action to put in place staff with the required technical and leadership skills and replacing those who do not, in the interests of the organisational community.
- An understanding that you are leading people. You must therefore proactively take into account and, equally importantly, be seen to take into account their expectations, aspirations, their views, tap into their knowledge, consult, in order to engender a sense of ownership.

We are not talking about playing "Happy Families" here. We are talking about the best way to achieve an organisation's long term objectives and optimal performance in terms and means acceptable to the requirements and aspirations of individuals and stakeholder groups who consider themselves part of the organisational community and significantly contribute to its operational effectiveness and performance.

Exercises

1. Imagine that you are the head of a division (e.g. finance, IT, marketing and sales). On the basis of your knowledge and perceptions of the organisation's long-term objectives develop a divisional vision and dominant logic of key principles, perspectives and

priorities which will act as the anchor and compass of all decisions made by the leadership of the division. Discuss in groups how this would be reflected in and affect the day to day operational processes, tasks and issues of the division. Conclude on the value, advantages and disadvantages of such an approach.

2. Consider a leadership issue of which you have intimate knowledge and experience (this may be in relation to your personal or business experience). Assess in groups the relevance and appropriateness of the principles, perspectives, priorities, practices and overall approach applied by the executive responsible for integration of the Hungarian organisation in relation to the leadership issue which you have selected.

3. Compare and contrast the importance of dedicated leadership perspectives, attributes and capabilities in the chief executive, divisional, departmental and unit heads' roles. Where is it most critical to have excellence in leadership in order to achieve optimal organisational effectiveness and long-term performance?

4. Consider two occasions when you first found yourself in a leadership situation without being officially appointed as a leader, when someone looked to you for guidance and advice, outside of purely technical support. Upon what principles, perspectives and priorities did you rely and base your response?

4 *Where Do I Start?*

The first stage in the operational application of practical and collaborative wisdom is to acknowledge that it is likely to be career threatening, unless you apply its principles, perspectives and priorities in a pragmatic, practical and realistic manner from the outset. It is important to continuously remind yourself that optimal individual and organisational success can only be based upon a marathon rather than sprint approach to decision-making and issue resolution, for the reasons which we have already detailed within the text. Part Four therefore offers insights on how you might successfully apply a collaborative wisdom mindset within the context of various stages in your career and various organisational contexts. Ultimately the application of practical and collaborative wisdom will also provide you with insights with regard to when your commitment and dedication is misplaced and your experience and judgement can be optimally applied elsewhere.

Collaborative wisdom concerns the application of practical wisdom in a collegiate and people-centric manner. This is based upon the realisation that the organisational community is best served, operates most effectively and optimises performance over the long term, this through the consistent application of a mindset which applies wisdom on the basis of the paramountcy of communicating a vision which all stakeholders support as consistent with their own personal aspirations and life objectives. Equally importantly, where each individual has a clear understanding of their specific contribution in the achievement of that vision, consider that they are involved in the decision-making process and are energised and excited by their involvement in its achievement.

The leader(s) who and organisation(s) which consistently apply collaborative wisdom acknowledge the critical impact on the organisation of satisfying the requirements and expectations of all stakeholders, with the resultant enhancement of cohesion, allegiance, dedication, motivation, excitement and energy. The result is a measure of productivity by the community of stakeholders on behalf of the organisation which is unattainable in the absence of a pervading atmosphere of collaborative wisdom. The role of the executive leadership cadre is to develop, manage and maintain this mindset and cohesive atmosphere. However, ultimately long-term success is based upon all stakeholders, not merely operational leaders, consistently applying the principles, perspectives and priorities of collaborative wisdom in their operational decisions, practices and actions.

The preceding chapters have described the perspectives, attributes and capabilities of the global leader who possesses practical and collaborative wisdom. Parts One and Two indicate that the practically wise are primarily nurtured rather than born in having the required mindset of perspectives, attributes and capabilities. Organisations which consistently apply the values and principles fundamental to the application of practical wisdom recruit individuals as potential leaders whose life experiences, attitudes and perspectives are conducive and make them receptive to the principles, priorities and practices of practical and collaborative wisdom. They then invest considerable development time, energy and financial resources to produce, over a sustained period, a cadre of global leaders, exposing them to many different situations, guiding, mentoring, challenging, until those individuals acknowledge and understand the relevance and impact of universal values and a community, people centric perspective on operational effectiveness and long-term organisational performance.

This final part of the book addresses the critical issue for the individual of the practical steps and obstacles to effective implementation, dependent upon their stage of career and the organisational context within which they find themselves. Effective leadership, like farming, requires fertile ground. This chapter therefore takes into account the reality that the individual alone, in the majority of cases, is largely impotent to change the organisational tide in the form of a dominant logic of principles, perspectives and priorities which are deeply embedded in the culture of the organisation. In this respect any focused, directed and coordinated challenge to embedded principles, perspectives, priorities and practices will, in the majority of cases, result in powerful, vehement and stolid resistance, likely to result in potentially career threatening repercussions. It is therefore appropriate to apply the principles and processes of practical wisdom to which we have referred in this book to achieve your leadership goals in an operationally pragmatic manner, utilising practical wisdom, founded on your leadership knowledge, experience, insight and judgement. By this means one gains a strong and firm footing from which to climb what is very likely to be a steep and arduous ascent. This mindset also invites you to take a holistic view of your career and look beyond the mechanical employment triggers which frequently guide choice of employer, particularly at the early stages of one's career. It thereby provides additional knowledge and insight, allowing you to be more proactive and selective in terms of future employers and/or quit before your career finds itself in the sidings.

8   *I Believe: Where Do I Join?*

No Quick Fix to a State of Practical and Collaborative Wisdom

To believe in the values, principles and priorities underpinning a practical and collaborative wisdom mindset is only the first of many significant steps in a long, boulder strewn journey towards its operational implementation. A clear understanding of the key priorities in its application and the fundamental disparities with the prevailing business logic within many organisations will act as a compass in navigating successfully towards creating an effective operational leadership context.

If the content of the preceding chapters seems logical and resonates with your mindset then you have taken the first steps towards the operational implementation of collaborative wisdom within your operational leadership context. However, a cursory consideration of the contents of preceding chapters makes it quite clear that the embedding of a culture of practical and collaborative wisdom amongst the leadership cadre, such that it pervades operational decision-making and daily practices, is not something which might be expected to be achieved within the timescales of the next 3-year plan, or the next, or the next in many if not the majority of business organisations. This is a long-term investment whose tangible benefits may not become clear and accepted by all stakeholder groups and embedded within all functions of the organisation within the time horizons which have increasingly become the expected norm for the implementation of business policies, plans and strategies. This is because we are operating at a more fundamental level, at the organisational mindset or logic, which has a more fundamental impact on those psychological and cognitive processes which direct decision making to ensure organisational survival and optimal performance over the long term.

Whilst these may appear merely to be words on a page, they are likely to resonate in the minds of former senior executives and board members of Enron, WorldCom, Lehman Brothers, Bear Stearns, Washington Mutual, RBS, HBOS, Northern Rock, CitiGroup, Anglo Irish Banking Corporation and many other organisations who many analysts and commentators conclude consistently took business decisions which sought to take a shorter route towards maximising profitability, this for reasons which I am sure appeared at the time to be both logical and justifiable on the basis of individual and peer group leader values, principles, priorities and practices. As Perlmutter (1969) stated, the first step is to be on the correct path, only then can you begin to make progress towards achieving a business vision geared towards survival and long-term optimal performance. Without wishing to synopsise the book in a few lines, allow me to give examples of the fundamental requirements towards achieving collaborative wisdom within an organisation:

KEY STEPS IN THE REALISATION OF A STATE OF COLLABORATIVE WISDOM

- Organisational founders and/or a dominant coalition comprised of individuals who have attained a state of practical and collaborative wisdom, primarily as a result of their personal experiences outside of the organisation.
- The development and consistent application of a single dominant logic based upon universal values.
- A realisation of the importance of holistic, marathon rather than sprint-based principles, perspectives and priorities of that dominant logic.
- The development of an inculcated cadre who can be relied upon to consistently apply this single dominant logic within the operational, functional context (e.g. finance, marketing, sales, HR, customer service, R&D, production).
- The development of a long-term training and development plan for the leadership cadre which engenders the required perspectives, attributes and capabilities of "quiet leadership", practical and collaborative wisdom.
- The development of a collegiate decision-making process in order to leverage knowledge and tacit knowledge in the decision-making process. Also to engender a sense of teamwork and involvement within the leadership cadre (note: this applies to decisions throughout the organisation, not merely at the executive committee level).
- The development and consistent operational application and continuous reinforcement of a soft-hearted, hard-headed, pragmatic, people-centric leadership approach. An understanding and acknowledgement that business leadership issues and solutions revolve around people and therefore decisions which resolve business issues must be centred around people.
- A recognition that survival and optimal performance of the organisation revolves around satisfying the requirements and expectations of individual stakeholders, resulting in enhanced allegiance, dedication to, motivation and energy on behalf of the organisation.
- The application of a leadership approach based on confidence, assertiveness, allied to the "quiet" attributes of pragmatism, persuasion, listening, open-mindedness and inclusion.
- Inculcation within the leadership cadre that their primary role and focus is the creation and proactive management of a cohesive organisational community of stakeholders rather than the generation of profit, which will be optimisedthrough the people/ community centric perspective.
- An operational leadership perspective based upon delegation with authority, confident that the inculcation process amongst the leadership cadre of a single dominant logic which ensures the consistent operational application of the principles, perspectives, priorities and practices underpinning collaborative wisdom.
- Consistent communication to all stakeholder groups of the organisational vision and its relevance to the individual's personal vision; also clarification of the importance of each individual's role in the achievement of that vision.

Such an approach achieves clarity, purpose, energy, excitement, motivation, allegiance, dedication, confidence and comfort amongst individuals and stakeholder groups. These are all critical ingredients in the attainment of optimal productivity, operational effectiveness, long-term survival and optimal performance.

It is evident from the above that effective implementation is a long-term project, albeit that benefits will gradually and incrementally accrue along the route in terms of enhanced cohesion, coordination, energy and allegiance, which will have knock on effects on stakeholder confidence, operational effectiveness and productivity. However, as an operational leader, albeit one who is convinced of the validity of a logic based upon collaborative wisdom, I am sure that you will agree the above list of organisational leadership priorities will be regarded by many leaders as anathema, an alien logic, contrary to the principles, perspectives and priorities, and operational reality in which they have been inculcated during their careers, specifically:

THE PERCEIVED REALITY OF THE OPERATIONAL LEADERSHIP CONTEXT

- The absence of a clear organisational vision which permeates to the operational, day to day management context.
- The absence of a defined and clearly communicated dominant logic of principles, perspectives and priorities which are understood, acknowledged and supported as consistent with how the individual leads their life and which are clearly seen to be so within the context of operational decision making.
- The recruitment and development of leaders primarily on the basis of technical capability and performance rather than a focus on the benefits of a collegiate and inculcated leadership cadre.
- The focus on short-term, unit profitability, rather than a long-term, holistic approach to performance and nurturing of knowledge and intellectual capital.
- A central operational focus on profit, revenue, sales, tasks, and projects rather than the achievement of organisational objectives and long-term vision through the management of people, which is regarded as a leadership skill, as a nice to have rather than a need to have.
- A focus on the analytical and logical as priorities and the absence of the consideration of the affective in decision making.
- A focus on key stakeholders within the community rather than seeking to satisfy the tangible and intangible expectations of the organisational community as a whole, with the resultant impact on cohesion, energy, allegiance and productivity.

This significant disparity in mindset makes the operational implementation of the practically and collaboratively wise leadership mindset highly problematic, requiring a re-indoctrination of the dominant coalition, the existing operational leadership cadre and the development and inculcation of a new generation of leaders. The results of this disparity in dominant logic are radical differences in perspectives and priorities during the operational, day to day, decision-making process, with a direct impact on issue resolution and operational practices, individual actions and practices, (in respect of such operational functions as R&D, production, sales, customer service, marketing, finance and HR), particularly in relation to day to day people interactions and responses. It is therefore easy to see why even those who are convinced of the organisational benefits of such a transition baulk at the perceived insuperable task of changing attitudes and perspectives of the organisational power base.

However, the task may in fact not in practice be so insuperable. The present financial and economic crisis has exposed serious deficiencies in the prevailing organisational leadership philosophy or culture. More important is the fact that many individual operational leaders have increasingly concluded that the absence of employees who understand the organisation's objectives and feel that they play a less than intrinsic part in their realisation, acts as a dead weight on the performance of the organisation in the midst of the knowledge economy. Individually then, many are therefore likely to be amenable to and perhaps already applying a more people-centric leadership approach, founded upon communicating principles based upon universal values, collaboration, cooperation, persuasion, albeit within the prevailing context of a more "mechanical", impersonal, organisational dominant logic.

It is therefore likely that in many organisations there are islands where operational leaders are, perhaps subconsciously and intuitively, exhibiting and applying the perspectives, attributes and capabilities of practical and collaborative wisdom and inculcating isolated cadres of leaders of today and tomorrow. What is possible in such circumstances is to gradually and purposefully join up these isolated units to create a cohesive movement which is able to influence and ultimately change the operational dominant logic. However, to persist with this approach in the face of a more dominant, pervasive and contrary leadership logic requires strong belief, self-confidence, courage, determination, tenacity and hope that at some juncture within the foreseeable future there will be a more widespread application of practical and collaborative wisdom. In their absence, individuals who base their leadership logic on practical and collaborative wisdom are likely to quickly exit or consider it judicious to join the majority for the sake of significant others and/or until such time as their self-confidence, courage and ability to influence are enhanced through further experience and credibility within the organisation.

It is quite possible that the credible, respected and confident leader of a department or division within the organisation might maintain and indeed extend the application of collaborative wisdom farther afield within the organisation, outside the area of their direct responsibility and authority. However, over the long term, the ideal strategy for embedding and inculcation throughout the organisation is for the dominant coalition to develop, manage and monitor all aspects of a dominant logic which fosters practical and collaborative wisdom, accepting the required long-term commitment and investment, cognisant of its impact on operational effectiveness and long-term organisational performance.

Be Honest: Understand and Assess Your Personal Perspectives and Priorities

Whilst some organisations may be committed to investing resources to develop the attributes and capabilities of global leadership in new recruits (although not necessarily recognising that these must be based on the principles and processes of practical and collaborative wisdom), the nascent perspectives, priorities and attitudes must already be in place prior to recruitment. It is therefore critical that as an individual you carefully and realistically consider whether your personal context has prepared you with the appropriate mindset to be a committed advocate for collaborative wisdom.

The application of practical and collaborative wisdom, with its attendant personal perspectives, priorities, personal attributes, capabilities and characteristics, is not something which resonates with, excites and enthuses everyone, to the extent of making it a central tenet of their leadership style. In many respects the application of practical and collaborative wisdom is part of a belief system which will be applied in every aspect of one's life; it is not a switch on/off approach applied only within the work context. Whilst you have individual free will it will tend to be limited by the values, principles and principles of the society to which you belong, relate and owe allegiance, and by what criteria success is defined. It is further moulded and refined by the views of family, school, college and other peer groups to which you are specifically connected and affiliated, with whom you have an affinity and have an affection. If these societal norms and peer groups have tended to emphasise, for instance:

• The benefit of the individual and a narrow group of stakeholders (e.g. family, college alumni, ethnic affiliates) and a focus on the tangible, analytical and logical.
• An assertive, no alternative views, talk, don't listen, follow me, I know what I'm doing interaction perspective.

Such a mindset will take much time to change and adapt (if ever) to a belief where practical and collaborative wisdom is considered fundamental to the prevailing dominant logic of organisational leadership. Indeed it is likely to cause personal confusion and adversely affect personal productivity and contribution to key organisational objectives until such inculcation has been achieved.

As stated previously, there is a requirement for the long-term successful organisation to inculcate recruits to the organisation in respect of the embedded values and principles of its dominant logic (which are based upon universal values), this in order to develop appropriate perspectives, attributes and capabilities through structured and focused career plans. However, as the first step in this process, they will seek to recruit individuals who have a mindset with a nascent affinity for the perspectives, priorities and practices required for the consistent operational implementation of practical and collaborative wisdom. It is the contention of this book that it is only at some later stage in the career of many leaders that they recognise the logic of practical and collaborative wisdom in optimising operational effectiveness and long-term organisational performance and, in addition, have developed the appropriate attributes and capabilities to implement within the operational leadership context. The objective of this book, however, is to fast forward this realisation and development of appropriate attributes and capabilities to the early career stages, when the nascent leader is in their mid to late-20s. It is therefore necessary that the embryonic mindset is activated and operationalised at an earlier stage in the career in order to deliver an optimal contribution to organisational performance.

The operational implementation of collaborative wisdom is complex and ambiguous, requiring an ability to consider a wide range of issues in a "balanced", multifaceted and relative manner, rather than in black or white. In this respect it mirrors the issue of whether ethical issues can be taught or more pertinently learned, absorbed or adequately critically reflected upon at this early life stage. In this respect I am reminded of a statement by Piper, Gentile and Parks when they considered the ability of postgraduate students to critically reflect upon ethical issues,

> *We found that these talented, highly motivated students have a strong sense of interpersonal accountability – of being trustworthy – in immediate face to face situations with colleagues and superiors. Yet perhaps because many of them had been insulated from diversity and failure, and have not heretofore been encouraged to critically reflect upon some of the important issues before them and their societies, they only have a limited consciousness of system harm and injustice, only a limited sense of what is at stake ... Unless they are effectively initiated into the public purposes and ethical norms of their profession, they will be ill-prepared to provide managerial leadership capable of engaging complex relationships among conflicting loyalties within a vision of the common good. They will not be able to provide ethical leadership in public life (Piper, Gentile and Parks, 1993, p. 19).*

The authors, however, contend that the exceptions to this general conclusion (as we mentioned in Part One) are those who have experienced trauma and crisis in their personal lives, which have caused them to undertake complex reflection. This has resulted in perspectives developed from their personal experience rather than on the basis of societal and peer group norms,

> *Leaders are people who have suffered significant and painful conflict ... that have led to an inward turning and estrangement from their environments from which they have emerged with a "created rather than an inherited sense of identity" (Piper, Gentile and Parks, 1993, p. 32).*

Within the context of these considerations, as a first step in the process of applying practical and collaborative wisdom, do you consider yourself ready, able and committed to act as an advocate within the day to day operational context?

HOW STRONGLY DO YOU BELIEVE?

- Has your social context prepared you to understand and relate to the values, perspectives, attributes and priorities of practical and collaborative wisdom?
- Has your personal experience prepared you to critically reflect on issues in a manner outside of the established norms of the societal framework of principles and priorities?
- Do you apply the values, principles, priorities and practices of practical and collaborative wisdom in your personal daily life outside of the business leadership context?
- Do you have the belief and confidence in practical and collaborative wisdom as a means of optimal operational effectiveness and long-term performance to advocate and consistently operationally implement within an organisational environment whose dominant logic is at fundamental odds with the core values, principles and priorities of collaborative wisdom?
- Do you consider that you have the required, innate personal characteristics, attributes and capabilities, knowledge, experience and insight to take decisions and resolve issues in a manner which creates credibility and respect for and understanding of practical and collaborative wisdom within the operational organisational context?

- If you considered that as an "early adopter" of practical and collaborative wisdom it was likely to adversely affect your career prospects, would you persist or cease to be a fervent advocate and switch to a leadership framework which was considered more in synch with the prevailing dominant logic?

For those readers who consider that practical and collaborative wisdom is the way ahead but conclude that they are not ready to be committed advocates (e.g. due to the absence of the appropriate levels of knowledge, experience, insight, judgment and/or confidence), that's OK. It is at least initially enough to be a "follower leader", aware of the nature and content of practical and collaborative wisdom, to benchmark other operational leadership perspectives, priorities and practices, and utilise this knowledge and insight to clarify personal goals in respect of developing appropriate core leadership attributes and capabilities. You will ultimately be ready and willing to seek out and support leaders whose belief, perspectives and attributes impel them towards an assertive approach to the communication and operational implementation of practical and collaborative wisdom, facilitating the linking of isolated islands to which we referred in the previous chapter section.

If, however, you are indeed a committed believer and advocate of the operational application of practical and collaborative wisdom, you are fortunately not limited in your options to a kamikaze approach to career progression. Fundamentally, the application of practical and collaborative wisdom is about being smart, pragmatic and practical about utilising your perspectives, priorities, knowledge and experience to develop insight and judgement for the long-term benefit of the organisation and the attainment of your personal aspirations within the wider community to which you relate and of which you are a part.

The following chapter sections therefore, offer advice and guidance on the options available, dependent upon what stage you have reached in your career development.

Just Starting? Look Around Carefully

Due to the significant impact on every aspect of your life it is important to be confident that any future employer is guided by principles and priorities which are in synch with your own. It is therefore not sufficient to make an initial list of potential employers on the basis of remuneration and credibility amongst family and friends. Whilst perhaps good for the ego and short-term pocket, the conflict, frustration, stress which results from a cursory selection process may significantly impact on your confidence and stall your career until, through critical reflection, you find an employer whose dominant logic is consistent with your "inner voice".

As stated above, a basic contention of this book is that at some stage in one's career, regrettably in the case of the majority towards the back end, there is a realisation amongst many of the relevance and importance of the framework of principles and priorities enshrined within that which we term practical and collaborative wisdom for effective operational leadership. It is the objective of this book to facilitate this realisation, more towards the front end of an individual's career.

When I graduated from college with a bachelor's degree in monetary economics, my job quest was dictated by a number of key factors:

- Those industries and organisations which were interested in my qualifications.
- Those organisations which advertised in the periodicals and compendia which were available on the subject of job opportunities for graduates.
- The organisation which offered the most money.
- My limited knowledge of "good" companies and those which boosted my self-esteem and credibility amongst significant others at the time by possible association.
- The organisation which seemed to offer ongoing career opportunities and training during the interview.

In the end I plumped for the one of the four offers (three in banking) which offered the most money (£200 per annum more in 1974 was a not inconsiderable sum). Soon I realised that whilst individuals were friendly and fair the organisational logic was rigid and imposed strict and unbending conformity, exhibiting little desire to listen to differing perspectives, with little regard for the interests of the bulk of customers or employees. After 2 years I had decided that this was not the organisation for me. Yet it took a further 3 years to mobilise myself to put me on the first stage of a more appropriate career trajectory. As a result of critical reflection based upon frustration, confusion, discomfort and discontent I had the opportunity to select an organisation more attuned to my, at the time, often subconscious principles, perspectives and priorities. It is apposite to note that this first organisation of my career was subsequently subsumed into another financial services organisation, which itself was largely " nationalised" during the 2008/2009 financial crisis in the UK.

I recount this piece of personal history to emphasise the value of not just being relieved that you have managed to get a job with decent money at a credible organisation. Most of us will spend some if not all of our careers working for organisations which operate on the basis of dominant logics which are inconsistent with our personal values, principles and beliefs. This is a useful, if painful learning experience, since it better clarifies what we wish for out of our employment career and emphasises the need to take personal control of our careers. We might, however, continue to cede control for too long (even until retirement) and for wholly justifiable reasons; to pay for the wedding, mortgage, car payments, school fees, to maximise our retirement pension, to offer our family stability and/or out of a fear of the unknown. The price of such a "hostage" perspective is annoyance, frustration, often fear and stress, perhaps depression, chronic and critical illness, with negative implications for significant others. In addition, more relevant to the theme of this book, you are likely to be inculcated with business and leadership principles, perspectives and priorities which, even if you subsequently consider them aberrant, will be increasingly difficult to shake off.

If you are someone whose personal experiences prior to employment have resulted in critical reflection, a confidence and clarity of vision, then this experience will ultimately help in defining the type of organisational dominant logic with which you are comfortable and compatible. You would, however, be wise to take a more structured and in-depth approach to early employment opportunities than salaries, graduate employment compendia, promotional blurb and the uninformed views of friends and relatives. In addition to offering consumer comments on the best computers, televisions, washing machines and lawnmowers, through various websites you will gain an impression from those who have or are still employed by various organisations of the core values, principles and priorities of organisations. Look at the league tables of the best organisations to work for, since these are based less on the financial and more on the people-centric aspects of the organisation. Given the impact which your employment context can have on your life and the potential difficulties of exiting, you should regard the task more akin to finding a spouse or soul mate, rather than just finding a first job to get you some decent money, at last. In any event, no matter the criteria applied in job selection (given the prevailing dismal employment opportunities for new entrants), it is critical that you practice proactive, single-minded control, rather than abrogation of your career development, as an intrinsic part of the tangibilisation of your inner beliefs and intuition, since this will ensure optimal productivity and performance in the interests of both self and employer.

Whilst so far this section has focused on pre-employment considerations, they apply equally well to the first 4–6 years of your career, when you are coming to understand the implications of the covenant which you have made with your employer. As I have mentioned previously in the book, there is a tendency on the part of both employee and employer to focus on the development and application of technical skills and competency within the operational context and no doubt this is a requirement to remain employed at this early juncture in your career. Some 2–4 years into your career, once the novelty of money in your pocket has receded, many employees will start to consciously or subconsciously, critically reflect on the nature of the organisation of which they are now a part.

Through the benefit of hindsight, although not at the time, many who did not choose wisely in respect of their initial employer will reflect on their good fortune in respect of their long-term career development, concluding their initial performance and contribution to their employer to have been stunted by fundamental differences in values, principles and priorities. Indeed in many cases their career prospects were effectively threatened by these fundamental differences, causing a form of personal crisis, compelling them to critically reflect on the embedded values, principles and priorities which they require of future employers and employment contexts. This caused them to take proactive steps to change employer, indeed to radically reorientate their career direction, guided by a new realisation of conscious or subconscious priorities and objectives. In this respect I am reminded of a quote by Steve Jobs,

Your time is limited, so don't waste it living someone else's life. Don't be trapped by dogma – which is living with the results of other people's thinking. Don't let the noise of others' opinions drown out your own inner voice. And most important, have the courage to follow your heart and intuition. They somehow already know what you truly want to become (Jobs, 2005).

Many others may, however, postpone any immediate and dramatic career moves, reflecting that for the moment they are content that any reservations with regard to the prevailing dominant logic of their employer are balanced by tangible benefits. However, the key point of this section is that given the impact on your broader life of the selection of organisation within whom to work, it is imperative that you develop and utilise your optimal powers of critical reflection, to proactively consider the extent of compatibility vis-à-vis values, principles and priorities between yourself and the organisation which employs you. The aim of this point is, however, less concerned with personal well-being, more with the resultant ability to make an optimal contribution to the performance of the organisational community over the long term. Practical and collaborative wisdom comprises, at this career juncture of, for the moment, disparate strands of and impulses in respect of values, principles and priorities which you are intuitively testing and developing into a cogent, defensible and for you logical belief system for consistent and proactive decision making, in preparation for future operational leadership contexts.

In Situ? Assess Organisational Leadership Principles and Perspectives – Then Quit

It is important to realise that at this stage in your career, as a trusted junior member of the leadership cadre, it will be assumed by your superiors, peers and, perhaps most importantly, subordinates, that you have embraced and will take decisions on the basis of the prevailing organisational dominant logic. As an operational leader you will be regarded as complicit in, if not culpable for any "unethical" practices resulting from the dominant logic. You therefore have not only a responsibility but personal interest in proactively communicating and implementing the principles, perspectives and priorities of practical and collaborative wisdom in a manner appropriate to the organisational leadership context.

Let us now assume that you have been in the organisation for some years (say, 7–10). You have attained technical proficiency and are accepted by management as having career potential and increasingly regarded as part of the organisation's management cadre, those who, by words and actions, have indicated an allegiance to the prevailing dominant logic. You are therefore trusted and for this reason appointed to a junior to medium leadership position which has some tangible impact on the direction, operational efficiency and performance of the organisation. Similarly, the longer you remain within the organisation you will increasingly be regarded by peers, also by subordinates, as at least a tacit supporter and advocate of the prevailing dominant logic. By the same token you have had the time and opportunity to ascertain and assess the values, principles and priorities which dominate the nature and direction of decision making within the organisation's senior leadership cadre and whether it is compatible or at significant variance with your personal dominant logic.

The nature of a state of practical and collaborative wisdom and a desire to apply its principles and processes requires that one applies a holistic and critically reflective mindset beyond the confines and requirements of a narrower "technical" approach. It requires that you consider, understand and acknowledge your role and responsibilities within the broader context, the vision and objectives of the organisation and the requirements and expectations of the broader stakeholder community. In this respect it is critical that you do not leave, much less abrogate, responsibility for the development and operational application of the organisation's dominant logic to someone else, anyone else, who has more stripes. You must rather accept as part of your operational leadership role and duty a responsibility to critically reflect on and proactively, assertively contribute to the business and leadership principles, perspectives and priorities which dictate the nature and direction of decision making within the organisation, no matter your leadership role or level. This may and generally does result in personal and interpersonal confusion and conflict regarding "turf" issues, based on silo rather than holistic perceptions of responsibility and authority. These are generally resolved through senior mentor support and personal credibility and respect as a general rather than technical manager and "engineer". In addition, at this career stage, when you have generated significant experience, self-confidence, insight and judgement as an operational leader of people you will begin to question and find it increasingly difficult to be directly responsible for the day to day implementation of decisions and actions which are at significant variance with personal principles, perspectives and priorities.

In many respects whether you are aware or not, whether you prefer to be a "mechanic" or an "engineer", the web of the organisation's dominant logic will embrace you all the more tightly the longer that you stay and the more senior you become as a leader. It is therefore important that you are reflecting critically on the implications of any widening gap between personal and organisational logic. Fundamentally, practical and collaborative wisdom reflects the process of applying a defined framework of values, principles, perspectives and priorities. In this respect it is very similar to the issues surrounding business ethics, which revolve around the application of a defined framework of values and principles. The key point for the leader who is a follower of practical and collaborative wisdom is that once you have become part of an organisation's leadership cadre, whether at the junior, middle or senior level, you are either culpable (meriting condemnation and blame), sponsoring and/or directing, or complicit (participating in a wrongful act), as a follower, aware of wrong but taking no action, in respect of the operational application of the organisation's dominant logic.

Complicit may sound the better of two evils. However, it is important to be aware that it is most often the junior or middle-ranking leader, directly responsible for operational tasks and functions, who is in the first instance disciplined for "unethical" operational actions and practices, which are the tangible end product and most apparent realisation of embedded aberrant values and principles. In this respect, from a personal perspective, this is why the individual operational leader needs to critically reflect on the values, and principles underpinning the dominant logic or prevailing culture of the organisation and whether they are only willing to "take the heat" on the basis of values, principles and priorities to which they ascribe and to which they are fully committed. This may seem a little far-fetched to some leaders, but in practice the values, principles and priorities enshrined within a dominant logic become tangibly and palpably reflected on a day to day basis in such operational and functional areas as accounting practices, advertising campaigns, product development (including pricing and charging, and attendant system programming), sales and service quality, HR practices, public relations, shareholder information, purchasing and health and safety. In practice the eye and hand falls primarily on those who are directly responsible for the practices rather than those directing the underlying principles. This later group of executives, standing a few steps from front of stage, at least initially, have a lot more wriggle room to escape from the glare of approbation and punishment, this on the basis of a defence in respect of misinterpretation, over-enthusiasm, inexperience or misjudgement by subordinates. Many of those who felt uncomfortable with the principles, perspectives and priorities of policies applied and decisions taken prior to and during the prevailing financial services crisis, but regarded it as ultimately the responsibility of superiors in the hierarchy, now find themselves unemployed, disciplined or moved to roles which do not satisfy their aspirations and self-esteem. Ultimately you can choose to be a global leader, and engineer, taking a proactive, holistic approach, actively utilising your experience, insight and judgment to take decisions on behalf of yourself, your dependants and those for whom you have a duty of responsibility due to the leadership role that you have accepted and for which you receive recompense Alternatively you must accept that you are a follower, held hostage by the decisions of others, at best a manager rather than a leader with no willingness or ability to influence or control what happens to the those who look to you for guidance and leadership.

It is important to recognise and acknowledge in a practical and pragmatic manner the complex reality of the individual operational leader. Whilst an avowed "believer" in practical and collaborative wisdom, you are continuously balancing this with career aspirations, enhancing the material support to family and dependents, incrementally increasing your levels of confidence and credibility, and the desire to be recognised by peer groups and their leaders. The use of the term practical is therefore critical in pragmatically selecting the right and most realistic time, place, means and method to apply the leadership perspectives, attributes and capabilities of practical and collaborative wisdom. This is not a cop-out but is rather the "smart" approach to global leadership. As a "believer" in practical and collaborative wisdom, having taken the first steps in undertaking a critical reflection of the dominant logic of the organisation, what options are therefore available to you to embed these principles and process into operational leadership practices? No matter the role that you find yourself in or option that you select, each requires awareness, pro-activity, commitment, courage and ownership, rather than an approach of following, waiting to react and respond to the decisions and actions of others. Believe that you are neither a follower nor a hostage, that your personal principles, perspectives and priorities have a significant contribution to make to organisational effectiveness and long term performance. Also that you have a personal responsibility to those stakeholders that you lead and represent and who rely upon you to support their aspirations. It is important to consider and indeed decide who you are working for, your immediate boss and his boss or the broader organisational community of stakeholders. Your response to this question largely defines your leadership perspectives, priorities and cognitive mental process during operational decision making and issue resolution.

I will address these options from the easier to the most dramatic for both organisation and career:

WHAT ROLES AND OPTIONS ARE AVAILABLE TO THE BELIEVER?

- **The supporter**: if you are fortunate to be a junior or middle-ranking operational leader within an organisation where collaborative wisdom is the foundation stone of its dominant logic, your role, as we have already briefly mentioned, is to consistently operationalise its values and principles within your area of direct responsibility. Also to proactively support its implementation in a holistic, but practical, realistic, pragmatic and incremental manner, where you consider that there exist staff or leaders who are unfamiliar, confused or in conflict with its perspectives and priorities.

- **The bridge builder**: if you are amongst the leadership cadre within an organisation where you consider that there is no strong dominant logic or, where there is, it is not dramatically at variance with the values of collaborative wisdom, then you should take steps to embed collaborative wisdom within the organisation.

  In the first instance you should define, consistently communicate and reinforce the principles and perspectives of practical and collaborative wisdom during the process of operational decision making, ensuring that staff within your direct area of responsibility are inculcated in these principles and priorities and are also taking decisions based upon this foundation.

  Due to the fact that no unit is an island and you normally have to liaise, cooperate and coordinate with other functions, internal and external to the organisation, the opportunity exists, through the application of the principles and practices of practical and collaborative wisdom and quiet leadership, to persuade and convince personnel across a broader front of its relevance for optimising effective operational management and long-term organisational performance.

  Again, the long-term, holistic perspective of the global leader requires the application of practical wisdom, critical reflection and pragmatism. The objective of the leader who consistently applies practical and collaborative wisdom is to take every opportunity to enhance operational effectiveness and organisational performance through persuasion and inculcation.

- **The innovator**: however, a problem arises in organisations without a pervasive dominant logic. In this scenario specific units and groups within the organisation are likely to be dominated by individuals in senior leadership positions with strong personal views, convictions and objectives. As a result, the junior or middle-ranking leader who does not have a mentor or sponsor from within this alpha group may not develop a following, even if personnel are supportive of the underlying perspectives and priorities.

  In such a situation the appropriate tactic is initially to apply the values and principles only within the orbit of your immediate area of direct responsibility and exhibit its ability to deliver in respect of operational effectiveness and optimal performance. Once you have achieved a modicum of credibility and respect and the support of your immediate superior you can consider extending the reach of practical and collaborative wisdom in the interests of a holistic leadership approach. This will be facilitated through making recommendations with respect to cross unit/functional issues where the solutions are most likely to be seen as offering the opportunity for optimal operational effectiveness and performance, whilst offering positive opportunities for the enhanced reputation and self-esteem of members of the dominant coalition.

  If you find that such forays do not meet with the support of your immediate superior and also results in the vehement opposition of a range of peer group leaders within the organisation then you should make plans for an exit from the organisation over the medium term, once you have found an organisation which is more in synch with your personal dominant logic.

- **The survivor**: the most difficult situation arises where you find that the organisational dominant logic is in conflict with your personal dominant logic, based upon practical and collaborative wisdom. This may occur as you gain insight following a sustained period within the organisation. It also sometimes occurs as a result of a change in the dominant coalition during your tenure, resulting in a change in organisational perspectives and priorities. This is a test of your status as a "believer".

  On the one hand, you may come to the conclusion that for all your beliefs and conviction, they are, for the present, outweighed by both the tangible and intangible rewards of maintaining and enhancing your position within the leadership cadre. In addition, due to your relatively junior leadership position the full negative effects on some stakeholder groups of the alternative dominant logic may not be clearly apparent and therefore not dramatically impact on your personal values and principles, until you attain more senior leadership positions. You may therefore consider that it is more realistic in terms of the interests of yourself, your family and dependents, your function and subordinates and the organisation that you hang in until such time as you have the personal capabilities and have attained a position within the organisation to persuade and convince stakeholders of the benefits of a dominant logic based upon the principles, perspectives and priorities of practical and collaborative wisdom. You will, however, take every opportunity to persuade and inculcate individuals and groups in the principles and mental process of practical and collaborative wisdom. The important point about the Survivor is that they recognise that the pervasive dominant logic is inconsistent with a global leadership mindset based upon practical and collaborative wisdom. They are aware, prepared and plan to take future opportunities for its application when they consider it appropriate and possible, rather than sitting back and going with the flow.

- **Breakout**: there will, however, be individuals who are believers and have attained a stage of critical reflection which compels them to conclude that they are unable to operate within an organisational dominant logic which contradicts and conflicts with the values, principles and priorities upon which practical and collaborative wisdom is founded. It is unlikely that where the two logics are in direct conflict you will be able to apply the principles and practices of practical and collaborative wisdom, even within your own area of responsibility, since your peers and subordinates will appreciate its inconsistency with the perspectives and priorities which prevail within the organisation. They will therefore feel disinclined to indicate or express their support through operational actions. In such a situation, where you consider that it is likely that your embedded logic, expressed in personal principles and priorities, characteristics, attributes and capabilities, cannot make a significant contribution to operational effectiveness and organisational performance. In addition, it is likely to lead to frustration, stress and a sense of diminishing self-esteem and respect. Your only option is to plan for an early exit, utilising the principles and processes of practical wisdom in the decision-making process towards finding appropriate alternative employment.

Sitting at the Top?

Holding a leadership position at or near the top potentially provides the opportunity and ability to effectively communicate and embed the principles, perspectives and priorities of a dominant logic based upon practical and collaborative wisdom which will provide vision, direction and purpose to energise stakeholders towards optimal performance. However, the nature of the opportunity is dependent upon your position and a constantly changing organisational context. All of the attributes and capabilities of the global leader are therefore required to achieve an effective inculcation of the leadership cadre and conversion of the prevailing dominant logic.

Sitting at the top of the organisation, as a member of the executive team (e.g. CEO, CFO, COO, CIO or CMO) or executive board member, the believer in collaborative wisdom appears to have an enviable opportunity to develop and embed the required values, principles, priorities, leadership attributes and capabilities of practical and collaborative wisdom throughout the organisation. However, perhaps even in this apparently dominant position the path may be strewn with boulders which require all your skills of practical wisdom and quiet leadership. Dependent upon the context and circumstances of your appointment depend the complexity and resistance to the implementation of your personal dominant logic, founded upon your belief in the values, principles, perspectives, attributes and capabilities of collaborative wisdom. I have split these into a number of role scenarios:

Implementer: if you have been appointed within an organisation which has embedded within it all of the traits of collaborative wisdom then you are likely to have risen from amongst the inculcated cadre of leader. Your objective as a believer will be to maintain the culture, develop the leadership cadre in the perspectives, the attributes and capabilities which energise staff and enhance their self-esteem, utilising practical wisdom to appropriately implement the framework of values, principles of priorities within the rapidly changing business context.

Saviour: you have been appointed as a "saviour" within an organisation to turn around the organisation, where collaborative wisdom has not been fundamental to the dominant logic of the organisation. In this scenario, until they have been persuaded and inculcated in its benefits to both organisation and individual your colleagues are likely to be reticent and have significant misgivings but at a minimum offer their conditional support, for as long as it delivers. Success in this scenario is likely to require a change in the perspectives of the dominant coalition from a focus on short-term shareholder and narrow stakeholder group benefit to a longer term, organisational community and people centric perspective. This reorientation will initially be facilitated by strong signs of recovery at the initial stages of your tenure, allied to a strong desire to support the survival initiatives of the appointed saviour. In such a scenario, during this "halo" period, it is important to embed the foundation stones of global leadership underpinned by practical and collaborative wisdom before the organisation is fully recovered (e.g. definition and communication of new dominant logic, development of framework to inculcate leadership cadre, embedding of holistic, long-term, nurturing perspectives, emphasis on quiet leadership, stakeholder, people-centric community, release of leaders unable or unwilling to adapt to new dominant logic), this in order to forestall the opportunity perceived by others to undertake initiatives to revert to the previous leadership framework once the organisation has recovered from its crisis.

Dominant logic changer: In this scenario, whilst you are accepted by the dominant coalition as possessing compatible perspectives and priorities, you have decided that optimal performance requires a change in dominant logic based upon the principles and practices of practical and collaborative wisdom. You, as a leader within the organisation might previously have been applying practical and collaborative wisdom within functions for which you were directly responsible, this is an organisation whose dominant logic was broadly compatible with its core values, principles and priorities. In many respects this change from within is the prevalent scenario in the manner of senior executive selection In the majority of appointments to membership of the dominant coalition you have either been:

– A respected member of the leadership cadre within the organisation, who can be trusted to take decisions consistent with the values, principles, vision and objectives of the dominant coalition.
– Appointed from outside of the organisation as a result of a selection process which ensures that your personal dominant logic of principles and priorities are not at variance with those of the dominant coalition. Equally importantly, that you have an unquestioned record of delivering on organisational effectiveness and performance.
– Unless you are courageous and/or stupid (which you are not, since you will have applied the principles and process of practical wisdom), you will not have selected an organisation and dominant coalition whose logic is dramatically at odds with the principles, priorities and key practices of practical and collaborative wisdom, of which you are a believer.

The implementation of collaborative wisdom within this scenario requires the application of practical wisdom, pragmatism and quiet leadership, in the form of a number of key tasks.

Task One: your first task is to gain the support of your immediate superior(s) (be it the board in the case of CEO/MD or CEO/MD in the case of a member of the executive committee) in order to apply your own leadership style, principles, perspectives and priorities within your already broad and impactful area of responsibility and authority within the organisation. This is likely to be granted on the basis of:

– The context and nature of the agreement of employment, to deliver on your performance targets and other key objectives for which you have been appointed.
– The unstated but assumed basis that your personal dominant logic broadly corresponds with that of the organisation's dominant logic. Your leadership approach will therefore not cause inter-functional mayhem and conflict at the interface, where coordination and cooperation is required to achieve overall organisational effectiveness and performance objectives.

Task Two: Your next task is to clearly and personally communicate, within your broad scope of personal responsibility and authority within the organisation, up front and personal, to your direct reports and also their direct reports, the values, principles, perspectives and priorities which will dominate the decisions, practices and actions of all operational leaders within your immediate area of responsibility. You will clearly communicate your interpretation of the vision of the organisation in terms consistent with the principles and priorities of practical and collaborative wisdom and the contribution of your area of responsibility to that vision. You will also take the time to effectively communicate, on a one to one basis, the individual contribution of each one of your direct reports. Thereafter you will monitor the response of your direct reports for 3–6 months in respect of the basis of their decision making and the nature and manner of cascading the principles, perspectives and priorities to be applied in decision making and the vision, which you have already communicated to them, to their subordinates.

If there is evidence of a fundamental resistance to the operational application of collaborative wisdom then you should offer advice and guidance and emphasise the importance of all leaders rowing behind a single dominant logic. If resistance continues beyond 12–15 months then replacements should be found who are "believers" or who indicate that their personal dominant logic is amenable to the values, principles and priorities of collaborative wisdom. Once you consider that your leadership cadre is in place then the proactive and directed process of developing over an extended period the perspectives, attributes and capabilities for practical and collaborative wisdom can begin in earnest.

Task Three: given the long-term, holistic perspectives and responsibilities of the "engineer" leader, to create an organisational community which is cohesive, energetic, with a single purpose, the leader who possesses and is directed by practical and collaborative wisdom will seek to extend their influence beyond his area of immediate responsibility. This is achieved through a confident, assertive, persuasive and listening approach. Success in "converting" across the organisation is dependent upon:

– The committed support of your immediate superior, which must be made obvious amongst the leadership cadre.
– The consistent achievement of objectives and targets for which you are responsible.
– The communication of solutions to issues which are founded upon values, principles, perspectives and priorities which resonate as logical and consistent with those which individuals apply in all aspects of their personal life.

This is a long-term process, extending over a period spanning from 3–7, perhaps as long as 10 years, requiring focus, application, determination, dedication and consistency.

Ultimately, dependent upon the response, you may gradually succeed in persuading individuals and groups within the organisation to apply the framework of principles and practices of collaborative wisdom. Alternatively you may fail in your endeavours due to the dynamics of organisational behaviour (see Snookered below) and be forced to move on.

Some readers may consider that the effort in respect of the application of collaborative wisdom, initially within your immediate area of responsibility and subsequently across the organisation, is reminiscent of a cult and a process of conversion, abiding no objectors. In many respects this is true, except to say that fundamental to the model is persuasion, listening, adaptation to context and collegiate decision making. Key words in the application of practical and collaborative wisdom are practical, pragmatic, context oriented and people centric, which requires a dynamic, complex, adaptable and flexible operational application of leadership perspectives, attributes and capabilities. These are geared to optimising the requirements and aspirations of all stakeholder groups within the organisational community. The practically wise leader provides clear direction and logical decision making within the context of inclusiveness. This, in order to optimise the benefits accruing to the organisational community through optimal access to the repository of knowledge, experience, insight and judgement, is available from each member.

The important difference between "Borg-like" inculcation and the proposed inculcation is the fundamental intentions behind its operational application and the absence of a predominant desire for individual power and influence. This is perhaps a fundamental difference which defines the global leader who achieves through collaborative wisdom. Power and influence is not sought as a primary motivation, rather it is an output, a result of the respect and credibility achieved due to the means by which optimal operational effectiveness and long-term performance has been achieved. Power and influence is worn like a cloak or gown by the global leader, rather than utilised as a mailed fist.

Snookered: due to the nature of the leadership of complex business organisations nothing stays the same for long. In this respect, no matter your role within the dominant coalition you may find that even as practical and collaborative wisdom is becoming accepted as fundamental to the organisation's dominant logic, a change in the composition of the dominant coalition places this achievement under threat. This can happen as a result of the appointment of a new chairman or members of the board, the appointment of a new chief executive or a key member of the executive committee within the evolving context of the market position of the organisation. Dependent upon your role, influence and/or credibility and the comparative influence, credibility, perspectives and characteristics of the new member within the dominant coalition you may choose to take time to consider whether there is value in continuing to expend time and energy seeking to implement a conversion or quit and move to an environment more fertile to the application of the principles, processes and principles upon which practical and collaborative wisdom are based..

Naturally the issue is operationally more complex than it sounds. Yet as someone for whom practical and collaborative wisdom is a fundamental belief and vision, given your limited lifespan you must, as Steve Jobs said, "have the courage to follow your heart and intuition" (Jobs, 2005). It is therefore appropriate that you apply your personal perspectives, attributes and capabilities in an environment most conducive to achieving optimal results through a dominant logic based upon the application of practical and collaborative wisdom.

As we have frequently stated, the global leader is a holistic thinker. Global leaders do not consider it inconsequential that they have not achieved optimal success in implanting the framework of practical and collaborative wisdom within the organisational dominant logic and operational leadership perspectives and priorities of an organisation. They will therefore not prefer to focus upon the material gains of remaining in situ. Ultimately the mindset of the global leader rather encompasses a bigger picture, a desire to contribute, to apply their knowledge, experience, principles, perspectives, insight, their judgement and wisdom to optimal effect. This might be within a single organisation where the environment is conducive or alternatively within a broader leadership context, perhaps a group of connected business organisations, a business sector or an economic and/or societal community. The global leadership objective and sense of achievement lies in its impact, to optimise the effectiveness and performance of the community to whom the global leader relates and considers they owe allegiance. The global leader is therefore compelled to move on to where his/her presence and efforts make the optimal contribution. This may lead to the suboptimal material benefit of the global leader and significant others, but this is more than balanced in the mind of the global leader by more intangible personal benefits and the perceived tangible benefits to the community(ies) to which he relates, owes allegiance and of which he considers himself a part.

Sounds Tough and Complicated: Is it Really Worth Risking my Career?

Effective operational leadership requires the courage to take decisions and resolve issues based upon critical reflection, which is itself founded upon knowledge, experience, insight and judgement. Only if during that process of critical reflection you are convinced that operational effectiveness and organisational performance (and the potential for career enhancement and personal satisfaction) is most likely to be optimised through a collegiate and collaborative leadership mindset, should you incrementally develop in yourself and the operational leadership cadre the principles, perspectives, priorities, the attributes and capabilities of practical and collaborative wisdom from the outset of and throughout the various stages of your career.

Collaborative wisdom comprises a simple proposition and a complex, long-term realisation. The proposition is that with a community-based, people-centric and collegiate perspective, priority and focus you will optimise operational effectiveness and long-term organisational performance. This is achieved through the application of practical and collaborative wisdom comprising a leadership mindset of perspectives, attributes, capabilities and mental processes which consistently delivers the collaborative proposition.

Practical and collaborative wisdom is not a philosophy, a theory, a concept, it is a practical, pragmatic operational leadership mindset, which guides and directs you in taking practical leadership decisions on a day to day basis. It is, however, not a plug and play option, because effective leadership is about starting with a foundation of values, principles and priorities, and applying them in a manner optimal to the prevailing context. Leaders fail because:

• They are not aware of and/or do not consistently apply this foundation.

and/or

• They have not developed the characteristics, attributes and capabilities to apply them in a contextually sympathetic manner.

Practical and collaborative wisdom brings clarity, direction and the ability to realise both requirements. The primary obstacles to the consistent application of collaborative wisdom within the operational leadership context are:

• The belief, conviction and commitment of existing and aspiring leaders;
• Prevailing business and leadership principles, perspectives and priorities;

both of which are inextricably linked.

We have gained insight from the preceding chapter sections how these obstacles can hinder your efforts to embed collaborative wisdom within the organisation at every stage of your career. However, in reality, this is the nature of the prevailing operational business leadership context. Differing personal dominant logics forever vying for supremacy and strong footholds on the mountain towards credibility, respect, influence and power whilst, almost as a subsidiary consideration, achieving the organisation's targets and objectives. Individuals who aspire to leadership positions are fundamentally driven by a lust for one, some, or all of these badges.

In contrast, practical and collaborative wisdom, founded on universal values and principles, whilst acknowledging the importance of individual aspirations, self-esteem, respect and credibility, discards power and influence as a primary individual objective, relegating it to a consequent result of achieving optimal operational effectiveness and organisational performance. This mindset makes the practice of operational leadership much less stressful and combative yet offers the opportunity and prospect of optimal effectiveness and performance. It does so because it fosters a collegiate and collaborative effort, utilising the experience, insight, knowledge and judgement of the community, whilst optimising its energy and motivation on behalf of the organisation. Whilst it does not guarantee optimal career advancement, for the reasons previously cited in this chapter, there is an innate logic upon which each reader should critically reflect within the context of their own beliefs, aspirations and how they prefer to lead and influence, and indeed lead their lives outside of their organisational role.

Readers should be clear on the central theme of this book. There has been much emphasis on the benefits of people leadership in order to achieve operational effectiveness and optimal long-term performance. However, this leadership focus is the output of critical reflection by the practically wise leader, based upon a cognitive mental process, developed through consistent long-term individual and organisational investment. Through this mental process the operational leader recognises critical values, principles, perspectives and priorities which must be considered in the operational decision-making process towards achieving operational effectiveness and the optimal performance of the organisational community.

Some of the key words in this book are anchor, compass, holistic, long term, practical and pragmatic and these are critical words towards consistently effective organisational leadership. They are also critical in respect of effective career development. My advice is that you develop and apply skills in collaborative wisdom consistently, over a sustained period and in a specific sequence, as noted below, according to your developing insights, judgement and leadership role, this in order to navigate your career towards a sense of optimal achievement and satisfaction throughout its various stages.

INITIAL CAREER STAGE PRIOR TO LEADERSHIP ROLE

- Accept the embedded values and principles of collaborative wisdom as the compass and anchor of your development as an effective leader.
- Whilst developing technical excellence in your area, look outside your immediate area and begin to look at the organisation in a holistic manner and how you might contribute to its operational effectiveness and performance within this holistic context.
- Begin to consider the priority issues which the organisation is presently addressing and critically reflect from the perspective of a people-centric mindset on how you might seek a resolution if you were in a leadership role.
- In your personal life practice critical reflection and apply the principles of practical and collaborative wisdom in taking personal decisions.

FIRST LEADERSHIP ROLE: BELIEVE AND SOW THE SEEDS

- Communicate in a confident and persuasive manner to your subordinate(s) the principles and priorities which you intend to apply in the decision-making process in order to resolve operational issues. Invite comment and buy-in.
- Become conversant with the tangible and intangible expectations and aspirations of subordinate(s).
- Explain to your subordinate(s) the means by which you see your unit contributing to the overall vision and objectives of the organisation and their specific contribution and responsibilities.
- Engender a sense of excitement in the achievement of unit objectives.
- Engender a sense of teamwork in the achievement of unit objectives and targets.
- Within the context of cross-functional tasks and projects clearly communicate in the joint analysis and decision-making process the principles and priorities which you consider appropriate for the optimal resolution of issues. Accept that given your junior role these may be ignored or only partially taken on board within the context of final decisions.

MIDDLE-RANKING LEADERSHIP ROLE – EXTEND IMPACT AND REACH

In addition to points made in First Leadership Role:

- Ensure that subordinates are applying the principles, priorities, processes and practices of collaborative wisdom in their own operational decision making. Regularly (i.e. weekly/fortnightly initially) take time to offer advice and guidance. Appraise and reward on the basis of collaborative wisdom parameters.
- Begin to develop a leadership development plan in order to embed perspectives, attributes and capabilities to support collaborative wisdom within key subordinates.
- On the basis of your extending credibility and respect outside of your area of immediate responsibility, through meetings, projects, presentations and other communications in respect of the resolution of business issues, put forward solutions which reflect the principles and perspectives, attributes and capabilities required for the application of collaborative wisdom. Be seen to be taking a long-term, holistic, people-centric approach to issue resolution, following the principles of quiet leadership, whilst achieving performance benchmarks.

EXECUTIVE LEADERSHIP POSITION – DIRECT AND REINFORCE

- Ensure that the vision of the organisation is clearly defined and communicated to all employees. Break down into functional contribution and responsibilities towards achievement and ensure that each individual is aware and excited and energised by their contribution.
- Develop and communicate to all stakeholder groups the set of business principles which lie at the heart of the organisation's dominant logic, thereby providing long-term confidence, comfort and predictability with respect to leadership decision making.
- Ensure that business principles are consistent with the application of collaborative wisdom and a people-centric leadership focus. Reinforce that all leadership decisions must tie back to both the content and tone of these principles.
- Emphasise to all stakeholders Emphasise to all stakeholders for whom you have direct responsibility or with whom you come into contact that the long-term survival and growth of the organisation is dependent upon a sense of living together (Kyosei) as an organisational community. This is achieved through recognition that the retention and nurturing of staff optimises and other stakeholder groups tacit knowledge and intellectual capital, creating a cohesive and innovative environment, resulting in optimal productivity and performance.
- Emphasise the collegiate and community-based objectives of the organisation in policy and organisation-wide decisions.
- Emphasise the requirement for leaders of the future to take a holistic, long-term, people-centric and quiet approach to leadership.
- Emphasise that this mindset is considered consistent with effective operational management and optimal long-term organisational performance.
- Institute a long-term leadership development plan which produces an inculcated cadre of leaders who exhibit the perspectives, attributes and capabilities required for the consistent operational application of practical and collaborative wisdom.

Exercises

1. Consider the contents of this chapter and provide six reasons why you consider yourself to be ready, willing and able, or not, as the case may be, to act as an effective advocate and operational implementer of practical and collaborative wisdom.
2. On the basis of your career stage explain, with examples based upon your personal context, how you might seek to operationally apply the framework of practical and collaborative wisdom.
3. Consider and explain why you conclude that the application of practical and collaborative wisdom can or cannot in practice act as the foundation for effective operational leadership, decision-making and issue resolution within the context of the business organisation of the twenty-first century.

Bibliography

Ali, A. J. (1995). Cultural Discontinuity and Arab Management Thought. *International Studies of Management and Organisation, 25* (3), 7–19.

Ali, A. J. (1996). Organizational Development in the Arab World. *The Journal of Management Development, 15* (5), 4–14.

Ali, A. J. and Amirshahi, M. (2002). The Iranian Manager: Work Values and Orientations. *Journal of Business Ethics, 40* (2), 133–143.

Ali, A. J. and Camp, R. C. (1995). Teaching Management in the Arab World: Confronting Illusions. *The International Journal of Educational Management, 9* (2), 10–17.

Al-Kazemi, A. A. and Zajac, G. (1999). Ethics Sensitivity and Awareness Within Organisations in Kuwait: An Empirical Exploration of Espoused Theory and Theory-in-Use. *Journal of Business Ethics, 20* (4).

Altunbas, Y. P., Molyneux, P. (1997). Big Bank Mergers in Europe: An Analysis of the Cost Implications. *Economica, 64*, 317–329.

Ardelt, M. (2004a) Where Can Wisdom Be Found: A Reply to the Commentaries by Baltes and Kunzmann, Sternberg, and Achenbaum. *Human Development, 47*, 304–307.

Ardelt, M. (2004b). Wisdom as Expert Knowledge System: A Critical Review of a Contemporary Operationalization of an Ancient Concept. *Human Development, 47*, 257–285.

Ardelt, M. (2005). How Wise People Cope with Crisis and Obstacles in Life. *ReVision, 28* (1), 7–19.

Aristotle. (1998). *The Nicomachean Ethics* (Oxford World's Classics ed.). (D. Ross, Trans.) Oxford: Oxford University Press.

Badarocco, J. J. (2002). *Leading Quietly: An Unorthodox Guide to Doing the Right Thing.* Harvard Business School Press.

Baltes, P. B. and Kunzmann, U. (2004). The Two Faces of Wisdom: Wisdom as a General Theory of Knowledge and Judgment about Excellence in Mind and Virtue vs. Wisdom as Everyday Realization in People and Products. *Human Development, 47*, 290–299.

Baltes, P. B. and Staudinger, U. M. (1993). The Search for a Psychology of Wisdom. *Current Directions in Psychological Science, 2* (1), 75–80.

Baltes, P. B. and Staudinger, U. M. (2000). Wisdom: A Metaheuristic (Pragmatic) to Orchestrate Mind and Virtue Toward Excellence. *American Psychologist, 55* (1), 122–136.

Banutu-Gomez, M. B. (2002). Leading and Managing in Developing Countries: Challenge, Growth and Opportunities for Twenty-First Century Organisations. *Cross Cultural Management, 9* (4), 29–41.

Barker, P. (1999, 15 November). Not Knowingly Undersold. *New Statesman*, pp. 29–30.

Barth, J. R. and Caprio, G. J. (2004). *Comparative International Characteristics of Banking.* Office of the Comptroller of Currency.

Bartlett, C. A. and Ghoshal, S. (1998). Beyond Strategic Planning to Organization Learning. *Strategy and Leadership, 26* (1), 34–39.

Bartlett, C. A. and Ghoshal, S. (2002). Building Competitive Advantage Through People. *MIT Sloan Management Review*, 34–41.

Bartlett, C. A., Ghoshal, S. and Birkinshaw, J. (2003). *Transnational Management: Text, Cases, and Readings in Cross-border Management* (International New York: McGraw Hill

Bassiry, G. R. and Jones, M. (1993). Adam Smith and the Ethics of Contemporary Capitalism. *Journal of Business Ethics, 12* (8), 621–627.

Bastick, T. (1982). *Intuition: How We Think and Act.* New York: Academic Press.

Bennis, W. (1999). *The Leadership Advantage, Leader to Leader, 12.* Retrieved 17 April 2011, from www.pfdf.org/leaderbooks/121/spring1999/bennis.html

Bennis, W. G. and O'Toole, J. (2000). Don't Hire the Wrong CEO. *Harvard Business Review, 78* (3), 171–176.

Berry, H., Guillen, M. F. and Zhou, N. (2010). An Institutional Approach to Cross-national Distance. *Journal of International Business Studies, 41* (9), 1460–1480.

Bilsky, W. and Schwartz, S. H. (1994). Values and Personality. *European Journal of Personality, 8,* 163–181.

Black, J. S. and Gregerson., H. B. (2000). High Impact Training: Forging Leaders for the Global Frontier. *Human Resource Management, 39* (2/3), 173–184.

Bloom, B. (1985). *Developing Talent in Young People.* New York: Ballantine.

Burgess, S., Schwartz, S. H. and Blackwell, R. D. (1993). Do Values Share Universal Content and Structure? A South African Test. *South African Journal of Psychology, 24* (1), 1–12.

Burrough, B. and Helyar, J. (1990). *Barbarians At The Gate.* London: Arrow Books.

Cartwright, S. and Cooper, C. (1993). The Role of Culture in Successful Organisational Marriage. *The Academy of Management Executive, 7* (2), 57–64.

Case, P. and Gosling, J. (2007). Wisdom of the Moment: Pre-modern Perspectives on Organizational Action. *Social Epistemology, 21* (2), 87–111.

Chang, S. J. and Ha, D. (2001). Corporate Governance in the Twenty-First Century: New Management Concepts for Supranational Corporations. *American Business Review, 19* (2), 32–44.

Chase, W. G. and Simon, H. A. (1973). The Mind's Eye in Chess. In Chase. W. G (ed.), *Visual Information Processing* (pp. 215–281). New York: Academic.

Clegg, S. and Kono, T. (2002). Trends in Japanese Management: An Overview of Embedded Continuities and Disembedded Discontinuities. *Asia Pacific Journal of Management, 19* (2/3), 269–285.

Croft, J. and Larsen, P. (2005, 29 November). Bond's Departure Heralds New Guard at HSBC. *Financial Times* .

Cross, R., Baker, W. and Parker, A. (2003). What Creates Energy in Organisations? *Sloan Management Review, 44* (4), 51–56.

Dale, E., Greenwood, R. S. and Greenwood, R. G. (1980). Donaldson Brown: GM's Pioneer Management Theorist and Practitioner. *Academy of Management Proceedings,* (pp. 119–123).

Dawes, R. M. (1980). Social Dilemmas. *Annual Review of Psychology,* 31 (1), 69-93..

Dayer, R. A. (1983). The Young Charles Addis: Poet or Banker? In F. H. King (ed.), *Eastern Banking: Essays in the History of the Hongkong and Shanghai Banking Corporation* (vol. I). London: Athlone Press.

Economist. (1992, 21 March). Hongkong Bank's Global Gamble. *Economist, 322* (7751), pp. 81–82.

Economist. (2008, 25 September). Into the Whirlwind. *Economist,* Book & Arts.

Ellis, C. D. (2008). *The Partnership: A History of Goldman Sachs.* London: Allen Lane – Penguin.

Endlich, L. (2007a). *Goldman Sachs: The Culture of Success.* London: Sphere – Little, Brown Book Group.

Endlich, L. (2007b). Inside Goldman Sachs: Making Partner, Having a Life – Forbes Life Executive. *Forbes, 180,* pp. 78–85.

Ericsson, K. A. and Charness, N. (1994). Expert Performance – Its Structure and Acquisition. *American Psychologist, 49* (8), 725–747.

Ericsson, K. A., Krampe, R. T., Tesch-Romer, C. (1993). The Rule of Deliberate Practice in the Acquisition of Expert Performance. *Psychological Review,* 100 (3), 363-406

Ericsson, K. A. and Lehmann, A. C. (1996). Expert and Exceptional Performance: Evidence of Maximal Adaptation to Task Constraints. *Annual Review of Psychology, 47*, 273–305.

Ericsson, K. A, Prietula, M. J. and Cokely, E. T. (2007). The Making of an Expert. *Harvard Business Review, July/August*, 114–121.

EyewitnesstoHistory. (2001). *The Death of Magellan, 1521.* Retrieved from www.eyewitnesstohistory.com.

Fan, Y. (2002). Guanxi's Consequences: Personal Gains at Social Cost. *Journal of Business Ethics, 38* (4), 371–380.

Geringer, J. M. and Herbert, L. (1989). Control and Performance of International Joint Ventures. *Journal of International Business Studies, 20* (2), 235–254.

Geus de, A. (1997). The Living Company. *Harvard Business Review, 75* (2), 51–59.

Ghoshal, S. and Bartlett, C. A. (1995). The Multinational Organisation as an Interorganisational Network. *Academy of Management Review* (January/February), 86–96.

Giddens, A. (1970). Durkheim as a review critic. *Sociological Review, 18*, 171–196.

Glaister, K. W. and Buckley, P. J. (1998). Measures of Performance in UK International Alliances. *Organisation Studies, 19* (1), 89–118.

Goldman Sachs. *Business Principles and Standards: Goldman Sachs Business Principles.* Retrieved 17 April 2012, from Goldman Sachs: www.goldmansachs.com/who-we-are/business-standards/business-principles/index.html.

Goodpaster, K. E. (2003). Some Challenges of Social Screening. *Journal of Business Ethics, 43* (3), 239–246.

Gould, S. J. (1995). The Buddhist Perspective in Business Ethics: Experiential Exercises for Exploration and Practice. *Journal of Business Ethics, 14* (1), 63–70.

Grant, R. M. (1996). Towards a Knowledge based Theory of the Firm. *Strategic Management Journal , Winter Special Issue*, 109–122.

Green, S. (2004). Speech: The Changing Balance of the World Economy: *The American European Community Association.*

Green, S. (2009). Good Value: Reflections on the Global Crisis and the Way Ahead. *APEC Summit*, (pp. 1–5). Singapore.

Green, S. (2010). What is Capitalism for in the 21st century? *27th Oxford Analytica International Conference*, (pp. 1–5). Blenheim Palace.

Gregersen, H. B. and Morrison, A. J. (1998). Developing Leaders for the Global Frontier. *Sloan Management Review, 40* (1), 21–32.

Groot de, A. D. ([1946] 1978). *Thought and Choice in Chess.* The Hague, Netherlands: Mouton Publishers.

Hayashi, A. M. (2001). When to Trust your Gut. *Harvard Business Review, 79* (2), 59–65.

Hayek, F. A. (1944). *The Road to Serfdom.* Routledge & Kegan Paul.

Hempel, P. S. and Chang, C. D. (2002). Reconciling Traditional Chinese Management with High-Tech Taiwan. *Human Resources Management Journal, 12* (1), 77–95.

Hofstede, G. (1997). *Cultures and Organisations: Software of the Mind.* New York: McGraw- Hill.

Hofstede, G. (1999). Problems Remain, But Theories Will Change: The Universal and the Specific in 21st Century Global Management. *Organisational Dynamics , 28* (1), 34–44.

Hursthouse, R. (2006). XI – Practical Wisdom: A Mundane Account. *Meeting of the Aristotelian Society, Senate House, University of London*, (pp. 283–307). London.

Isaacson, W. (1997, 13 January). In Search of the Real Bill Gates. *Time Magazine US*.

Jobs, S. (2005). Text of Commencement Address by Steve Jobs, CEO of Apple Corporation and Pixar Animation Studios June 2005. *Stanford Report*. Stanford: Stanford University.

Kellaway, L. (2006, 10 April). The Tale of "an ordinary bloke who got lucky". *Financial Times*, p. 10.

Kerr, S. L. (2004). Using Stretch Goals to Promote Organizational Effectiveness: General Electric and Goldman Sachs. *Academy of Management Executive, 18* (4), 134–138.

King, C. E. (1983). The First Trip East – P&O Via Suez. In F. H. King (ed.), *Eastern Banking: Essays in the History of the Hongkong and Shanghai Banking Corporation* (vol. I). London: Athlone Press.

King, F. H. (1969). British Chartered Banking: Climax in the East – An Inaugural Lecture. *University of Hong Kong Supplement to the Gazette, XVI* (6), 1–10.

Klein, S. (2003). The Natural Roots of Capitalism and Its Virtues and Values. *Journal of Business Ethics, 45* (4), 387–401.

Korbin, S. (1994). Is there a Relationship Between a Geocentric Mind-Set and Multinational Strategy? *Journal of International Business Studies, 25* (3), 493–511.

Kupers, W. M. (2007). Phenomenology and Integral Pheno-Practice of Wisdom in Leadership and Organization. *Social Epistemology, 21* (2), 169–193.

Littrell, R. F. (2002). Desirable Leadership Behaviours of Multi-national Managers in China. *The Journal of Management Development, 21* (1), 65–74.

Lubatkin, M., Calori, R., Very, P. and Veiga, J. F. (1998). Managing Mergers Across Borders: A Two Nation Exploration of a Nationally Bound Administrative Heritage. *Organization Science, 9* (6), 670–684.

Margolis, J. D. and Walsh, J. P. (2003). Misery Loves Companies; Rethinking Social Initiatives by Business. *Administrative Science Quarterly, 48* (2), 268–306.

McAdams, D. P. (2005). The Wisdom of Experience: Autobiographical Narratives Across Adulthood. *International Journal of Behavioural Development, 29* (3), 197–208.

McCall, M. W. and Hollenbeck, G. P. (2008). Developing the Expert Leader. *People & Strategy, 31* (1), 20–28.

McLelland, S. (1994). Gaining Competitive Advantage Through Strategic Management Development. *The Journal of Management Development, 13* (5), 4–13.

Metwally, W. W. (1997). Economic Consequences of Applying Islamic Principles in Muslim Societies. *International Journal of Social Economics, 24* (7/8/9), 941–953.

Microsoft News Center. (1997). *Remarks by Bill Gates*. Retrieved from http:www.microsoft.com/presspass/exec/billg/speeches/1997

Miroshnik, V. (2002). Culture and International Management: A Review. *The Journal of Management Development, 21* (7/8), 521–544.

Montagu-Pollock, M. (1991). All The Right Connections. *Asian Business, 27* (1), 20–24.

Myers, D. G. (2002). *Intuition: Its powers and perils*. New Haven and London: Yale University Press.

Nahapiet, J. and Ghoshal, S. (1998). Social Capital, Intellectual Capital, and the Organisational Advantage. *The Academy of Management Review, 23* (2), 242–266.

Nakano, C. (1997). A Survey Study in Japanese Managers' Views of Business Ethics. *Journal of Business Ethics, 16* (16), 1737–1751.

Naughton, S. and Naughton, T. (2000). Religion, Ethics and Stock Trading: The Case of an Islamic Equities Market. *Journal of Business Ethics, 23* (2), 145–159.

Nonaka, I. and Toyama, R. (2007). Strategic Management as Distributed Practical Wisdom (phronesis). *Industrial and Corporate Change, 16* (3), 371–394.

Nyberg, D. (2008). The Morality of Everyday Activities: Not The Right, But the Good Thing To Do. *Journal of Business Ethics, 81*, 587–598.

Ogbor, J. O. and Williams, J. (2003). The Cross-Cultural Transfer of Management Practices: the Case for Creative Synthesis. *Cross Cultural Management, 10* (2), 3–23.

Owen, G. (2011, 28 April). When the workers take over. *Financial Times*, p. 16 Business Life.

Park, G. R. (2006). *Thesis: An Exploration of Cross-Cultural Adaptability and its Relevance for Effective Cross-Border Acquisition and Integration: Towards an Understanding of the Effective Operational Management of the Cross-Border Financial Services Organisation.* Dublin, Ireland: Michael Smurfit Graduate School of Business, University College Dublin.

Parnell, J. A., Shwiff, S., Yalin, L. and Langford, H. (2003). American and Chinese Entrepreneurial and Managerial Orientations: A Management Education Perspective. *International Journal of Management, 20* (2), 125–137.

Paul, H. (2000). Creating a Mindset. *Thunderbird International Business Review, 42* (2), 187–200.

Pava, M. (2001). The Many Paths to Covenantal Leadership: Traditional Resources for Contemporary Business. *Journal of Business Ethics, 29* (1/2), 85–93.

Perlmutter, H. V. (1969). The Tortuous Evolution of the Multinational Corporation. *Columbia Journal of World Business*, 9–18.

Peters, T. (1988). *Thriving on Chaos: Handbook for a Management Revolution.* New York: Harper Paperbacks.

Piper, T. R., Gentile, M. C. and Parks, S. D. (1993). *Can Ethics Be Taught? Perspectives, Challenges, and Approaches at Harvard Business School.* Boston: HBS Press.

Prahalad, C. K. and Bettis, R. A. (1986). The Dominant Logic: A New Linkage Between Diversity and Performance. *Strategic Management Journal, 7* (6), 485–501.

Prahalad, C. K. and Mashelkar, R. A. (2010). Innovation's Holy Grail. *Harvard Business Review* (July/August), 132–141.

Prahalad, C. K. and Oosterveld, J. P. (1999). Transforming Internal Governance: The Challenge for Multinationals. *MIT Sloan Management Review, 40* (3), 31–39.

Primeaux, P. and Vega, G. (2002). Operationalising Maslow: Religion and Flow as Business Partners. *Journal of Business Ethics, 38* (1/2), 97–108.

Pucik, V. (1997). Human Resources in the Future: An Obstacle or a Champion of Globalization? *Human Resource Management, 36* (1), 163–167.

Redding, S. G. (1983). Organisational and Structural Change in the Hongkong and Shanghai Banking Corporation 1950–1980. In F. H. King (ed.), *Eastern Banking: Essays in the History of the Hongkong and Shanghai Banking Corporation* (vol. III, p. 791). London: Athlone Press.

Reed, A. M. (2002). Corporate Governance Reforms in India. *Journal of Business Ethics, 37* (3), 249–268.

Reed, D. (2002). Corporate Governance Reforms in Developing Countries. *Journal of Business Ethics, 37* (3), 223–247.

Rooney, D. and McKenna, B. (2005). Should the Knowledge-based Economy be a Savant or a Sage? Wisdom and Socially Intelligent Innovation. *Prometheus, 23* (3), 307–323.

Rooney, D. and McKenna, B. (2007). Wisdom in Organizations: Whence and Whither. *Social Epistemology, 21* (2), 113–138.

Ross, P. E. (2006). The Expert Mind. *Scientific American, 295* (2), 64–71.

Rowan, R. (1986). *The Intuitive Manager.* Boston MA: Little Brown.

Sadler-Smith, E. and Shefy, E. (2004). The Intuitive Executive: Understanding and Applying "Gut Feel" in Decision Making. *Academy of Management Executive, 18*, 76–91.

Sandberg, M. (1978). Operations of HSBC Bank Group. *Internal Executive Seminar*, (pp. 1–12).

Schwartz, B. and Sharpe, K. E. (2006). Practical Wisdom: Aristotle Meets Positive Psychology. *Journal of Happiness Studies*, 377–395.

Schwartz, S. H. (1992). Universals in the Content and Structure of Values: Theoretical Advances and Empirical Tests in 20 Countries. In M. Zama (ed.), *Advances in Experimental Psychology* (vol. 25, pp. 1–65). New York: Academic Press.

Schwartz, S. H. (1994a). Are There Universal Aspects in the Structure and Contents of Human Values? *Journal of Social Sciences, 50* (4), 19–45.

Schwartz, S. H. (1994b). Beyond Individualism/Collectivism – New Cultural Dimensions of Values. In U. Kim, C. Triandis, C. Kagitcibasi, S. C. Choi and G. Yoon (eds), *Individualism and Collectivism: Theory Method and Application* (pp. 85–110). Newbury Park, California: Sage Publications.

Schwartz, S. H. and Bardi, A. (2001). Value Hierarchies Across Cultures: Taking a Similarities Perspective. *Journal of Cross-Cultural Psychology, 32* (3), 268–290.

Schwartz, S. H. and Bilsky, W. (1987). Toward a Universal Psychological Structure of Human Values. *Journal of Personality and Social Psychology, 53* (3), 550–562.

Schwartz, S. H. and Bilsky, W. (1990). Towards a Theory of the Universal Content and Structure of Values: Extensions and Cross-Cultural Replications. *Journal of Personality and Social Psychology, 58* (5), 878–891.

Schwartz, S. H. and Melech, G. (2001). Extending the Cross-Cultural Validity of the Theory of Basic Human Values with a Different Method of Measurement. *Journal of Cross-Cultural Psychology, 32* (5), 519–542.

Senge, P. M. (1990). The Leader's New Work: Building Learning Organisations. *MIT Sloan Management Review, 32* (1), 7–23.

Simon, H. A. (1996). *TheSciences of the Artificial* (3rd edn). Cambridge MA: MIT Press.

Simon, H. A. (1997). *Administrative Behaviour* (4th edn). New York: MacMillan.

Sir Bond, J. (1996). Speech: The City: A Newcomer's Perspective. *Sir Kenneth Cork Memorial Lecture*, (p. 19). London.

Sir Bond, J. (1998). Speech: HSBC – What's in a Name? *London Manager's Club*.

Sir Bond, J. (1999). HSBC – A View of Business Values and Culture from Newcastle to New Delhi. *University of Newcastle*, (p. 5). Newcastle.

Sir Bond, J. (2000a). Speech: In Pleasant Company: Working for the 21st Century Corporation. *Institute of Management, Jersey*, Jersey.

Sir Bond, J. (2000b). HSBC – Characteristics and Commitment. *Economic Forum*. Cairo.

Sir Bond, J. (2000c). CCF Reunion Intern. Carrousel du Louvre, Paris

Sir Bond, J. (2001). Speech: Managing an International Business in the 21st Century. *China Center for Economic Research*, (pp. 1–5). Peking University, Beijing.

Sir Bond, J. (2003). Speech: Acceptance of Foreign Policy Association Medal. *Foreign Policy Association Financial Services Dinner*, (p. 5).

Sir Bond, J. (2004, 7 May). Goldman Sachs Conference. (pp. 1–5).

Sir Bond, J. (2005, 13 June). Managing Corporate Social Responsibilities. *Pacific Basin Economic Council, 38th International General Meeting*. Hong Kong.

Snoeyenbos, M., Almeder, R. and Humber, J. (eds). (2001). *Business Ethics* (3rd edn). New York: Prometheus Books.

Spiro, L. N. and Reed, S. (1997, 22 December). Inside the Money Machine. *Business Week* (3558), pp. 86–90.

Stanek, M. B. (2000). The Need for Global Managers; A Business Necessity. *Management Decision, 38* (4), 232–242.

Stanfield, J. R. (1980). The Institutional Economics of Karl Polanyi. *Journal of Economic Issues, 14* (3), 593–614.

Staudinger, U. and Baltes, P. B. (1996). Interactive Minds: A Facilitative Setting for Wisdom-Related Performance? *Journal of Personality and Social Psychology, 71* (4), 746–762.

Staudinger, U. M., Maciel, A. G., Smith, J. and Baltes, P. B. (1998). What Predicts Wisdom-Related Performance? A First Look at Personality, Intelligence, and Facilitative Experiential Contexts. *European Journal of Personality, 12*, 1–17.

Sternberg, R. J. (1985). *Beyond IQ: A Triarchic Theory of Human Intelligence*. New York: Cambridge University Press.

Sternberg, R. J. (2001). Why Schools Should Teach for Wisdom: The Balance Theory of Wisdom in Educational Settings. *Educational Psychologist, 36* (4), 227–245.

Sternberg, R. J. (2005). WICS: A Model of Leadership. *The Psychologist-Manager Journal, 8* (1), 29–43.

Stewart, M. (2006, June). The Management Myth. *Atlantic Magazine*, 80-87..

Swan, J., Newell, S., et al. (1999). Knowledge Management and Innovation: Networks and Networking. *Journal of Knowledge Management, 3* (4), 262–274.

Tarantino, D. A. (1998). Principled Business Leadership – Global Business and the Caux Round Table at a Crossroads. *64* (18), 559–562.

Tayeb, M. (1997). Islamic Revival in Asia and Human Resource Management. *Employee Relations, 19* (4), 352–361.

Toffler, B. L. (2003). *Final Accounting: Ambition, Greed and trhe Fall of Arthur Andersen*. New York: Broadway Books.

Trompenaars, F. and Hampden-Turner, C. (2003). *Riding the Waves of Culture – Understanding Cultural Diversity in Business*. London: Nicholas Brearley Publishing.

Tsai, W. and Ghoshal, S. (1998). Social Capital and Value Creation: The Role of Intrafirm Works. *Academy of Management Journal, 41* (4), 464–476.

Very, P., Lubatkin, M. and Calori, R. (1996). A Cross-National Assessment of Acculturative Stress in Recent European Mergers. *International Studies of Management & Organisation, 26* (1), 59–86.

Westcott, M. R. (1968). *Toward a Contemporary Psychology of Intuition: A Historical, Theoretical and Empirical Inquiry*. New York: Holt, Rinehart and Winston.

Westwood, R. (1997). Harmony and Patriarchy: The Cultural Basis for "Paternalistic Headship" Among the Overseas Chinese. *Organisation Studies, 18* (3), 445–480.

White, B. (2008, 17 December). Goldman Sachs Reports $2.1 Billion Quarterly Loss. *The New York Times*, p. B4.

Whitson, K. R. (2001). What's Bred in the Bone ... Managing HSBC. *Institute of Directors*, (pp. 1–7).

Worthy, J. C. (1955). Education for Business Leadership. *Journal of Business, 28* (1), 76–82.

Index

For Product Safety Concerns and Information please contact our EU
representative GPSR@taylorandfrancis.com Taylor & Francis Verlag GmbH,
Kaufingerstraße 24, 80331 München, Germany

Printed and bound by CPI Group (UK) Ltd, Croydon, CR0 4YY

01/05/2025

01858422-0016